Big Data: Concepts, Technology and Architecture

Big Data: Concepts, Technology and Architecture

Edited by
Felicity Jackson

www.statesacademicpress.com

Published by States Academic Press,
109 South 5th Street,
Brooklyn, NY 11249, USA

ISBN: 978-1-63989-073-6

Cataloging-in-Publication Data

Big data : concepts, technology and architecture / edited by Felicity Jackson.
      p. cm.
Includes bibliographical references and index.
ISBN 978-1-63989-073-6
1. Big data. 2. Data sets. I. Jackson, Felicity.
QA76.9.B45 B54 2022
005.7--dc23

For information on all States Academic Press publications
visit our website at www.statesacademicpress.com

Contents

Preface

This book has been an outcome of determined endeavour from a group of educationists in the field. The primary objective was to involve a broad spectrum of professionals from diverse cultural background involved in the field for developing new researches. The book not only targets students but also scholars pursuing higher research for further enhancement of the theoretical and practical applications of the subject.

Big data is a field that deals with the ways to analyze, systematically extract information from, or otherwise deal with data sets that are too large or complex to be dealt with using traditional data-processing application software. Data with many columns offer greater statistical power, while data with higher complexity may lead to a higher false discovery rate. Challenges associated with big data analysis comprise capturing data, data storage, data analysis, sharing, transfer, visualization, querying, updating, information privacy, and data source. It is associated with three key concepts of volume, variety, and velocity. It has applications for government, international development, healthcare, education, insurance, media, the internet of things, and IT. This book outlines the principles and applications of big data in detail. It discusses the fundamentals as well as modern approaches of this field. As big data is emerging at a rapid pace, the contents of this book will help the readers understand the modern concepts and applications of the subject.

It was an honour to edit such a profound book and also a challenging task to compile and examine all the relevant data for accuracy and originality. I wish to acknowledge the efforts of the contributors for submitting such brilliant and diverse chapters in the field and for endlessly working for the completion of the book. Last, but not the least; I thank my family for being a constant source of support in all my research endeavours.

Editor

Big Data Reduction and Optimization in Sensor Monitoring Network

Bin He and Yonggang Li

School of Electronics and Information Engineering, Tongji University, Shanghai 201804, China

Correspondence should be addressed to Bin He; hebin@tongji.edu.cn

Academic Editor: X. Zhang

Wireless sensor networks (WSNs) are increasingly being utilized to monitor the structural health of the underground subway tunnels, showing many promising advantages over traditional monitoring schemes. Meanwhile, with the increase of the network size, the system is incapable of dealing with big data to ensure efficient data communication, transmission, and storage. Being considered as a feasible solution to these issues, data compression can reduce the volume of data travelling between sensor nodes. In this paper, an optimization algorithm based on the spatial and temporal data compression is proposed to cope with these issues appearing in WSNs in the underground tunnel environment. The spatial and temporal correlation functions are introduced for the data compression and data recovery. It is verified that the proposed algorithm is applicable to WSNs in the underground tunnel.

1. Introduction

It is well known that traditional structural health monitoring mainly relies on manual work, which is a labor-intensive and time-consuming process. Utilizing wireless sensor networks (WSNs) is considered as a promising solution to address these issues. WSNs have been installed in some sections of the London underground, Prague Metro, and Barcelona Metro to perform a task of structural health monitoring [1, 2].

At the same time, as an emerging technology, there are some limitations for the application of WSNs in subway tunnel monitoring, such as big data communication, transmission, and storage. Data compression is considered as a promising method to overcome these limitations, which reduces data capacity prior to data transmission and also reduces power consumption. A variety of data compression approaches appeared in the literature: a distributed data compression approach [3] and a local data compression approach [4]. Distributed compression approaches are broadly classified into four main techniques: distributed source modeling (DSM), distributed transform coding (DTC), distributed source coding (DSC), and compressed sensing (CS) techniques [5]. In general, distributed data compression approaches in WSNs are usually applied in dense sensor networks. Ciancio et al. introduced energy-aware distributed wavelet compression algorithms for WSN. However, the proposed algorithm only considers the spatial redundancy in sensor data [3]. Ji et al. proposed Bayesian compressive sensing to estimate the original signal based on the compressive-sensing measurements [6]. But the number of the compressive-sensing measurements in their study is relatively small, resulting in a corresponding higher recovery error.

Meanwhile, in order to achieve satisfactory coverage, typical WSNs are densely deployed in sensor field [7]. As a result, spatially proximal sensors observations about a single event are highly correlated. Moreover, WSNs are also required to periodically perform observations and transmission of the sensed event features, thus constituting the temporal correlation between consecutive sensor measurements of sensor node [8]. The existence of spatial and temporal correlations poses a significant challenge for data compression and data recovery. Chou et al. developed a simple DSC to adaptively compress spatially and temporally correlated sensor readings [9]. However, the proposed DSC schemes are not efficient in terms of coding efficiency.

Based on the analysis above, we develop an optimization algorithm for WSNs in the underground tunnel, which takes

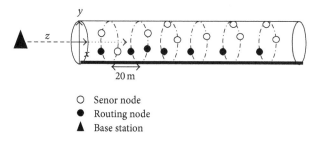

○ Senor node
● Routing node
▲ Base station

FIGURE 1: Wireless sensor network deployment model in subway tunnel.

into account two properties: temporal correlation property and spatial correlation property. Our algorithm is considered as an extension to spatial and temporal data compression algorithms [10], lying in the fact that we further explore the correlation property among sensor nodes to carry out the corresponding data compression and recovery based on the correlation degree [11, 12].

In this paper, we proposed an optimization algorithm based on the temporal and spatial data compression. The temporal and spatial correlation functions are introduced to measure the correlation degree of sensing data. The temporal and spatial correlation degree of sensing data determines the transmission contents of sensor nodes. Transmitting the variation of the sensing signals, rather than the original signals, to the base station can reduce the volume of data stream in the routing path and save the energy, thereby prolonging the lifetime of the network.

The remainder of the paper is organized as follows. Section 2 presents a model of WSNs installation in the underground tunnel. In Section 3, an optimization algorithm based on the temporal and spatial data compression is provided to address these issues emerging from data communication and transmission in WSNs. Section 4 verifies the effectiveness of the algorithm through some experiments carried out using the data acquired from a real WSN used for subway structural health monitoring system. The energy consumption for baseline data transmission is analyzed based on the proposed algorithm. The last section summarizes the conclusions of this paper.

2. Wireless Sensor Network Deployment Model

We deployed a WSN in a Shanghai tunnel. Figure 1 shows a model of the tunnel and the sensor nodes deployed. Here the base station is 50 meters away from the tunnel entrance and is perpendicular to the tunnel mouth. In order to obtain the specific distribution location, we establish a Cartesian coordinate system, in which the x-axis is parallel to the ground, the y-axis is perpendicular to the ground, and the z-axis is perpendicular to the x- and y-axes.

Each circle in Figure 1 contains one or two sensor nodes and a routing node which serve as a single unit. One circle is allowed to communicate with an adjacent circle along z-axis negative direction. The last circle contains all the data from

the other circles and itself and transmits this data to the base station. This completes the transmission process.

For a circle, we consider the temporal correlation between sensor nodes, whereas we consider spatial correlation between two adjacent circles. Two functions are introduced to show the correlation degree: temporal correlation function $R_v(\cdot)$ and spatial correlation function $R_h(\cdot)$. And two correlation thresholds ε and δ are set to detect the degree of the correlation. $R_v(\cdot)$ is used to measure the degree of correlation of the same node at different moments, while $R_h(\cdot)$ is used to measure the degree of correlation of the different nodes at the same moment:

$$R_v\left(S_I^{T_a}, S_I^{T_b}\right) = \sum_{k=0}^{m} D_k\left(S_{I,k}^{T_a}, S_{I,k}^{T_b}\right) W_k + D_{m+1}\left(T_a, T_b\right) W_{m+1}$$

$$R_h\left(S_I^{T_j}, S_L^{T_j}\right) = \sum_{k=0}^{m} D_k\left(S_{I,k}^{T_j}, S_{L,k}^{T_j}\right) W_k + D_{m+1}\left(I, L\right) W_{m+1},$$

$$(1)$$

where S_I^T denotes the sensing information of node I at moment T and contains m sensing information components, $D(\cdot)$ denotes the spatial and temporal correlation function for the sensing information components, distributed in the closed set $[0, 1]$ and expressed in (2), and W_k is the weighted value at component k under the condition of $\sum_{k=0}^{m+1} W_k = 1$. Consider

$$D\left(x_1, x_2\right) = e^{-|x_1 - x_2|/\max(x_1, x_2)}. \quad (2)$$

If $R_v(\cdot) < \varepsilon$, which shows that the correlation degree is low, it means that the sensing values largely change from the moment T_a to T_b.

If $R_v(\cdot) > \varepsilon$, which shows that the correlation degree is high, it means that the sensing values remain almost stable from the moment T_a to T_b.

Similarly, δ is employed as the threshold to evaluate the spatial correlation function. It should be noted that the values of ε and δ are determined by awareness information requirements, distributed in the open set $(0, 1)$. The proper choice for the values helps ensure effective compression performance and high recovery degree.

3. Optimization Algorithm Based on Temporal and Spatial Correlation

Every circle in Figure 1 is seen as a cluster which contains many sensor nodes. The whole data compression algorithm is called cluster compression. Every sensor node in the cluster experiences the temporal and spatial data compression. In every cluster, one sensor node is chosen as a reference node responsible for data transmission based on the power saving. From the moment T_a to T_b, every sensor node needs to compute the temporal correlation degree used as a criterion to determine data transmission content in the link. At the moment T_b, two sensor nodes in the same cluster need to compute the spatial correlation degree utilized as a criterion to determine transmission content in the link.

Temporal correlation data compression

If $R_v\left(S_I^{T_a}, S_I^{T_b}\right) < \varepsilon$

Then record and transmit the changes

$$\Delta S_I^{T_a \to T_b} = S_I^{T_b} - S_I^{T_a}$$

And update the original sensing information

$$S_I^{T_b} = S_I^{T_a}$$

If $R_v\left(S_I^{T_a}, S_I^{T_b}\right) > \varepsilon$ and $D_k(\cdot) < \varepsilon_k$

Then record the changes

$$\Delta S_{I,k}^{T_a} = S_{I,k}^{T_b} - S_{I,k}^{T_a}$$

And update the original sensing information

$$S_{I,k}^{T_a} = S_{I,k}^{T_b}$$

Spatial correlation data compression

If $R_h\left(S_I^{T_j}, S_L^{T_j}\right) < \delta$

Then record and transmit the changes

$$\Delta S_I^{T_j} = S_I^{T_j} - S_L^{T_j}$$

And update the original sensing information

$$S_I^{T_j} = S_L^{T_j}$$

If $R_h\left(S_I^{T_j}, S_L^{T_j}\right) > \delta$ and $D_k(\cdot) < \delta_k$

Then record the changes

$$\Delta S_{I,L}^{T_j} = S_I^{T_j} - S_L^{T_j}$$

And update the original sensing information

$$S_{I,k}^{T_j} = S_{I,L}^{T_j}$$

ALGORITHM 1: Data compression based on the temporal and spatial correlation.

These reference nodes combined with routing nodes located in the cluster form a routing path and are in charge of data transmission.

3.1. Cluster Compression Algorithm. For each sensor node, the temporal correlation function $R_v(\cdot)$ is used to measure the degree of temporal correlation with respect to itself located in the circle during a specific time interval. $R_h(\cdot)$ is used to measure the degree of spatial correlation with respect to two nodes at the same moment. The variation of the temporal and spatial sensing value is transmitted through routing node to the next cluster, thus completing the cluster compression. The temporal and spatial correlation compression algorithm is expressed in Algorithm 1.

It is noted that the variation of the temporal and spatial sensing values, $\Delta S_I^{T_a}$ and $\Delta S_I^{T_j}$, rather than the original sensing values, is transmitted through routing node to the next cluster.

3.2. Analysis of Optimization Algorithm. At the moment T_a, the variation of the spatial sensing information between node I and node L is $\Delta S_{I,L}^{T_a}$; at the moment of T_b, the variation of the spatial sensing information between node I and node L is $\Delta S_{I,L}^{T_b}$. During the period from T_a and T_b, the variation value of the temporal sensing information of node I is $\Delta S_I^{T_a \to T_b}$; the variation of the temporal sensing information of node L is $\Delta S_L^{T_a \to T_b}$. If the distance between node I and routing node in the same cluster is shorter than that between node L and routing node, node I will be chosen as a reference node based on power saving and will be responsible for forwarding the variation values of the sensing data ($\Delta S_{I,L}^{T_a}$, $\Delta S_{I,L}^{T_b}$, $\Delta S_I^{T_a \to T_b}$, $\Delta S_L^{T_a \to T_b}$) through routing node to the next cluster. The situation for node Z is the same. It should be pointed out that if the correlation degree is high, the variation values of the sensing data are equal to 0. There is no need for the reference node to transmit the sensing information to another node.

From Figure 1, we see that there are many circles located in the deployment model. Every circle serves as a single unit with multiple inputs and one output. Input means sensing data of sensor nodes; output refers to the variation of the sensing data. Circle C_1 transmits the variation to circle C_2, and circle C_2 transmits the variation from both circle C_1 and itself to circle C_3. In the same way, circle C_N is responsible for forwarding all of the variation from nodes to the base station. The output of the first circle is expressed as follows:

$$C_1 = \begin{bmatrix} \Delta S_{I,L}^{T_a} & \Delta S_{I,L}^{T_b} & \Delta S_I^{T_a \to T_b} & \Delta S_L^{T_a \to T_b} \end{bmatrix}^T. \tag{3}$$

Likewise, the output of circle C_2 is obtained as follows:

$$C_2 = \begin{bmatrix} \Delta S_{U,V}^{T_a} \\ \Delta S_{U,V}^{T_b} \\ \Delta S_{U}^{T_a \rightarrow T_b} \\ \Delta S_{V}^{T_a \rightarrow T_b} \end{bmatrix} + \begin{bmatrix} \Delta S_{I,L}^{T_a} \\ \Delta S_{I,L}^{T_b} \\ \Delta S_{I}^{T_a \rightarrow T_b} \\ \Delta S_{L}^{T_a \rightarrow T_b} \end{bmatrix}. \qquad (4)$$

Along the routing path, the base station finally receives all the data from all the circles. A matrix $G(\cdot)$ can be used to represent the data received by the base station. Consider

$$G\left(S^{T_b}\right) = \begin{bmatrix} \Delta S_{I,L}^{T_a} & \Delta S_{I,L}^{T_b} & \Delta S_{I}^{T_a \rightarrow T_b} & \Delta S_{L}^{T_a \rightarrow T_b} \\ \Delta S_{U,V}^{T_a} & \Delta S_{U,V}^{T_b} & \Delta S_{U}^{T_a \rightarrow T_b} & \Delta S_{V}^{T_a \rightarrow T_b} \\ \vdots & \vdots & \vdots & \vdots \\ \Delta S_{Y,Z}^{T_a} & \Delta S_{Y,Z}^{T_b} & \Delta S_{Y}^{T_a \rightarrow T_b} & \Delta S_{Z}^{T_a \rightarrow T_b} \end{bmatrix}, \qquad (5)$$

where each row of sensing formation matrix $G(S^{T_b})$ represents the corresponding output of each cluster. Based on the recovery algorithm, the data will be recovered later with a close approximation to the original data. Based on the recovery data, we are further familiar with current situation of each node in the underground tunnel.

3.3. The Routing Strategy. The sensor nodes in Figure 1 are numbered according to their locations and are projected in a square area with their fixed relative distance. Routing nodes and sensor nodes close to these routing nodes form a routing path on which all the data is delivered to the base station. The choice of the routing path is decided by minimal energy consumption. Some sensor nodes are selected in the route, while others are not selected in the route. Coefficient α_i is used to show the relationship between node I and the routing path. The output model is formulated as follows:

$$Y_i = \sum_{i=1}^{17} \alpha_i x_i, \quad \alpha_i = \begin{cases} 1, & \text{If node } I \text{ is in the route} \\ 0, & \text{Otherwise.} \end{cases} \qquad (6)$$

3.4. Data Recovery. The process of data recovery is contrary to that of data compression. The process of data acquisition by base station consists of two phases.

At the moment T_a, the original sensing data are transmitted to the base station without data compression. These data construct an initial sensing matrix denoted by $G_{\text{ori}}(S^{T_a})$.

At the moment T_b, the compressed data are transmitted to the base station. These data form a compressed sensing matrix denoted by $G(S^{T_b})$.

The recovery data matrix at the moment T_b is obtained below:

$$G_{\text{rec}}\left(S^{T_b}\right) = G_{\text{ori}}\left(S^{T_a}\right) + G\left(S^{T_b}\right). \qquad (7)$$

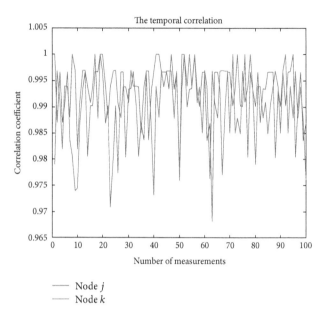

FIGURE 2: Temporal correlation of node j and node k.

Meanwhile, the recovery error is introduced to evaluate the recovery effect and defined as follows:

$$\gamma = \frac{\left\| G_{\text{ori}}\left(S^{T_b}\right) - G_{\text{rec}}\left(S^{T_b}\right) \right\|_2}{\left\| G_{\text{ori}}\left(S^{T_b}\right) \right\|_2}, \qquad (8)$$

where $G_{\text{ori}}(S^{T_b})$ is the original data from the sensor nodes, while $G_{\text{rec}}(S^{T_b})$ is recovery value.

4. Simulation and Experimental Results

Our wireless inclinometers monitoring system is currently installed at Shanghai Metro Line 12 Lijin Road station. The function of the monitoring system is to detect the deformation of the underground tunnel in the early stage.

4.1. Temporal and Spatial Correlation. All the data comes from sensor nodes located in the underground tunnel. We perform the following simulations based on the sensing data from node h, node j, and node k located underground.

At the moment T_a, we got two sets of the sensing data of node j and node k, respectively. At the moment T_b, we got the other two sets of the sensing data of node j and node k. Based on these data, we obtained the temporal correlation of node j and node k (see Figure 2). It can be seen that the temporal correlation degree is very high with the correlation coefficient being larger than 0.965. High temporal correlation degree means that the sensing data of different moments is almost stable irrespectively of time. Our optimization algorithm just makes uses of the high correlation degree property to reduce amount of data transmission, hence saving energy.

At the moment T_c, we obtained three sets of sensing data of node h, node j, and node k, respectively. Node h was chosen as a reference node to achieve the spatial correlation

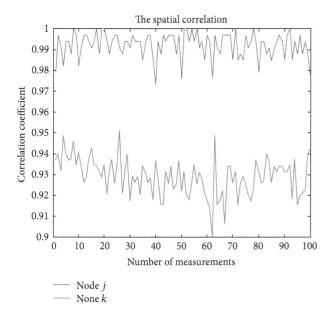

FIGURE 3: Spatial correlation of node j and node k.

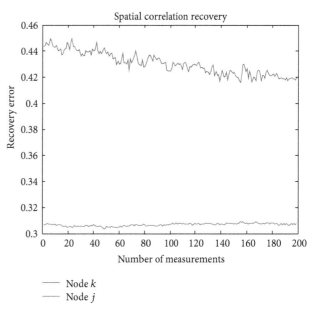

FIGURE 5: Spatial correlation recovery of node j and node k.

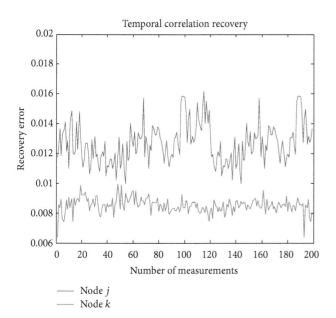

FIGURE 4: Temporal correlation recovery of node j and node k.

with regard to node j and node k. From Figure 3, the spatial correlation values of node j are bounded below by 0.9731, while those of node k are bounded above by 0.9514 and below by 0.9003. According to these data analyzed above, we can conclude that the sensing data of node j and node k is less influenced by the space position. So the sensing data of reference node in combination with the variation values are used to recover the original sensing data of the latter.

4.2. Temporal Recovery of Sensor Nodes. Figure 4 shows the temporal recovery error ε versus the number of measurements corresponding to node j and node k. We can see that the recovery error of node j is a little larger than that of node

k. Our recovery error is an order magnitude lower than that of the other data compression and recovery methods proposed in the literatures [13, 14]. Moreover, bounded fluctuation of recovery error curve of node j fails to influence the recovery performance. When the number of measurements gradually increases, the recovery errors still remain in a certain range. Therefore, it can be concluded that the data compression scheme is effective in terms of the relative recovery error level.

4.3. Spatial Recovery of Sensor Nodes. Figure 5 represents the spatial recovery error δ versus the number of measurements corresponding to node j and node k. The reason why the spatial correlation error of node j is lower than that of node k shown in Figure 5 is that node j has higher spatial correlation degree than node k illustrated above. Moreover, for node k or node j, its temporal recovery performance is superior to spatial recovery performance based on the fact that the temporal recovery error is an order magnitude lower than the spatial recovery error. When the number of measurements increases, the spatial recovery errors are bounded above by some constants. Forasmuch, the proposed algorithm is applicable to the underground tunnel environment.

WSNs are used to monitor the structural health of the underground tunnel. When the underground tunnel is subject to the vibrations that mainly resulted from passage of trains, the sensor nodes deployed in the underground tunnel begin to sample these signals. When the underground tunnel is free of vibrations mentioned above, these sensor nodes still sample these unchanged signals. Rather than the original signals, the variation of these signals is forwarded to base station along the routing path.

Low recovery error means that the recovery values are very close to the original values. It can be seen that the performance of the temporal recovery has an advantage over the spatial recovery based on the former's low recovery

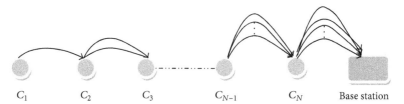

FIGURE 6: Baseline data transmission.

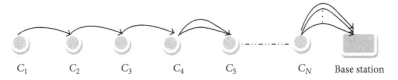

FIGURE 7: Data transmission based on spatial correlation property.

error. When sensing signals vary with time and space, the proposed algorithm captures only the variation to complete the data recovery; when sensing signals are irrespective of time and space, the proposed algorithm makes use of high correlation property to achieve a complete recovery with a high approximation to the original signals. Meanwhile, high correlated property helps eliminate redundant information of WSNs and reduce data volume needed to forward to the base station.

4.4. Energy Consumption Optimization Analysis. Figure 6 shows such a network where sensors are densely deployed in the region of interest and monitor the environment on a regular basis. Suppose N sensors, denoted as C_1, C_2, ..., C_N, form a multihop route to the base station. Let d_j denote the readings obtained by node C_j. The intuitive way to transmit d_j, $j = 1, 2, ..., N$ to the base station is through multihop relay as depicted in Figure 1. Node C_1 transmits its reading to C_2, and C_2 transmits both its reading d_2 and the relayed reading d_1 to C_3. At the end of the route, C_N transmits all N readings to the sink. We can observe that C_N carries more traffic load compared with other nodes due to the much more amount of data transmission. Obviously, node C_N will soon use up its energy and lifetime of sensor network will be significantly shortened. In Figure 6, the total number of reading d_1 transmission is $(N - 1)$ and that of reading d_2 transmission is $(N - 2)$. The total number of data transmission in baseline data transmission model is $N(N + 1)/2$.

Due to the dense deployment in the region of interest, sensing readings from all the nodes are spatially correlated. Assume that readings among C_1, C_2, and C_3 have high spatial correlation, while readings between C_3 and C_4 are not spatially correlated. Based on the data compression algorithm mentioned above, the model of data transmission is changed as follows. Node C_2 receives the reading from node C_1 and finds spatial correlation degree between its reading and the reading of node C_1; then it transmits only its reading to node C_3. In the same way, node C_3 transmits only its reading to node C_4. Due to the fact that the readings between C_3 and C_4

are uncorrelated, node C_4 needs to transmit both its reading and the variation between C_3 and C_4 to node C_5. The model of data transmission is depicted as shown in Figure 7.

Compared with Figure 6, the total number of data transmission in Figure 7 is greatly reduced, thus saving energy consumption and prolonging the lifetime of WSNs. The more correlated the readings are, the more energy the wireless sensor network saves. The network can achieve very high energy efficiency.

In the paper, the energy model considered only the energy consumption during the data reception and transmission. $E_{TX}(l, r)$ stands for the energy cost that a single node is sending L bits data of r distance, and $E_{RX}(l)$ represents the energy consumption that a single node is receiving L length data. In order to evaluate the approach, we chose the "first order radio model" [15]; thus,

$$E_{TX}(l, r) = E_{\text{elec}}l + \varepsilon_{\text{amp}}lr^{\sigma}$$
$$E_{RX}(l) = E_{\text{elec}}l. \tag{9}$$

In our work, we assume a simple model where a radio dissipates $E_{\text{elec}} = 50$ nJ/bit to run the transmitter or receiver circuitry; the communication channel is assumed to be multipath fading with a path-loss exponent $\sigma = 2$; then $\varepsilon_{\text{amp}} = 0.1$ nJ/bit/m^2 for the transmitter amplifier. The unit transmission range is 20 m. The length of unit data is 400 bits. In Figure 6, each node will require $(j - 1)$ and j represent the number of data reception and transmission for node j. The total energy consumption of each node is expressed as follows:

$$E_{\text{Total}} = (j - 1) \times E_{\text{elec}}l + j \times \left(E_{\text{elec}}l + \varepsilon_{\text{amp}}lr^{\sigma}\right). \tag{10}$$

In Figure 6, node C_j will require $(j - 1)$ receives and j transmits. In Figure 7, node C_1 will require only one transmit. Node C_2 and node C_3 have one receive and one transmit. Node C_4 has one receive and two transmits. Node C_5 has two receives and three transmits.

From Figure 8, it can be observed that the energy consumption increases linearly with the increase on the node

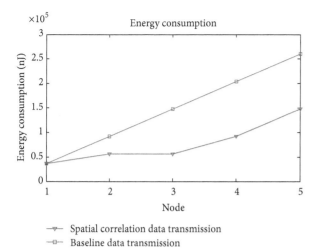

FIGURE 8: Energy consumption comparison.

number in the baseline data transmission. However, energy consumption remains stable if readings between nodes are spatially correlated. Generally, data compression based on spatial correlation property, which is applicable to the case where sensor nodes are densely deployed, can lower the total energy consumption of WSNs based on the decrease on the amount of data transmission. On the other hand, dense deployment of sensor nodes leads to the emergence of redundant information, which increases the overall power consumption of WSNs. Spatial correlation analysis provides new insights into optimal sensors placement and helps avoid the sensor field overlap. According to spatial correlation property, the optimal number of sensors is placed in the proper location to achieve satisfactory coverage.

5. Conclusion and Future Work

Aiming at many issues such as data communication, transmission, and storage in large size WSNs, we propose an optimization algorithm based on the temporal and spatial data compression to address these issues. Transmitting the variation of the sensing signals, rather than the original signals, to the base station can reduce the volume of data stream in the routing path and save the energy consumption, thereby prolonging the lifetime of the network. It is verified through simulations performed above that the data compression algorithm is feasible to WSNs of underground tunnel. Meanwhile, efficient recovery performance ensures the accuracy of the recovery data, and these recovery data are very effective and reliable in performing an analysis of the structural health in underground tunnel.

This paper is only concerned with a multiple-hop data transmission mode. In the future, the single-hop data transmission mode is our primary concern. Besides, the influence of time delay of data transmission on the wireless sensor network will be taken into account.

Conflict of Interests

The authors declare that there is no conflict of interests regarding the publication of this paper.

Acknowledgment

This work is supported by the National Basic Research Program of China (973 Program: Grant no. 2011CB013803).

References

[1] A. Hada, K. Soga, R. Liu, and I. J. Wassell, "Lagrangian heuristic method for the wireless sensor network design problem in railway structural health monitoring," *Mechanical Systems and Signal Processing*, vol. 28, pp. 20–35, 2012.

[2] C. Hirai and K. Soga, "An experimental model of relay deployment planning tool for a wireless sensor network system to monitor civil engineering structures," in *Proceeding of the 19th IASTED International Conference on Parallel and Distributed Computing and Networks (PDCN '10)*, pp. 164–171, February 2010.

[3] A. Ciancio, S. Pattem, A. Ortega, and B. Krishnamachari, "Energy-efficient data representation and routing for wireless sensor networks based on a distributed wavelet compression algorithm," in *Proceedings of the 5th International Conference on Information Processing in Sensor Networks (IPSN '06)*, pp. 309–316, April 2006.

[4] C. M. Sadler and M. Martonosi, "Data compression algorithms for energy-constrained devices in delay tolerant networks," in *Proceedings of the 4th International Conference on Embedded Networked Sensor Systems (SenSys '06)*, pp. 265–278, November 2006.

[5] T. Srisooksai, K. Keamarungsi, P. Lamsrichan, and K. Araki, "Practical data compression in wireless sensor networks: a survey," *Journal of Network and Computer Applications*, vol. 35, no. 1, pp. 37–59, 2012.

[6] S. Ji, Y. Xue, and L. Carin, "Bayesian compressive sensing," *IEEE Transactions on Signal Processing*, vol. 56, no. 6, pp. 2346–2356, 2008.

[7] I. F. Akyildiz, W. Su, Y. Sankarasubramaniam, and E. Cayirci, "Wireless sensor networks: a survey," *Computer Networks*, vol. 38, no. 4, pp. 393–422, 2002.

[8] J. Kusuma, L. Doherty, and K. Ramchandran, "Distributed compression for sensor networks," in *Proceedings of the IEEE International Conference on Image Processing (ICIP '01)*, vol. 1, pp. 82–85, October 2001.

[9] J. Chou, D. Petrovic, and K. Ramchandran, "A distributed and adaptive signal processing approach to exploiting correlation in sensor networks," *Ad Hoc Networks*, vol. 2, no. 4, pp. 387–403, 2004.

[10] L. Wang, Y. Guo, C. Chen, and Y. Yan, "A spatio-temporal data compression algorithm," in *Proceedings of the 4th International Conference on Multimedia Information Networking and Security (MINES '12)*, pp. 421–424, Nanjing, China, November 2012.

[11] M. C. Vuran, O. B. Akan, and I. F. Akyildiz, "Spatio-temporal correlation: theory and applications for wireless sensor networks," *Computer Networks*, vol. 45, no. 3, pp. 245–259, 2004.

[12] I. F. Akyildiz, M. C. Vuran, and O. B. Akan, "On exploiting spatial and temporal correlation in Wireless sensor networks," in *Proceedings of the 2nd International Symposium on Modeling*

and Optimization in Mobile, Ad-Hoc and Wireless Networks (WiOpt '04), 2004.

[13] X. Wang, Z. Zhao, Y. Xia, and H. Zhang, "Compressed sensing based random routing for multi-hop wireless sensor networks," in *Proceedings of the International Symposium on Communications and Information Technologies (ISCIT '10)*, pp. 220–225, Tokyo, Japan, October 2010.

[14] M. Roughan, Y. Zhang, W. Willinger, and L. Qiu, "Spatio-temporal compressive sensing and internet traffic matrices (extended version)," *IEEE/ACM Transactions on Networking*, vol. 20, no. 3, pp. 662–676, 2012.

[15] C. Efthymiou, S. Nikoletseas, and J. Rolim, "Energy balanced data propagation in wireless sensor networks," *Wireless Networks*, vol. 12, no. 6, pp. 691–707, 2006.

2

Information-Balance-Aware Approximated Summarization of Data Provenance

Jisheng Pei and Xiaojun Ye

Department of Computer Science and Technology, Tsinghua University, Beijing, China

Correspondence should be addressed to Jisheng Pei; pjs07@mails.tsinghua.edu.cn

Academic Editor: Chi-Hung Chi

Extracting useful knowledge from data provenance information has been challenging because provenance information is often overwhelmingly enormous for users to understand. Recently, it has been proposed that we may summarize data provenance items by grouping semantically related provenance annotations so as to achieve concise provenance representation. Users may provide their intended use of the provenance data in terms of provisioning, and the quality of provenance summarization could be optimized for smaller size and closer distance between the provisioning results derived from the summarization and those from the original provenance. However, apart from the intended provisioning use, we notice that more dedicated and diverse user requirements can be expressed and considered in the summarization process by assigning importance weights to provenance elements. Moreover, we introduce information balance index (IBI), an entropy based measurement, to dynamically evaluate the amount of information retained by the summary to check how it suits user requirements. An alternative provenance summarization algorithm that supports manipulation of information balance is presented. Case studies and experiments show that, in summarization process, information balance can be effectively steered towards user-defined goals and requirement-driven variants of the provenance summarizations can be achieved to support a series of interesting scenarios.

1. Introduction

With the development of data-generating devices and services such as intelligent mobile phones, tablets, sensor networks, and large-scale social network sites, it has become a common and important practice to collect, store, and aggregate large amount of data from multiple sources to generate useful information for users. Real-world examples include scientific workflow systems and crowd-sourcing applications such as open-source encyclopedia and crowd rating websites. The results produced by these applications are often used to help users make various kinds of decisions in both life and business. Therefore, as the stakeholders in these scenarios are desiring to get more information about how the application comes up with its results and how different data are contributing to them, questions such as how and why data were derived have often been raised [1, 2]. For example, how are different group of users (e.g., younger/senior users, male/female users, and users from different expertise areas)

contributing the results? Furthermore, in order to get a feeling of the derivation process in a hands-on manner, users may also want to try discarding some of the contributions to see their original influence on the results. For example, users may discard some parts they consider to be scams or irrelevant, or they may discard some parts until only what they are interested in are among the inputs.

To answer questions like these, we may refer to the provenance of the data derivation process, as it records the context of data input and how the information was derived. For example, movie rating websites such as IMDB usually present estimated movie ratings by aggregating ratings submitted by a large number of users, whose diverse demographic characteristics, preferences, and previous reviews are all recorded as part of the provenance. We may use such information to analyze why the data derivation process has been executed in certain way or what are the influences applied onto the final result by different groups of users. To achieve this, provenance semiring [2] has been proposed and used to support both the storage and the analytical manipulations to analyze the influence of various data elements. For example, based on provenance semiring, we can support provisioning of the result according to hypothetical insertions, removals, or modifications to the input.

However, listing all recorded provenance in full all at once is not the proper way for users to understand the messages contained by the provenance, as the size and the complexity of detailed provenance information could be overwhelming. Approximated summarization of data provenance has therefore been proposed in [3] to reduce the provenance size by grouping multiple "similar" data provenance annotations as a single annotation through mapping. Intuitively, as annotations are being merged to form new feasible annotations, each annotation would have to symbolize more and more annotations from the original provenance. Thus, the information in each provenance annotations will become ambiguous. Although this would lead to a more concise and high-level representation, it might also cause possible losses in information content or ambiguity, since the grouped annotation no longer makes distinctions between the original annotations. Therefore, we need to find a way to retain useful information for the users in the summaries as much as possible.

Previously, semantic constraints that keep the grouped annotations make sense semantically are imposed such that only "similar" or "related" annotations may be grouped together. However, these are relatively loose constraints (e.g., annotations sharing at least one attribute in common may be grouped together) that are meant to keep the grouped annotations make sense, rather than to retain information that is useful for the users. On the other hand, to achieve a balance between provisioning accuracy and the size of provenance summarization, it has been proposed in [3] that the provisioning results derived from the provenance summary should be retained as much as possible compared to the one derived from the original provenance. Based on this requirement, the current provenance summarization algorithm in [3] searches for an approximated optimal provenance summary, by grouping semantically feasible annotations that will lead to maximum size reduction and minimal distance increment (combined with some weights), one pair at a time in a step-wise manner. However, in this constraint, only the deviation in provisioning results, which is but one of the consequences of the information loss, is considered. But again, the loss of information caused by annotation grouping has not yet been evaluated or dealt with.

Actually, in general data grouping tasks, where raw data are grouped in classes to cope with complexity, balancing the information amount and homogeneity of the grouped classes has for long been recognized as one of the key requirements by users [4]. We believe that this should also be the case for provenance annotation grouping. Users may want to have the freedom to express what kind of information they want to include (or exclude) in the summary. In other words, when choosing from different options of annotation groupings, the influence of size reduction and distance increment should be considered in the context of the information balance. Consequently, among some possible provenance summaries

of similar size and distance, the one that preserves more "useful" provenance items for the users should be more favorable than the others. It would be of interest to investigate how we could take control of the loss of information content during provenance summarization and to see how it might affect the quality outcome of the summarization.

Contribution in this article is as follows: we present a novel algorithm for provenance summarization that adopts information balance as an additional factor for provenance summarization quality control. The new summarization process not only takes semantic constraint and provisioning distance into consideration but also uses information balance to dynamically assess the "usefulness" of the summary contents for users. We define a dynamic entropy based heuristic function that keeps the balance between information amount loss and homogeneity according to user requirement inputs as weights assigned to each provenance tuple. Case studies and comparative experiments on real-world datasets are conducted to show that, by controlling information balance during provenance summarization, our approach can allow provenance summarization results meet customized user requirements while achieving comparable or even better size-distance performance with the previous works.

2. Preliminaries

We first recall some background of provenance information management, semiring provenance model, and the summarization of provenance from [1–3] before discussing our motivation and proposal.

2.1. Collection and Storage of Provenance Information. Provenance information can be collected in various forms including scientific workflow logs, data access logs, file system records, and relational query logs. In other words, the raw form of provenance information can be highly heterogeneous (e.g., text files, tables, relational graphs, and time series) and both structured and unstructured information can be involved. In order to cope with the complexities and heterogeneity of these captured provenance information, we need to organize them in structural format. In the experiment part of this article, we consider the case of movie rating websites and adopt the widely used MovieLens dataset, in which users ratings from multiple sources are collected with automatic crawlers along with demographic information of the users. As Figure 1 shows, the raw provenance information collected is stored and managed in a relational database management system as a rating table, a movie information table, and a user information table. These three tables together provide information on which users rated which movies and the ratings they assign. We match the relations of the rows in these tables to the notations in semiring provenance model (e.g., Example 1) so as to reflect how each individual rating influences the eventual aggregation analysis result of movie ratings. To achieve this, we implement semiring algebraic structures (e.g., Figure 1) in our programs by organizing data items from these tables as different attributes of a semiring element class and indicating their roles in the provenance semiring expression (e.g., tuple annotation, value, and tensor).

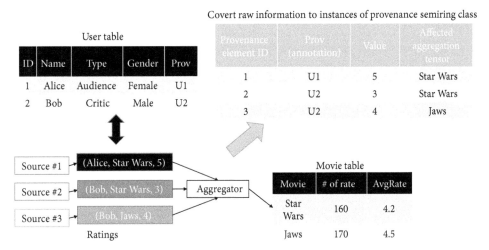

FIGURE 1: Raw provenance information collected from applications is converted to provenance semiring structures.

Thus, a set of instances of such semiring element class may be used to represent and store a provenance expression. In next subsection, we will introduce these roles and symbols as well as their meaning.

2.2. Semiring Provenance Model. Our study focuses on the semiring provenance model [1, 2, 4], but the same result can also be easily extended to other types of models [5, 6]. Semiring provenance model records provenance information with a finite set X of provenance annotations, which can be understood as the basic data items or elements. For example, an annotation may be used to symbolize a row or a field in databases, a user of an information system, or a transaction recorded by the system, and so forth. The provenance information is recorded using these annotations as basic identifiers and organized as an algebraic structure called provenance semiring. Provenance semiring has been used to capture provenance for positive relational queries. In provenance semiring structure, the + symbol is used to describe the fact that some of the data item connected by the symbol are chosen for use, whereas data items connected by • will always be used together; the presence and absence of data during derivation are marked by 1 and 0 in the expression, respectively. As provenance semiring develops, descriptions of aggregation functions in the form like $\sum_i t_i \otimes v_i$ are proposed to capture aggregate queries. In such forms, v_i records the value to be aggregated (e.g., SUM, AVG, and MAX), and t_i symbolizes the provenance (annotation) attached on it. They are paired together with $\otimes$ to indicate the fact that t_i describes the provenance of v_i. The pair $t_i \otimes v_i$ as a whole is called a tensor. Tensors are collected together by the symbol Σ and symbolize the derivation process of aggregation. We use the following example similar to the one used in [1] to illustrate the use of provenance semiring.

2.3. Valuations and Provisioning. Supporting the operation of provisioning is the main reason why provenance semiring is proposed and also its main design goal. Provisioning is the operation of computing the changes to the results by applying some user-specified modifications to the data. We

may do this by alternating the truth valuations applied to semiring expressions. For example, in the expression P_2 of Example 1, if we suspect UID_2 to be an abnormal user, we can then map UID_2 to false and calculate a new result based on the modified expression, thus discarding the contribution of UID_2. In existing literatures, such operation is formalized as the notation of $V : N[X] \rightarrow \{true, false\}$.

2.4. Summarization through Grouping and Mapping. As the derivation process gets more complex, the length and complexity of the corresponding provenance expression become more and more difficult for users to understand. Instead of offering the whole expressions to the users as raw information, provenance expressions should be summarized to reduce its size and highlight the major messages that need to be conveyed. It has been proposed [1] that the summarization of data provenance be achieved through a series of mapping of annotations. Put in simple words, multiple annotations are mapped to one common annotation so as to reduce the size of provenance expression (such mapping is denoted as $h(x)$). The mapped expression serves as a homomorphic but smaller form of the original provenance. During this process, the distinction between some original annotations is sacrificed for the reduced size of the whole expression.

2.5. Evaluate and Control Summarization Quality. Previous approaches evaluate the quality of provenance summarization mainly by size, distance, and semantic relatedness of the grouped annotations. It is worthwhile to first recall these three existing considerations. The first and most obvious consideration size is simply the number of annotations of a provenance expression, which largely determines its complexity. The second consideration is the semantic similarities between annotations to be grouped together. To ensure that the grouping process and summarization outcome make sense, only similar annotations pairs should be considered for mapping. In Example 1, for example, we allow ID_2 and ID_3 to be grouped together only because they share the *female* gender attribute. In other words, we allow two annotations

x_1, x_2 to be grouped together as one annotation when they share some common attribute or characteristics.

The third consideration is the distance between the original and summarized expression depending on the output value of the expressions under the hypothetical manipulations specified by users. Given a set of user-specified valuation V_X, a mapped valuation of V_X will be built for the summarized provenance expressions (denoted as V'_X). In [3] a function φ (combiner function) is provided to perform this mapping. In simple words φ provides descriptions about how summarized annotations will be discarded or retained in the mapped valuation according to valuation choices of the original provenance. For example, φ may decide that a summarized annotation would be discarded only if all original annotations it corresponds are discarded by the original valuation. The original valuation and the mapped valuation are applied on the provenance expression p and its summary $h(p)$, respectively, and the differences of the resulting between p and $h(p)$ are then collected and aggregated as the distance between them regarding the valuation. In detail, a function named VAL-FUNC would be needed to describe how such differences are collected and aggregated. Various sorts of function instances have been proposed to implement VAL-FUNC. For example, we may use the absolute difference between the two expressions values under the valuation as VAL-FUNC. Alternatively, we may introduce a function that returns zero if the two expressions produce the same output and one if any difference exits. For more choices of distance measures we refer readers to [3].

Apart from the three existing considerations listed as above, we propose to introduce *information amount* as an additional consideration to reflect and support more user requirement. The distance between original and summarized expression measures the error introduced by annotation grouping in terms of end-to-end provisioning result value. On the other hand, in terms of overall information loss, we lose track of the information about the original provenance annotations and elements every time we group some annotations together, as the grouped annotation make no distinction between them and consequently the underlying provenance elements (e.g., tuples and tensors) would have to be mixed together. Due to users' changing requirements in various real-world applications, there are a lot of scenarios in which user requirements can be better satisfied by retaining or reducing the information amount of certain kind of provenance elements or annotations during the summarization. This quality factor has not been considered in the work of [3, 5], and we will discuss more about how to measure the quality of the summarization in terms of its information amount in the next section.

Example 1. Consider three provenance expressions (inspired by and adapted from [3])

$$P = \mathrm{ID}_1 \otimes (1,1) \oplus \mathrm{ID}_2 \otimes (3,1) \oplus \mathrm{ID}_3 \otimes (5,1)$$

$$P' = \mathrm{ID}_1 \otimes (1,1) \oplus \mathrm{Female} \otimes (5,2) \qquad (1)$$

$$P'' = \mathrm{Audience} \otimes (3,2) \oplus \mathrm{ID}_3 \otimes (5,1).$$

In this case, P' and P'' are both summarized version of P in the sense that ID_2 and ID_3 are mapped to an abstract annotation "Female" and $\mathrm{ID}_1, \mathrm{ID}_2$ are mapped to an abstract annotation "Audience."

Both P' and P'' incur decrease of information amount since information about the original annotations and tensors are mixed in the new provenance expression. However, whether such decrease is good or bad to the users depends on use cases and requirements.

Since computing an optimal summarization is #P-hard, [3] has proposed an absolute approximation algorithm for computing the distance between two provenance expressions, by sampling the possible valuations and an approximation algorithm to compute optimal summarization with respect to the first three considerations, but not the fourth, that is information amount.

3. Capturing User Requirements with Weighted Information Balance

Observing that user requirements for the provenance summarizations can be expressed as importance weights assigned to each provenance element, we could include information amount as part of the quality consideration of provenance summarization. To do this, we need a quantitative measurement to evaluate the amount of remaining information during annotation grouping and provenance summarization. In this work, we introduce a generalization of entropy proposed by Guiaşu in [7, 8]. Intuitively, as the process of data grouping goes on, the distinctive power provided by the initial symbols or elements is gradually lost and converted to the homogeneity of the newly grouped symbols or elements. Consequently, information amount represented using the grouped annotations as a whole will decrease. We could quantify the information loss by computing the difference of information amount contained in the initial provenance annotation set and the one after summarization.

Let us suppose that we need to perform an analysis of a set of raw data items, for example, the set of provenance annotations. In this paper, we denote them as the set $X = \{x_1, \ldots, x_N\}$. In order to allow users to specify their preferences over the annotations for being preserved, we allow a corresponding set of weights $w_1, \ldots, w_N$ to be associated with the elements in X, respectively. In order to reduce the complexity of X, we consider the possibility that X is partitioned into a partition (scheme of annotation grouping) consisting of n sets with the form of

$$\mathscr{P}_n = \{X_1, \ldots, X_n\}, \qquad (2)$$

where X_i are nonoverlapping subsets of X whose union is the set of X itself.

The initial amount of information supplied by X is defined in the form of the following:

$$\mathscr{I}(X) = -\sum_{k=1}^{N} w_k p_k \log_2 p_k, \qquad (3)$$

where $P_1, \ldots, P_N$ are the probability distribution that elements in X are subject to.

However, as the original dataset is partitioned, the information amount contained in the partitioned symbols decreases. More specifically, the relation between the original raw data set X and the partition can be described as follows (information balance [7]):

$$\mathscr{I}(X) = \mathscr{I}(\mathscr{P}_n) + \mathscr{H}(\mathscr{P}_n). \qquad (4)$$

Here $\mathscr{I}(\mathscr{P}_n) = -\sum_{i=1}^{n} w_k(X_i) p(X_i) \log_2 p(X_i)$ is the amount of information supplied by the classes of partition $\mathscr{P}_n$ (e.g., the provenance annotations after summarization), and $\mathscr{H}(\mathscr{P}_n)$ is the degree of homogeneity of the partition $\mathscr{P}_n$. After grouping, an amount $\mathscr{I}(X) - \mathscr{I}(\mathscr{P}_n)$ of information is removed as the distinction between the annotations mapped to the same summarized annotation is lost. On the other hand, this lost part is added to the data homogeneity $\mathscr{H}(\mathscr{P}_n)$. For detailed definition and discussions on how to compute $\mathscr{I}(\mathscr{P}_n)$, we refer readers to the related work of [7, 8].

Now let us consider how the variation of $\mathscr{I}(\mathscr{P}_n)$ and $\mathscr{H}(\mathscr{P}_n)$ may affect the outcome of provenance summarization in as the annotations are grouped together. It has been proved in [7] that $\mathscr{I}(\mathscr{P}_n)$ decreases as the grouping goes on whereas $\mathscr{H}(\mathscr{P}_n)$ increases. Therefore [7] also argues that when $\mathscr{I}(\mathscr{P}_n) = \mathscr{H}(\mathscr{P}_n)$, that is, when the amount of remaining information is equal to the amount of information converted into homogeneity, some kind of balance is reached. However, in the problem of provenance annotation summarization, users may want to specify their preferred degree of balance between annotation preserving and grouping. For example, when users want to have a more high-level view of the provenance information on certain aspects of the provenance data, higher homogeneity values may be more preferable. On the other hand, users may also want to reduce the loss of information on certain part of the information which he might deem to be interesting or helpful.

When $\mathscr{I}(\mathscr{P}_n) < \mathscr{I}(X)/2$, we have $\mathscr{I}(\mathscr{P}_n) < \mathscr{H}(\mathscr{P}_n)$, which can be understood as more information is retained rather than being converted to homogeneity. On the other hand, when $\mathscr{I}(\mathscr{P}_n) > \mathscr{I}(X)/2$, we have $\mathscr{I}(\mathscr{P}_n) > \mathscr{H}(\mathscr{P}_n)$ suggesting that more information is being converted to homogeneity than is remaining. Therefore, we could measure the balance between information preservation and information homogeneity using $\mathscr{I}(X)/2$ as a pivot point. To do this, we introduce the notation of *information balance index* as follows:

$$\mathrm{IB}(\mathscr{P}_n) = \frac{\mathscr{I}(\mathscr{P}_n) - \mathscr{I}(X)/2}{\mathscr{I}(X)/2} = \frac{2\mathscr{I}(\mathscr{P}_n)}{\mathscr{I}(X)} - 1. \qquad (5)$$

It is easy to prove that $-1 \leq \mathrm{IB}(\mathscr{P}_n) \leq 1$. Intuitively, smaller $\mathrm{IB}(\mathscr{P}_n)$ value suggests that more information amount has been retained whereas greater $\mathrm{IB}(\mathscr{P}_n)$ value suggests that less information has been retained and the homogeneity is higher. In other words, $\mathrm{IB}(\mathscr{P}_n)$ measures the information balance status of a given partition $\mathscr{P}_n$.

Let us now consider how IBI is relevant in our problem of provenance summarization. As provenance annotations are being mapped together, the underlying provenance elements (e.g., tensors and tuples) will also be grouped into partitions. If we treat each element of our provenance expression as one data element and the grouping of the elements due to annotation grouping as the partitions in [7], we may then quantitatively measure the change of information amount during summarization.

Example 2. For example, if we treat each element in the expression $P = \mathrm{ID}_1 \otimes (1, 1) \oplus \mathrm{ID}_2 \otimes (3, 1) \oplus \mathrm{ID}_3 \otimes (5, 1)$ as a data element, then we have a dataset $X_P = \{x_1, x_2, x_3\} = \{\mathrm{ID}_1 \otimes (1, 1), \mathrm{ID}_2 \otimes (3, 1), \mathrm{ID}_3 \otimes (5, 1)\}$. By grouping ID_1 and ID_2 as Female, the grouped dataset becomes $X_{P'} = \{\mathbf{X}_1', \mathbf{X}_2'\}$ where $\mathbf{X}_1' = \{x_1, x_2\}$ and $\mathbf{X}_2' = \{x_3\}$. Based on the probability (uniformed distribution or specified by users) and weights assigned to x_1, x_2, x_3 by the users, we may compute the information balance index of $X_{P'} = \{\mathbf{X}_1', \mathbf{X}_2'\}$, $\mathrm{IB}(X_{P'})$, according to (5).

By continuously computing the information balance index of these groups, we may dynamically assess the amount of remaining information so as to support the decision-making of next annotation grouping operation. Therefore, users may express their requirements or preferences by assigning their preferred weights to each element. For example, users might assign higher weights to the "useful" provenance elements and lower weights to the "less useful" ones. Under this setting, provenance summarizations with higher amount of remaining information should be more desirable for the users. There exist many alternative ways for users to express their requirement; for example, users may assign higher weights to the items they are less interested in and encourage the amount of remaining information to be as low as possible.

Figures 2 and 3 show the curve of IBI with respect to the iteration steps of the summarization algorithm in [3] under different configurations of aggregation function and combination functions. IBI grows as the provenance summarization algorithm iterates, since more and more annotations are being grouped and the amount of remaining information decreases. We notice that different aggregation function or combination functions may lead to different speeds or patterns of information balance index growth. To deliberately alter this trend towards users' requirements, we could choose mapping candidate based on the additional factor of information balance index.

4. Balanced Provenance Summarization Computation Algorithm

In [3], candidates' mapping is chosen based on their candidate mapping scores defined as

$$\mathrm{CandidateScore} = w\mathrm{Dist} \cdot r\mathrm{Dist} + w\mathrm{Size} \cdot r\mathrm{Size}, \qquad (6)$$

where $w\mathrm{Dist}$ and $w\mathrm{Size}$ are the weights for size and distance and $r\mathrm{Dist}$ and $r\mathrm{Size}$ are the rank of size and distance of summary after performing the candidate mapping. To include information balance into consideration, we could extend the original definition of candidate mapping score to

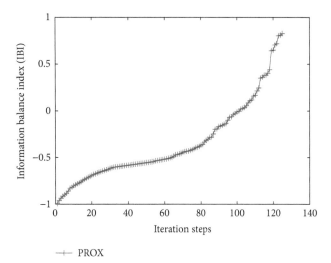

—+— PROX

FIGURE 2: Using expression from MovieLens dataset, AVG aggregation, and "cancel one annotation" valuation, wSize $= w$Dist $= 0.5$, using conjunction as combination function.

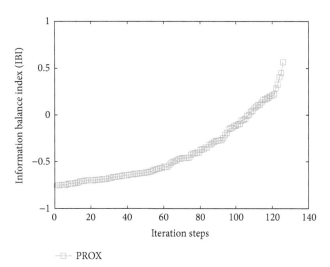

—☐— PROX

FIGURE 3: Same setting as in Figure 2, but using MAX as congruence aggregation function.

have an extra item involving the influence of the information balance index, as the following definition shows:

$$CandidateScoreInf = w\text{Dist} \cdot r\text{Dist} + w\text{Size} \cdot r\text{Size} + scoreIBI. \qquad (7)$$

The influence of information balance index (scoreIBI) here can be defined in various forms to satisfy user requirements. One of the simplest forms could be

$$scoreIBI = w\text{IBI} \cdot r\text{IBI}, \qquad (8)$$

where wIBI and rIBI stand for the weight and rank (in ascending order or descending order) of the information balance index. When using the ascending order, candidate mappings that lead to lower information balance (i.e., more useful information is retained) will be encouraged, whereas

the using of a descending order will encourage higher homogeneity. Generally, users can alternate the definition of scoreIBI to a form that suits their requirements best; for example, to dynamically adjust the influence of IBI, we could even make scoreIBI a function of the current information balance index value and number of steps as

$$scoreIBI = f\left(r\text{IBI}, i\right), \qquad (9)$$

where i denotes the current step number of summarization.

On the other hand, in our experiment we notice that the introduction of information balance index score (scoreIBI) sometimes has negative impacts on the size-distance quality of the provenance summarization, since it partially undermines the impact of the original size score and distance score in choosing a locally optimal candidate mapping. To counterbalance this negative influence, we propose to guarantee the size-distance quality by considering the candidate mappings with top k (or k percent) best size-distance quality only. That is, we choose candidate that has the highest CandidateScoreInf among those with the k (or k percent) best original CandidateScore.

Based on the above considerations, we present a new provenance summarization algorithm (see Algorithm 1). To satisfy their requirements, users can provide their preferred ranking function, weight function, and top-k-percent selection function as input to the algorithm.

Algorithm 1 extends the existing approximated provenance summarization algorithm in [3] by supporting the additional functionality of consideration information balance, by computing additional IBI information on a selected set of candidate mappings. Since the remaining information amounts matters in our algorithm, we do not perform equivalence grouping at the beginning as is done in [3]. The algorithm constructs the homomorphism h gradually in a greedy manner. The greedy decision is made according to the evaluation score consisting of considerations including not only size and distance but also our proposed IBI values. At each iteration, we examine a set of possible single-step mappings of two annotations to a new abstract annotation. For each mapping a homomorphism $h(p')$ of the current expression p' is computed so as to evaluate its candidate score and support the greedy decision. After that candidates of top-k percent size-distance performance are selected and evaluated for their IBI scores. Notice that since it is #P-hard to compute the exact distance between p_0 and $h(p')$, we approximate the distance value by sampling as is done in [3]. Right after that, the IBI scores of these k (k percent) candidates are computed and the candidate with the best total score is chosen and used for annotation mapping in the current iteration. Of course, the consideration of size and distance is still involved here, and they need to be combined according to some user-specified weights. Our algorithms differ from the original summarization algorithm in [3] in the sense that we perform a two-stage search to find first some promising candidates in terms of size-distance performance before computing and comparing their IBI performances. This will help the algorithm remain temporally efficient in spite of the additional computation requirement of IBI. We

Require: p_0 (original provenance), Ann (annotations in p_0), φ (combiner
        function) and V_{Ann} (VAL-FUNC function), the weight for distance,
        size, definition and weight of IBI score, selection size k, size bound
        TSIZE, distance bound TDIST
Returns: Summarized expression p_1
(1)   Initialize p' as p_0
(2)   **While** Size(p') > TSIZE or dist(p_0, p', V_{Ann}) < TDIST **Do**
(3)   candidateSet = $\varnothing$
(4)   **For** every $h \in$ FeasibleMapping(p') **Do**
(5) $p_{cand} = h(p')$
(6)   Add p_{cand} to candidate set
(7)   **End For**
(8)   selectedSet = p_{cand} from candidateSet with top k percent size-
            distance performance
(9)   **For** every p_{cand} **in** selectedSet **Do**
(10)   **If** candScoreWithScoreIBI(p_0, p_{cand}) is optimal **Then**
(11) $p'_{prev} = p'$
(12) $p' = p_{cand}$
(13)   **End if**
(14)   **End For**
(15)   **End While**
(17)   **If** dist(p_0, p', V_{Ann}) > TDIST **Then**
(17)   return p'_{prev}
(18)   **End If**
(19)   return p'

ALGORITHM 1: Information-Balance-Aware Approximated Provenance Summarization Algorithm (IB-PROX).

keep performing the mapping of annotations and reducing the size of provenance annotations set and stop when TSIZE is reached or the distance exceeds TDIST.

5. Evaluation

We conduct evaluations on two typical use cases to validate the effectiveness of our IBI-driven algorithm (Algorithm 1) in terms of its ability to steer IBI curve towards user requirements and also the application potentials of the proposed approach. In Use Case 1, we observe how IBI-driven algorithm could effectively retain the information amount of "useful" items at reasonable costs of size-distance performance. In Use Case 2, we pay a first visit to the possibility of using IBI to improve size-distance performance of provenance summarization.

5.1. Use Case 1 (Retain Useful Items Using IBI). In provenance expressions, there are often interesting or useful provenance tuples that users may prefer to be kept in the summary. For example, when provenance tuples annotated with some previously unobserved annotations start to occur in the retrieved provenance expressions, users would like to keep them in the summary to see how they differ with the previously seen ones. Another example is that users may want to retain some highly influential provenance elements (e.g., elements with outlier values and frequent attribute patterns), which could lead to significant deviations to provisioning results. To do this, users may assign higher importance weights to those tuples

of higher interestingness and lower weights to the rest. In this way, grouping interesting tuples with the less interesting ones would lead to a more significant loss of information amount than grouping the less interesting ones only. Under this setting, it is obvious that provenance summarization with higher remaining information amount is more favorable.

This case study is to validate the effectiveness of information loss reduction by our IBI-driven algorithm and also observe the negative impact on size-distance performance by such reduction. The experiments for this case study were conducted using the MovieLens dataset for various configurations of weight, VAL-FUNC, and aggregation functions. We would like to point out that although only a subset of results are shown, the rest of the results which are not featured in this paper actually have similar characteristics.

In the experiment shown by Figures 4 and 5, we assume that users choose "Cancel Single Annotation" valuation and the AVERAGE aggregation function. We assign equal weights to wSize, wDist, and wIBI and randomly pick 25% of the tuples in the provenance expression as "interesting" tuples and make their weights one magnitude larger than the rest. In Figure 4, we choose a provenance expression with 200 tuples and compare the size-distance performance and information balance index curve of the results produced by the original provenance summarization algorithm in [3] (labelled as "PROX") and ours ("IB-PROX"). The blue plots and green plots stand for the results produced by our algorithm under the setting of $k = 5$ (selecting only candidates with top 5 size-distance performance for information balance index

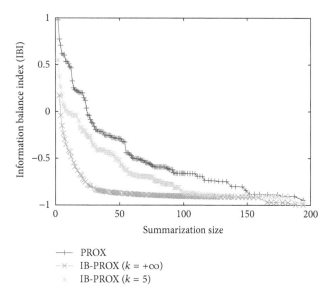

—+— PROX
—✕— IB-PROX ($k = +\infty$)
       IB-PROX ($k = 5$)

FIGURE 4: IBI curve can be effectively altered.

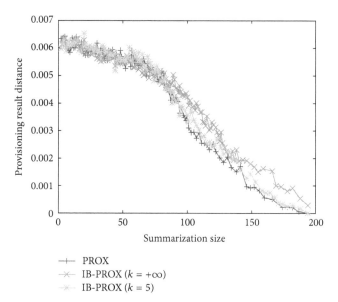

—+— PROX
—✕— IB-PROX ($k = +\infty$)
—✕— IB-PROX ($k = 5$)

FIGURE 5: Negative impacts on size-distance performance can be counter-balanced by the select-top-k strategy.

comparison at each iteration) and $k = +\infty$ (selecting all candidate for information comparison). The red plots stand for the results produced by the original algorithm in [3].

By observing the balance index curves, we may observe how effectively information balance has been controlled by our algorithm. In Figure 4, information balance index curves of IB-PROX (green and blue) are significantly lower for summarization at all sizes than the original algorithm PROX (purple) (meaning more information content amount is retained).

From this trend, we may conclude that, by considering the information balance score, our algorithm can effectively alter the information balance index curve towards our desired bias (lower information balance index) to retain more information amount. Figure 5 shows the negative impact on size-distance performance. It can be observed that the negative impact is not quite significant until the size of summarization is less than 100. On the other hand, by using the select-top-k strategy, we can partially counterbalance this negative impact by sacrificing a certain amount of information loss reduction.

5.2. Use Case 2 (Better Summarization Quality Using IBI). In Use Case 1, we show that information balance index curve can be effectively "pushed down" to encourage interesting items to be retained (or not mixed with the lower-weight items as much as possible), by sacrificing a certain amount of size-distance performance. Seeing this, one might naturally come up with the question "Instead of worsening the size-distance performance, could we alternate the information balance index curve to improve size-distance performance? If possible, how?" It is reasonable to assume that if we could identify the "right" information that, when put together by grouped annotations, would incur less size-distance costs, then we are able to improve the size-distance performance by carefully choosing the weights assigned to each annotation. Admittedly, the definition or properties of the "right" information inevitably might vary due to the selection of valuation

classes, aggregation function, datasets, and so forth. But it is still important to notice that we could build small successes one at a time in establishing specific correlations between information balance index and size-distance quality for some useful scenarios.

In this case study, we illustrate this point using the case of AVG aggregation. In this experiment we choose the "Cancel One Tuple" valuation class; that is, users may cancel one tuple (or more accurately, a tensor) from the provenance expression at a time for provisioning, and the combination rule is that if any tuple related to the grouped annotation is cancelled, the congruence tuple of the grouped annotation should be cancelled. In this case, we could notice an intuitive correlation between information balance and the size-distance performance. That is, higher homogeneity (higher information balance index value) in each grouped annotation may have positive impact on the size-distance performance. This is because, by creating higher homogeneities, more "raw" tuples will be grouped and considered in the tensor congruencies of the grouped annotations. Consequently, for each provisioning operation involving the cancellation of tuples related to the grouped annotations, the congruence value of the grouped tuples to be cancelled is closer to the global average. Therefore, the inaccuracies introduced by cancelling the congruence value rather than the original tuple will be smaller.

To validate this, we perform experiments to check the effect of information balance manipulation on the size-distance performance with multiple combinations of weights and information bias settings. All combinations demonstrate that, by encouraging higher homogeneity (i.e., higher information balance index values), the size-distance performance of the provenance summarization process can be improved. Due to space constraint, we show the representative results of the information balance index curve and size-distance

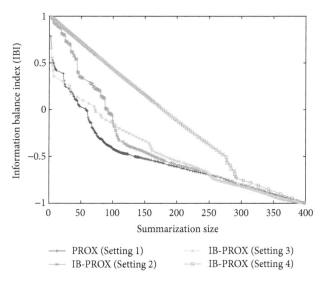

FIGURE 6: IBI curve under different settings.

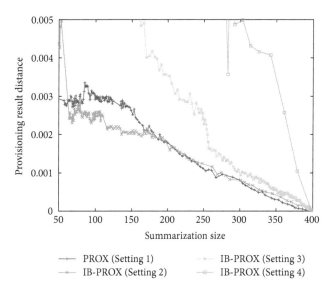

FIGURE 7: Size-distance performance under different settings.

performance produced by 4 settings of the summarization processes: (1) the original PROX process with $wSize = Dist = 0.5$, (2) IB-PROX with $wSize = 0.25$, $wDist = 0.25$, $wIBI = 0.5$, $k = +\infty$, and a bias towards "raised" information balance index curve, (3) the same configuration as in (2) but with a bias towards "lowered" information balance index curve, and (4) IB-PROX with $wSize = 0$, $wDist = 0$, $wIBI = 1$, and a bias towards "raised" information balance index curve.

We could observe from Figure 6 that although setting (3) tried to lower the information curve and successfully did that until the summary size drops to around 200, it failed to keep the trend and became even higher than the original summarization process (Setting 1). This can be explained by the fact that we still have $wSize = 0.25$ and $wDist = 0.25$ in Setting 3, so the bias towards a lower information balance index curve is counterbalance by the requirements of better size-distance performance, which favors higher homogeneity. This in a way reflects that there indeed exists a correlation between higher homogeneity and better size-distance performance.

We can see from Figure 7 that, by "raising" the information balance index curve (Setting 2), the size-distance performance is significantly improved after when the summary size dropped under 150. Although a small amount of negative impact on size-distance performance can be observed from the diagram, the overall improvement by Setting 2 is still highly significant. Among the settings which deliberately alter the information balance index curve, Setting 2 is the only setting that performs better than the original provenance summarization process. The other two settings (Settings 3 and 4) both create negative impact on the size-distance performance. Moreover, from the performance of Setting 4 we may conclude that although higher homogeneity may help to improve the size-distance performance, it is not the unique determining factor that can settle the size-distance performance once and for all. The size-distance performance can be improved only when the goal of higher homogeneity

is considered and balanced in the context of size and distance ranking information.

The above results are representative for the summarization of provenance expressions involving AVG aggregation function only. For other scenarios with different aggregation functions and combination functions, the IBI-driven strategies and weight values would have to be redesigned to fit the scenario. Users may further apply machine learning techniques to automatically generate such strategies.

6. Discussion

Being analogous to the data grouping process in statistical analysis, the summarization of provenance through annotation mapping causes loss of information as the data provenance is summarized. With the analysis and the alternative provenance summarization algorithm presented in this work, we show that such losses could be well defined, measured, and controlled with the concept of information balance during provenance summarization (e.g., Figures 2 and 3). Consequently, information balance and the weights assigned to each provenance elements can serve as methods for users to specify and control the amount of information loss caused by abstract annotation mappings. The perspective provided by information balance differs from the traditional quality considerations used in [3] in the sense that it does not only focus on the end-to-end valuation error caused by the annotation mapping but quantitatively and statistically track the loss of information amount from the perspective of importance weight and information entropy.

In Use Case 1 of our evaluation, we observe that sometimes there exists a trade-off between users' preferred information balance bias and better size-distance performance of the provenance summarization. But still, information balance index (IBI) can be effectively alternated towards users' preferences at acceptable costs of size-distance performance deterioration if we could balance different considerations properly by tuning the heuristic weights used by the search algorithm. On the other hand, in Use Case 2, we may also observe that under certain cases the importance weights and information balance goals can be carefully chosen such that we could achieve an even better performance in terms of both size and valuation error distance by heuristically optimizing the information balance goal. It turns out that the performance of our algorithm in Use Case 2 can be even better in terms of size-distance ratio than the previous algorithms which considers only size and distance as heuristics information.

With these observations, we may come to the realization that *information balance index* is a promising additional measurement of provenance summary quality that can be effectively optimized according to users' requirements and that it is a powerful way for users to specify their additional goals during provenance summarization and even a promising way to improve traditional quality goals such as summary size and valuation error distance when skillfully used. These findings imply that it would be an interesting and fruitful research direction to explore other sophisticated ways of specifying and optimizing the information balance goals in provenance summarization. As the incentives of the changes in *information balance index* and importance weights assigned to each provenance elements may largely determine the outcome of the provenance summarization process, they may serve useful tools for domain-specific provenance summarization solutions to adaptively observe and manipulate so as to reach their additional quality goals.

7. Related Work

Data provenance [9, 10] has been proposed to record how data is generated, propagated, and modified by different users or system modules. Many studies have demonstrated the wide scope of application that data provenance is capable of [11–13] and also the challenges [14, 15] we are faced with while applying provenance technologies. Among these challenges, the evergrowing size and complexity of provenance data have become a significant obstacle for users to understand the messages inside. Therefore, several provenance summarization or compression approaches have been proposed. In [16], an interactive way for exploring large provenance graph has been proposed to control the complexities presented to the users. In [17] the authors proposed to compress provenance graphs in a lossless manner so as to reduce spatial cost. In [18], abstract provenance graphs have been proposed to provide a homomorphic view of the provenance data to help users spot useful information. The most recent work of [3] proposed summarizing provenance data through a series of annotation mapping. However, to the best of our knowledge no existing works on provenance summarization consider the variation of information amount during provenance summarization, and none of the existing approaches allows users to control the loss of information or balance between homogeneity and information completeness by controlling entropy-like indices.

On the other hand, although the concept of entropy and its related derivatives have been successfully applied to a wide range of problems related to summary and compression [19–23], our work is the first attempt to try to involve the computation and control of entropy measurements with the user requirement specification during approximated provenance summarization. We believe that by allowing more flexible control of approximated data provenance summarization using entropy measurements, a wide scope of provenance-related tasks, for example, provenance based access control rules retrieval [24], provenance visualization [25], and provenance storage [26, 27], can be performed both more effectively and more efficiently.

8. Conclusion

More dedicated and diverse user requirements can be expressed and considered by the provenance summarization process by assigning importance weights to provenance elements. Information balance is introduced to measure the change of information content amount during provenance summarization process and included as part of the quality evaluation to achieve user goals defined in terms of biases on information balance. Experiment results show that IBI can be effectively manipulated at reasonable size-distance costs. As future work, promising directions include exploring more possible use cases of information balance driven provenance summarization and consequently new definitions of IBI score, weight evaluation function, and scenario-specific information balance index manipulation strategies, using domain knowledge and even machine learning techniques. It is also an important potential direction to explore how information balance information can be used to improve provenance summarization quality in more general cases.

Conflicts of Interest

The authors declare that there are no conflicts of interest regarding the publication of this paper.

Acknowledgments

This research was supported by the National Key Research and Development Program of China (no. 2016YFB0800901) and the program of China Scholarship Council (CSC) (no. 201606210384).

References

[1] Y. Amsterdamer, D. Deutch, and V. Tannen, "Provenance for aggregate queries," in *Proceedings of the 30th Symposium on Principles of Database Systems, PODS'11*, pp. 153–164, May 2011.

[2] T. J. Green, G. Karvounarakis, and V. Tannen, "Provenance semirings," in *Proceedings of the 26th ACM SIGMOD-SIGACT-SIGART Symposium on Principles of Database Systems, PODS 2007*, pp. 31–40, June 2007.

[3] E. Ainy, P. Bourhis, S. B. Davidson, D. Deutch, and T. Milo, "Approximated summarization of data provenance," in *Proceedings of the 24th ACM International Conference on Information and Knowledge Management, CIKM 2015*, pp. 483–492, October 2015.

[4] Y. Amsterdamer, S. B. Davidson, D. Deutch, T. Milo, J. Stoyanovich, and V. Tannen, "Putting lipstick on pig: Enabling database-style workflow provenance," in *Proceedings of the VLDB Endowment 5.4*, pp. 346–357, 2011.

[5] P. Missier, K. Belhajjame, and J. Cheney, "The W3C PROV family of specifications for modelling provenance metadata," in *Proceedings of the 16th International Conference on Extending Database Technology, EDBT 2013*, pp. 773–776, March 2013.

[6] L. Moreau and M. Paolo, "PROV-DM: The PROV Data Model," 2013.

[7] S. Guiaşu, "Weighted entropy," *Reports on Mathematical Physics*, vol. 2, no. 3, pp. 165–179, 1971.

[8] S. Guiaşu, "Grouping data by using the weighted entropy," *Journal of Statistical Planning and Inference*, vol. 15, no. 1, pp. 63–69, 1986.

[9] P. Buneman, S. Khanna, and W. Tan, "Data Provenance: Some Basic Issues," in *FST TCS 2000: Foundations of Software Technology and Theoretical Computer Science*, vol. 1974 of *Lecture Notes in Computer Science*, pp. 87–93, Springer Berlin Heidelberg, Berlin, Germany, 2000.

[10] Y. L. Simmhan, B. Plale, and D. Gannon, "A survey of data provenance in e-science," *ACM SIGMOD Record*, vol. 34, no. 3, pp. 31–36, 2005.

[11] J. Park, D. Nguyen, and R. Sandhu, "A provenance-based access control model," in *Proceedings of the 10th Annual International Conference on Privacy, Security and Trust (PST '12)*, pp. 137–144, Paris, France, July 2012.

[12] R. Lu, X. Lin, X. Liang, and X. Shen, "Secure provenance: the essential of bread and butter of data forensics in cloud computing," in *Proceedings of the 5th ACM Symposium on Information, Computer and Communication Security (ASIACCS '10)*, pp. 282–292, Beijing, China, April 2010.

[13] I. M. Abbadi, "A framework for establishing trust in Cloud provenance," *International Journal of Information Security*, vol. 12, no. 2, pp. 111–128, 2013.

[14] I. M. Abbadi and J. Lyle, "Challenges for provenance in cloud computing," in *Proceedings of the 3rd USENIX Workshop on the Theory and Practice of Provenance (TaPP)*, 2011.

[15] K.-K. Muniswamy-Reddy, P. Macko, and M. Seltzer, "Provenance for the cloud," in *Proceedings of the 8th USENIX Conference on File and Storage Technologies (FAST)*, vol. 10, 2010.

[16] P. Macko, D. Margo, and M. Seltzer, "Provenance map orbiter: Interactive exploration of large provenance graphs," in *Proceedings of the 3rd USENIX Workshop on the Theory and Practice of Provenance (TaPP)*, 2011.

[17] Y. Xie, K.-K. Muniswamy-Reddy, D. D. E. Long, A. Amer, D. Feng, and Z. Tan, "Compressing Provenance Graphs," in *Proceedings of the 3rd USENIX Workshop on the Theory and Practice of Provenance (TaPP)*, 2011.

[18] D. Zinn and B. Ludäscher, "Abstract provenance graphs: Anticipating and exploiting schema-level data provenance," *Lecture Notes in Computer Science (including subseries Lecture Notes in Artificial Intelligence and Lecture Notes in Bioinformatics)*, vol. 6378, pp. 206–215, 2010.

[19] L. Ferrier, *A maximum entropy approach to text summarization*, School of Artificial Intelligence, Division of Informatics, University of Edinburgh, 2001.

[20] H. Karloff and K. E. Shirley, "Maximum entropy summary trees," *Computer Graphics Forum*, vol. 32, no. 3, pp. 71–80, 2013.

[21] G. Ravindra, N. Balakrishnan, and K. R. Ramakrishnan, "Multi-document Automatic Text Summarization Using Entropy Estimates," in *Proceedings of the International Conference on Current Trends in Theory and Practice of Computer Science*, Springer Berlin Heidelberg, Berlin, Germany, 2004.

[22] J. Lin, "Divergence measures based on the Shannon entropy," *Institute of Electrical and Electronics Engineers. Transactions on Information Theory*, vol. 37, no. 1, pp. 145–151, 1991.

[23] D. S. Ornstein and B. Weiss, "Entropy and data compression schemes," *Institute of Electrical and Electronics Engineers. Transactions on Information Theory*, vol. 39, no. 1, pp. 78–83, 1993.

[24] J. Pei and X. Ye, "Towards policy retrieval for provenance based access control model," in *Proceedings of the 13th IEEE International Conference on Trust, Security and Privacy in Computing and Communications, TrustCom 2014*, pp. 769–776, September 2014.

[25] P. Chen and B. A. Plale, "Big data provenance analysis and visualization," in *Proceedings of the 15th IEEE/ACM International Symposium on Cluster, Cloud, and Grid Computing, CCGrid 2015*, pp. 797–800, May 2015.

[26] Z. Bao, H. Köhler, L. Wang, X. Zhou, and S. Sadiq, "Efficient provenance storage for relational queries," in *Proceedings of the 21st ACM International Conference on Information and Knowledge Management, CIKM 2012*, pp. 1352–1361, November 2012.

[27] Y. Xie, D. Feng, Z. Tan et al., "A hybrid approach for efficient provenance storage," in *Proceedings of the 21st ACM International Conference on Information and Knowledge Management, CIKM 2012*, pp. 1752–1756, November 2012.

3

Routing Optimization Algorithms Based on Node Compression in Big Data Environment

Lifeng Yang,[1] **Liangming Chen,**[2] **Ningwei Wang,**[2] **and Zhifang Liao**[2]

[1]*School of Continuing Education, Yunnan Open University, Yunnan, China*
[2]*School of Software, Central South University, Hunan, China*

Correspondence should be addressed to Zhifang Liao; zfliao@csu.edu.cn

Academic Editor: Wenbing Zhao

Shortest path problem has been a classic issue. Even more so difficulties remain involving large data environment. Current research on shortest path problem mainly focuses on seeking the shortest path from a starting point to the destination, with both vertices already given; but the researches of shortest path on a limited time and limited nodes passing through are few, yet such problem could not be more common in real life. In this paper we propose several time-dependent optimization algorithms for this problem. In regard to traditional backtracking and different node compression methods, we first propose an improved backtracking algorithm for one condition in big data environment and three types of optimization algorithms based on node compression involving large data, in order to realize the path selection from the starting point through a given set of nodes to reach the end within a limited time. Consequently, problems involving different data volume and complexity of network structure can be solved with the appropriate algorithm adopted.

1. Introduction

The single source shortest path problems in graph theory are very typical questions that enjoy wide applications in real life, such as network routing path selection, vehicle navigation, and travel routes. The classic algorithm to solve such problems is Dijkstra's Algorithm [1] proposed by Dijkstra in 1959 and a lot of researchers focus on this research area [2–4]. However, Dijkstra fails to solve problems where routes are required to go from the starting point, pass the specified intermediate node, and finally reach the destination—far more practical problems exemplified as follows:

(1) "Postman problem": the postman starts from the post office, sends letters to residents, and returns home, where we need to find the postman a shortest path within a given time.

(2) "Limited time problem": within a limited time, activities designed for staff members who tracked consent using depth sensors were proposed and they were carefully reminded of noncompliant activities [5], and a collaborative smartphone task model is proposed, which is called Collaboration-Based Intelligent Perception Task Model (CMST) [6].

(3) "Traveler problem": calculate a travel route for the traveler within the specified time, who needs to go from a designated location, pass a designated scenery spot, and visit a given place. The total distance should be the shortest or the total expense should be the lowest [7, 8].

(4) "Compression problem": a new compression method for large data environment is proposed, which can effectively reduce the data compression of single nodes and ensure the quality of data [9]. Due to the large amount of web service data, a data-driven scheme is based on kernel least mean squares (KLMS) algorithm [10]. In order to compress the input to further improve the learning effect, a new QKLMS is based on entropy-guided learning [11].

(5) "Network routing problem": find an efficient routing algorithm to solve the problem of path optimization of wireless sensor network, considering the influences of some practical factors such as the consumption of the energy of the nodes and recovery time of routing [12–14].

(6) "Laguerre neural network" [15]: it intends to propose a novel automatic learning scheme to improve the tracking efficiency while maintaining or improving the data tracking accuracy. A core strategy in the proposed scheme is the design

of Laguerre neural network- (LaNN-) based approximate dynamic programming (ADP).

(7) "Energy of the sensor nodes" [16]: a novel prediction-based data fusion scheme using grey model (GM) and optimally pruned extreme learning machine (OP-ELM) is proposed. The proposed data fusion scheme called GM-OP-ELM uses a dual prediction mechanism to keep the prediction data series at the sink node and sensor node synchronous.

These problems can be summarized as one graph theory problem; that is, in a weighted directed graph, a route goes from a starting point, passes through the designated intermediate node, and reaches a destination. It is required to find valid paths within a specified time, calculate the weight of these paths, and select a path with the lowest weight as the final result.

To solve this kind of problems, we may traverse the whole graph and find a shortest path, although theoretically this traversal algorithm will eventually sort out the optimal solution; however the time complexity remains high. In view of this, this paper proposes a node compression routing algorithm with considered time limits. The study pays attention to node compression and applies useful information obtained in path finding to search conditions, readjusting the order of subnodes and other methods as well. Additionally, the high time complexity in traditional algorithm is improved, offering an effective solution to this type of problem.

2. Problem Description

2.1. Mathematical Model of the Problem. Given a weighted graph $G(V, E)$ where $V = \{1, 2, 3, \ldots, n\}$ is the vertex set, $E = \{e_{ij} = (i, j) \mid i, j \in V, i \neq j\}$ is the edge set. d_{ij} $(i, j \in V, i \neq j)$ is the weight of vertexes i to j, where $d_{ij} > 0$ and $d_{ij} \neq \infty$; while d_{ij} and d_{ji} may be unequal, $V' = \{1', 2', \ldots, n'\} \in V$. We need to find the sequence $A = \{a_1, a_2, a_3, \ldots, a_n\}$ within a given time, where s is starting point and t is the destination, $s, t \in V$ and s, t do not belong to V', all of the elements in V' must appear in sequence A, making the sum of the weights of all edges of the path formed in sequence A minimal, and loop is not allowed in any path. The mathematical model of the problem is defined as follows.

Under the condition of Time $= t$, solve $\min C = \sum_{i \neq j} d_{ij} \times X_{ij}$, in order to define the starting point s and the destination t and make sure that there's only one in-edge and out-edge on each vertex except the edges of starting point and the destination paths; we make the following constraints:

$$X_{ij} = \begin{cases} 1, & \text{edge } e_{ij} \text{ is along the result path} \\ 0, & \text{edge } e_{ij} \text{ is out of the result path,} \end{cases} \tag{1}$$

where X_{ij} is an integer of 0 or 1, 1 represents edge e_{ij} on the result path, and 0 represents edge e_{ij} out of the result path, and X_{ij} is used to calculate the weight of the resulting path.

$$\sum_{i \neq j} X_{ij} = 1, \quad j \in V', \tag{2}$$

where $i \neq j$ means that the result path cannot contain the edges that the starting node and the end node are the same

node, which means the point in the intermediate node set on the result path can only occur once and must occur once.

$$\sum X_{sj} = 1, \quad j \in V, j \neq s. \tag{3}$$

The formula defines an edge that begins with the starting nodes which should appear in the result path, and the starting node in the edge cannot be the end node.

$$\sum X_{js} = 0, \quad j \in V, j \neq s. \tag{4}$$

The formula restricts that the starting node s can only be the starting node in an edge, and it cannot be any other kind of nodes, such as end node or intermediate nodes.

$$\sum X_{it} = 1, \quad i \in V, i \neq t. \tag{5}$$

The formula restricts that the result path must have an edge ended with the end node t, which means the edge cannot start with the end point t.

$$\sum X_{ti} = 0, \quad i \in V, i \neq t. \tag{6}$$

The formula restricts that the resulting path cannot contain the edge beginning with the end node t; that is, the end node t can only be used as the final node on the resulting path.

$$\sum_{i, j \in V} X_{ij} = |A|. \tag{7}$$

This formula defines the number of edges on the resulting path which can be the number of nodes minus one; that is, the resulting path cannot appear with unrelated edges and loops.

For the convenience of subsequent description, the following two definitions are given.

Definition 1 (key nodes). The nodes in V' include other must-pass nodes except starting point s and destination t.

Definition 2 (free nodes). All other nodes except the key nodes are included.

2.2. Simple Example. In the weighted graph G shown in Figure 1, four nodes can be found, namely, 0, 1, 2, and 3; therefore $V = \{0, 1, 2, 3\}$, and there are seven edges 0, 1, 2, 3, 4, 5, and 6, so $E = \{0, 1, 2, 3, 4, 5, 6\}$, where the weight of the edge is $\{d_{01} = 1, d_{02} = 2, d_{03} = 1, d_{21} = 3, d_{31} = 1, d_{23} = 1, d_{32} = 1\}$. To find a path from 0 to 1 via vertexes 2 and 3, we have $V' = \{2, 3\}$. Two paths can be found to solve this problem: $0 \rightarrow 2 \rightarrow 3 \rightarrow 1$ and $0 \rightarrow 3 \rightarrow 2 \rightarrow 1$. Since the weight of edges on the first route is 4, and the weight of the other is 5, the optimal solution should be $0 \rightarrow 2 \rightarrow 3 \rightarrow 1$.

3. Improved Backtracking Algorithm: IBA

If using the backtracking method to solve this problem, theoretically, we can have the optimal solution and of course other solutions. However, the backtracking method does not effectively use information constructed in the search process or the optimal solution to lay a foundation for optimization condition of the next-step search. In this section, an

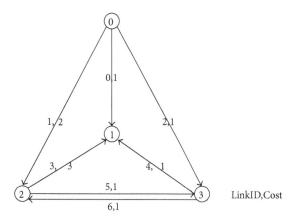

FIGURE 1: A simple example of the problem.

```
Improved-Backtrack (G)
(1) node=start
(2) while usedtime< t &&
(node!=end && !A' ∈ nodes)
(3) nodes.add(node)
(4) record information include
route and weigths
(5) for i = 1 to children.length
(6) add search rule
(7) Improvedacktrack (children[i])
(8) if result !=null-B
(9) return result and weight
(10) else
(11) return NA
```

ALGORITHM 1: The key pseudocode of the improved backtracking algorithm.

improved backtracking method (OPT-Backtrack Algorithm) is proposed based on traditional backtracking method. The new IBA retrieves known information and valid results from the previous search and adds them up to the next search rules before searching from other nodes. In this way, the search method and algorithms can be improved, since existing information and possible results are taken into consideration for a higher search efficiency.

The addition rule in the improved backtracking algorithm is shown below.

Rule 1. If the next node happens to be the destination, yet the current path has not gone through every must-pass node in the node set, the path will track back and begin searching for the next node. This rule avoids the generation of many invalid solutions thus improving the algorithm efficiency.

Rule 2. If the current path weight and the weight of the edge to the next node is greater than or equal to the minimum weight of the available solution, the path will track back and continue searching for the next node. If current path has been found whose current weight and the weight of edge to the next node is no more than the existing weight, then there is no need to search for the next node, because initially the problem is to find the smallest possible weight of the path.

Rule 3. For those nondestination nodes with zero child nodes, we should avoid entering the search. If a node is not destination and has no child nodes, the path shall not continue; therefore, it is not necessary to search at such nodes or rather they can be simply deleted from the graph.

The key pseudocode of the improved backtracking algorithm is shown in Algorithm 1.

4. Node Compression Based Search Algorithm

Although search efficiency can be enhanced by the improved backtracking algorithm to a certain degree, the negative complexity of the improved backtracking method will also increase as scale of the graph and solution domain expand.

To reduce algorithm complexity, this paper proposes a new algorithm, node compression based search algorithm: NCSA.

As the scale of graph increases, paths will expand accordingly. The same problem would be finding a path from a start point, reaching an intermediate node halfway and finally the destination. To reduce the algorithm complexity, we may preprocess the graph. The method is to compress the total number of nodes, remove useless nodes and low-value path fragments, and then save the only paths that are necessary to simplify the entire graph; the goal is to compress solution domain and ultimately improve search efficiency.

4.1. Node Compression Algorithm (NCA). The algorithm is applicable to the following circumstance: If a node is relatively remote which only reaches one other node, that is, a node followed only by one child node, in this case, the search will follow down the only child node route and will repeat this wherever there is such a node during the searching process. What we want to do is to avoid the simple and repeated calculations in this kind of situation.

Solution to this problem is Node Compression Algorithm (NCA). NCA records the paths through the above-mentioned nodes when the algorithm is applied for the first time and will remove the nodes but retain the path information; therefore, when the next search continues at this node, only stored path information will be used to avoid duplicated counting. As a result, the total number of nodes is compressed and reduced, making it easier to search for a better solution.

The process is shown in Figure 2.

In Figure 2, node 1 is followed by the only child node 2, the weight from nodes 1 to 2 is 2, marked as path 1; the compression process means transferring node 1 information to node 2 so that node 2 becomes the direct child node of node 0. If compressed, the weight from nodes 0 to 2 is 3, and path from nodes 0 to 2 is "0 | 1." This means node 1 is removed while the path information from nodes 1 to 2 is retained solely in node 2. When the next search algorithm reaches node 0, information retained in node 2 can be used directly without going back to node 1. So the number of nodes is reduced and the path will not be searched again.

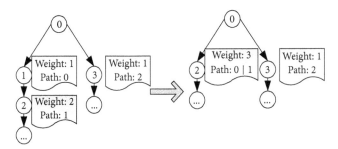

FIGURE 2: The basic idea of compression search algorithm.

4.2. Complete Compression Algorithm: CCA. Since Node Compression Algorithm (NCA) is used mainly to solve free nodes with only one child node, if such nodes are many in the graph, the algorithm efficiency will be significantly improved. However, if the scale of such nodes is limited, the basic compression algorithm will take less or no effect, which limits the effectiveness of compression search algorithm.

In view of the problem of NCA, this paper proposes a more efficient compression strategy, which compresses all free nodes in the graph to reduce the complexity of the graph, improving the search efficiency.

The problem is finding a noncircle path from the starting node to the destination node while passing through the intermediate node sets so that the weights of the edges on paths are as small as possible. When the reachability of nodes is complex, there will be many more possible paths to reach nodes of one and another. Since the problem requires that intermediate node set V' be passed and, within the set, there are multiple reachable paths between nodes, yet only one path will be selected within the set as one fragment of the final solution, therefore, we should find out all reachable paths while saving the path with the smallest weight. As the search algorithm reaches a corresponding node, the valid path will be retrieved from the stored information while the original nodes on the path can be removed from the graph, reducing useless nodes and repetitive counting. With this compression method, only the starting point, destination, the intermediate node set, and their interconnected path information will remain, simplifying the entire graph to a large extent with excellent compression efficiency.

Just like Figure 1, it can be seen as a simplified graph, and only the starting point, destination, and intermediate node set are preserved. In this way, we can achieve good compression efficiency by selecting the reachable path with the smallest path.

4.3. Improved Complete Compression Algorithm: ICCA. In order to further improve compression efficiency, this section continues to adjust and improve node compression by the three steps.

4.3.1. Adjusting Child Nodes Order by Weight. In the search process, algorithm can be done based on the weight of feasible solutions (see Rule 2 of IBA). First the order of subnodes is sorted according to the weight size from small to large. When algorithm searches the path, subnodes carrying smaller weight are searched with priority so that paths with smaller weight are easily obtained. As a result of this search strategy, other paths with larger weight can be skipped. This certainly reduces unnecessary search processes with greater efficiency.

4.3.2. Adjusting Child Nodes Order by the Sequence of Passing Nodes (from Small to Large). From the perspective of probability, when a new node is inserted into a graph, the more nodes a path passes, the more likely the repeated path will be generated. Therefore, under the condition of same weight, the nodes with fewer subnodes will be given priority since the paths that follow will make fewer repeated attempts, making it easier to find the solution path.

4.3.3. Removing Child Nodes with Larger Weight. This strategy is only applicable to high-complexity graphs. After compression, the remaining nodes will connect one and another to form paths; complexity of the graph might be still high. There would be the case where one path might be an effective solution but the nodes it passes carry excessive weight, so the path will not be considered the final solution. In this case, removing large weight nodes will lower the graph complexity and improve search efficiency. In addition, it will save time and figure out a better solution with a lower weight path.

By analysis, the spatial complexity of IBA is $O(n)$, while the spatial complexity of NCA, CCA, and ICCA is $O(n^2)$, where n is the total number of nodes in the graph. ICCA can quickly select the shortest paths according to the weights of nodes and the nodes with smaller weights and delete the nodes with larger weights from the compression of large networks efficiently.

5. Experimental Analysis

5.1. Data Description and Analysis. Without loss of generality, experiment data are from the cases of *2016 Huawei Software Elite Competition*; these quoted examples are based on the network topological graph of Huawei's network routers, switches, and other network elements when Huawei established its own network facilities.

5.1.1. Problem Description. Given a weighted graph $G = (V, E)$, V is the vertex set, E is the directed edge set, and each directed edge contains the weight. For a given vertex s, t, and a subset V' of V, find a nonringing directed path P from s to t within a given time so that P passes through all vertices in V' (the order of passing is not required), making the total weight of all directed edges on path P as small as possible.

5.1.2. Data Description. (1) All weights in the graph are integers within $[1, 20]$.

(2) The starting point of any directed edge is not destination.

(3) The number of directed edges connecting vertex A to vertex B may be more than one, whose weight may or may not be the same.

(4) The total number of vertices of the directed graph will not exceed 600, and the number of each vertex out-degree

(the number of directed edges with these points as the starting point) does not exceed 8.

(5) The number of elements in V' does not exceed 50.

(6) The nonringing directed path P starts from s to t, where P is a directed connected path consisting of a series of directed edges from s to t, with no repeated path allowed.

(7) The weight of a path is the sum of all weights on the directed edges of the path.

5.1.3. Data Format. (1) In the graph, each line contains the following information:

$$\{LinkID, SourceID, DestinationID, Cost\},$$

where LinkID is index of directed edge, SourceID is index of the starting vertex of the directed edge, DestinationID is the index of destination vertex of the directed edge, Cost is the weight of the directed edge. The index of vertex and that of directed edge are numbered from 0 (not necessarily continuous, but the case ensures that the index does not repeat).

(2) Path information includes

$$\{SourceID, DestinationID, IncludingSet\},$$

where SourceID is the starting point of the path, DestinationID is the destination of the path, and IncludingSet represents the must-pass vertex set V', and different vertex indexes are segmented with "|."

5.1.4. Experiment Environment. Windows 7 64-bit operating system, with Intel core i5 processor, jre1.6, 32-bit java virtual machine, up to 4 G memory, is used.

5.2. Experiment Methods and Result Analysis

5.2.1. IBA, NCA, and CCA Comparison. To verify backtracking method and IBA, NCA, and CCA algorithms, four sets of experiments will be conducted with the solution time limited to 10 seconds. From Experiments 1–4, the total number of nodes and edges in the graph will be gradually increased, while the number of intermediate nodes will be kept unchanged. Experiment results will be compared by the weight of final path result and time spent.

Experiment 1. Total nodes are 10; must-pass nodes are 3; edges are 39.

Figure 3 shows the experimental result from Experiment 1 and it presents the fact that IBA has higher efficiency than the backtracking method. Efficiency difference is not remarkably obvious in NCA and CCA because the compression process takes time and also the efficiency becomes even less obvious if the complexity of the graph is low.

Experiment 2. Total nodes are 20; must-pass nodes are 5; edges are 55.

Figure 4 shows the experimental result from Experiment 2 and it presents the fact that IBA, NCA, and CCA have a greater efficiency than backtracking method. Efficiency

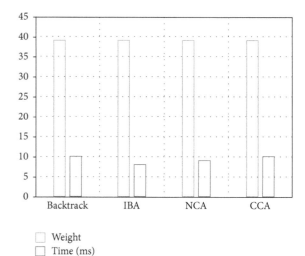

Figure 3: Experimental results of Experiment 1.

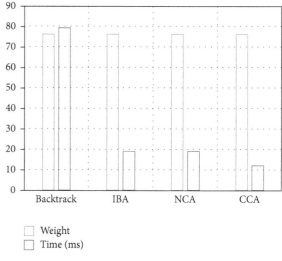

Figure 4: Experimental results of Experiment 2.

of CCA is the highest while IBA and NCA have a similar efficiency because of few remote nodes.

Experiment 3. Total nodes are 30; must-pass nodes are 10; edges are 135.

Figure 5 shows the experimental result from Experiment 3 and it presents the fact that the superiority of CCA proves obvious as graph complexity gradually improves.

Experiment 4. Total nodes are 40; must-pass nodes are 10; edges are 229.

Figure 6 shows the experimental result from Experiment 4 and it presents the fact that backtracking method indicates low efficiency if complexity of the graph is even higher; in contrast, CCA efficiency performs reasonably well.

Experiment results have shown that IBA has a higher efficiency than backtracking method judged by either weights

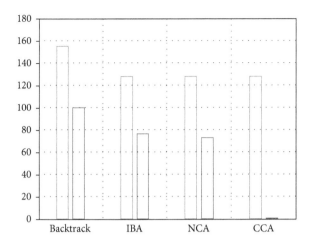

Weight

Time (100 ms)

FIGURE 5: Experimental results of Experiment 3.

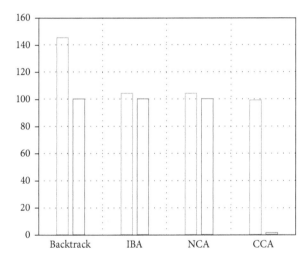

Weight

Time (100 ms)

FIGURE 6: Experimental results of Experiment 4.

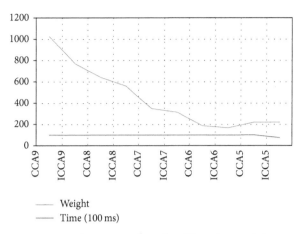

—— Weight

—— Time (100 ms)

FIGURE 7: Experimental results of Experiments 5–9.

nodes and edges, while the size of intermediate nodes set will also increase. Comparison will be based on the following five experiments.

Experiment 5. Total nodes are 60, must-pass nodes are 10, and edges are 285.

Experiment 6. Total nodes are 100, must-pass nodes are 15, and edges are 516.

Experiment 7. Total nodes are 200, must-pass nodes are 20, and edges are 997.

Experiment 8. Total nodes are 400, must-pass nodes are 28, and edges are 2178.

Experiment 9. Total nodes are 600, must-pass nodes are 50, and edges are 3418.

Figure 7 shows the experimental results which have indicated that compared to CCA, ICCA obtains better solutions. Therefore, the improved strategy in Section 4.3 is proved to be effective.

6. Conclusion

Problems like postman problem, traveler problem, bus line design, network routing problem, and other similar cases can be abstracted as the path finding graph model as discussed in this study. IBA and NCA are applicable to medium-sized problems. NCA is recommended to solve graphs that contain many remote nodes, while CCA and ICCA are more efficient in dealing with large-scale problems with great algorithm complexity. Additionally, ICCA is able to promote search efficiency when subnodes are readjusted.

As the size of problem becomes larger, CCA and ICCA may not be able to search the whole solution space completely with the optimal solution within a given time. In this case, the compression idea will be integrated into heuristic algorithms such as genetic algorithm and ant colony algorithm to expect a far more efficient search algorithm so as to resolve routing problems with larger scales.

or search time. NCA shows only a slight advantage over IBA because remote nodes in the graph are very limited. In particular, judging from all dimensions, CCA has proved significant quality in searching the results with superior efficiency to other algorithms, indicating the effectiveness of CCA in solving such problems.

5.2.2. CCA and ICCA Comparison. It is observed from the previous four experiments that the respective efficiency of backtracking method, IBA, and NCA decreases drastically as the sum of nodes increases. Therefore, there is no research value to add up more nodes to the graph. This section continues to compare between CCA and ICCA.

Experiment environment will remain the same as those of Experiments 1–4; experiment will gradually increase total

Conflicts of Interest

The authors declare that there are no conflicts of interest regarding the publication of this paper.

References

[1] E. W. Dijkstra, "A note on two problems in connexion with graphs," *Numerische Mathematik*, vol. 1, pp. 269–271, 1959.

[2] D.-Y. Zhang, W.-L. Wu, and C.-F. Ouyang, "Top-k shortest-path query on RDF graphs," *Tien Tzu Hsueh Pao/Acta Electronica Sinica*, vol. 43, no. 8, pp. 1531–1537, 2015.

[3] H. Y. Cao, Y. Yuan, and Z. Q. Liu, "Routing algorithm for WSNs based on residual energy of node and the maximum angle," *Transducer & Microsystem Technologies*, 2015.

[4] L.-Y. Feng, L.-W. Yuan, W. Luo, R.-C. Li, and Z.-Y. Yu, "Geometric algebra-based algorithm for solving nodes constrained shortest path," *Tien Tzu Hsueh Pao/Acta Electronica Sinica*, vol. 42, no. 5, pp. 846–851, 2014.

[5] W. Zhao, R. Lun, C. Gordon et al., "A human-centered activity tracking system: toward a healthier workplace," *IEEE Transactions on Human-Machine Systems*, vol. 47, no. 3, pp. 343–355, 2017.

[6] T. Li, Y. Liu, L. Gao, and A. Liu, "A cooperative-based model for smart-sensing tasks in fog computing," *IEEE Access*, vol. 5, pp. 21296–21311, 2017.

[7] Y.-H. Qi, Y.-G. Cai, H. Cai, Y.-L. Tang, and W.-X. Lv, "Chaotic Hybrid Discrete Bat Algorithm for Traveling Salesman Problem," *Acta Electronica Sinica*, vol. 44, no. 10, pp. 2543–2547, 2016.

[8] Y. Z. Wang, Y. Chen, and J.-S. Zhang, "Novel Fruit Fly Algorithm Based on Learning and Memory for Solving Traveling Salmesman Problem," *Journal of Chinese Computer Systems*, vol. 37, no. 12, pp. 2722–2726, 2016.

[9] C. Yang, X. Zhang, C. Zhong et al., "A spatiotemporal compression based approach for efficient big data processing on Cloud," *Journal of Computer and System Sciences*, vol. 80, no. 8, pp. 1563–1583, 2014.

[10] X. Luo, J. Liu, D. D. Zhang, and X. Chang, "A large-scale web QoS prediction scheme for the Industrial Internet of Things based on a kernel machine learning algorithm," *Computer Networks*, vol. 101, pp. 81–89, 2016.

[11] X. Luo, J. Deng, J. Liu, W. Wang, X. Ban, and J. Wang, "A quantized kernel least mean square scheme with entropy-guided learning for intelligent data analysis," *China Communications*, vol. 14, no. 7, pp. 127–136, 2017.

[12] A. Fernández-Fernández, C. Cervelló-Pastor, and L. Ochoa-Aday, "Improved Energy-Aware Routing Algorithm in Software-Defined Networks," in *Proceedings of the 41st IEEE Conference on Local Computer Networks, LCN 2016*, pp. 196–199, UAE, November 2016.

[13] N. Li, J.-F. Martínez, and V. H. Díaz, "The balanced cross-layer design routing algorithm in wireless sensor networks using fuzzy logic," *Sensors*, vol. 15, no. 8, pp. 19541–19559, 2015.

[14] L. Lei, W. F. Li, and H. J. Wang, "Path optimization of wireless sensor network based on genetic algorithm," *Journal of University of Electronic Science & Technology of China*, vol. 38, no. 2, pp. 227–230, 2009.

[15] X. Luo, Y. Lv, M. Zhou, W. Wang, and W. Zhao, "A laguerre neural network-based ADP learning scheme with its application to tracking control in the Internet of Things," *Personal and Ubiquitous Computing*, vol. 20, no. 3, pp. 361–372, 2016.

[16] X. Luo and X. Chang, "A novel data fusion scheme using grey model and extreme learning machine in wireless sensor networks," *International Journal of Control, Automation, and Systems*, vol. 13, no. 5, 2015.

4

Developing a Novel Hybrid Biogeography-Based Optimization Algorithm for Multilayer Perceptron Training under Big Data Challenge

Xun Pu,[1] ShanXiong Chen,[1] XianPing Yu,[1] and Le Zhang ⓘ[1,2]

[1]*College of Computer & Information Science, Southwest University, Chongqing, China*
[2]*College of Computer Science, Sichuan University, Chengdu, China*

Correspondence should be addressed to Le Zhang; zhangle06@scu.edu.cn

Academic Editor: Anfeng Liu

A Multilayer Perceptron (MLP) is a feedforward neural network model consisting of one or more hidden layers between the input and output layers. MLPs have been successfully applied to solve a wide range of problems in the fields of neuroscience, computational linguistics, and parallel distributed processing. While MLPs are highly successful in solving problems which are not linearly separable, two of the biggest challenges in their development and application are the local-minima problem and the problem of slow convergence under big data challenge. In order to tackle these problems, this study proposes a Hybrid Chaotic Biogeography-Based Optimization (HCBBO) algorithm for training MLPs for big data analysis and processing. Four benchmark datasets are employed to investigate the effectiveness of HCBBO in training MLPs. The accuracy of the results and the convergence of HCBBO are compared to three well-known heuristic algorithms: (a) Biogeography-Based Optimization (BBO), (b) Particle Swarm Optimization (PSO), and (c) Genetic Algorithms (GA). The experimental results show that training MLPs by using HCBBO is better than the other three heuristic learning approaches for big data processing.

1. Introduction

The term big data [1–3] had been developed to describe the phenomenon of the increasing size of massive datasets in scientific experiments, financial trading, and networks. Since big data is always of big volume and has multiple varied types and fast update velocity [4], it is urgent for us to develop such a tool that can extract the meaningful information from big data. Neural networks (NNs) [5, 6] are one of popular machine learning computational approaches, which are composed of several simple and interconnected processing elements and good at loosely modeling the neuronal structures of the human brain. A neural network can be represented as a highly complex nonlinear dynamic system [5], which has some unique characteristics: (a) high dimensionality, (b) extensive interconnectivity, (c) adaptability, and (d) ability to self-organize.

In the last decade, feedforward neural networks (FNNs) [6] have gained popularity in various areas of machine learning [7] and big data mining [1] to solve classification and regression problems. While the two-layered FNN is the most popular neural network used in practical applications, it is not suitable for solving nonlinear problems [7, 8]. The Multilayer Perceptron (MLP) [9, 10], a feedforward neural network with one or more hidden layers between the input and the output layers, is more successful in dealing with nonlinear problems such as pattern classification, big data prediction, and function approximation. Previous research [11] shows that MLPs with one hidden layer are able to approximate any continuous or discontinuous function. Therefore, the study of MLPs with one hidden layer has gained a lot of attention from the research community.

Theoretically, the goal of the learning process of MLPs is to find the best combination of weights and biases of the connections in order to achieve minimum error for the given train and test data. However, one of the most common problems of training an MLP is that there is a tendency for the algorithm to converge on a local minimum. Since an MLP can consist of multiple local minima, it is easy to be trapped in one of them rather than converging on the global minimum. This is a common problem in most gradient-based learning approaches such as backpropagation (BP) based NNs [12]. According to Mirjalili's research [13], the initial values of the learning rate and the momentum can also affect the convergence in case of BP based NNs, with unsuitable values for these variables resulting in their divergence. Thus, many studies focus on using novel heuristic optimization methods or evolutionary algorithms to resolve the problems of MLP learning algorithms [14]. Classical applied approaches are Particle Swarm Optimization (PSO) algorithms [15, 16], Ant Colony Optimization (ACO) [17], and Artificial Bee Colony (ABC) [18]. However, the No Free Lunch (NFL) theorem [19, 20] states that no heuristic algorithm is best suited for solving all optimization problems. Most of them have their own side effects and overall there has been no significant improvement [13] using these approaches. For example, Genetic Algorithms (GA) may reduce the probability of getting trapped in a local minimum, but they still suffer from slow convergence rates.

Recently, a novel optimization method called Biogeography-Based Optimization (BBO) [21] has been proposed. It is based on the motivation that geographical distribution of biological organisms can be represented by mathematical equations. It is a distributed paradigm, which seeks to simulate the collective behavior of unsophisticated individuals interacting locally with their environment to efficiently identify optimum solutions in complex search spaces. There are many related works of research [22–25] which show that the BBO algorithm is a type of evolutionary algorithm which can offer a specific evolutionary mechanism for each individual in a population. This mechanism makes the BBO algorithm more successful and robust on nonuniform training procedures than gradient-based algorithms. Moreover, compared with the PSO or ACO, the mutation operator of the BBO algorithm can enhance their exploitation capability. This allows the BBO algorithm to outperform PSOs in training MLPs. This has led to a great interest in applying the efficiency of BBO in training MLPs. In 2010, Ovreiu and Simon [24] trained a neuro-fuzzy network with BBO for classifying P-wave features for the diagnosis of cardiomyopathy. Research [13] used 11 standard datasets to provide a comprehensive test bed for investigating the abilities of the BBO algorithm in training MLPs. In this paper, we propose a hybrid BBO with chaotic maps trainer (HCBBO) for MLPs. Our approach employs chaos theory to improve the performance of the BBO with very little computational burden. In our algorithm, the migration and mutation mechanisms are combined to enhance the exploration and exploitation abilities of BBO, and a novel migration operator is proposed to improve BBO's performance in training MLPs.

The rest of this paper is organized as follows. In Section 2, a brief review of the MLP notation and a simple first-order training method are provided. In Sections 3 and 4, the HCBBO framework is introduced and analyzed. In Section 5, the computational results to demonstrate the effectiveness of the proposed improved hybrid algorithm are provided. Finally, Section 6 provides concluding remarks and suggests some directions for future research.

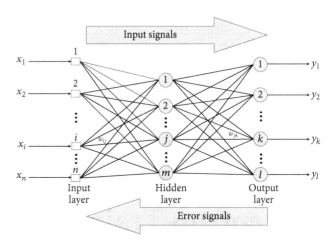

FIGURE 1: An MLP with one hidden layer.

2. Review of the MLP Notation

The notation used in the rest of the paper represents a fully connected feedforward MLP network with a single hidden layer (as shown in Figure 1). This MLP consists of an input layer, an output layer, and a single hidden layer. The MLP is trained using a backpropagation (BP) learning algorithm. Let n denote the number of input nodes, m denote the number of hidden nodes, and l denote the number of output nodes. Let the input weights $w_{i,j}$ connect the ith input to the jth hidden unit and output weights $w_{\text{out}(j,k)}$ connect the jth hidden unit to the kth output. The weighted sums of inputs are first calculated by the following equation:

$$s_j = \sum_{i=1}^{n} \left(w_{ij} x_i \right) - \theta_j, \quad j = 1, 2, \ldots, m, \tag{1}$$

where n is the number of the input nodes, w_{ij} is the connection weight from the ith node in the input layer to the jth node in the hidden layer, x_i indicates the ith input, and θ_j means the threshold of the jth hidden node.

The output of each hidden node is calculated as follows:

$$f(j) = \frac{1}{\left(1 + \exp\left(-s_j \right) \right)} \quad j = 1, 2, \ldots, m. \tag{2}$$

After calculating outputs of the hidden nodes, the final output can be defined as follows:

$$o_k = \sum_{j=1}^{m} W_{jk} \cdot f(j) - \theta'_k \quad k = 1, 2, \ldots, l, \tag{3}$$

where W_{jk} is the connection weight from the jth hidden node to the kth output node and θ'_k is the bias of the kth output node.

The learning error E (fitness function) is calculated as follows:

$$E_k = \sum_{i=1}^{l} \left(o_i^k - d_i^k \right)^2,$$

$$\tag{4}$$

$$E = \sum_{k=1}^{q} \frac{E_k}{q},$$

where q is the number of training samples, l is the number of outputs, d_i^k is the desired output of the ith input unit when the kth training sample is used, and o_i^k is the actual output of the ith input unit when the kth training sample is used.

From the above equations, it can be observed that the final value of the output in MLPs depends upon the parameters of the connecting weights and biases. Thus, training an MLP can be defined as the process of finding the optimal values of the weights and biases of the connections in order to achieve the desirable outputs from certain given inputs.

3. The Proposed Hybrid BBO for Training an MLP

Biogeography-Based Optimization (BBO) is a population-based optimization algorithm inspired by evolution and the balance of predators and preys in different ecosystems. Experiments show that results obtained using the BBO are at least competitive with other population-based algorithms. It has been shown to outperform some well-known heuristic algorithms such as PSO, GA, and ACO on some real-world problems and benchmark functions [21].

The steps of the BBO algorithm can be described as follows. In the beginning, the BBO generates a random number of search agents named habitats, which are represented as vectors of the variables in the problem (analogous to chromosomes in GA). Next, each agent is assigned emigration, immigration, and mutation rates which simulate the characteristics of different ecosystems. In addition, a variable called HSI (the habitat suitability index) is defined to measure the fitness of each habitat. Here, a higher value of HSI indicates that the habitat is more suitable for the residence of biological species. In other words, a solution of the BBO with a high value of HSI indicates a superior result, while a solution with a low value of HSI indicates an inferior result.

During the course of iterations, a set of solutions is maintained from one iteration to the next, and each habitat sends and receives habitants to and from different habitats based on their immigration and emigration rates which are probabilistically adapted. In each iteration, a random number of habitants are also occasionally mutated. That makes each solution adapt itself by learning from its neighbors as the algorithm progresses. Here, each solution parameter is denoted as a suitability index variable (SIV).

The process of BBO is composed of two phases: migration and mutation. During the migration phase, immigration (λ_k) and emigration (μ_k) rates of each habitat follow the model as depicted in Figure 2. A high number of habitants in a habitat increase the probability of emigration and decrease the probability of immigration. During the mutation phase, the mutation factor in BBO keeps the distribution of habitants in a habitat as diverse as possible. In contrast with the mutation factor in GA, the mutation factor of BBO is not set randomly; it is dependent on the probability of the number of species in each habitat.

The mathematical formula of immigration (λ_k) and emigration (μ_k) can be written as follows:

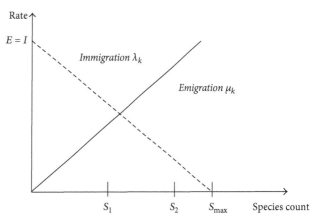

FIGURE 2: Species model of a habitat.

$$\lambda_k = I\left(1 - \frac{S_k}{S_{\max}}\right),$$
$$\mu_k = E\left(\frac{S_k}{S_{\max}}\right), \tag{5}$$

where I is the maximum immigration rate, E is the maximum emigration rate, $S_{\max}$ is the maximum number of habitants, and S_k is the habitant count of k.

The mutation of each habitat, which improves the exploration of BBO, is defined as follows:

$$m(s) = m_{\max} \times \left(1 - \frac{P_n}{P_{\max}}\right). \tag{6}$$

Here $m_{\max}$ is the maximum value of mutation defined by user, $P_{\max}$ is the greatest mutation probability of all the habitats, and P_n is the mutation probability of the nth habitat, which can be obtained as

$$\dot{P}_n$$
$$= \begin{cases} -(\lambda_n + \mu_n)P_n + \mu_{n+1}P_{n+1}, & n = 0; \\ -(\lambda_n + \mu_n)P_n + \mu_{n+1}P_{n+1} + \lambda_{n-1}P_{n-1}, & 1 \le n \le S_{\max} - 1 = 0; \\ -(\lambda_n + \mu_n)P_n + \lambda_{n-1}P_{n-1}, & n = S_{\max}. \end{cases} \tag{7}$$

The complete process of the BBO algorithm is described in Algorithm 1; here $I : \phi \rightarrow \{H^n, \text{HSI}^n\}$ initializes an ecosystem of habitats and computes each corresponding HSI and $\Gamma = (n, m, \lambda, \tau, \Omega, M)$ is a transition function which modifies the ecosystem from one optimization iteration to the next. The elements of the 6-tuple can be defined as follows: n is the number of habitats; m is the number of SIVs; λ is the immigration rate; τ is the emigration rate; Ω is the migration operator; and M is the mutation operator.

4. The Proposed Hybrid CBBO Algorithm for Training an MLP

There are three different approaches for using heuristic algorithms for training MLPs. In the first approach, heuristic algorithms are employed to find a combination of weights

$$I : \phi \rightarrow \{H^n, \text{HSI}^n\}$$
$$\text{While (condition} = T)$$
$$\Gamma = (n, m, \lambda, \tau, \Omega, M)$$
$$\text{end}$$

ALGORITHM 1: Pseudocode of BBO for optimization problems.

and biases to provide the minimum error for an MLP. In the second approach, heuristic algorithms are utilized to find the proper architecture for an MLP to be applied to a particular problem. In the third approach, heuristic algorithms can be used to tune the parameters of a gradient-based learning algorithm.

Mirjalili et al. [13] employed the basic BBO algorithm to train an MLP using the first approach, and the results demonstrate that BBO is significantly better at avoiding local minima compared to PSO, GA, and ACO algorithms. However, the basic BBO algorithm still has some drawbacks, such as (a) the large number of iterations needed to reach the global optimal solution and (b) the tendency to converge to solutions which may be locally the best. Many methods have been proposed to improve the capabilities for the exploration and exploitation of the BBO algorithm.

4.1. Chaotic Systems. Chaos theory [26] refers to the study of chaotic dynamical systems, which is embodied by the so-called "butterfly effect." As nonlinear dynamical systems, chaotic systems are highly sensitive to their initial conditions, and tiny changes to their initial conditions may result in significant changes in the final outcomes of these systems.

In this paper, chaotic systems are applied to BBOs instead of random values [25–27] for their initialization. This means that chaotic maps substitute the random values to provide chaotic behaviors to heuristic algorithms. During the processing of the BBO algorithm, the most important random values are calculated to choose a habitat for emigrating the new habitants during the migration phase. We utilize chaotic maps, which use the logistic model in (8), and choose a value from the interval of $[0, 1]$, whenever there is a need for a random value.

$$x_{n+1} = f(x_n) = \frac{\mu}{4} \sin(\pi x_n); \qquad (8)$$

here $x_{n+1} \in [0, 1]$ and μ are named logistic parameters. When μ equals 4, the iterations produce values which follow a pseudorandom distribution. This means that a tiny difference in the initial value of x_1 will give rise to a large difference in its long-time behavior. We employ this feature to avoid a local convergence of the BBO algorithm.

4.2. Habitat Suitability Index (Fitness Function). During the training phase of an MLP, each training data sample should be involved in calculating the HIS of each candidate solution.

In this work, the Mean Square Error (MSE) is utilized for evaluating all training samples. The MSE is defined as follows:

$$E = \sum_{k=1}^{q} \frac{\sum_{i=1}^{l} \left(o_i^k - d_i^k\right)^2}{q}; \qquad (9)$$

here q is the number of training samples, l is the number of outputs, d_i^k is the desired output of the ith input unit when the kth training sample is used, and o_i^k is the actual output of the ith input unit when the kth training sample is used. Thus, the HSI value for the ith candidate is given by $\text{HSI}(c_i) = E(c_i)$.

4.3. Opposition-Based Learning. To improve the convergence of BBO algorithm during the mutation phase, a method named opposition-based learning (OBL) has been used in [22]. The main idea of opposition-based learning is to consider an estimate and its opposite at the same time to achieve a better approximation of the current candidate solution.

Assuming that $X = (x_1, x_2, \ldots, x_n)$ represents a vector of the weights and biases in the MLP, with $x_i \in R$ and $x_i \in [\min_i, \max_i] \; \forall i \in \{1, 2, \ldots, n\}$, then the definition of the opposite vector is $X' = (x_1', x_2', \ldots, x_n')$ with its elements as $x_i' = \min_i + \max_i - x_i$. The algorithm for the OBL method can be described as follows:

(1) Generate a vector $X = (x_1, x_2, \ldots, x_n)$ and its opposite $X' = (x_1', x_2', \ldots, x_n')$, in an n-dimensional search space.

(2) Evaluate the fitness of both points, $\text{HSI}(X)$ and $\text{HSI}(X')$.

(3) If $\text{HSI}(X) \leq \text{HSI}(X')$, then replace X with X'; otherwise, continue with X.

Thus, the vector and its opposite vector are evaluated simultaneously to obtain the fitter one.

4.4. Outline of HCBBO for MLP. In this section, the main procedure of HCBBO is described. To guarantee an initial population with a certain quality and diversity, the initial population is generated using a combination of the chaotic system and the OBL approach. By fusing the local search strategies with the migration and mutation phases of the BBO algorithm, the exploration and exploitation capabilities of the HCBBO can be well balanced. The main procedure of our proposed HCBBO to train an MLP can be described as Algorithm 2.

5. Experimental Analysis

This study focuses on finding an efficient training method for MLPs. To evaluate the performance of the proposed HCBBO algorithm in this paper, a series of experiments were developed using the Matlab software environment (V2009). The system configuration is as follows: (a) CPU: Intel i7; (b) RAM: 4 GB; (c) operating system: Windows 8. Based on the works described in [13, 28, 29], we choose four publicly available classification big datasets to benchmark our system: (1) balloon, (2) iris, (3) heart, and (4) vehicle. All these datasets are freely available from the University of California at Irvine (UCI) Machine Learning Repository [30], thus ensuring replicability. And the characteristics of these datasets are listed in Table 1.

(1) **input**: habitat size n, maximum migration rate E and I (emigration and immigration rate), the maximum mutation rate M_{max};

(2) Initialize set of MLPs (habitats) by chaos maps on formula Eq. (8);

(3) For each habitat, calculate its mean square error by relative parameters based on formulas (9). And the basic rule of fitness function is the better performance maintains the smaller value of MSE. Then elite habitats are identified by the values of HSI.

(4) Combing MLPs according to immigration and emigration rates based on Eq. (6)
Probabilistically use immigration and emigration to modify each non-elite habitat based on Eq. (7).

(5) Select number of MLPs and recomputed (mutate) some of their weights or biases by chaos maps.

(6) Save some of the MLPs with low MSE;

(7) This loop will be terminated if a predefined number of generations are reached or an acceptable problem solution has been found, otherwise go to step (3) for the next iteration.

(8) **output**: the MLP with minimum MSE (HSI).

ALGORITHM 2: The framework of HCBBO algorithm.

TABLE 1: Classification datasets.

Classification datasets	Number of attributes	Number of training samples	Number of test samples	Number of classes
Balloon	4	16	16 as training samples	2
Iris	4	150	150 as training samples	3
SPECT Heart	22	80	187	2
Vehicle	18	400	446	4

TABLE 2: The main parameters of BBO and HCBBO.

Maximum number of generations: $T = 300$	Maximum mutation rate: $M_{max} = 0.005$
Elitism parameter: $e = 5$	Maximum possible emigration rate: $E = 1$
Population size: $P_{max} = 200$	Maximum possible immigration rate: $I = 1$

TABLE 3: MLP structure parameters.

	Balloon	Iris	SPECT Heart	Vehicle
Input	4	4	22	18
Hidden	9	9	45	52
Output	1	3	1	4

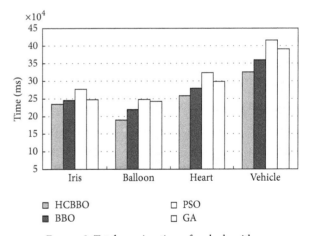

FIGURE 3: Total running time of each algorithm.

In this paper, we compare the performances of 4 algorithms, BBO, PSO, GA, and HCBBO, over the benchmark datasets described in Table 1. Since manually choosing appropriate parameters for each of these algorithms is time-consuming, the initial parameters and property structures for both the classical BBO algorithm and HCBBO algorithms (which were adjusted as Table 2) were chosen as in paper [13].

In order to increase the accuracy of the experiment, each algorithm was run 20 times, and different MLP structures will be used to deal with different datasets, which were listed in Table 3.

The running time (RT) and convergence curves of each algorithm are shown in Figures 3–7. From Figure 3, it can be observed that the average computational time of HCBBO is 8 to 13% lower than the best time obtained for the BBO. It is also lower than the computational time of all the other algorithms compared in this experiment. This decrease in the running time can be attributed to the fact that the HCBBO's search ability was enhanced by OBL.

The convergence curves in Figures 4–7 show that, among all the algorithms, HCBBO has the fastest convergence behavior on all the datasets. In Figure 4, under the same experimental conditions, HCBBO achieved the optimal values for its parameters after 150 generations while BBO could not converge to an optimal value even after 200 generations. The same pattern in faster convergence for the HCBBO was observed for the other classical problems (Figures 5–7). Statistically speaking, HCBBO performs the best on all the classification datasets, since it is able to avoid local minima better than any

TABLE 4: Experimental results for classification rate.

Algorithm	Iris Classification rate	Heart Classification rate	Balloon Classification rate	Vehicle Classification rate
HCBBO	93%	81.2%	100%	76.2%
BBO	90%	75.4%	100%	71.7%
PSO	38%	66.5%	100%	56.8%
GA	88.2%	56.9%	100%	59.9%

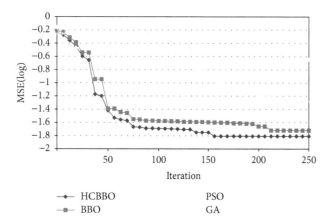

FIGURE 4: Convergence curves of algorithms for iris dataset.

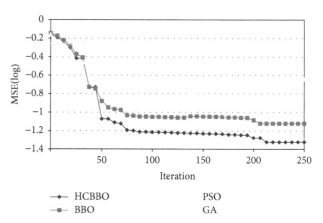

FIGURE 7: Convergence curves of algorithms for vehicle dataset.

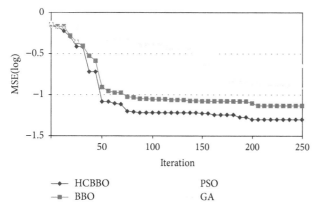

FIGURE 5: Convergence curves of algorithms for heart dataset.

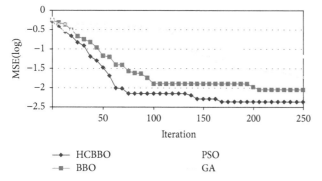

FIGURE 6: Convergence curves of algorithms for balloon dataset.

other algorithm. And the classification results obtained by HCBBO are better than all other algorithms for the chosen datasets.

The experimental results of mean classification rate are provided in Table 4. Statistically speaking, HCBBO has the best results in all of the classification datasets because it avoids local minima better.

6. Discussion and Conclusions

In this paper, a HCBBO algorithm was presented for training an MLP. Four benchmark big datasets (balloon, iris, heart, and vehicle) were employed to investigate the effectiveness of HCBBO in training MLPs. The performance results were statistically compared with three state-of-the-art algorithms: BBO, PSO, and GA. The main contributions and innovations of this work are summarized as follows: (a) this is the first research work combining a hybrid chaos system with the BBO algorithm to train MLPs; (b) the method named OBL was used in the mutation operator of HCBBO to improve the convergence of the algorithm; and (c) the results demonstrate that HCBBO has better convergence capabilities than BBO, PSO, and GA. In the future, we will apply the trained neural networks to analyze the big medical data and integrate more novel data mining algorithms [29, 31–35] into HCBBO.

Conflicts of Interest

The authors declare that they have no conflicts of interest.

References

[1] C. Kacfah Emani, N. Cullot, and C. Nicolle, "Understandable big data: a survey," *Computer Science Review*, vol. 17, pp. 70–81, 2015.

[2] F. J. Alexander, A. Hoisie, and A. Szalay, "Big data [Guest editorial]," *Computing in Science & Engineering*, vol. 13, no. 6, Article ID 6077842, pp. 10–12, 2011.

[3] D. Boyd and K. Crawford, "Critical questions for big data: provocations for a cultural, technological, and scholarly phenomenon," *Information Communication and Society*, vol. 15, no. 5, pp. 662–679, 2012.

[4] P. Hitzler and K. Janowicz, *Linked Data, Big Data, and the 4th Paradigm*, IOS Press, 2013.

[5] B. Irie and S. Miyake, "Capabilities of three-layered perceptrons," in *Proceedings of 1993 IEEE International Conference on Neural Networks (ICNN '93)*, pp. 641–648, San Diego, CA, USA, 1988.

[6] T. L. Fine, "Feedforward neural network methodology," *Information Science & Statistics*, vol. 12, no. 4, pp. 432-433, 1999.

[7] C. W. Deng, G. B. Huang, J. Xu, and J. X. Tang, "Extreme learning machines: new trends and applications," *Science China Information Sciences*, vol. 58, no. 2, pp. 1–16, 2015.

[8] M. H. Hassoun, *Fundamentals of Artificial Neural Networks*, MIT Press, 1995.

[9] R. C. Odom, P. Paul, S. S. Diocee, S. M. Bailey, D. M. Zander, and J. J. Gillespie, "Shaly sand analysis using density-neutron porosities from a cased-hole pulsed neutron system," in *Proceedings of the SPE Rocky Mountain Regional Meeting*, Gillette, Wyoming, 1999.

[10] N. A. Mat Isa and W. M. F. W. Mamat, "Clustered-hybrid multilayer perceptron network for pattern recognition application," *Applied Soft Computing*, vol. 11, no. 1, pp. 1457–1466, 2011.

[11] K. Hornik, M. Stinchcombe, and H. White, "Multilayer feedforward networks are universal approximators," *Neural Networks*, vol. 2, no. 5, pp. 359–366, 1989.

[12] D. Rumelhart and J. Mcclelland, *Learning Internal Representations by Error Propagation*, MIT Press, 1988.

[13] S. Mirjalili, S. M. Mirjalili, and A. Lewis, "Let a biogeography-based optimizer train your multi-layer perceptron," *Information Sciences*, vol. 269, pp. 188–209, 2014.

[14] A. Van Ooyen and B. Nienhuis, "Improving the convergence of the back-propagation algorithm," *Neural Networks*, vol. 5, no. 3, pp. 465–471, 1992.

[15] I. A. A. Al-Hadi, S. Z. M. Hashim, and S. M. H. Shamsuddin, "Bacterial foraging optimization algorithm for neural network learning enhancement," in *Proceedings of the 2011 11th International Conference on Hybrid Intelligent Systems, HIS 2011*, pp. 200–205, Malaysia, 2011.

[16] V. G. Gudise and G. K. Venayagamoorthy, "Comparison of particle swarm optimization and backpropagation as training algorithms for neural networks," in *Proceedings of the IEEE Swarm Intelligence Symposium (SIS '03)*, pp. 110–117, Indianapolis, Ind, USA, 2003.

[17] C. Blum and K. Socha, "Training feed-forward neural networks with ant colony optimization: an application to pattern classification," in *Proceedings of the 5th International Conference on Hybrid Intelligent Systems (HIS '05)*, pp. 233–238, 2005.

[18] M. Karacor, K. Yilmaz, and F. Erfan Kuyumcu, "Modeling MCSRM with artificial neural network," in *Proceedings of the 2007 International Aegean Conference on Electrical Machines and Power Electronics (ACEMP) and Electromotion '07*, pp. 849–852, Bodrum, Turkey, 2007.

[19] I. Boussaïd, J. Lepagnot, and P. Siarry, "A survey on optimization metaheuristics," *Information Sciences*, vol. 237, no. 237, pp. 82–117, 2013.

[20] D. H. Wolpert and W. G. Macready, "No free lunch theorems for optimization," *IEEE Transactions on Evolutionary Computation*, vol. 1, no. 1, pp. 67–82, 1997.

[21] D. Simon, "Biogeography-based optimization," *IEEE Transactions on Evolutionary Computation*, vol. 12, no. 6, pp. 702–713, 2008.

[22] M. Ergezer and D. Simon, "Oppositional biogeography-based optimization for combinatorial problems," in *Proceedings of the 2011 IEEE Congress of Evolutionary Computation, CEC 2011*, pp. 1496–1503, New Orleans, LA, USA, 2011.

[23] S. S. Malalur, M. T. Manry, and P. Jesudhas, "Multiple optimal learning factors for the multi-layer perceptron," *Neurocomputing*, vol. 149, pp. 1490–1501, 2015.

[24] M. Ovreiu and D. Simon, "Biogeography-based optimization of neuro-fuzzy system parameters for diagnosis of cardiac disease," in *Proceedings of the 12th Annual Genetic and Evolutionary Computation Conference, GECCO-2010*, pp. 1235–1242, New York, NY, USA, 2010.

[25] W. Zhu and H. Duan, "Chaotic predator-prey biogeography-based optimization approach for UCAV path planning," *Aerospace Science and Technology*, vol. 32, no. 1, pp. 153–161, 2014.

[26] S. H. Kellert, "Books-received - in the wake of chaos - unpredictable order in dynamical systems," vol. 267, Science, 95 edition, 1995.

[27] L. Zhang, Y. Xue, B. Jiang et al., "Multiscale agent-based modelling of ovarian cancer progression under the stimulation of the STAT 3 pathway," *International Journal of Data Mining and Bioinformatics*, vol. 9, no. 3, pp. 235–253, 2014.

[28] S. Mirjalili, S. Z. Mohd Hashim, and H. Moradian Sardroudi, "Training feedforward neural networks using hybrid particle swarm optimization and gravitational search algorithm," *Applied Mathematics and Computation*, vol. 218, no. 22, pp. 11125–11137, 2012.

[29] L. Zhang and S. Zhang, "Using game theory to investigate the epigenetic control mechanisms of embryo development: comment on: epigenetic game theory: how to compute the epigenetic control of maternal-to-zygotic transition "by Qian Wang et al"," *Physics of Life Reviews*, vol. 20, pp. 140–142, 2017.

[30] C. J. M. C. Blake, *Repository of Machine Learning Databases*, http://archive.ics.uci.edu/ml/datasets.html.

[31] B. Jiang, W. Dai, A. Khaliq, M. Carey, X. Zhou, and L. Zhang, "Novel 3D GPU based numerical parallel diffusion algorithms in cylindrical coordinates for health care simulation," *Mathematics and Computers in Simulation*, vol. 109, pp. 1–19, 2015.

[32] H. Peng, T. Peng, J. Wen et al., "Characterization of p38 MAPK isoforms for drug resistance study using systems biology approach," *Bioinformatics*, vol. 30, no. 13, pp. 1899–1907, 2014.

[33] Y. Xia, C. Yang, N. Hu et al., "Exploring the key genes and signaling transduction pathways related to the survival time of glioblastoma multiforme patients by a novel survival analysis model," *BMC Genomics*, vol. 18, no. Suppl 1, 2017.

[34] L. Zhang, M. Qiao, H. Gao et al., "Investigation of mechanism of bone regeneration in a porous biodegradable calcium phosphate (CaP) scaffold by a combination of a multi-scale agent-based model and experimental optimization/validation," *Nanoscale*, vol. 8, no. 31, pp. 14877–14887, 2016.

[35] L. Zhang, Y. Liu, M. Wang et al., "EZH2-, CHD4-, and IDH-linked epigenetic perturbation and its association with survival in glioma patients," *Journal of Molecular Cell Biology*, 2017.

5

Deployment Strategy for Car-Sharing Depots by Clustering Urban Traffic Big Data Based on Affinity Propagation

Zhihan Liu ⓘ, Yi Jia, and Xiaolu Zhu

State Key Laboratory of Networking and Switching Technology, Beijing University of Posts and Telecommunications, Beijing, China

Correspondence should be addressed to Zhihan Liu; zhihan@bupt.edu.cn

Academic Editor: Youngjae Kim

Car sharing is a type of car rental service, by which consumers rent cars for short periods of time, often charged by hours. The analysis of urban traffic big data is full of importance and significance to determine locations of depots for car-sharing system. Taxi OD (Origin-Destination) is a typical dataset of urban traffic. The volume of the data is extremely large so that traditional data processing applications do not work well. In this paper, an optimization method to determine the depot locations by clustering taxi OD points with AP (Affinity Propagation) clustering algorithm has been presented. By analyzing the characteristics of AP clustering algorithm, AP clustering has been optimized hierarchically based on administrative region segmentation. Considering sparse similarity matrix of taxi OD points, the input parameters of AP clustering have been adapted. In the case study, we choose the OD pairs information from Beijing's taxi GPS trajectory data. The number and locations of depots are determined by clustering the OD points based on the optimization AP clustering. We describe experimental results of our approach and compare it with standard K-means method using quantitative and stationary index. Experiments on the real datasets show that the proposed method for determining car-sharing depots has a superior performance.

1. Introduction

Big data exists everywhere and is providing with kinds of large data sets which can make people's life more convenient and realize sustainable development [1]. Big data usually requires a set of techniques and technologies with new forms of integration to reveal insights from datasets that are diverse, complex, and of a massive scale [2]. Over the last few years, urban traffic data have been exploding, and we have truly entered the age of big data for transportation [3]. This situation inspires us to make some new attempts on urban traffic big data. In the paper, we propose a new attempt of urban traffic big data to determine the locations of car-sharing depots.

Car-sharing systems intend to offer an alternative model of car rental, by which users are permitted to use vehicles charged by hours [4]. These respects are used to evaluate car-sharing systems, namely, urban traffic environment, depots' layout, and rental mode. As for the urban traffic environment, intuitively big cities are a good choice because they have high demand for public transportation. With regard to

depot locations, car sharing is a most important long-term decision owing to the fact that it has a direct impact on quality, efficiency, and cost of service and affects profit and market competitiveness. Deploying car-sharing depots based on demand has been a big challenge due to the lack of realistic vehicle operational data. Therefore, a detailed study of determining depot locations precisely would be necessary.

To maximize profits by distributing the depots rationally, the following three respects should be considered. (1) Consumers aspect: the ideal distance of walking on foot is 0–3 km. If the distance is too long, the willingness of users to rent vehicles will decrease significantly. (2) Return on investment aspect: good locations of depots will significantly improve overall earnings. From existing car-sharing systems, we know that car sharing is overwhelmingly concentrated in metropolitan cores; around 95% of members are found in these settings [5]. For example, Autolib' is a full electric car-sharing service in Paris. Up to July 2016, it offers over 1000 depots that can be found within a 5-minute walk in Paris. (3) Feasibility of depots construction aspect: generally speaking, car-sharing depots should be located in hot spots, such as shopping malls, office building parking lot, and transport hub. These sites usually have enough available parking, and cost of construction is relatively low. On the whole, consumers hope they can rent vehicles as conveniently as possible. However, car-sharing service providers aspire to earn more and spend fewer on constructing depots at the same time. Considering these factors in an integrated manner, a frequently visited area by taxis is a good choice, namely, taxi hotspots. With widespread traffic sensors, urban traffic data is easily acquired and becomes of large scale. There are many methods to discover taxi hotspots from taxi GPS trajectory data. However, not all taxi hotspots are well suited for car-sharing depots. Having available parking spots is necessary for building car-sharing depots. Origin and Destination points (OD points) of users' trips can be extracted from taxi GPS trajectory data, which reflect traffic hotspots and indicate the potential demand of car sharing. Based on the above theory, we propose a method to discover the traffic hotpots by clustering taxi OD points and determine the locations of car-sharing depots.

As there are so many clustering algorithms, different clustering algorithm gives different clusters. It is important to choose an appropriate clustering algorithm to make a balance between time cost and performance. One of the most popular clustering algorithms is K-means. However, K-means works well only when the number of clusters is known before clustering. It is exciting that another popular clustering algorithm, AP (Affinity Propagation) clustering algorithm, can determine the number of clusters spontaneously. Nevertheless, the complexity of AP is unacceptable, particularly when the dataset is of large scale. To improve the computing complexity of AP, this paper proposes an optimization method based on administrative region segmentation and sparse representation of similarity matrix. The results of this study demonstrate the benefit of large-scale data to determine the locations of car-sharing depots. The results can provide some guidance and suggestion to government and car-sharing service providers in the early stage of car-sharing system construction. Although this study only uses a specific city as a case, the proposed method and framework are also applicable to other cities.

The contributions of this paper mainly lie in the following two aspects:

(i) We propose a novel optimization approach to determine the depot locations by clustering massive OD points with AP algorithm based on administrative region segmentations. We propose a method based on density to optimize the parameter of AP and briefly introduce the principle and application range of AP clustering method for sparse similarity matrix.

(ii) We implement experiments on a large-scale dataset about containing ninety thousand OD points extracted from taxi GPS trajectories generated by about 12,000 taxis in Beijing. Our method produces about 50 points suited for the car-sharing depots. Then we evaluate our model with the net similarity between optimized AP and K-means. The results show that our AP has an advantage over K-means.

All the experiments show that our method is feasible and effective in determining car-sharing depots by clustering.

The remainder of the paper is organized as follows. Section 2 introduces some related works about locations of depots and taxi GPS data briefly. Section 3 presents the details of our method to determine the locations of car-sharing depots. Section 4 discusses the experimental results and analyzes the results. Conclusions and future work are discussed in Section 5.

2. Related Works

The majority of researches on determining the locations of car-sharing depots are dealing with urban traffic big data. In this section, we review some of the existing works.

2.1. Determining the Location of Depots. Urban big data enables a highly granular and longitudinal system, and it can help us understand city system and service better [6–10]. It can be used in many fields such as planning and governing cities, and business. For example, [3] applies big data to traffic flow prediction. Reference [11] presents a model to evaluate train timetable from the viewpoint of passengers' data on rail transit lines. Reference [12] proposes a study about public electric vehicle charging stations using traffic big data.

Many kinds of urban traffic big data are used for the depot locations problem. Reference [13] presents an approach to optimize locations of depots in one-way car-sharing systems in which vehicle stock imbalance issues are solved by three trip selection schemes. Reference [14] presents a method to optimize the locations of bike sharing stations and the fleet dimension and measures the bicycle relocation activities required in a regular operation day. Reference [15] develops a simulation model that considers demand variability and one-vehicle relocation policy and tests the solutions provided by the previous MIP model. Reference [16] analyzes the performance of the car sharing service across all stations, estimates the key drivers of demand, and uses these drivers to identify future locations of depots. Reference [17] determines the locations of depots based on the predicted car-sharing demand. The basis and premise of determining the candidate depots have been given. However, it is still difficult to determine the candidate depots so that a detailed study is extremely necessary.

2.2. Analyzing Taxi GPS Trajectory Data. Taxi GPS trajectory data is an important and effective type of urban traffic big data for analyzing some certain problems about transportation. More and more researches begin to focus on taxi GPS data in recent years. There are a number of works on analyzing taxi GPS data. Reference [18] uses taxi GPS data to analyze traffic congestion changes around the Olympic games in Beijing. Reference [19] presents a method to construct landmarks-nodes graph. Landmarks are defined as frequently traversed road segments by taxis. They present an approach to split adaptively a day into different time segments based on the entropy and variance of the travel time between landmarks. This brings up an estimative distribution of the travel times

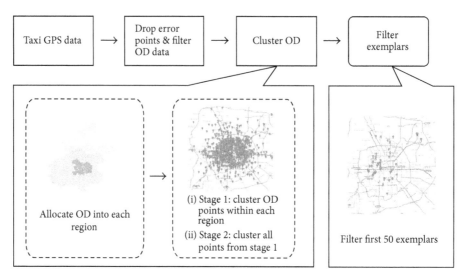

FIGURE 1: The framework of our proposed method.

between landmarks. Reference [20] proposes a method to construct a model of traffic density based on a large scale of taxi trips, which can be used to predict the traffic conditions and estimate the effect of emissions on the city's air quality. Reference [21] develops a method to identify traffic hotspots based on taxis GPS data, which is based on the method of clustering taxi GPS data by K-means algorithm. However, the most obvious problem of K-means is that it needs an input parameter K, which means you must know how many traffic hotspots in advance. From above all, for depot locations problem, more attention to taxi GPS data analyzing is needed.

3. Methodology

This section focuses on introducing our method in detail, which aims at finding suitable locations and the number of car-sharing depots while satisfying consumers demand and minimizing the total cost. Assuming that the total demand of car-sharing depots is unknown but positively associated with taxi flows, our approach is to cluster taxi OD points and then find hotspots from continuous taxi GPS trajectories, which could be considered as the locations of car-sharing depots. Our architecture of this paper is shown in Figure 1. The framework consists of three major components: filtering raw data, clustering OD points, and the final exemplars filter. The detailed process will be introduced in the following sections.

3.1. Filtering Raw Data. Filtering the efficient points from taxi GPS trajectory data is the necessary preparation, because not all the trips are efficient. For example, some error data caused by the breakdown of the GPS-equipment or some invalid data cannot reflect the character of traffic flows validly. The location of car-sharing depots is determined by the travel demand of travelers. We just filter the origin and destination points of passengers' trips which reflect the travel demand to some extent. And the OD points can be extracted from the continuous GPS trajectories according to trigger event.

Each taxi GPS point is described by a set of six elements: taxi id, trigger event, operation status, time, longitude, and latitude of GPS. "Taxi id" is the license of the car, which is a unique identifier for each taxi. "Trigger event" is the event that represents the taxi's trigger status. When the trigger event is equal to 0, that means the taxi turns to the "no-load" status from others. And 1 means turning to "load," 2 means "fortified," 3 means "withdraw garrison." "Operation status" is the operation status of the taxi. 0 means "no-load," 1 means "load," 2 means "Parking," and 3 means "off-the-line." "Time" is taxi's current time (SGT), the format is "mm-dd-hh-mm-ss". "Longitude" is the GPS coordinates of the taxi (East longitude and North latitude). For example, a data record (1143, 1, 1, 1106123843, 116.556101, 39.963646), it means the taxi 1143 was turning to "no-load" and the current time is 12:38:43 6th November, Beijing Time, and the taxi was located at $116.556101°E$ and $39.963646°N$. To satisfy our demand, we need to filter points which trigger event has a sudden jump from 1 to 0 or 0 to 1, namely, OD points. It is worth mentioning that all the OD points are sorted by birth time.

3.2. Clustering the OD Points. In order to determine the locations of car-sharing depots, we make the cluster analysis on OD points based on AP clustering algorithm.

3.2.1. New Preference $\{s(k,k)\}$ in AP Clustering. Firstly, we review the standard AP model [22]. For N data points, the input is a set of pairwise similarities $\{s_{ij}\}$, where s_{ij} is the similarity of point j to point i, and a set of exemplar preferences $\{p_j\}$, where p_j is the preference for choosing point j as an exemplar. Generally, preference p_j is set as the similarity s_{jj} and influences the final number of identified exemplars. The goal is to select a subset of data points as exemplars and assign every nonexemplar points to the corresponding exemplar, so as to maximize the overall sum of similarities between points and their exemplars. There are two kinds of message exchanged between data points, namely,

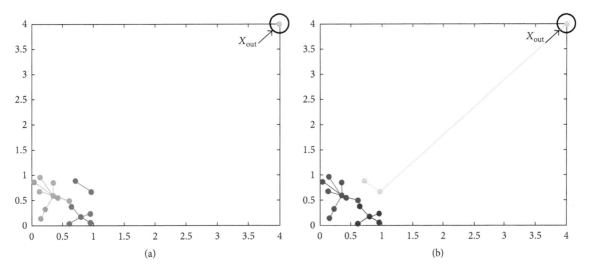

FIGURE 2: Outliers belonging to in different preference.

responsibility $r(i, k)$ and availability $a(i, k)$. To begin with, the availability values $a(i, k)$ are set to zero and the responsibility values $r(i, k)$ are set to the input similarity between point i and k. The message's updates of AP are computed as follows:

$$r(i, k) \longleftarrow s(i, k) - \max_{k' \text{ s.t. } k' \neq k} \left\{ a(i, k') + s(i, k') \right\} \tag{1}$$

$$a(i, k)$$

$$\longleftarrow \begin{cases} \min \left\{ 0, r(k, k) + \sum_{i' \text{ s.t. } i' \notin \{i, k\}} \max \left\{ 0, r(i', k) \right\} \right\} & i \neq k \\ \sum_{i' \text{ s.t. } i' \neq i} \max \left\{ 0, r(i', k) \right\} & i = k, \end{cases} \tag{2}$$

where $r(i, k)$ represents the evidence for how well point x_k serves as the exemplar of x_i. $a(i, k)$ reflects the evidence for how appropriate x_i choosing x_k as its exemplar. Equation (1) indicates that the update of $r(i, k)$ decreases the similarity $s(i, k)$ by removing the corresponding candidate exemplars from competition. Equation (2) represents the update process of $a(i, k)$ and gathers evidence from data points as to whether each candidate exemplar would make a good exemplar.

The above update rules require only simple, local computations that are easily implemented, and messages need only be exchanged between pairs of points with known similarities. At any point during affinity propagation, availabilities and responsibilities can be combined to identify exemplars. For point i, the value of k that maximizes $a(i, k) + r(i, k)$ either identifies point i as an exemplar if $k = i$, or identifies the data point that is the exemplar for point i.

AP considers all data points as potential exemplars. It takes as input a set of similarity $s(i, k)$, while $s(k, k)$ is set by input preferences. In this paper, similarity is set to be negative Euclidean distance: for points x_i and x_k, $s(i, k) = -\|x_i - x_k\|^2$. Note that the preference can be used to control the number of final exemplars, with low preferences leading to small number of exemplars and high preferences leading to large number of exemplars. Generally, the preferences of all data points are set to be the median of the input similarities so that all

data points are equally suitable as exemplars. That declares no prior inclination toward particular data points as exemplars.

However, it would lead some outliers to generate corresponding clusters which consist only relatively small data points in traditional AP algorithm. For example, Figure 2(a) shows the outliers in the AP clustering procedure, and the data points in the upper right corner would form a single cluster far from with the other clusters. However considering the scenario of this paper, outliers are the points where taxis seldom pass by. From the economic point of view, the outliers are not suitable to be individual candidate car-sharing depots. Therefore, we prefer to merge outliers into nearest high-density cluster. Based on the purpose, we propose a new formulation of the input preference as follows:

$$s(k, k) = \frac{1}{N-1} \sum_{i=0, i \neq k}^{N} s(k, i), \quad \forall k \in N. \tag{3}$$

The new preference $\{s(k, k)\}$ is set to be the average of similarities between point x_k and others. This value is related to density around the point. The higher the density, the bigger the value; meanwhile the point is more like to be chosen as the exemplar. Figure 2(a) presents the cluster result which preferences are set to be the median of all the input similarities. We can see outlier X_{out} becomes a cluster consisting only itself. Figure 2(b) presents the cluster result in which preferences are set followed by (3). Obviously, X_{out} belongs to the nearest relative high-density cluster.

3.2.2. AP Clustering Based on Administrative Region Segmentation. It is intuitively plausible that AP's runtime is $O(N^3)$ per iteration. However, as [23] presents, sharing computations allow us to compute messages efficiently which can reduce runtime within $O(N^2)$ per iteration. Figure 3 presents the curve of runtime with the total number N ranging from 5000 to 30000 by 5000 per step. We can find that the runtime increases dramatically with N rising. Results of experiments confirm the conclusion. While the N is thirty

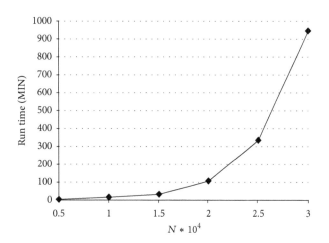

FIGURE 3: Runtime curve over the number of data points.

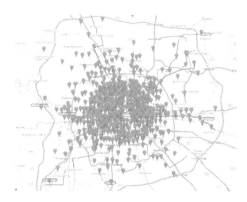

FIGURE 4: All exemplars in map.

thousand, runtime is about 15 hours. If the N becomes larger, it is unacceptable. For example, the number of OD points within twenty-four hours is about one hundred thousand, and it may cost hundreds of hours.

In order to solve the above problem, we propose an optimized AP clustering method based on administrative region segmentation. Suppose that N OD points are distributed uniformly in R administrative regions. There are four following major steps of our method:

(1) Allocate all OD points into different sets by administrative regions. The set of OD points in each region is named as AdminRegion[x], $x = 1, 2, \ldots, R$. Each region has nearly N/R OD points.

(2) Implement standard AP in each AdminRegion[x], and then we get a set of exemplars named AdminRegionCenter[x] for each AdminRegion[x]. The time complexity of this step is $O(RT(N/R)^2) = O((1/R)TN^2)$, where T is the number of iterations.

(3) Repeat the two steps above for every day's OD points. Then we have each region's exemplars in each day: AdminRegionCenter[day][x], day = $1, 2, \ldots, D$, $x = 1, 2, \ldots, R$.

(4) For each region, put all the exemplars of AdminRegionCenter[day][x] to a set, day = $1, 2, \ldots, D$. Implement AP on these sets separately. Then we have the final exemplars of each region.

For simplicity, we mark step (1) to (3) as stage 1 and step (4) as stage 2.

While AP based on administrative region segmentation works well, it still takes too much time due to the mass data. For example, the iterations of Haidian District in Beijing need 12 hours, which is obviously unacceptable. One improvement is that sparse similarity matrix to AP is applied. AP exchanges message between each point. If the similarity between two points is too low, the message between them is so few that we can set it to zero. In other words, we can set a minimal

and acceptable similarity threshold ε, then the computational formula of similarity becomes as follows:

$$s(i, j) = \begin{cases} s(i, j) & \text{if, } (s(i, j) > \varepsilon) \\ -\infty & \text{if } (s(i, j) < \varepsilon). \end{cases} \quad (4)$$

Then, we transform similarity matrix $\{s(i, j)\}$ to sparse matrix. That means we just need to compute the nonempty elements. We can use triples to store the sparse matrix and calculate based on some techniques to reduce the complexity. For N OD points, $\{s(i, j)\}$ have N^2 elements. Through above method, it becomes M elements. Obviously, $M < N^2$. The time complexity of step (2) can be decreased to $O((1/R)TM)$ from $O((1/R)TN^2)$. When the scale of dataset is quite large and the dataset is widely distributed, the method is obviously efficient.

Despite the fact that the sparse method can shorten the time, it also brings some problems. The similarity between two points involved in the calculation is limited in sparse threshold ε. The procedure of finding exemplars limited in a certain distance will increase the number of exemplars.

After above optimization procedure, AP clustering method based on administrative region segmentation now can be implemented to get a set of exemplars. These exemplars are selected from actual data points, informally called "centers." It can be considered as a subset of representative points of all the points. So we take these exemplars as traffic hotspots. These traffic hotpots can be regarded as potential candidate depots.

Figure 4 shows clustered exemplars from thirty thousand OD points of Beijing. We find that 82 percent exemplars are located within the Fifth Ring Road. As we all know, the Fifth Ring Road is the boundary of densely populated area. At the macroscopic level, these cluster exemplars results conform to the reality very well.

3.3. Exemplars Filter. Based on the previous steps, we have a set of exemplars. However, we cannot simply regard all the exemplars as car-sharing depots. In some cases, some exemplars are so close that they almost overlap (Figure 4). What is more, the number of points in each cluster is different. Some exemplars can represent many points while others represent only a few. Therefore, we count the point number

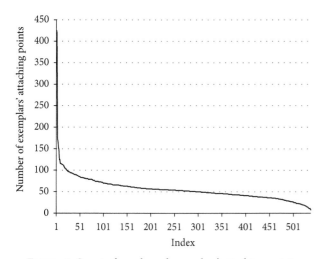

FIGURE 5: Count of number of exemplars' attaching points.

FIGURE 7: One of first 24.

FIGURE 6: Exemplars overlap.

FIGURE 8: Exemplars first 24.

of each cluster and rank it from the largest to the smallest. As shown in Figure 5, the x-axis is the indexes of exemplars, and the y-axis is the number of points, which have be clustered to the exemplar. We find a turning point in Figure 5, and it is about (24, 100). It means that only 24 exemplars have 100 or more attaching points. This interesting result is caused by the principle of AP. AP aspires to find an exemplar for each point, and it cannot remove outliers spontaneously. Considering the goal of this paper is to find high-density areas, we can only take the first 24 exemplars to make a brief analysis and evaluation.

Figure 6 shows part of the points in Terminal 3 Building of Beijing Capital International Airport before filtering. Figure 7 shows the points after filtering. Compared with Figure 6, points in Figure 7 are no longer overlapping. Figure 8 shows the positions of the first 24 exemplars. We can find out that the most of exemplars are hotspots in our life. It is especially sensitive to train stations, large-scale business, and residence districts.

4. Experiment and Results

In order to prevent noise interference and determine appropriate locations of car-sharing depots, we take a week's taxi GPS data consisting of seven hundred thousand points in Beijing. Thus, the target of this section is to apply "administrative region segmentation" model to the large-scale dataset.

In the following sections, we describe the datasets used for the experiment in Section 4.1. Section 4.2 presents the details of the experiment based on the large-scale dataset, and finally we analyze the results in several respects.

4.1. Case Study Datasets. To determine the locations of car-sharing depots, we need to obtain two types of data, namely, OD points obtained from taxi GPS trajectory data and the boundaries of administrative regions.

TABLE 1: The results of our method.

Region	N	1st stage K (mean preference)	1st stage K (new preference)	2nd stage K (sparse AP)	2nd stage K (standard AP)
Haidian	237820	21094	9125	4075	304
Chaoyang	206602	14457	9009	3355	268
Fengtai	176047	11534	6845	2625	219
Xicheng	100602	4890	3492	1190	159
Dongcheng	93261	4313	3134	1042	146
Shijingshan	40137	1848	1816	582	84
Daxing	15901	1612	1577	605	73
Shunyi	15385	1321	825	325	32
Tongzhou	4936	715	664	281	43
Mentougou	3185	304	271	97	25
Fangshan	1263	267	236	104	26
Sum	895139	62355	36994	14281	1379

(1) Taxi GPS Trajectory Data. The GPS trajectory data acquired in GPS-equipped vehicles represents the mobility patterns of the citywide human, from which we can get the origin and destination points of each taxi trip. The OD points can be extracted from continuous GPS trajectory data by trigger event.

In this paper, we utilized a GPS trajectory dataset generated by 12,000 taxis in Beijing from 5 to 11 November 2012. The GPS trajectory dataset consists of about seven hundred thousand GPS points. And we extracted 895,139 OD points from GPS trajectory dataset. We define the following notations for simplicity:

(i) $Q = \{1, 2, \ldots, q, \ldots, Q\}$: set of taxi GPS trajectory data

(ii) $N = \{1, 2, \ldots, n, \ldots, N\}$: set of OD points which are filtered out from Q

(iii) $K = \{1, 2, \ldots, k, \ldots, K\}$: set of locations of car-sharing depots

(2) The Boundaries of Administrative Regions. The boundaries of administrative regions are used to divide the OD points, which consist of polygon vertexes. We obtain it from Baidu map API (https://api.map.baidu.com/library/CityList/1.4/docs/symbols/BMapLib.CityList.html).

4.2. The Results. In this paper, OD points are of large scale and dense, and the span of space is large. It satisfies the specification and requirement of sparse AP completely. Therefore, we use the sparse AP in stage 1 of Section 3.2. Following the steps in Section 3, the results of different input preference and divided two stages are summarized in Table 1. Firstly, we focus on the comparison between different input preferences. The "mean preference" means that the input preference is the mean of all similarities in stage 1. The "new preference" means that the input preference of stage 1 is the expected value of similarities calculated by (4). We found that the number of clustering exemplars based on mean preference is larger than that based on new preference, because the new preference

results in allocating the outliers into corresponding high-density areas and decreasing the total number K. Secondly, compared with the results of sparse AP and standard AP of stage 2, we find that the total number of sparse AP is larger than standard AP's. The average elements in clusters of the sparse AP are 2.59, while the average elements in clusters of standard AP are 26.83. The former looks so bad because of incorrect use of sparse AP. We have mentioned that we use the sparse AP in stage 1, which causes the similarity between any two points of the input data in stage 2 and is limited over the sparse threshold. Therefore, in stage 2, it is difficult to find exemplars over the sparse threshold validly once more. When we adopt the standard AP in stage 2, the cluster results become better. Therefore, it is important to verify whether the dataset is suitable to use sparse AP. In summary, stage 1 with new preference and stage 2 with standard AP are the best choice.

For more information, we compare the results between AP and K-means in net similarity, which is defined as follows:

$$netSimilarity = \sum_k \left(s(k, k) + \sum_i s(i, k) \right). \quad (5)$$

Net similarity measures the appropriateness degree of how exemplars explain the data. It is the objective function that AP and K-means try to maximize. We can use the net similarity to evaluate the performance of the clustering methods. As we can see in Figure 9, the net similarity of AP based on administrative region is a little larger than K-means in each region, especially in big regions such as Haidian District. This is due to sparse AP used in stage 1 is more suitable to large-area regions. Meanwhile in smaller regions, such as Xicheng District, our method does not show an outstanding advantage.

The results present that there are 1379 exemplars alternative to car-sharing depots. However, as we know, not all the exemplars are suitable, and we need to filter these exemplars manually. Following the method in Section 3.3, we analyze the number of points which should be clustered to the 1379

TABLE 2: Comparison with AP and K-means in time cost (min).

N	K	K-means	AP
5000	160	0.006457	3.503131
10000	262	0.016079	16.63446
15000	339	0.019477	33.17552
20000	402	0.027256	107.2591
25000	463	0.047055	335.4124
30000	535	0.059033	945.0208

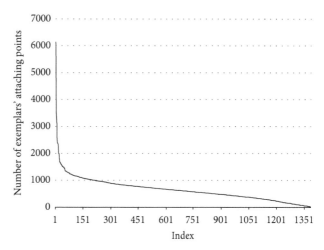

FIGURE 10: Count of number of exemplars' attaching points.

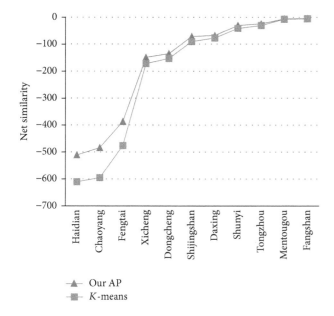

FIGURE 9: Net similarity.

FIGURE 11: Exemplars first 50.

exemplars, respectively, as shown in Figure 10. Similarly, we find a turning point and its coordinate is about (43, 1500). Therefore, we take first 50 exemplars to make a brief analysis and evaluate. As Figure 11 presents, we can find that our method is sensitive to most of the traffic hotpots, especially to stations, airports, shopping centers, and hospitals. From the most direct sense, this result is as expected.

To evaluate the time cost of our AP and K-means method, we make another experiment with 5000 to 30000 OD points based on the steps above. The results of time cost are summarized in Table 2. Apparently, the time cost of AP far outweighs the K-means. It is noteworthy that the results showed in Line 3 time cost of K-means, which just executes for just once, where we set K as a result of AP. That is to say, we set the final cluster number of AP as the input K of K-means. In fact if there is no result of AP, we must determine the approximate K value through different attempts and experiments iteratively. It is hard to predict the range of K on the premise of massive data. However, the results do not convince that the time complexity of K-means performs better than AP. If we perform K-means iteratively

to determine the approximate K, in the worst case scenario, the time complexity of K-means would be

$$\sum_{k=1}^{N} O(T * N * K) = O\left(T * N * \frac{N(N+1)}{2}\right)$$
$$= O(N^3),$$

(6)

and meanwhile the time complexity of AP is $O(N^2)$, which is less than K-means. Therefore, the combination of AP and K-means is the future direction of this paper to reduce the time complexity of K-means.

5. Conclusions

In this paper, we do a new trial on urban traffic big data about the determination of car-sharing depots. Experiments are implemented on the taxi GPS trajectory data in Beijing consisting of large-scale taxi OD points to study deployment strategy for car-sharing depots. To solve the highly complex problem caused by the large-scale data set, we present an optimization AP clustering method based on administration region segmentation. We define a new preference formula to solve the outliers problem in the process of clustering. In addition, we apply sparse AP on our method to decrease time cost. Combining theories and practices, we present the scope of application of our method. Meanwhile we have compared the objective function of AP and K-means in common, namely, net similarity. AP can not only overcome the biggest weakness of K-means, which is that K-means cannot determine K (the number of clusters) by itself, but also perform better in the net similarity. In spite of some measures taken to minimize the runtime of AP, it still takes too long. Thus, in practical applications, we can combine AP with K-means to achieve better performance. Although this study only takes Beijing as a case, the result of this paper indicates that this method has good versatility, because the method is not restricted to the data set itself. The methodological framework is applicable to any city only if the data set is available.

Owing to the fact that our method is simply based on clustering using taxi OD points, we have not considered much about whether the hotpots have the capacity to be car-sharing depots. Meanwhile, simply dividing dataset by regions is not rigorous. It maybe breaks some relevance especially in high-density areas. In this case, AP clustering based on grid segmentation is more reasonable. The grid segmentation means that taxi OD points are partitioned into multiple nonoverlapping grids to simplify representation of huge data points into smaller subsets. We plan to make further studies in these aspects.

Conflicts of Interest

The authors declare that there are no conflicts of interest regarding the publication of this paper.

Acknowledgments

This work is supported by the National Science and Technology Major Project (2016ZX03001025-003) and Special Fund for Beijing Common Construction Project.

References

[1] M. Batty, "Big data and the city," *Built Environment*, vol. 42, no. 3, pp. 321–337, 2016.

[2] I. A. T. Hashem, I. Yaqoob, N. B. Anuar, S. Mokhtar, A. Gani, and S. Ullah Khan, "The rise of 'big data' on cloud computing: review and open research issues," *Information Systems*, vol. 47, pp. 98–115, 2015.

[3] Y. Lv, Y. Duan, W. Kang, Z. Li, and F.-Y. Wang, "Traffic flow prediction with big data: a deep learning approach," *IEEE Transactions on Intelligent Transportation Systems*, vol. 16, no. 2, pp. 865–873, 2015.

[4] T. D. Schuster, J. Byrne, J. Corbett, and Y. Schreuder, "Assessing the potential extent of carsharing a new method and its implications," *Transportation Research Record*, no. 1927, pp. 174–181, 2005.

[5] A. Millard-Ball, G. Murray, J. Schure T et al., "Car-Sharing: Where and How It Succeeds," *Tcrp Report Transportation Research Board of the National Academies*, 2005.

[6] R. Kitchin, "Urban Big Data," *The Planner*, 2016.

[7] D. Tian, Y. Yuan, H. Qi et al., "A dynamic travel time estimation model based on connected vehicles," *Mathematical Problems in Engineering*, vol. 2015, Article ID 903962, 11 pages, 2015.

[8] D. Tian, J. Hu, Z. Sheng, Y. Wang, J. Ma, and J. Wang, "Swarm Intelligence Algorithm Inspired by Route Choice Behavior," *Journal of Bionic Engineering*, vol. 13, no. 4, pp. 669–678, 2016.

[9] X. Cao and X. Zhang, "Anomaly digging approach based on massive RFID data in transportation logistics," *International Journal of Big Data Intelligence*, vol. 1, no. 3, p. 166, 2014.

[10] F. Yang, S. Wang, J. Li, Z. Liu, and Q. Sun, "An overview of internet of vehicles," *China Communications*, vol. 11, no. 10, pp. 1–15, 2014.

[11] Z. Jiang, C.-H. Hsu, D. Zhang, and X. Zou, "Evaluating rail transit timetable using big passengers' data," *Journal of Computer and System Sciences*, vol. 82, no. 1, part B, pp. 144–155, 2016.

[12] H. Cai, X. Jia, A. S. F. Chiu, X. Hu, and M. Xu, "Siting public electric vehicle charging stations in Beijing using big-data informed travel patterns of the taxi fleet," *Transportation Research Part D: Transport and Environment*, vol. 33, pp. 39–46, 2014.

[13] G. H. D. A. Correia and A. P. Antunes, "Optimization approach to depot location and trip selection in one-way carsharing systems," *Transportation Research Part E: Logistics and Transportation Review*, vol. 48, no. 1, pp. 233–247, 2012.

[14] L. M. Martinez, L. Caetano, T. Eiró, and F. Cruz, "An Optimisation Algorithm to Establish the Location of Stations of a Mixed Fleet Biking System: An Application to the City of Lisbon," *Procedia - Social and Behavioral Sciences*, vol. 54, pp. 513–524, 2012.

[15] D. Jorge, G. Correia, and C. Barnhart, "Testing the Validity of the MIP Approach for Locating Carsharing Stations in One-way Systems," *Procedia - Social and Behavioral Sciences*, vol. 54, pp. 138–148, 2012.

[16] V. P. Kumar and M. Bierlaire, "Optimizing locations for a vehicle sharing system," in *Proceedings of the in Swiss Transport Research Conference*, 2012.

[17] X. Zhu, J. Li, Z. Liu, and F. Yang, "Optimization Approach to Depot Location in Car Sharing Systems with Big Data," in *Proceedings of the 4th IEEE International Congress on Big Data, BigData Congress 2015*, pp. 335–342, USA, July 2015.

[18] H. Wen, Z. Hu, J. Guo, L. Zhu, and J. Sun, "Operational Analysis on Beijing Road Network during the Olympic Games," *Journal of Transportation Systems Engineering and Information Technology*, vol. 8, no. 6, pp. 32–37, 2008.

[19] J. Yuan, Y. Zheng, C. Zhang et al., "T-drive: driving directions based on taxi trajectories," in *Proceedings of the 18th International Conference on Advances in Geographic Information Systems ACM SIGSPATIAL (GIS '10)*, pp. 99–108, November 2010.

[20] P. S. Castro, D. Zhang, and S. Li, "Urban traffic modelling and prediction using large scale taxi GPS traces," in *Pervasive Computing*, vol. 7319 of *Lecture Notes in Computer Science*, pp. 57–72, Springer, Berlin, Germany, 2012.

[21] Z. Yunpeng, Z. Gang, and L. Jian, "A novel method for traffic hotspots recognition based on taxi GPS data," *Journal of Beijing Information Science & Technology University*, vol. 31, no. 1, pp. 43–47, 2016.

[22] B. J. Frey and D. Dueck, "Clustering by passing messages between data points," *American Association for the Advancement of Science: Science*, vol. 315, no. 5814, pp. 972–976, 2007.

[23] I. Givoni, C. Chung, and B. J. Frey, *Hierarchical affinity propagation*, 2012, https://arxiv.org/abs/1202.3722.

6

Performance of a Code Migration for the Simulation of Supersonic Ejector Flow to SMP, MIC, and GPU Using OpenMP, OpenMP+LEO, and OpenACC Directives

C. Couder-Castañeda,[1,2] H. Barrios-Piña,[3] I. Gitler,[1] and M. Arroyo[1]

[1]Departamento de Matemáticas, Centro de Investigación y Estudios Avanzados del Instituto Politécnico Nacional (ABACUS-CINVESTAV-IPN), P.O. Box 14-740, 07000 México, DF, Mexico
[2]Centro de Desarrollo Aeroespacial del Instituto Politécnico Nacional, Belisario Domínguez 22, 06010 México, DF, Mexico
[3]Tecnológico de Monterrey, Avenida General Ramón Corona 2514, 45201 Zapopan, JAL, Mexico

Correspondence should be addressed to H. Barrios-Piña; hector.barrios@itesm.mx

Academic Editor: Jan Weglarz

A serial source code for simulating a supersonic ejector flow is accelerated using parallelization based on OpenMP and OpenACC directives. The purpose is to reduce the development costs and to simplify the maintenance of the application due to the complexity of the FORTRAN source code. This research follows well-proven strategies in order to obtain the best performance in both OpenMP and OpenACC. OpenMP has become the programming standard for scientific multicore software and OpenACC is one true alternative for graphics accelerators without the need of programming low level kernels. The strategies using OpenMP are oriented towards reducing the creation of parallel regions, tasks creation to handle boundary conditions, and a nested control of the loop time for the programming in offload mode specifically for the Xeon Phi. In OpenACC, the strategy focuses on maintaining the data regions among the executions of the kernels. Experiments for performance and validation are conducted here on a 12-core Xeon CPU, Xeon Phi 5110p, and Tesla C2070, obtaining the best performance from the latter. The Tesla C2070 presented an acceleration factor of 9.86X, 1.6X, and 4.5X compared against the serial version on CPU, 12-core Xeon CPU, and Xeon Phi, respectively.

1. Introduction

Currently, the development of parallel applications in science is conducted for heterogeneous architectures which are a set of distinct processing units that share one memory system. Usually, these units are a set of processors with multiple cores or processing units such as graphics cards (GPUs) or coprocessors, like the Xeon Phi, also known as Many Integrated Core (MIC), designed to accelerate the computing time.

Due to the diversity of architectures, the type of parallel programming employed is heavily dependent on the type of hardware. For this reason, when developing a parallel application to be migrated for various platforms, the programmer must have three fundamental questions in mind: the performance regarding the programming effort, that is, the evaluation of the development cost in terms of the execution time reduction, the energy efficiency, and the ease of maintenance/modification of the source code.

For example, the parallel programming at low level on Graphics Processing Units (GPUs) (at the kernel level) can be complicated and requires much development time. This type of programming can lead to a lack of productivity and error prone, thereby usually not being acceptable for industrial projects where the development time is a critical decision factor. In order to mitigate the development effort, the next-generation compilers help to create low-level code through directives written in a higher level of abstraction. However, even when these compilers are currently more advanced and simplify the developer's work, they still require good coding design to achieve an efficient parallel algorithm. Benefits of the compiler can be evidenced by simplifying the tedious low-level coding work.

Within the methodology of a parallel application, the most difficult part begins even before the first line is coded. Having a successful parallel algorithm is essential to improve performance, thereby reducing processing time. If the design of the application is not significantly converted to parallel, the implementation on a GPU or MIC will not have much benefit. Other options and different possibilities for parallelization should be explored [1].

Currently, OpenMP could be considered as standard for scientific programming on symmetric multiprocessing systems (SMP), and even it can be used transparently in the Xeon Phi architecture [2]. OpenMP is sustained by a combination of function and compiler directives [3, 4]. OpenMP has proven to be a powerful tool for SMP due to several reasons: it is highly portable; it allows medium granularity; each thread can access the same shared memory; it has its own private memory; and it also has a greater level of abstraction than MPI models [5]. Specifically for Computational Fluid Dynamics (CFD), applications of OpenMP have proven their effectiveness better than MPI [6]. Meanwhile, OpenACC, with a very similar methodology than OpenMP, has recently appeared as a viable alternative for specialized low-level languages, such as CUDA C and OpenCL for fluid dynamics GPU based applications, with very good results [7, 8]. The granularity in OpenACC is considered fine for its origin linked to CUDA.

The application to be accelerated in the present work is a serial code for simulating an ejector supersonic flow, commonly used in oil and gas industry. The ejectors confine a fluid flow under controlled conditions and then discharge it to an intermediate pressure between high pressure fluid from the nozzle and low pressure fluid from the suction. The flow through an ejector is governed by the principle of momentum conservation. Ejectors are seen like a venturi that works on the transmission of energy caused by the impact of a fluid moving with a very high velocity against another slow-moving or steady flow. This impact generates a mixture of fluids moving at a moderately high velocity, finally obtaining a higher pressure than the slow-moving fluid.

Ejectors are commonly employed to extract gases from the reservoirs where vacuums are produced, appliances such as condensers, evaporators, vacuum-based distillation towers, and refrigeration systems, where the extracted gases are generally noncondensable, as air. Ejectors are also used for mixing flows in sulfitation processes of sugar mills. Figure 1 shows the components of a typical ejector.

Previous numerical simulations for the ejector diffuser using the present source code were conducted by Couder-Castañeda [9], where the geometry of the diffuser, the numerical scheme, and the initial and boundary conditions are described in detail. Couder-Castañeda parallelized the code using a message-passing methodology based on the JPVM; however, the code was tested only in four processors because the required number of messages is intensive. Thus it is not scalable. After the work of Couder-Castañeda, convolutional PML boundary conditions were improved in the code to absorb pressure waves at the outflow boundary [10]. The simulations have been costly in terms of computing time, resulting in undesirable time-delays to get results. For

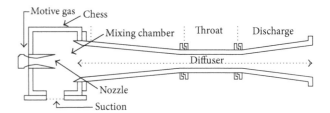

FIGURE 1: Different parts of a typical ejector.

example, on an Intel Xeon 2.67 GHz, 3 seconds of real-time simulation consumes about 35 hours of serial computing time. For this reason, in this work other coding alternatives to reduce the computing time are sought, while maintaining the source code intact due to the complexity of the numerical scheme.

This paper is organized as follows. Section 2 focuses on the design of the parallel algorithm, where both OpenMP and OpenACC designs are described in detail. In Section 3, performance experiments of the designs are shown for different architectures, that is, OpenMP on conventional multicore CPU and Xeon Phi and OpenACC on GPU. Section 4 shows validation tests of the code porting for the case of the ejector flow, where the total energy and the Mach number are compared. The paper ends with the conclusions in Section 5.

2. Design of the Parallel Algorithm

Details of the numerical scheme used in the original source code can be consulted in [9]. As an explicit finite difference numerical method is used and the set of equations is solved by a predictor-corrector scheme, the code is highly parallelizable. However, it is necessary to be cautious about the parallel implementation in order to get a significant reduction of computing time. First, the number of loops to be parallelized must be analyzed. Figure 2 illustrates the flow diagram which corresponds to the predictor step and demonstrates the execution of the loops labelled as C_1, C_2, C_3, C_4, C_5, C_6, and C_7. On the other hand, Figure 3 shows the corrector step where the loops are C_8, C_9, C_{10}, C_{11}, C_{12}, C_{13}, C_{14}, C_{15}, and C_{16}.

In the predictor step, the loops are used as follows:

  (i) One loop to calculate the predicted values of the flow primitives with backward finite differences (C_1).

  (ii) Four light loops to apply boundary conditions (from C_2 to C_5).

  (iii) One loop to calculate stress forces (C_6).

  (iv) One loop to calculate the predicted flow variables (C_7).

In the corrector step, the loops are used as follows:

  (i) One loop to calculate the new corrected values of the flow primitives with forward finite differences (C_8).

  (ii) Four light loops to apply boundary conditions (from C_9 to C_{12}).

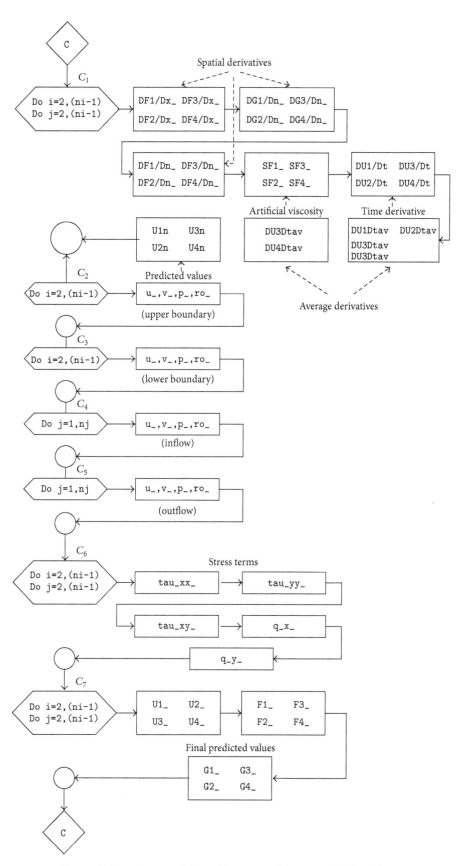

FIGURE 2: Flow diagram of the predictor step of the numerical algorithm.

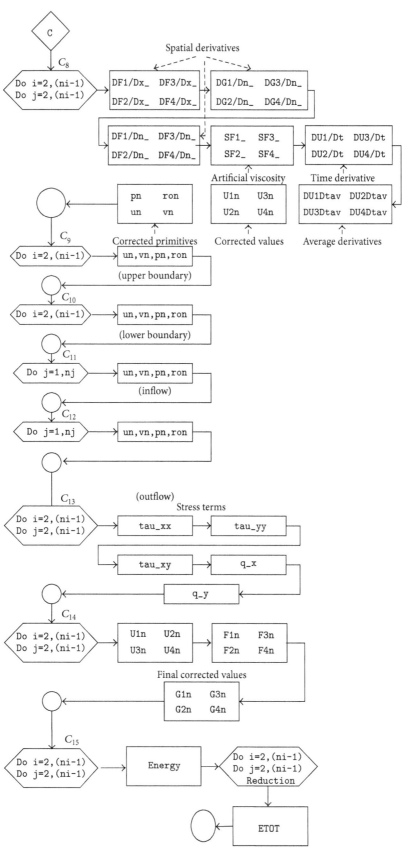

FIGURE 3: Flow diagram of the corrector step of the numerical algorithm.

TABLE 1: Intensity values of loops of the original source code. The underlined intensities correspond to loops candidates to be parallelized.

Loop	Intensity
C_1	<u>1.63</u>
C_2	0.50
C_3	0.50
C_4	0.36
C_5	0.00
C_6	<u>2.69</u>
C_7	<u>1.86</u>
C_8	<u>1.86</u>
C_9	0.50
C_{10}	0.50
C_{11}	0.36
C_{12}	0.00
C_{13}	<u>2.14</u>
C_{14}	<u>2.69</u>
C_{15}	<u>1.86</u>
C_{16}	<u>1.40</u>

(iii) One loop to calculate stress forces (C_{13}).

(iv) One loop to calculate the final flow variables (C_{14}).

Additionally, one more loop is considered to calculate the energy per cell (C_{15}), and another loop with a sum reduction serves to calculate the total energy (C_{16}). Thus, the code requires 16 loops to complete one time step. In order to get a significant reduction in computing time, the loops must be computationally intensive. Intensity is not the only metric, but for codes that use finite differences it is very useful. The intensity of a loop is the ratio of floating point operations to the memory accesses required by the loop.

In the PGI FORTRAN compiler, the parameter -Minfo=intensity can be employed to calculate intensity I. The intensities obtained for loops C_1 to C_{16} are shown in Table 1. It is necessary to clarify that the intensity I is defined as $I = f/m$, where f is the number of floating point operations and m is the number of data movements; for example, A(:)=B(:)+C(:) has an intensity of 0.333 (3 memory accesses, 1 operation) or A(:)=C0+B(:)*(C1+B(:)*c2) has an intensity of 2.0 (2 memory accesses, 4 operations); more examples could be seen in [11]. All the intensities in the loops were calculated manually following this definition to verify the results given by the PGI compiler. Additionally, the computing time required by loops was measured using the PGI profiling tool. We observe that intensity is directly proportional to computing time, which means that loops with greater intensity are loops that consume more computing time.

The intensities obtained are shown in Table 1. The implications of these results have to be managed carefully, because it is necessary to take into account the characteristics of the hardware. For this problem we consider that every loop with an intensity level $I \geq 1.0$ is a candidate to be parallelized, but it is also possible to parallelize them if they are part of a larger program. Loops with $I \leq 1.0$ generally are loops for which accelerating is not recommended but it depends on the platform properties. The loops of the present source code with intensities greater than 1.0 (values underlined in Table 1) are ready to be parallelized. The loops with intensities less than 1.0 are those where the boundary conditions are handled (values boxed in Table 1). In these cases, the loops are data dependent, which means that once one loop has finished, the next can start, with the exception of specific loops of boundary conditions that can be executed concurrently.

2.1. Design in OpenMP. The methodology begins with the OpenMP design, since it is more widely used and is compiled directly for multicore systems. Currently, OpenMP is considered the de facto standard to express parallelism in symmetric multiprocessing systems. According to Calvin et al. [2], OpenMP can be employed transparently in the Xeon Phi architecture. Furthermore, it is based on a combination of compilation directives and functions. OpenMP has proven to be a powerful tool for the development of scientific applications requiring parallelization, because (1) it is highly portable across multiple platforms, (2) it allows the development of applications with medium granularity, (3) each processing thread created with the same directive has its own private memory while also being able to access the shared memory, and (4) it is considered to have a higher level of abstraction than the message-passing model [3, 12, 13]. Two possible disadvantages that the use of OpenMP can has are that the application can be affected by problems of cache coherence, and uncontrolled and simultaneous access to the shared memory can lead to false sharing problems between execution threads.

The main characteristics of OpenMP are as follows:

(i) The OpenMP codes run on shared memory machines. It could be expected that they run also in GPUs in the 4.0 specification.

(ii) It has high portability.

(iii) It permits both medium grain and fine grain parallelism (vectorization level).

(iv) Each thread sees the same global memory but has its own private memory.

(v) It has implicit messaging (through shared variables).

Some disadvantages we can find are as follows:

(i) The placement policy of data can cause problems for not experts developers.

(ii) Overheads can become an issue when the size of the parallel loop is too small.

(iii) Threads are executed in a nondeterministic order.

(iv) Explicit synchronization is required.

In order to use OpenMP, the code should include the compilation directives to generate the parallel loops, thereby distributing the computation automatically [13]. The loops could be parallelized using Listing 1 or Listing 2. The computing is distributed implicitly; therefore the partitioning of

```
!$OMP PARALLEL DO SHARED(···) &
!$OMP & FIRSTPRIVATE(···)
      ···
!$OMP END PARALLEL
```

LISTING 1: The parallel DO is implemented more efficiently than a general parallel region containing a loop.

```
!$OMP PARALLEL SHARED(···) &
!$OMP & FIRSTPRIVATE(···)
   !$OMP DO
      ···
   !$OMP END DO
!$OMP END PARALLEL
```

LISTING 2: Parallel region containing a loop.

```
!$OMP PARALLEL DO
!$OMP END PARALLEL DO
!$OMP PARALLEL DO
!$OMP END PARALLEL DO
```

LISTING 3: Opening and closing of the parallel region.

```
!$OMP PARALLEL
   !$OMP DO
   !$OMP END DO

   !$OMP DO
   !$OMP END DO
!$OMP END PARALLEL
```

LISTING 4: Parallel region persistent between loops.

the loop is effectuated automatically using a balancing algorithm. It can be specified by the developer but for our application the decision is left to the scheduler.

We have two options for parallelizing the loops that have to be considered; the first is the handling of loops inside a parallel region (Listing 3), and the second is to create one parallel DO for each loop (Listing 4). Both options are viable because even when a parallel region is closed the threads remain active and when a new parallel region is reopened the overhead is not significant.

On the other hand, the parallelization of the loops DO/FOR in the highest possible level can lead to a better performance, thereby implying the parallelization of the outer-most loop and the encompassing of multiple loops in the parallel region. In general, the creation of loops inside

parallel regions reduces the overload for the parallelization by avoiding the creation of a parallel DO.

For example, the code showed in Listing 1 is more efficient than the code showed in Listing 2.

Nevertheless, the parallel constructor in OpenMP of the FORTRAN code shown in Listing 3 is less efficient than the code shown in Listing 4, because of the creation of the parallel DO; however the overhead creation is minimal, but, in finite difference codes for fluid flows, where millions of iterations are necessary over the time, a minimal overhead creation could not be negligible.

Implementations using Listing 3, Figure 4(a), can be seen in high-performance algorithms based on finite difference methods, as the SEISMIC_CPML algorithm [14, 15]. However, it misses the benefits shown in Listing 4, Figure 4(b), where a better performance can be obtained. In this case, the parallel region is persistently maintained throughout the time iteration. Additionally, we prefer to code by the way of Listing 4 because the readability of the code could be improved. This is due to the behavior of the variables that are only declared once at the beginning of the parallel region (SHARED, PRIVATE...). With the use of the scheme of Listing 4, the code contains 16 execution loops in one time iteration and only closes and reopens at the beginning of the time iteration. In this way, the opening and closing of 16 parallel regions on each iteration are avoided. It is important to clarify that the compiler cannot joint parallel regions automatically, because it could modify the logic of the flow work. If the parallel region is continuously opened and closed, it is obvious that the creation of a parallel region (spawning in multiple threads) will imply computational resources consumption, even if the threads are not destroyed. The time consumption to create a parallel region depends on compiler optimizations; thus this is a responsibility of the developer.

The scheme shown in Figure 4(b) uses only one parallel region. This scheme was selected to develop the code with the OpenMP directives. For the loops for boundary conditions, C_2 to C_5 and from C_9 to C_{12}, where intensities are $I < 1.0$, we have two options. The first is to perform parallelization by distributing the loop between available processing units (cores), as with the other loops with intensities greater than 1. This first alternative could not be convenient because a false sharing can occur; nevertheless as the loops are part of a large program, it seems to be a viable alternative. The second option, which is preferred in the present work, is to create one task for one loop (four loops to manage the boundary conditions). In our case, from one thread up to four can be assigned to perform the tasks. If the task is considered computationally nonintensive, one thread can perform all the tasks (all the loops), or if the task takes much time to be completed by one thread, other threads could be assigned to other tasks (see Figure 5).

Finally, it is possible to maintain the parallel region open, even during the time iteration. As shown in Figure 6(b), all the threads have control of the time iteration, thereby maintaining the parallel region open during the entire simulation time. It means that just one parallel region is created during all the execution. In this way, the possibility of overhead is reduced to a minimum. With this last design, only one

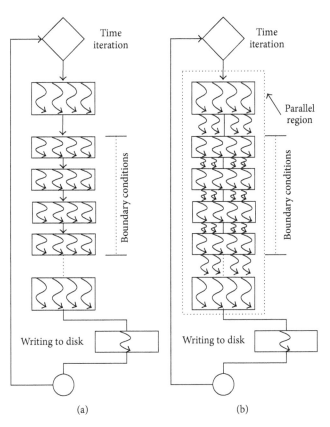

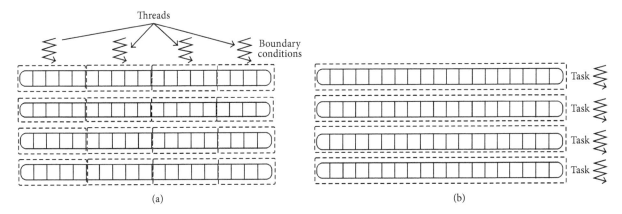

FIGURE 4: Design in OpenMP. (a) Opening and closing of parallel regions between loops, (b) persistent parallel regions between loops.

FIGURE 5: Implementation of the boundary conditions. (a) Distribution of the loops among the threads, (b) assignment of one loop to one task to avoid possible false sharing due to a computational intensity < 1.

parallel region is opened during the whole execution of the program and the loops with intensities below 1 are managed with tasks; however it is necessary to mention that there are more than one design possibilities.

Another important issue taken into account is the collapsing of loops. The collapse directive is used to increase the total number of iterations that will be partitioned across the available number of threads. By reducing the granularity, the number of parallel iterations to be done by each thread is therefore increased. If the amount of work to be done by each

thread is not vectorizable (after collapsing is applied), the parallel scalability of the application may be improved. This technique was compared against vectorization of the inner loop.

When the loops are collapsed, the number of iterations distributed among the threads is $(nj-1) \times (ni-1)$ (see Listing 5). Without collapsing, the number of iterations distributed among the threads is $(nj-1)$. In Listing 6 the loops are collapsed and the operations are vectorized; however, the number of floating point operations should be sufficient to

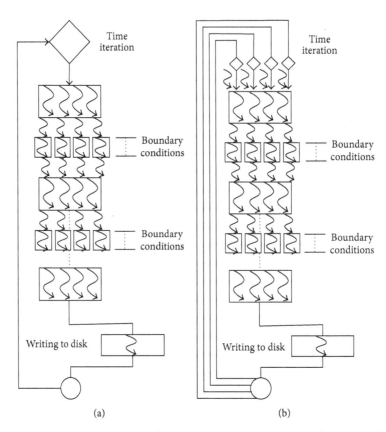

FIGURE 6: Design in OpenMP with boundary condition handling via tasks. (a) A boundary condition is handled by only one thread; (b) all threads handle the time iteration creating only one parallel region for the entire program execution.

```
!$OMP DO COLLAPSE(2)
DO j=2,(nj-1)
    DO i=2,(ni-1)
        ...
    END DO
END DO
```

LISTING 5: Iterations of the loops are joined to be executed in parallel by the team of threads.

```
!$OMP DO SIMD COLLAPSE(2)
DO j=2,(nj-1)
    DO i=2,(ni-1)
        ...
    END DO
END DO
```

LISTING 6: Iterations of the loops are joined to be executed in parallel and the internal operations are intended to be vectorized.

```
!$OMP DO SIMD
DO j=2,(nj-1)
    DO i=2,(ni-1)
        ...
    END DO
END DO
```

LISTING 7: Iterations of the outer loop are distributed among the threads and the operations are intended to be vectorized; as the inner loop exists, it is intended to be vectorized.

For this reason the directive OMP DO SIMD COLLAPSE(2) cannot be used. The Intel FORTRAN Compiler version 15.0 produces the warning #13379: loop was not vectorized with "simd" and the PGI compiler produces the warning Loop not vectorized: may not be beneficial. In Listing 8, the directive OMP DO SIMD COLLAPSE(2) could be applied with better success because an additional inner loop is included.

To distribute the iterations of the outer loop among the threads and to vectorize the operations (in general the inner loop), the directive OMP DO SIMD (Listing 7) could be used. For some compilers, the clause SIMD is not necessary because an automatic vectorization is applied.

achieve the vectorization. If the operations are not sufficient, the compiler is not able to generate a vectorized code and a warning would be shown. In our code this is the case.

```
!$OMP DO SIMD COLLAPSE(2)
DO j=2,(nj-1)
    DO i=2,(ni-1)
        DO k=2,(nz-1)
            ...
        END DO
    END DO
END DO
```

LISTING 8: Iterations of the outer loops are joined to be executed in parallel and the internal operations are intended to be vectorized. As the inner loop exists, it is intended to be vectorized.

The possibilities to parallelize the loops applicable to our present code are shown in Listings 5 and 7.

2.1.1. OpenMP on the Xeon Phi. One advantage of the parallel implementation in OpenMP is the possibility of migrating to a MIC type architecture practically without modification [4, 16]. The migration only requires the transfer of variables and data to the coprocessor and then the transfer of the execution of the parallel region. When the parallel regions are opened, it is important to avoid the transfer of data between CPU and coprocessor because this produces latency, which will significantly reduce the overall performance of the application. For this reason, the code should avoid any transfers during the execution of a time iteration.

Since the GPUs have been on the market during much time, more scientific applications have been migrated and tried on them than on the MICs. Specifically, the efficiency of the GPUs has been proven for finite difference-based algorithms [17–19]. MPI with CUDA C is used in [19]. There exist some similarities because the authors solve a PDE on time as we do, but their implementation is low level (kernels) for elastodynamic equations in a huge domain. Our application is for fluid flow equations in a relatively small domain; however, the flow chart shown is analogous. The GPUs do not offer an easy programming when they are used with low-level kernels, available on the Xeon Phi coprocessors, because the GPUs are not complete cores. In fact, the GPU cores can be seen as a group of small mathematical coprocessors that efficiently handle applications with very fine granularity. Similarly, we expect that applications which show a positive result using GPUs should benefit even more than the Xeon Phi architecture due to the presence of the vectorization concept, which is similar to CUDA architecture. The flexibility of the Xeon Phi allows the migration and provides support to a large number of applications requiring multiprocessing without the vectorization concept. Additionally, code generation for the GPU requires more refinement of the application to achieve the desired performance. This refinement means much development time, but, with the use of OpenACC, the job of coding low-level kernels is reduced.

One important aspect to be considered for understanding the expected performance of a Xeon Phi is the MT technology. With MT, each core can handle four threads for reducing the inherent latency to a micro-architecture multicore. This should not be confused with hyper threading (HT), defined as rapidly commutating between two threads that use the same core; HT can be deactivated via BIOS (for CPU). The Xeon Phi multithread technology cannot be deactivated and therefore we have to deal with it. Due to the inherent MT, available on the Xeon Phi coprocessor, the testing will consist of 1 up to 4 threads per core, the maximum that can be efficiently handled.

Although the Xeon Phi coprocessors are a complete computer by itself, they are able to execute programs natively independent of the CPU. The programming model recommended by Intel is the offload, where the CPU controls the Xeon Phi card, sending the tasks to be completed while the results are transferred back to the CPU. This model is employed since it is considered the most flexible, similar to the one used with the GPU. It is necessary to clarify that LEO extensions were preferred to offload the data, because although OpenMP 4.0 has capabilities of offloading, not all compilers implement it entirely. For example, OpenMP 4.0 will be apparently implemented completely in GCC 5.0 but in earlier versions it is partially implemented.

As happens in OpenMP for the CPU, what must be minimized is the number of parallel regions that are created in the loop of time, because unlike the CPU the threads created in the MIC for a parallel region are destroyed when the control returns to the CPU. However, the information must be registered on the CPU every certain number of iterations in order to write the simulation data to permanent storage. In this way, in a given instant, the parallel region must be abandoned in order to give back the control to the CPU. For this reason, it is not possible to use the model of Figure 6(b), where the parallel region is persistent throughout the whole program execution.

To minimize the number of parallel regions is important because much computing time is needed to create them. Schmidl et al. [20] showed that, to create a parallel region on an Intel Xeon Phi with 240 threads, 27.56 microseconds were needed. In the present code, we have 16 loops and, for example, a numerical simulation of 3 million of iterations implies 48 millions of `parallel for/DO`, which means 22 minutes of overload approximately (environ 2% of the overall time).

It is possible to use a design whereby the region is maintained open when disk writing is necessary. In Figure 7(a) we show a conventional design, where for each time iteration a parallel region is created on the MIC (this design will be denoted by D1 herein). In Figure 7(b) an improved design is shown, designed by reducing the number of created parallel regions. This is achieved by abandoning the execution of the MIC when disk writing is needed (this design will be denoted by D2 herein). In other words, control is given to the CPU only when transferring data from simulation to disk is effectuated. The corresponding implementation of Figure 7(b) can be seen in the Listing 9.

2.2. Design in OpenACC. Once the OpenMP model is completed and since this algorithm is a finite difference algorithm

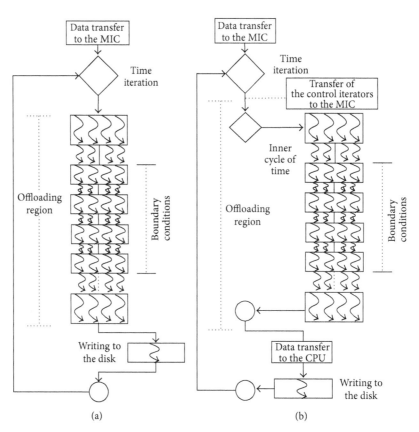

FIGURE 7: Design in OpenMP for the MIC architecture. (a) For each time iteration, one parallel region is opened and unloaded; (b) the parallel region is maintained until it is necessary to write data to the permanent memory; at that point control is returned to the CPU followed by a reentry to the MIC.

without complex reductions, it seems easy to migrate it to the OpenACC model. Both models have many similarities that can be consulted extensively in [21].

Researches have shown that, to obtain the best performance on the GPU, the transfers between CPU and GPU must be reduced at minimum. These transfers are transfers between kernels of the persistent variables. In OpenACC, the directive data specifies a region of the code where the data will be persistent on the GPU. Any region enclosed in the data region will use a persistent variable on the GPU, without the necessity of transferring the variables themselves to the compute region (kernel). The design used in this work is shown in Figure 8. This design is analogous to the one shown previously in Figure 7(a). However, the GPU has a limited residence time of the functions; that is, the card necessarily returns the control to the CPU after executing the kernel, in contrast to MIC.

The code structure which corresponds to the design of Figure 8 is shown in Listing 10.

The format of the loop (C_{16}) to calculate the total energy with a reduction is shown in Listing 11.

3. Performance Experiments

This section is focused on the experiments to evaluate both the performance of OpenMP on the conventional multicore CPU and Xeon Phi and the performance of OpenACC on the TESLA C2070 GPU. The time step Δt is 1×10^{-6} s and the code is executed to simulate 3.0 s of real time, requiring 3 millions of time iterations. The computational domain is composed of 1121×41 discrete points in x and y directions, respectively. Based on this mesh size, the computational domain can be considered as small, which has to be taken into account for the calculation of the performance.

This problem is considered as strong-scaling, because the computational domain is fixed and the number of processing elements is increased (threads mapped to cores); therefore the problem is governed by Amdahl's law. In strong-scaling, a program is considered to scale linearly if the speed-up is equal to the number of the processing elements used. In general, it is hard to achieve good strong-scaling with a big number of processes, since the communication overhead for most algorithms increases in proportion to the number of processes used. For the present problem the processes are threads.

3.1. Experiments on CPU. The configuration of the workstation is

(i) Dual Intel(R) Xeon(R) CPU X5650 @ 2.67 Ghz,

(ii) 12 real cores (one core can handle two threads when HT is enabled),

```
! dir$offload_transfer target(mic:0)
in(U1,U2,U3,U4: alloc_if(.true.)
free_if(.false.))
!dir$offload_transfer target(mic:0)
in(U1_,U2_,U3_,U4_: alloc_if(.true.)
free_if(.false.))
!dir$offload_transfer target(mic:0)
in(F1,F2,F3,F4: alloc_if(.true.)
free_if(.false.))

DO WHILE (.TRUE.)
...
!dir$ offload target(mic:0)
nocopy(DF1Dx,DF2Dx,DF3Dx,DF4Dx) &
& nocopy(F1,F2,F3,F4,U1,U2,U3,U4,
G1,G2,G3,G4) &
& nocopy(a_x,b_x,K_x,deltae) &
...
& in(k,Timetotal) out(k_shared) &
& out(Timetotal_shared,etot) &
& out(ro,u,v,P,T,M,ET)

!$OMP PARALLEL DEFAULT(NONE) &
!$OMP & SHARED(DF1Dx,DF2Dx,DF3Dx,DF4Dx) &
!$OMP & SHARED(F1,F2,F3,F4,
U1,U2,U3,U4,G1,G2,G3,G4) &
!$OMP & SHARED(a_x,b_x,K_x,deltae) &
...
DO WHILE (K <= nk)
!$OMP DO COLLAPSE(2)
DO j=2,(nj-1)
        DO i=2,(ni-1)
          ...
        END DO
END DO
...
!$OMP END PARALLEL
PRINT *, 'EXITING THE MIC TO WRITE DATA';
...
...
IF (k_shared >=nk) exit;
    k = k_shared+1;
    TimeTotal = TimeTotal_shared;
END DO;
```

LISTING 9: Code fragments corresponding to Figure 7(b); first all the variables are transferred to the MIC.

(iii) 12 GB RAM,

(iv) CentOS 6.6 Operating System,

(v) Intel FORTRAN Compiler 15.0.0.

Before the performance experiments begin, the developer should keep in mind the effects of the HT and the vectorization on the performance [22]. Thus, the experiments are conducted with HT enabled and HT disabled. Since there are 12 physical cores, from 1 to 12 kernel threads are created to analyze the behavior of the performance when HT is disabled. On the other hand, when HT is enabled, from 1 to 24 kernel threads are created. It is not necessary to create more threads

than cores (or logical cores) in the system; otherwise only overhead will be created.

For experiments with HT disabled, the strategy is to assign one thread to one core, and the compact scheduling affinity was used (see Figure 9). The compact strategy keeps all threads running on a single physical processor mapped one to one. Performance experiments for only 30,000 time iterations show that the scatter affinity is slower than the compact affinity by 30% to 10% (from 2 to 12 threads); therefore it is not included in the performance experiments. The compact affinity is desirable as long as all threads in the application repeatedly access different parts of a large array

```
    !$acc data &
    !$acc copyin(deltae,a_x,b_x,K_x) &
     !$acc local(DF1Dn,DF2Dn,DF3Dn,DF4Dn) &
...

    !WHILE OF TIME
...

    !$acc kernels
...

      !$acc loop independent
      DO j=2,(nj-1)
              !$acc loop independent
              DO i=2,(ni-1)
                   ...
              END DO
      END DO
...

    !$acc end kernels

    IF (MOD(k,it_display) == 0) THEN
    !$acc update host(U,V,ro,P,T,M,ET) async
    CALL LAYER_WRITE(DBLE(k))
    END IF

    END DO ! end of while in time

    !END OF WHILE

    !$acc end data
```

LISTING 10: Format of the OpenACC directives used to parallelize the loops.

```
    DO i=2,(ni-1)
    !$acc loop reduction(+:ETOT)
        DO j=2,(nj-1)
            ETOT = ETOT + (ET(i,j)*VOL(i,j));
        END DO
    END DO
```

LISTING 11: Format of the OpenACC directives used when a reduction is required. For the outer loop the directive acc loop has to be deleted.

(the case of the present application). When HT is enabled (see Figure 10), the scatter and the compact affinities give similar performance when the 24 kernel threads are created. However, the behavior of the performance of scatter affinity is similar to the performance with HT disabled until 12 threads, because the physical allocation is equal.

The performance experiments were carried out with vectorization of the inner loop and collapsing the loops. Sometimes the performance of nested loops can be improved by collapsing them, since this increases the total number of iterations that will be distributed over the available threads,

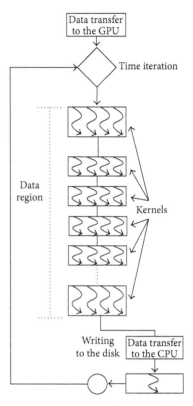

FIGURE 8: Design of the OpenACC for the GPU architecture.

thereby increasing the granularity. Nevertheless, for this problem the vectorization of the inner loop results in a better performance than collapsing by 5% to 7%. Vectorization is the process by which the implementation of an algorithm is converted from scalar to vectorial such that one single operation is executed over a group of contiguous values, all at the same time. In our particular case, the vectorization only applies to large floating point operations (inner loop) [23]. Thus, when the loops are collapsed, the granularity is reduced and the vectorization could not be applied; that is, by collapsing the loops, computing is insufficient for vectorization.

For the handle of the boundary conditions, an improvement by 1% and 1.5% was obtained using tasks, compared with loops parallelized conventionally; thus the gain is low. About the use of a persistent parallel region the gain is by 0.5% and 1.0%. Thus, there is not a noticeable overhead when many parallel regions are used, and therefore one or many parallel regions could be used.

The best performance is gathered when the compact affinity, vectorization of the inner loop, tasks for the boundary conditions, and HT disabled were considered. The corresponding computing times with their respective speed-up factors are shown in Table 2 for 1 to 12 threads.

The behavior of the computing time with HT enabled and disabled is shown in Figures 11(a) and 11(b), respectively. We denote that there is a difference in computing time when the HT is enabled and disabled. When the HT is enabled the serial execution is slower by 20%. This result is in

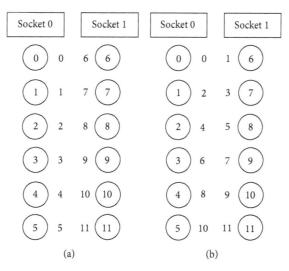

FIGURE 9: Affinities behavior on a SMP with 2 sockets and 6 cores by socket, with the HT disabled; (a) compact affinity, (b) scatter affinity.

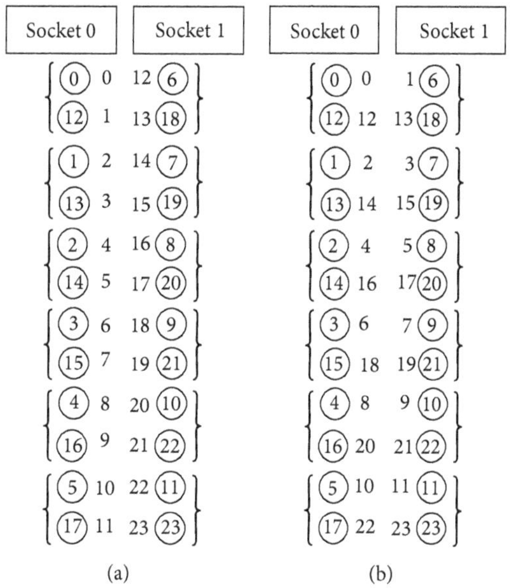

FIGURE 10: Affinities behavior on a SMP with 2 sockets and 6 cores by socket, with the HT enabled; (a) compact affinity, (b) scatter affinity. Curly brackets mean that the virtual cores are handled by the same physical core.

agreement with Zhang et al. [13], who found that sometimes it is better to execute an OpenMP application using only a single thread per physical processor. Leng et al. [24] also confirmed that the HT can lead to performance degradation for some HPC applications. Empirical studies showed that when HT is used for intensive floating point calculation codes, which need to share variables among the threads, an overhead can be introduced. To achieve similar performance with only one thread without the HT, it is necessary to create two threads and assign them to the same core. Nevertheless, for applications where the threads do not share the computational domain a gain in performance was observed by Couder-Castañeda et al. [25].

The graph of Figure 12(a) depicts a behavior governed by Amdahl's law with a maximum speed-up factor of 6.14X.

The speed-up factors obtained let us to approximate the serial fraction of our code between 0.05 and 0.10. This also was estimated by measuring the computing time of the different parts of the code.

With HT enabled each core can handle 2 threads and reports 24 logic cores; therefore execution threads from 1 to 24 are created to analyze the performance behavior. In this way, we tried to determine if a better performance can be achieved with HT [26–29]. When HT is enabled, the best speed-up factor obtained is 6.72 for the scatter affinity and 7.40 for the compact affinity, considering as reference the computing time of the optimized serial version executed with the HT enabled. In this case, the use of HT does not increase the performance; thus the HT does not really provide a benefit for this case. This behavior seems to be normal

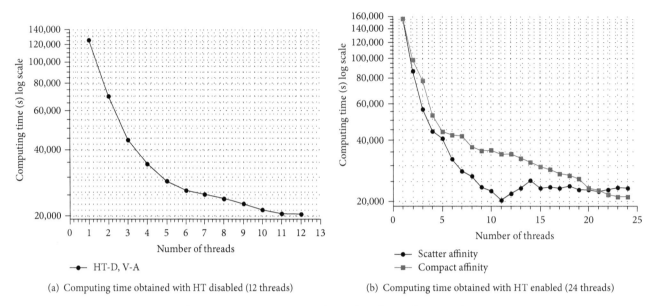

(a) Computing time obtained with HT disabled (12 threads)

(b) Computing time obtained with HT enabled (24 threads)

FIGURE 11: Computing times obtained on the Dual Xeon CPU.

TABLE 2: Computing times and speed-up factors obtained using OpenMP on the Xeon CPU with HT disabled. The speed-up factors are calculated with best optimized serial version as reference. With HT: hyper threading, V: vectorization, D: deactivated, and A: activated.

Threads	HT-D V-A	Speed-up
1	34 h 48 m 32 s	(1.00X)
2	19 h 26 m 58 s	(1.79X)
3	12 h 20 m 02 s	(2.82X)
4	09 h 35 m 11 s	(3.63X)
5	07 h 58 m 53 s	(4.36X)
6	07 h 15 m 54 s	(4.79X)
7	06 h 58 m 14 s	(4.99X)
8	06 h 40 m 30 s	(5.21X)
9	06 h 18 m 21 s	(5.52X)
10	05 h 55 m 56 s	(5.87X)
11	05 h 41 m 52 s	(6.11X)
12	05 h 40 m 23 s	(6.14X)

because the application is floating point intensive and two threads are sharing the same core FPU (floating point unit).

These results showed in Table 3 emphasize the effects of the vectorization which works correctly when the number of floating point operations by core is sufficient and can be vectorized.

3.2. Experiments on the Xeon Phi. The code with OpenMP directives was also tested for performance on the Xeon Phi (model 5110P) with the following general characteristics:

(i) 60 active cores (each core can handle 4 threads),

(ii) frequency 1 GHz,

TABLE 3: Computing times and their corresponding speed-up factors obtained with HT enabled for the compact and scatter affinities. HT: hyper threading, V: vectorization, and A: activated.

Threads	HT-A, V-A, compact	HT-A V-A, scatter
1	43 h 22 m 22 s (1.00X)	43 h 19 m 58 s (1.00X)
2	27 h 17 m 46 s (1.59X)	24 h 05 m 16 s (1.80X)
3	21 h 38 m 07 s (2.00X)	15 h 41 m 05 s (2.76X)
4	14 h 37 m 51 s (2.96X)	12 h 15 m 17 s (3.54X)
5	12 h 12 m 27 s (3.55X)	11 h 18 m 27 s (3.83X)
6	11 h 44 m 25 s (3.69X)	08 h 55 m 26 s (4.86X)
7	11 h 36 m 13 s (3.74X)	07 h 46 m 44 s (5.57X)
8	10 h 15 m 49 s (4.23X)	07 h 21 m 59 s (5.88X)
9	09 h 49 m 17 s (4.42X)	06 h 31 m 26 s (6.64X)
10	9 h 51 m 28 s (4.40X)	06 h 16 m 28 s (6.91X)
11	09 h 26 m 09 s (4.60X)	05 h 33 m 41 s (7.79X)
12	09 h 27 m 33 s (4.59X)	06 h 03 m 58 s (7.14X)
13	09 h 01 m 54 s (4.8X)	06 h 29 m 24 s (6.68X)
14	08 h 37 m 13 s (5.03X)	07 h 01 m 00 s (6.18X)
15	08 h 12 m 43 s (5.28X)	06 h 27 m 47 s (6.70X)
16	07 h 56 m 28 s (5.46X)	06 h 31 m 54 s (6.63X)
17	07 h 35 m 52 s (5.71X)	06 h 26 m 55 s (6.72X)
18	07 h 27 m 38 s (5.81X)	06 h 35 m 04 s (6.58X)
19	07 h 09 m 47 s (6.06X)	06 h 20 m 00 s (6.84X)
20	06 h 26 m 38 s (6.73X)	06 h 19 m 51 s (6.84X)
21	06 h 18 m 32 s (6.87X)	06 h 12 m 58 s (6.97X)
22	06 h 00 m 01 s (7.23X)	06 h 20 m 40 s (6.83X)
23	05 h 51 m 48 s (7.40X)	06 h 24 m 12 s (6.77X)
24	05 h 51 m 49 s (7.40X)	06 h 27 m 04 s (6.72X)

(iii) 8 GB of DDR5 memory,

(iv) up to one theoretical Teraflop in double floating point precision.

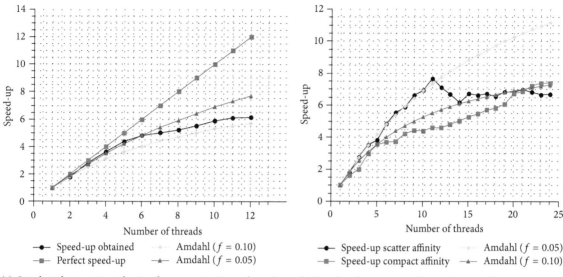

(a) Speed-up factor estimated using the computing times showed in Figure 11(a)

(b) Speed-up factor estimated using the computing times showed in Figure 11(b)

FIGURE 12: Comparison of the obtained speed-up factors versus Amdahl's law with a serial fraction of $f = 0.05$ and $f = 0.10$.

The first consideration regarding this implementation is that the Xeon Phi coprocessor supports 4 threads per processing core; therefore the optimum number of execution threads per core is necessary to be determined. Generally, this optimal number of threads greatly depends on the algorithm and the memory management within the application [30, 31]. Moreover, on the Phi architecture, more than one thread per core helps to hide the inherent latencies in the applications. For example, while one thread awaits its memory resource assignment, other threads could be scheduled on the core. On the conventional Xeon CPU architecture, various developers have found that in general HPC applications do not benefit from the HT technology [32]. Nevertheless, this is not applicable to the Phi technology where the multithreading (MT) can not be disabled as the HT can be disabled via BIOS.

The Xeon Phi could be used in native or offload mode. In native mode the Phi could be seen as stand-alone computer and the applications can run directly on the coprocessor. In the offload mode the Phi operates as a slave computer and the information and control are transferred and handled by the hosts. In the present case, the Phi is used in the same manner as a conventional GPU.

When the Xeon Phi coprocessor is used in offload mode, the method to observe the performance begins with the creation of different numbers of threads from $(n - 1)$ up to $4 \times (n - 1)$, where n is the number of physical cores in the Phi. Then, as recommended by Intel, four experiments should be executed creating $(n - 1)$, $2 \times (n - 1)$, $3 \times (n - 1)$, and $4 \times (n - 1)$ threads, respectively. This serves to determine if the increasing number of threads per core improves the performance. Multiples of $(n - 1)$ are employed instead of multiples of n because one core is left available for the operating system services. Therefore, we conducted the experiments using 59, 118, 177, and 236 execution threads on the Xeon Phi with a balanced affinity, since each core

can handle up to 4 threads. Regarding the vectorization, the $SIMD directive was required to vectorize the internal loop. Table 4 reports the results obtained in execution time of the different configurations.

Figure 13 shows the graphs which correspond to Table 4. In this case, the condition of 59 execution threads was considered as reference to calculate the speed-up factors. If the conventional design D1 is used, the number of threads is increased from 59 up to 236 threads, since 4 threads per core is the optimal number handled by the Phi cores. The experiments were conducted in a similar way for the collapsed design and the vectorized design D2.

From Figure 13, the best speed-up factor is reached by the collapsed design D2, as expected, since the times the parallel region has created were reduced. With this, the improvement in performance is between 0.05X and 0.34X. This result suggests that the overload for creating one parallel region on the coprocessor can be considered lightweight, but when several parallel regions are created (millions) this can cause overhead for this case by 2%. If this design is implemented in algorithms where the number of iterations is much higher [33], the benefit would be even more evident, for example, wave-propagation models.

The maximum speed-up factor obtained when using four threads per core is 2.30X, in reference with the one-thread-per-core design on the Phi and 4.30X in reference with the serial version on the CPU. This is a result of the low number of data. Effects of vectorization are not denoted in the performance, because the data handled by the internal loops are not too many. Moreover, the number of data is not sufficient to continue scaling. For this reason, in contrast with the experiments carried out on the conventional CPU, the best performance is shown by collapsing the loops without vectorization. Table 5 compares the speed-up factors for the MIC

TABLE 4: Computing times and the corresponding speed-up factors obtained by using OpenMP mounted on the Xeon Phi coprocessor. D1: design 1, D2: design 2, C: collapsed, and V: vectorized.

Threads	D1-C	D2-C	D2-V
59	37 h 07 m 47 s (1.00X)	27 h 47 m 51 s (1.34X)	28 h 52 m 20 s (1.29X)
118	18 h 54 m 38 s (1.91X)	18 h 54 m 38 s (1.96X)	24 h 43 m 53 s (1.50X)
177	20 h 09 m 13 s (1.84X)	19 h 24 m 13 s (1.91X)	22 h 24 m 06 s (1.66X)
236	16 h 40 m 19 s (2.23X)	16 h 10 m 10 s (2.30X)	22 h 07 m 53 s (1.68X)

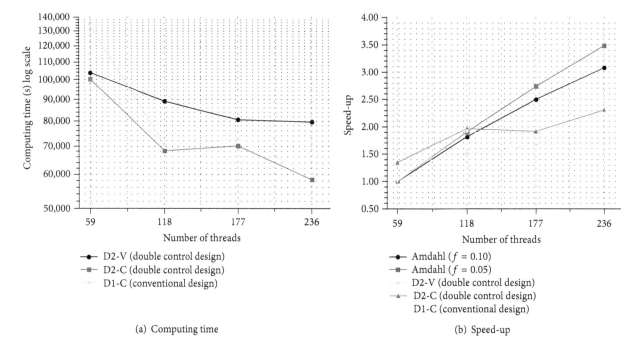

(a) Computing time

(b) Speed-up

FIGURE 13: Computing times and the corresponding speed-up factors compared to Amdahl's law with $f = 0.05$ and $f = 0.10$. As can be seen, the Xeon Phi stops scaling in two threads per core for all the proposed designs (for this domain size). Unlike the conventional CPU the Phi does not show improvements with the vectorization, due to the decrease of vectorization effects with many cores; that is, there are no sufficient floating point operations per core.

against the other architectures in their best version regarding the performance.

3.3. Experiments on the GPU.

The GPU experiments were carried out using a Tesla C2070 card with the following characteristics:

(i) 14 multiprocessors (SM),

(ii) 32 cores per multiprocesador (448 GPU cores total),

(iii) 6 GB of DDR5 global memory,

(iv) up to 515 theoretical Gflops in double floating point precision,

(v) up to one theoretical Teraflop in single floating point precision,

(vi) 1.15 GHz frequency of the GPU cores.

The experiment used the PGI version 15.3 64-bit compiler with the compilation flags: `-Minline -Minfo=acc, accel, intensity -acc -fast`. The execution time obtained was 3 h 31 m 47 s, which is the best execution

time reached for all architectures. Table 6 compares the speed-up factors for the C2070 against the other architectures in their best version regarding the performance.

4. Validation of the Code Porting

The level of decomposition (granularity) is highly influenced by the type of architecture employed. This work employed three different architectures and two programming paradigms to obtain the maximum performance from each platform. Moreover, the validation of the code is a work that must be addressed as well, since inherent errors can occur during program development.

The supersonic ejector flow is a very complex problem due to the physics of the flow and the geometry of the ejector. A transformation of grid coordinates has to be used to characterize the expansion section of the diffuser. Thus, an appropriate transformation to generate a boundary-fitted coordinate system was implemented and validated [9]. On the other hand, as the flow is supersonic, pressure waves are present on the flow and have to be absorbed at the open

TABLE 5: Comparison of the speed-up factors taking as reference the MIC.

MIC	Computing time	Versus CPU serial vectorized without HT	Versus CPU (HT) OpenMP vectorized	GPU C2070
5110P	16 h 10 m 10 s (1.0X)	2.15X	−3.5X	−4.5X

TABLE 6: Comparison of the speed-up factors taking as reference the GPU.

GPU	Computing time	Versus CPU serial vectorized without HT	Versus CPU (HT) OpenMP vectorized	Versus MIC
C2070	03 h 31 m 47 s (1.0X)	9.86X	1.6X	4.5X

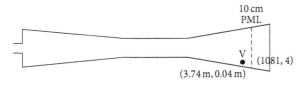

FIGURE 14: Location of the numerical visor near the outflow region. The thickness of the CPML absorbing zone is 10 cm ($10 \times \Delta x$).

TABLE 7: Total energy and Mach number obtained in the visor V for all three architectures at the end of the 3 s of simulation period.

	E_t (m^2/s^2)	M
Reference	3366417302.615026	1.644826
GPU	3366759849.759678	1.644971
MIC	3367625209.964143	1.643896
CPU multicore	3366417302.615055	1.644826

TABLE 8: Relative percentage error for total energy and for Mach number obtained in the visor V for all three architectures at the end of the 3 s simulation period.

	Error for E_t (%)	Error for M (%)
GPU	1.01754×10^{-4}	8.81552×10^{-5}
MIC	3.58811×10^{-4}	5.65409×10^{-4}
CPU	8.92365×10^{-15}	0.00000

boundaries, which is not trivial. For this reason, an unsplit convolutional PML boundary condition was developed to absorb pressure waves [10]. Moreover, the numerical scheme considers Direct Numerical Simulation (DNS), which implies high computational cost even at low Reynolds numbers. This is one of the reasons that an algorithm with a high level of optimization must be used for this problem.

Time series signals of the primitive flow variables were stored to analyze the quality of the calculations. For this reason, a numerical visor was located near one of the sloped walls, where the diffuser section is expanded (see Figure 14). The visor was located at the near flow region walls, a critical region where distortions of the flow structure could appear due to the presence of spurious fluxes coming from the open boundary. The simulations were carried out over 3 millions of iterations and the data were stored each 30,000 iterations, thereby generating 100 data points per primitive flow variable. The 10 cm zone at the end of the ejector is highlighted, where a Convolutional Perfectly Matched Layer (CPML) of the open boundary is employed to absorb pressure waves.

A numerical simulation using a serial processing of one core provided the reference solution to be compared with the parallel solution of the same core. To compare the serial and the parallel solutions, the computed total energy of the system (E_t) was analyzed, since this physical quantity integrates all the primitive variables as follows:

$$E_t = \frac{1}{2}\left(u^2 + v^2\right) + \frac{1}{\gamma - 1}\frac{p}{\rho}, \tag{1}$$

where u and v are the vector velocity components in the x and y directions, respectively, p is the pressure, ρ is the density of the fluid, and γ is the adiabatic dilation coefficient. The first term of the right hand of (1) represents the kinetic energy per unit of mass and the second term represents the internal energy per unit of mass.

In addition, the computed Mach number (M) from both solutions was also compared, because it characterizes the flow under consideration.

For the sake of clarity, only the results of the experiments which reached the best performance from the GPU and MIC platforms are discussed (see Figures 15 and 16). The curves of Figures 15 and 16 together with the calculated correlation coefficients show good agreement between the porting parallel solutions and the serial reference solution. However, we observe small differences among the results of the platforms. Even within the same platforms where we introduced processing threads, variations are observed.

The numerical algorithm must be robust and stable enough during long periods of time in order to demonstrate numerical stability. Table 7 shows the differences between the magnitudes of total energy and Mach number computed in the visor V at the end of the 3 s of simulation, for all three architectures. The corresponding relative percentage errors are also shown in Table 8 regarding the reference serial solution. It can be observed that the CPU multicore architecture provides the most accurate solution regarding the reference serial solution, where the error is negligible for both the total energy and the Mach number. For the GPU and MIC architectures, the MIC has the greatest error for both the total energy (3.58811×10^{-4}) and the Mach number (5.65409×10^{-4}).

Figure 17 shows different snapshots of the Mach number in the diffuser of the ejector at different times. Patterns were obtained on the GPU C2070. Snapshots of the Mach number in the ejector diffuser are reproduced at 0.75 s, 1.5 s, 2.25 s, and 3 s of real time. The contour levels show the instants when the compression, transfer, and expansion occur in the diffuser.

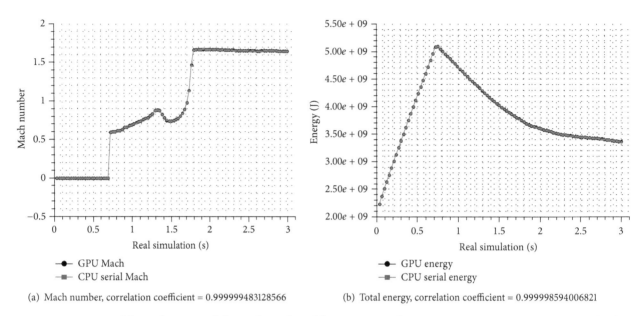

(a) Mach number, correlation coefficient = 0.999999483128566

(b) Total energy, correlation coefficient = 0.999999594006821

FIGURE 15: Comparison of the total energy and the Mach number of the visor V. Simulations on GPU compared against the serial reference solution.

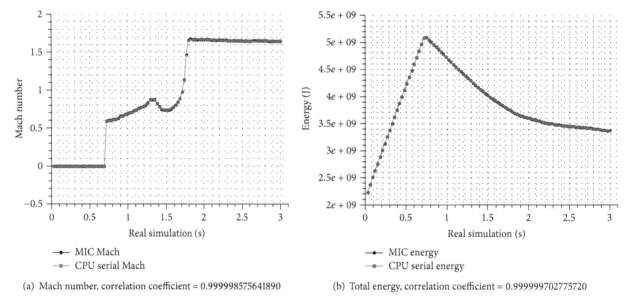

(a) Mach number, correlation coefficient = 0.999998575641890

(b) Total energy, correlation coefficient = 0.999999702775720

FIGURE 16: Comparison of the total energy and the Mach number of the visor V. Simulations on MIC running with the design D2 at 236 threads compared against the serial reference solution.

5. Conclusions

The need of reducing computing time of scientific applications led to the development of accelerators and coprocessors to meet this demand. There are now tools based on directives as OpenACC and OpenMP that reduce the arduous task of low-level programming. However, in spite of the fact that a methodology based on directives reduces the programming work, it is necessary to explore different design strategies to take advantage of the maximum potential of the available architectures. The application ported in this work was a serial source code for a supersonic ejector flow. This work showed

the effectiveness of OpenMP, by reducing the computing time in very good agreement with Amdahl's law. Regarding OpenACC, the well-known strategy that could be applied is to maintain the data regions active among calls to the kernels, thereby avoiding the data transfer between CPU and GPU. Similarly, the persistent variables are maintained when working on the MIC in offload mode. The overload, caused by adding directives in OpenMP for the parallel programming on CPU and on the MIC, is relatively low and does not limit scalability.

In terms of programmability and productivity, we show that OpenMP and OpenACC are viable alternatives for

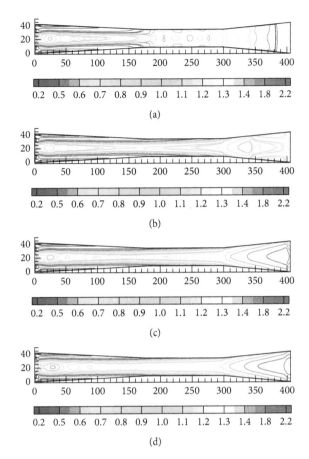

FIGURE 17: Snapshots of the Mach number obtained at different times: (a) 0.75 s, (b) 1.5 s, (c) 2.25 s, and (d) 3.0 s.

the development of parallel codes for scientific applications. The expected performance is satisfactory, considering that OpenMP and OpenACC are paradigms that express parallelism and the parallel code is generated by the compiler, which finally implies less development time with an acceptable performance.

6. Future Work

As future work, OpenMP and OpenACC can be mixed in order to port the application to a multi-GPU or multicoprocessor architecture integrated in the same node.

Conflict of Interests

The authors declare that there is no conflict of interests regarding the publication of this paper.

Acknowledgments

This work has been supported in part by the project ABACUS-CONACyT under Grant no. EDOMEX-2011-C01-165873. The authors would like to thank the CNS (National Supercomputing Center, http://www.cns-ipicyt.mx/) for the facilities given for using the Xeon Phi coprocessor.

References

[1] I. Foster, *Designing and Building Parallel Programs: Concepts and Tools for Parallel Software Engineering*, Addison-Wesley Longman, Boston, Mass, USA, 1995.

[2] C. Calvin, F. Ye, and S. Petiton, "The exploration of pervasive and fine-grained parallel model applied on Intel Xeon Phi coprocessor," in *Proceedings of the 8th International Conference on P2P, Parallel, Grid, Cloud and Internet Computing (3PGCIC '13)*, pp. 166–173, IEEE, Compiègne, France, October 2013.

[3] L. Dagum and R. Menon, "OpenMP: an industry standard API for shared-memory programming," *IEEE Computational Science and Engineering*, vol. 5, no. 1, pp. 46–55, 1998.

[4] M. Curtis-Maury, X. Ding, C. D. Antonopoulos, and D. S. Nikolopoulos, "An evaluation of openmp on current and emerging multithreaded/multicore processors," in *OpenMP Shared Memory Parallel Programming: Proceedings of the International Workshops, IWOMP 2005 and IWOMP 2006, Eugene, OR, USA, June 1–4, 2005, Reims, France, June 12–15, 2006*, vol. 4315 of *Lecture Notes in Computer Science*, pp. 133–144, Springer, Berlin, Germany, 2008.

[5] H. Brunst and B. Mohr, "Performance analysis of large-scale openmp and hybrid mpi/openmp applications with vampir ng," in *OpenMP Shared Memory Parallel Programming*, M. Mueller, B. Chapman, B. Supinski, A. Malony, and M. Voss, Eds., vol. 4315 of *Lecture Notes in Computer Science*, pp. 5–14, Springer, Berlin, Germany, 2008.

[6] A. Amritkar, S. Deb, and D. Tafti, "Efficient parallel CFD-DEM simulations using OpenMP," *Journal of Computational Physics*, vol. 256, pp. 501–519, 2014.

[7] B. P. Pickering, C. W. Jackson, T. R. Scogland, W.-C. Feng, and C. J. Roy, "Directive-based GPU programming for computational fluid dynamics," *Computers & Fluids*, vol. 114, pp. 242–253, 2015.

[8] A. Kucher and G. Haase, "Many-core sustainability by pragma directives," in *Large-Scale Scientific Computing*, vol. 8353 of *Lecture Notes in Computer Science (Including Subseries Lecture Notes in Artificial Intelligence and Lecture Notes in Bioinformatics)*, pp. 448–456, Springer, 2014.

[9] C. Couder-Castañeda, "Simulation of supersonic flow in an ejector diffuser using the jpvm," *Journal of Applied Mathematics*, vol. 2009, Article ID 497013, 21 pages, 2009.

[10] R. Martin and C. Couder-Castaneda, "An improved unsplit and convolutional perfectly matched layer absorbing technique for the navier-stokes equations using cut-off frequency shift," *Computer Modeling in Engineering and Sciences*, vol. 63, no. 1, pp. 47–77, 2010.

[11] J. Levesque and G. Wagenbreth, *High Performance Computing: Programming and Applications*, CRC Press, 2010.

[12] Z. Krpic, G. Martinovic, and I. Crnkovic, "Green HPC: MPI vs. OpenMP on a shared memory system," in *Proceedings of the 35th International Convention on Information and Communication Technology, Electronics and Microelectronics (MIPRO '12)*, pp. 246–250, 2012.

[13] Y. Zhang, M. Burcea, V. Cheng, R. Ho, and M. Voss, "An adaptive OpenMP loop scheduler for hyperthreaded SMPs," in *Proceedings of the International Conference on Parallel and Distributed Computing Systems (PDCS '04)*, 2004.

[14] R. Martin, D. Komatitsch, and A. Ezziani, "An unsplit convolutional perfectly matched layer improved at grazing incidence for seismic wave propagation in poroelastic media," *Geophysics*, vol. 73, no. 4, pp. T51–T61, 2008.

[15] D. Komatitsch, G. Erlebacher, D. Göddeke, and D. Michéa, "High-order finite-element seismic wave propagation modeling with MPI on a large GPU cluster," *Journal of Computational Physics*, vol. 229, no. 20, pp. 7692–7714, 2010.

[16] T. Cramer, D. Schmidl, M. Klemm, and D. an Mey, "Openmp programming on intel r xeon phi tm coprocessors: An early performance comparison," 2012.

[17] J. Zhou, D. Unat, D. J. Choi, C. C. Guest, and Y. Cui, "Hands-on performance tuning of 3D finite difference earthquake simulation on GPU fermi chipset," in *Proceedings of the 12th International Conference on Computational Science (ICCS '12)*, pp. 976–985, June 2012.

[18] P. Micikevicius, "3D finite difference computation on GPUs using CUDA," in *Proceedings of the 2nd Workshop on General Purpose Processing on Graphics Processing Units (GPGPU-2 '09)*, pp. 79–84, ACM, New York, NY, USA, March 2009.

[19] D. Michéa and D. Komatitsch, "Accelerating a three-dimensional finite-difference wave propagation code using GPU graphics cards," *Geophysical Journal International*, vol. 182, no. 1, pp. 389–402, 2010.

[20] D. Schmidl, T. Cramer, S. Wienke, C. Terboven, and M. Muller, "Assessing the performance of OpenMP programs on the intel xeon phi," in *Euro-Par 2013 Parallel Processing*, F. Wolf, B. Mohr, and D. an Mey, Eds., vol. 8097 of *Lecture Notes in Computer Science*, pp. 547–558, Springer, Berlin, Germany, 2013.

[21] S. Wienke, C. Terboven, J. C. Beyer, and M. S. Müller, "A pattern-based comparison of OpenACC and OpenMP for accelerator computing," in *Euro-Par 2014 Parallel Processing*, F. Silva, I. Dutra, and V. Santos Costa, Eds., vol. 8632 of *Lecture Notes in Computer Science*, pp. 812–823, Springer International Publishing, Cham, Switzerland, 2014.

[22] D. K. Ojha and G. Sikka, "A study on vectorization methods for multicore SIMD architecture provided by compilers," in *ICT and Critical Infrastructure: Proceedings of the 48th Annual Convention of Computer Society of India- Vol I*, vol. 248 of *Advances in Intelligent Systems and Computing*, pp. 723–728, Springer, 2014.

[23] J. Francés, S. Bleda, A. Márquez et al., "Performance analysis of SSE and AVX instructions in multi-core CPUs and GPU computing on FDTD scheme for solid and fluid vibration problems," *The Journal of Supercomputing*, vol. 70, no. 2, pp. 1–13, 2013.

[24] T. Leng, R. Ali, J. Hsieh, V. Mashayekhi, and R. Rooholamini, "An empirical study of hyper-threading in high performance computing clusters," in *Proceedings of the Linux HPC Revolution Conference*, 2002.

[25] C. Couder-Castañeda, J. C. Ortiz-Alemán, M. G. Orozco-del-Castillo, and M. Nava-Flores, "Forward modeling of gravitational fields on hybrid multi-threaded cluster," *Geofísica Internacional*, vol. 54, no. 1, pp. 31–48, 2015.

[26] U. Ranok, S. Kittitornkun, and S. Tongsima, "A multithreading methodology with OpenMP on multi-core CPUs: SNPHAP case study," in *Proceedings of the 8th Electrical Engineering/Electronics, Computer, Telecommunications and Information Technology (ECTI '11)*, pp. 459–463, IEEE, Khon Kaen, Thailand, May 2011.

[27] J. H. Abdel-Qader and R. S. Walker, "Performance evaluation of OpenMP benchmarks on Intel's quad core processors," in *Proceedings of the 14th WSEAS International Conference on Computers*, vol. 1, pp. 348–355, July 2010.

[28] W. Zhong, G. Altun, X. Tian, R. Harrison, P. C. Tai, and Y. Pan, "Parallel protein secondary structure prediction schemes using Pthread and OpenMP over hyper-threading technology," *Journal of Supercomputing*, vol. 41, no. 1, pp. 1–16, 2007.

[29] G. Bernabé, R. Fernández, J. M. García, M. E. Acacio, and J. González, "An efficient implementation of a 3D wavelet transform based encoder on hyper-threading technology," *Parallel Computing*, vol. 33, no. 1, pp. 54–72, 2007.

[30] A. E. Eichenberger, C. Terboven, M. Wong, and D. an Mey, "The design of openmp thread affinity," in *OpenMP in a Heterogeneous World*, vol. 7312 of *Lecture Notes in Computer Science*, pp. 15–28, Springer, Berlin, Germany, 2012.

[31] C. Allande, J. Jorba, A. Sikora, and E. César, "A performance model for openMP memory bound applications in multisocket systems," *Procedia Computer Science*, vol. 29, pp. 2208–2218, 2014.

[32] P. Gepner, M. F. Kowalik, D. L. Fraser, and K. Waćkowski, "Early performance evaluation of new six-core intel xeon 5600 family processors for HPC," in *Proceedings of the 9th International Symposium on Parallel and Distributed Computing (ISPDC '10)*, pp. 117–124, July 2010.

[33] M. Araya-Polo, F. Rubio, R. de la Cruz, M. Hanzich, J. M. Cela, and D. P. Scarpazza, "3D seismic imaging through reverse-time migration on homogeneous and heterogeneous multi-core processors," *Scientific Programming*, vol. 17, no. 1-2, pp. 185–198, 2009.

7

Text Summarization Using FrameNet-Based Semantic Graph Model

Xu Han,[1,2] **Tao Lv,**[1,2] **Zhirui Hu,**[3] **Xinyan Wang,**[4] **and Cong Wang**[1,2]

[1]*School of Software Engineering, Beijing University of Posts and Telecommunications, Beijing 100876, China*
[2]*Key Laboratory of Trustworthy Distributed Computing and Service, Beijing University of Posts and Telecommunications, Beijing 100876, China*
[3]*Department of Statistics, Harvard University, Cambridge, MA, USA*
[4]*Air Force General Hospital, Beijing, China*

Correspondence should be addressed to Xinyan Wang; wangxinyan@china.com

Academic Editor: Xiong Luo

Text summarization is to generate a condensed version of the original document. The major issues for text summarization are eliminating redundant information, identifying important difference among documents, and recovering the informative content. This paper proposes a Semantic Graph Model which exploits the semantic information of sentence using FSGM. FSGM treats sentences as vertexes while the semantic relationship as the edges. It uses FrameNet and word embedding to calculate the similarity of sentences. This method assigns weight to both sentence nodes and edges. After all, it proposes an improved method to rank these sentences, considering both internal and external information. The experimental results show that the applicability of the model to summarize text is feasible and effective.

1. Introduction

With the era of big data, text resources are becoming more and more abundant. Natural Language Processing (NLP) techniques have developed rapidly. Text summarization is a research tool that has widely applied in NLP. It gives a summary which can help us understand the whole article immediately with least words. Text summarization is to generate a condensed version of the original documents by reducing documents in size while retaining the main characteristics [1]. But artificial text summarization needs much background knowledge and often requires long processing time, while qualities of summaries are not always good enough. For this reason, people began to focus on automatic text summarization. Automatic text summarization was first studied almost 60 years ago by Luhn [2] and has gained much attention in recent years. This method is faster than artificial ones and performs better than the average level. With the rapid growth of text resources online, various domains of text summarization are applied. For instance,

a Question Answering (QA) System produces a question-based summary to offer information. Another example is the search result snippets in web search engine which can assist users to explore more [3]; short summaries for News Articles can help readers to obtain useful information about an event or a topic [4]; speech summarization automatically selects indicative sentences from original spoken document to form a concise summary [5].

Automatic text summarization is mainly facing the following two problems: one is to reduce redundancy and the other is to provide more information with less words. Sentences in-summary are those which can stand for parts of the whole article. So the repeated information should be reduced, while the main information should be maintained. The major issues for text summarization are as follows. To begin with, information included in text is often redundant, so it is crucial to develop a method to eliminate redundancy. It is very common that different words are used to describe the same object in a text. For that reason, naive similarity measures between words cannot faithfully describe the content

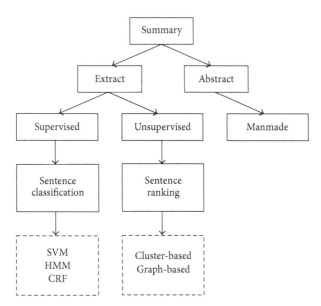

FIGURE 1: Summarization Approach Categories.

similarity. Another issue is identifying important difference among documents and covering the informative content as much as possible [6].

In this paper, to handle these issues, it proposes a Semantic Graph Model using FrameNet (FSGM) for text summarization that exploits the semantic information of sentence. FSGM treats sentences as vertexes while the semantic relationship between sentences as the edges. Firstly, it uses FrameNet to classify all sentences and then calculates the relevance values between sentences using semantic analysis and takes the values as weights of edges. Word embedding is used to combine similar sentences more accurately. Then based on the FSGM, sentences' values are scored by a variant of the improved PageRank graph ranking algorithm [7], considering both internal and external information. The experiments have been conducted on the DUC2004 data sets, and the results show that our model improves graph-based sentence extraction algorithms under various settings. So it can be used to enhance the performance. The experimental results show our model can be used for sentence extraction effectively.

The rest of the paper is organized as follows. Sections 2 and 3 briefly review the related work of current approaches about text summarization and the prepare work for experiments. The proposed Semantic Graph Model using FrameNet and word embedding is presented in Section 4 in detail. Section 5 is about the experiment, results, and relevant discussion. Finally, conclusion for this paper is in Section 6.

2. Related Work

Figure 1 shows the main summarization approaches [8]. There are two categories of summarization: abstract-based and extract-based. The abstractive summarization methods mostly generate the summary by compressing and reformulating the sentence. By this way, summary can keep its

original length but has more effective information. However, the method requires complex linguistic processing, while the extract-based summarization measures various statistical significance for the words to locate the most central sentences in documents [9].

Extract-based approaches can be further categorized by supervised and unsupervised approaches. Supervised method proposes summarizing text as a classification problem in which all the sentences can be divided into either in-summary or not-in-summary. These methods are based on an essential assumption that each sentence should be independent. Naturally, it ignores the dependence between sentences. And then, there are additional approaches to build the relationship between sentences, such as using Hidden Markov Model (HMM) or Conditional Random Field (CRF).

Unsupervised method is to generate summaries by ranking sentences. Cluster-based approaches can classify sentences into groups and then choose the important ones in each group to form the final summary. Radev et al. [10] present MEAD with cluster centroids leverage. MEAD makes score for sentences by various features, assigning a representative centroid-based approach. Sentence-level semantic analysis (SLSS) and Symmetric Non-Negative Matrix Factorization (SNMF) are used in summarization by Wang et al. [11]. Mei and Chen [12] adapt fuzzy medoid-based clustering approach to produce subsets of similar sentences. Moreover, Latent Semantic Analysis (LSA), which helps adding and analyzing hidden topic features, is employed by Gong and Liu's work [13]. Wang et al. [14] generate summaries via discriminative sentence selection. He et al. [15] consider sentences in documents as a kind of signals from the perspective of compressive sensing. However, cluster-based approaches only considered the relationship between sentences, which may cause the semantic gap.

Another approach of unsupervised extract-based summarization [11, 16] uses graph-based model. TextRank [17] and LexRank [18] are first two graph-based models applied in text summarization, which use the PageRank-like algorithms to mark sentences. Then, other researchers have integrated the statistical and linguistic features to drive the sentence selection process, for example, the sentence position [19], term frequency [20], topic signature [21], lexical chains [22], and syntactic patterns [7, 23]. Ko and Seo [24] composed two sentences nearby into a bigram. Those bigrams were supposed to be context information. First, they extracted the bigrams by using the sentence extraction model. Then they used another extraction module to extract sentences from them. The ClusterCMRW and ClusterHITS models calculated the sentences scores by considering the cluster-level information in the graph-based ranking algorithm. Canhasi and Kononenko [25] improve matrix decomposition by employing the archetypal analysis for generic multidocument summarization. While coming to the document set, there must be more consideration about the document-level influence. But it did not consider the relationship between words and sentences. The DsR model [26] achieved it by using document-sensitive graph-based ranking model. But this method did not get a satisfied result. Yin et al. improved the summarization quality by adding extra information which came from the query-extraction scenario. Goyal et al. [27] take Bernoulli model of randomness to index weights of sentences taking the context into consideration. The method proposed in [28] decomposed sentences by semantic role analysis, but while building the model, it did not use graph-based algorithms.

However, most of these graph-based methods only consider the relation of keyword cooccurrence, without considering the sentence-level dependency syntax. Those papers which use semantic information do not utilize the semantic information in the sentence-level. Thus, how to take advantage of the relationship between sentences needs further research. In this paper, it proposes sentence-level Semantic Graph Model. FSGM can build the relationships between sentences in a better way. Several experiments show ideal results in our model.

3. Preliminaries

In this section, it introduces related works for the experiments: firstly, the graph sorting algorithm, then the FrameNet, and finally word embedding.

3.1. Graph Sorting Algorithm. Graph sorting algorithm can calculate the nodes importance based on the graph structure. PageRank is one of its classical algorithms. The basic idea concerns the webpages' weight impacted both by usual links and reverse links, which means the more reverse links are, the heavier webpages' weight is. It builds graphs by using links structure, while the links are edges and webpages are nodes. The formula is as follows:

$$PR(p_i) = \frac{1-d}{N} + d \sum_{p_j \in M(p_i)} \frac{PR(p_j)}{L(p_j)}, \quad (1)$$

where $p_1, p_2, \ldots, p_n$ are all nodes, $M(p_i)$ is a set which connect to p_i, $L(p_i)$ is p_i out-degree, N is the total number of nodes, and d is damping coefficient, usually set by 0.85.

In automatic text summarization, the graph is built by Natural Language Processing, text units are nodes, and the relationship of text units is edges. These relevancies often have its meaning, so the graph is basically unweighted undirected graph.

In undirected graph, every node has same in-degree and out-degree. In sparse condition, the convergence speed in undirected graph is faster than directed graph. The stronger the graph can connect, the faster it can converge. If the graph connectivity is strong enough, the convergence curves undirected and directed are nearly overlapped [29].

In weighted graph, the weight between nodes can be used; the formula is as follows:

$$PR(p_i) = \frac{1-d}{N} + d \sum_{p_j \in M(p_i)} \frac{w_{ij} PR(p_j)}{L(p_j)}. \quad (2)$$

In graph sorting algorithm, the relevance between nodes is very important. In LexRank, if Cosine similarity between sentences is larger than the threshold, there is an edge. TextRank

has another weight parameter comparing with PageRank. It gives edges weights and builds weighted graph. These two methods are simple and ignore some effective factors, such as semantic information and linguistic knowledge. Above all [30, 31], these methods are all considered more similar to judge the relevance between nodes. Corresponding solutions of these limitations are proposed in this paper. It used FrameNet combining the word embedding, to calculate the relevance between sentences; it will give more details in next section.

3.2. FrameNet. Traditional semantic sentence representations employ WordNet [17] or a corpus-based measure [9] in a classic bag of words, without considering sentence-level semantic information and word order. The proposed semantic sentence representation uses semantic frames instead of words to take both sentence-level semantic information and word order into account.

FrameNet, a lexical database based on a theory called frame semantics, contains a wealth of semantic lexical resources. Frame semantics studying the meaning of words and syntactic structure based on real corpus is proposed by Charles J. Fillmore. This theory uses empirical methods to find the close relationship between language and the human experience and tries to describe this relationship with a possible way. The basic idea is straightforward: the meanings of most words can best be understood on the basis of a semantic frame, a description of a type of event, relation, or entity, and the participants in it.

In the context of FrameNet, "frame" is a linguistic term that refers to a set of concepts to understand when people use natural language to describe an event or a semantic scene. Words that evoke a frame are called "lexical units" (LUs); for example, bike, carry, and drive are the LUs of the BRINGING frame. Each frame contains a series of semantic roles containers which called Frame Elements (FEs). FEs are related to words described in the context of events or objects in real corpus. There are two classes of FEs, core and noncore elements, which are determined by their importance to the corresponding frame. Different frames have different types and numbers of Frame Elements, and these differences can reflect semantic information in natural language. Figure 2 is an illustration of the BRINGING frame.

Frame-to-frame relation describes an overview semantic relationship, which is an asymmetric directional relation. Eight frame relations are defined, which are inheritance, perspective_on, subframe, precedes, causative_of, inchoative_of, using, and see_also.

Each frame is directly related to two frames, based on the orientation relationship; one is called super_frame and the other is called sub_frame. The BRINGING frame-to-frame relation is as follows:

Inherits from:

Is Inherited by: *Smuggling*

Perspective on:

Is Perspectivized in:

Uses: *Cause_motion, Motion*

BRINGING

Definition:

This frame concerns the movement of a Theme and an Agent and/or Carrier. The Agent, a person or other sentient entity, controls the shared Path by moving the Theme during the motion. In other words, the Agent has overall motion in directing the motion of the Theme. The Carrier may be a separate entity, or it may be the Agent's body. The Constant_location may be a subregion of the Agent's body or (a subregion of) a vehicle that the Agent uses.

Karl CARRIED the books across campus to the library on his head.

The FEs include Path, Goal, and Source. Area is an area that contains the motion when the path is understood as irregular. This frame emphasizes the path of movement as opposed to the FEs Source or Goal as in Filling or Placing.

FE core set(s):
{Goal, Path, Source}, {Agent, Carrier}

Lexical units:

airlift.v, bear.v, bike.v, bring.v, bus.v, carry.v, cart.v, convey.v, drive.v, ferry.v, fetch.v, fly.v, get.v, haul.v, hump.v, jet.v, lug.v, mobile.a, motor.v, paddle.v, portable.a, row.v, schlep.v, shuttle.v, take.v, tote.v, transport.n, transport.v, truck.v, trundle.v, wheel.v

FIGURE 2: Definition of the frame.

Is Used by: *Convoy, Sending*

Subframe of:

Has Subframe(s):

Precedes:

Is Preceded by:

Is Inchoative of:

Is Causative of:

See also: *Cause_motion, Motion, Passing, Sending*

To sum up, the strengths of FrameNet are as follows.

(a) It contains a wealth of semantic information (semantic roles) and specifies the scene of semantic roles appeared under predicates.

(b) The definitions of semantic roles are intuitive and straightforward.

(c) It defines relationships between the predicates.

The weaknesses are listed below.

(a) Frames are determined by predicates, so new predicates need to define new frame.

(b) The expression of the semantic predicates is determined by other related words; the selection of frames is a thorny problem, especially in the case of polysemy.

(c) FrameNet may parse some phrases directly into semantic roles, but these phrases may be separable.

3.3. Word Embedding. Word embedding is a core technique, which brings deep learning into NLP research. In the past, it often uses a simple method, called one-hot representation, to transfer words into vectors. Every word is shown as a long vector; the dimension of the vector is the length of the thesaurus. It is represented by sparse matrix. For example, word "mic" is saved as $[0, 0, 0, 0, 1, \ldots, 0, 0]$ and word "microphone" is saved as $[0, 0, 0, 1, 0, \ldots, 0, 0]$. It is simple but has a fatal weakness; it cannot distinguish synonym, such as "microphone" and "mic." This phenomenon is called semantic gap. Meanwhile, the curse of dimensionality will appear when the dimension is large enough [32].

Hinton [33] proposed "distributed representation" in 1986. It uses low dimension real numbers to represent word vectors; the length of the dimension used to be 50 or 100. For example, word "mic" can be saved as $[0.58, 0.45, -0.15, 0.18, \ldots, 0.52]$. This method avoids the semantic gap by calculating the distances between words. Word embedding can give words similarity at the semantic level, which is an effective addition for FrameNet. At first, it used FrameNet to compute sentence similarity at a sentence-level. Although it achieved good results, the similarity between sentences calculation relies only on simple comparison within the framework of words. Word embedding transfers all the words in the sentence. In the calculation of sentence similarity, it can effectively reduce the redundancy of sentences by combining the subject or object [34]. In this paper, it uses the lexicon generated by Wikipedia words.

4. FrameNet-Based Semantic Graph Model

Sarkar [35] uses selected key phrases as key concepts identified from a document to create summary of document, while Sankarasubramaniam et al. [36] leverage Wikipedia as the knowledge base to understand the salient concepts of documents. However, the above techniques may fail to semantically analyze newly coined words; Heu et al. [37] employ the tag clusters used by Flickr, a Folksonomy system. Inspired by above researchers, FSGM adapts FrameNet to detect key concepts from documents.

In FSGM, it utilizes the semantic information while considering automatic text summarization, to avoid semantic gap as well as ignorance of grammatical structure by other methods. FrameNet is the basis of FSGM to represent semantic information. The Frame Elements in FrameNet can express rich semantic information of the framework. And FSGM requires the relationship between frames to calculate similarities between sentences. In order to make full use of semantic information, word embedding is applied in computation of sentence similarity. In construction of the semantic graph, sentences should be aggregated when sentence similarity value is greater than the threshold α, and the aggregated sentence should assign new aggregated weights. Thus, the number of nodes in the semantic graph n is not greater than the number of sentences in the text. Graph

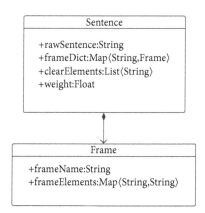

FIGURE 3: UML form of the structure.

FIGURE 4: Semantic parsing.

sorting algorithm is then applied to the semantic graph. After the calculation, the aggregation and nodes weights are combined to select the most representative sentence. Detailed steps are as follows.

(a) Use FrameNet to parse the text, to identify the frame, and annotate the sentences with LUs and FEs, and generate the sentence node.

(b) Calculate the similarity between sentence nodes by combining the FrameNet with the word embedding.

(c) Aggregate sentences when the similarity value is greater than threshold α.

(d) Calculate the weight of sentence nodes by graph ranking algorithm.

(e) The final weights of the sentence nodes are calculated by using the method of combination of aggregate weights and relationship weights.

(f) Select the most representative sentence to generate summary.

4.1. Structure of Sentence Node. In order to facilitate further steps after preprocessing, sentences should be stored in specific structure. The structure of sentence node in FSGM must include original text, recognized frame, Frame Elements, lexical elements after preprocessing, and sentence weight. It should be noted that a sentence may contain multiple frames, and it designs the most basic data structure for storing the semantic representation of the sentence. Figure 3 shows the UML form of the structure.

In Figure 3, frame structure includes frame name and collection of Frame Elements. Sentence structure includes original sentence, collection of frames, collection of lexical elements after preprocessing, and sentence weight.

After computing sentence similarity, FSGM will aggregate appropriate sentences, for the purpose of reducing redundancy and promoting diversity while generating summary.

4.2. Sentence Semantic Parsing. When FSGM parses sentences, it first annotates LUs in sentences to identify frames inside, then locates other FEs in sentences according to the FEs defined in the frames, and stores parsed semantic

information in predefined sentence structure. FSGM uses an open-source semantic parser SEMAFOR. It first analyzes sentence with a rule-based system to recognize target LUs and then identifies frames by using a statistical model. FEs are captured by another statistical model at the last step. Figure 4 is an example of semantic parsing.

For the sentence "Kate drove home in a stupor." two frames are identified from the sentence: BRINGING and FOREIGN_OR_DOMESTRIC_COUNTRY. Moreover, Frame Elements Agent and Theme are annotated in the frame BRINGING.

4.3. Sentence Semantic Similarity. Sentence semantic similarity is the kernel of the FSGM, which describes differences between sentences in semantic level by combining the FrameNet and word embedding. Lin et al. [38] propose a similarity measure for text by computing the similarity between two documents with respect to a feature. FSGM regards frame as the feature between sentences and takes following three cases into account.

If frames identified in both sentences are the same and the Frame Elements defined in the frames are also the same, the similarity between two sentences is 1, indicating in the sight of FrameNet that the semantics is the same. If the frame is different, it defined similarity as

$$\text{Sim}\left(S_i, S_j\right) = \frac{\sum_{k=0}^{n} \theta_k \times \text{Distance}\left(\text{SF}_{ik}, \text{SF}_{jk}\right)}{\sum_{k=0}^{n} \theta_k}, \quad (3)$$

where SF is word vector of the lexicon elements and θ is the coefficient of lexicon elements, which has 3 types. The first is that elements are under the same frame, the second is that elements are under the 8 frames mentioned above, and the third is all the other conditions. In this paper, θ is set by 1.2, 1.1, and 1.0. n is the smaller number in lexicon elements, set by $\min(\text{num}(\text{SF}_i), \text{num}(\text{SF}_j))$. Lexicon elements either are under frame or are not.

Word vectors are as follows:

$$\text{SF} = \frac{\sum_{i=0}^{n} E_i}{n}, \quad (4)$$

where n is the number of elements in lexicon setting and E_i is the number of i's word vector.

$\text{Distance}(\text{SF}_i, \text{SF}_j)$ is the Cosine distance:

$$\text{Distance}\left(\text{SF}_i, \text{SF}_j\right) = \frac{\sum_{k=0}^{n} v_{ik} \times v_{jk}}{\sqrt{\sum_{k=0}^{n} v_{ik}^2} \sqrt{\sum_{k=0}^{n} v_{jk}^2}}, \quad (5)$$

where v_{ik} is SF_i's value in k dimension.

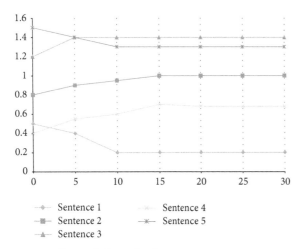

FIGURE 5: Example of convergence curves.

Word embedding generates a multidimension word vector for each word; [34] proved that adding up all the word vectors in one sentence and calculating the Cosine distance is an effective method to get the sentence similarity.

4.4. Construct Semantic Graph. After transforming sentences into semantic sentence representation and calculating of the semantic similarity between pairwise sentences, the sentence nodes need to be merged for variability and diversity. The threshold of the similarity is 1, which means FSGM only merges the same sentences.

FSGM builds a weighted undirected semantic graph $G = \{V, E\}$, where V is the vertex set and E is the edge set of the graph. Each sentence in documents is represented in frames and is built to be a graph vertex. If the semantic similarity between them is larger than some threshold, these representative vertexes in the semantic graph will be linked by edges and the edge weight is assigned by the value of the pairwise semantic similarity.

Based on the weighted undirected graph, every sentence is evaluated by applying the PageRank-like algorithm. Equation (6) shows how to calculate the weight of each vertex in graph,

$$\text{weight}\left(V_i\right) = (1 - d) + d$$
$$\times \sum_{V_j \in \ln(V_i)} \frac{\text{Sim}\left(S_i, S_j\right) \times \text{weight}\left(V_j\right)}{\sum_{V_k \in \text{Out}(V_j)} \text{Sim}\left(S_j, S_k\right)}, \quad (6)$$

where weight(V_i) represents the weight of V_i which also represents the sentence S_i, d represents the damping factor, usually set to 0.85, $\ln(V_i)$ is the set of vertexes which is connected to V_i, since the graph is undirected, Out(V_i) = $\ln(V_i)$, and Sim(S_i, S_j) is the semantic similarity between S_i and S_j. The convergence threshold η is set to 10^{-5}. In actual calculation, an initial value is given for V_i and then updated by (6). Experiments show that (6) usually converges in 20–30 iterations in a sentence semantic graph.

Figure 5 shows the weight change of five sentences in a document with a given initial value C. The abscissa represents

the number of iterations; the ordinate represents the sentence weight of current state. In the undirected weighted graph, vertex weight converges very quickly. After a few iterations, the difference between the vertex weight values is far less than η.

With sentence-level semantic graph, it can obtain the weight of each sentence in the document. After calculating the similarity, it gathers the sentences if the values are larger than the threshold α and generate a new node. Given the new node its weight is based on the number of combining sentences. Then, if the similarity values are larger than the threshold β, we link these two sentences. After that, it generates a weighted graph. The convergence results in graph ranking model are irrelevant with the initial weight vector. After iteration, it finally gets a FSGM.

4.5. Sentence Semantic Weight. Word embedding can represent word senses in word embedding vectors. As the dimension of word embedding vectors is consistent between words, words in a sentences can sum their word embedding vectors up to represent the sentence. Also sentences in a document can sum their vectors to represent the document. So the semantic representation of document can be word embedding vectors.

The vectors of the document contain all semantic information. The sentence semantic weights should be the amount of information that the vectors of sentence contained. So the weight is calculated by the Cosine distance between the document vectors and the sentence vectors.

4.6. Sentence Selection. It should consider both the semantic weight and the weight in the text structure when generating summary. FSGM combined the semantic weight and the relation weight; the formula is as follows:

$$W = \mu W_s + (1 - \mu) W_g, \quad (7)$$

where μ is the coefficient of semantic weight, $(1 - \mu)$ is coefficient of relation weight, W is the final weight, W_s is the semantic weight for sentence node, and W_g is the relation weight for sentence node.

5. Experiments

In this section, it introduces the data set, the evaluation metric, and the result of text summarization using proposed FSGM.

5.1. Setup. Firstly, to compare our methods, it uses several document summarization baseline systems. The definitions of these systems are as follows.

Lead. For each topic, it would return the leading sentences of every document.

Random. For each topic, it would select sentences randomly.

GraphRank. Rank sentences by graph-based algorithms using traditional bag-of-word.

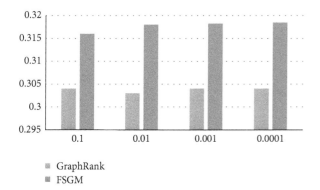

FIGURE 6: Sensitivity of ROUGE-1 with respect to threshold η.

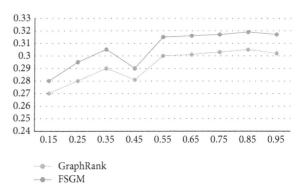

GraphRank
FSGM

FIGURE 7: Sensitivity of ROUGE-1 with respect to damping factor d.

5.2. Data Set. In the experiments, it chooses DUC 2004 dataset for text summarization. It is the collections of newspaper documents from TREC. It has the original summaries. Besides, the datasets are public. Therefore, lots of researchers select DUC 2004 to study text summarization. For each document, NIST human assessors wrote two summaries: one is 200 words and the other is 400 words. And for each task, there are two summarizer models. There are 5 tasks in DUC 2004; each task has 15 clusters. It has chosen 15 clusters randomly from the 75 clusters.

5.3. Evaluation Metrics. ROUGE is a performance evaluation method widely applied by DUC. It chooses this method to measure our FSGM. It measures the summary quality by counting the overlaps between a set of reference summaries and candidate summary. After that, there are several kinds of automatic evaluation methods, such as ROUGE-N, ROUGE-W, ROUGE-L, and ROUGE-SU. Equation (8) shows the compute step for ROUGE-N which is a n-gram recall:

ROUGE-N

$$= \frac{\sum_{S \in \{\text{RefSum}\}} \sum_{n\text{-gram} \in S} \text{Count}_{\text{match}} (n\text{-gram})}{\sum_{S \in \{\text{RefSum}\}} \sum_{n\text{-gram} \in S} \text{Count} (n\text{-gram})}, \quad (8)$$

where n is the length of the n-gram and Ref is the reference summaries. In a candidate summary and the reference summary, $\text{Count}_{\text{match}}(n\text{-gram})$ is the max of n-gram, and in the reference summaries, the number of n-gram is $\text{Count}(n\text{-gram})$. The longest common subsequence (LCS) has been used in ROUGE-L statistics; while ROUGE-W is based on weighted LCS, ROUGE-SU is on the basis of skip-bigram plus unigram. All these four evaluation methods in ROUGE can form three scores, which are recall, precision, and F-measure.

It uses the ROUGE toolkit 1.5.5 for evaluation. It calculates these scores by our FSGM method and compared with three other systems, (Lead, Random, and GraphRank). It uses the scores of ROUGE-1, ROUGE-2, and ROUGE-L.

5.4. Result and Discussion. For graph-based text summarization method, the value of threshold η and damping factor d will affect the performance of the graph-based algorithm. It analyzes the sensitivity of both parameters for two

TABLE 1: Performance comparison of FSGM with word embedding and without word embedding.

Method	FSGM (with word embedding, default settings)	FSGM (without word embedding, default setting)
ROUGE-1	0.325	0.315
ROUGE-2	0.052	0.049
ROUGE-L	0.298	0.293

graph-based systems involved in our experiment including GraphRank and FSGM. The threshold η is varied in the set $\{0.1, 0.01, 0.001, 0.0001\}$ and damping factor d is varied in the range between 0.05 and 0.95 with an interval of 0.1. From Figure 6, it can be inferred that the choice of threshold η in the set $\{0.1, 0.01, 0.001, 0.0001\}$ is quite insensitive to both systems. And the experiments show that when η is set to 0.0001, both systems gave the best results. Figure 7 shows that the results are not sensitive to the damping factor d in the range between 0.65 and 0.95 of both systems.

$d = 0.85$ is chosen for further experiments as it gave the best results.

In order to investigate the effects of performance by different parameters, it compares the default setting of several parameters with designed parameters.

Table 1 illustrates the performance comparison of FSGM with and without word embedding. The table clearly shows that word embedding can better utilize the semantic information to calculate similarity between sentences. It should mention that although word embedding can finitely improve the performance of generating summary, the option of adapting word embedding or not should be considered thoroughly.

Different settings of coefficients of lexical elements in the semantic similarity are compared in Table 2. The coefficient is a vector of the three elements. Each element is the weight of the related collections of lexical elements. It can be inferred from the table that the default setting achieved the best performance. The default setting assigns reasonable weights to three types of lexical elements collections. The θ_3 assigns all types of lexical elements with the weight of one, but it mixes different types of collections without consideration.

TABLE 2: Performance comparison of FSGM with different coefficients of lexical elements.

Parameter	θ_{default} (1.2, 1.1, 1.0)	θ_1 (2, 1.5, 1.0)	θ_2 (1.5, 1.3, 1.0)	θ_3 (1.0, 1.0, 1.0)	θ_4 (0.5, 0.8, 1.0)
ROUGE-1	0.325	0.315	0.322	0.310	0.298
ROUGE-2	0.052	0.049	0.049	0.047	0.042
ROUGE-L	0.298	0.305	0.303	0.293	0.289

TABLE 3: Performance comparison of FSGM with different thresholds of combining sentences.

Parameter	α_{default} (1)	α_1 (0.95)	α_2 (0.90)	α_3 (0.85)	α_4 (0.5)
ROUGE-1	0.325	0.320	0.320	0.317	0.198
ROUGE-2	0.052	0.049	0.052	0.046	0.019
ROUGE-L	0.298	0.300	0.295	0.293	0.135

TABLE 4: Performance comparison of FSGM with different thresholds of estimating sentence relationship.

Parameter	β_{default} (0.5)	β_1 (0.9)	β_2 (0.7)	β_3 (0.3)	β_4 (0.1)
ROUGE-1	0.325	0.167	0.240	0.214	0.156
ROUGE-2	0.052	0.019	0.032	0.024	0.013
ROUGE-L	0.298	0.126	0.145	0.156	0.113

TABLE 5: Performance comparison of FSGM with different coefficients of estimating semantic weight.

Parameter	μ_{default} (0.3)	μ_1 (0.9)	μ_2 (0.7)	μ_3 (0.5)	μ_4 (0.1)
ROUGE-1	0.325	0.298	0.320	0.307	0.306
ROUGE-2	0.052	0.043	0.051	0.049	0.045
ROUGE-L	0.298	0.270	0.295	0.293	0.273

Table 3 is the performance comparison of FSGM with different thresholds of combining sentences. When the threshold is set by 1, the performance is the best. When it comes lower, all parameters are worse. And when it comes to 0.5, which means that it combines two sentences when they are only half same, ROUGE parameters make no sense. The more similar the two sentences are when combined, the better their performance is.

Table 4 is the performance comparison of FSGM with different thresholds of estimating sentence relationship. The best performance appears on 0.5. This line almost obeys the normal distribution, while the sentences should not be too similar nor too dissimilar. When β is small, there are little edges; when β is too big, nearly all lines link between nodes.

Table 5 is the performance comparison of FSGM with different coefficients of estimating semantic weight. This parameter has less influence than others. The best setting is $\mu = 0.3$.

Moreover, this paper analyzes and compares the FSGM performance on the DUC2004 with several baseline systems. Table 6 presents the results that are achieved by Lead, Random, GraphRank, and FSGM. The table clearly shows the proposed FSGM outperformed other systems. It can be inferred from the results that text summarization gets better performance using sentence-level semantic information.

It should notice that Lead's performance outperformed Random in every ROUGE measure, and its results of measure ROUGE-2 and ROUGE-L even approach graph-based system GraphRank. Lead method only chooses the first sentence of the document as the abstract, while the result is similar to GraphRank. It means that the location of sentences must be considered when generating abstract. Although Lead method is simple, its performance is instable, because it greatly depends on the context.

Unlike Lead, GraphRank analyzes the context based on relations of words. It builds a graph model based on sentence similarity and analyzes their occurrence relations. So the performance is much better than baseline. But it is not enough to consider the sentence-level semantic similarity. It only focuses on the relationship between sentences, ignoring sentence itself as basic morpheme. On such basis, FSGM considers the semantic similarity between sentences, so it gets the best performance. Meanwhile, as it considers the relationship between sentences, the performance is very stable.

While there are multiple choices of graph ranking algorithm, it choses PageRank-like algorithm as the default ranking algorithm of FSGM. It choses another famous graph ranking algorithm HITS for performance comparison, which is also widely applied in measuring the importance of graph vertexes. Both HITS and PageRank-like algorithm applied in the FSGM achieve the best results. It can be inferred from Table 6 that taking sentence-level semantic information into consideration can improve the performance of general graph ranking algorithm. The reason why PageRank-like algorithm does better than HITS in the experiment may be because that the former is topic independent while the latter is topic related. The FSGM based on HITS may be more suitable in query-based tasks.

6. Conclusion

In this paper, it reviews the common methods of text summarization and proposes a Semantic Graph Model using FrameNet called FSGM. Besides the basic functions, it particularly takes sentence meaning and words order into consideration, and therefore it can discover the semantic relations between sentences. This method mainly optimizes the sentences nodes by combining similar sentences using word embedding. Also, giving the sentences its weight and optimizing the PageRank can make the model more rigorous. The results show that FSGM is more effective from the understanding of sentence-level semantic.

Above all, if it can take more semantic information into account, it may probably get a better result. In the future work, it prepares to build a multiple-layer model to further show the

TABLE 6: Performance comparison on DUC2004 using ROUGE evaluation methods.

Parameter	Lead	Random	GraphRank	FSGM (PageRank-like)	FSGM (HITS-like)
ROUGE-1	0.292	0.290	0.304	0.325	0.310
ROUGE-2	0.043	0.041	0.041	0.052	0.045
ROUGE-L	0.271	0.264	0.265	0.298	0.280

accuracy rate of application in text summarization. And in this paper, it only applies FSGM to a test corpus. Nowadays, text from social media is the main resource. And there will be more serious problems about the credibility. It will research on the social media content in the future.

Disclosure

This paper is based on the authors' paper "Text Summarization Using Sentence-Level Semantic Graph Model" from 2016 4th IEEE International Conference on Cloud Computing and Intelligence Systems.

Competing Interests

The authors declare that there is no conflict of interests regarding the publication of this article.

Acknowledgments

This work is supported by Basic Research of the Ministry of Science and Technology, China (2013FY114000).

References

[1] K. S. Jones, "Automatic summarising: factors and directions," in *Advances in Automatic Text Summarization*, I. Mani and M. Maybury, Eds., pp. 1–12, MIT Press, Cambridge, Mass, USA, 1999.

[2] K. M. Svore, L. Vanderwende, and C. J. C. Burges, "Enhancing single-document summarization by combining RankNet and third-party sources," in *Proceedings of the Joint Conference on Empirical Methods in Natural Language Processing and Computational Natural Language Learning (EMNLP-CoNLL '07)*, pp. 448–457, June 2007.

[3] T. Hirao, Y. Sasaki, and H. Isozaki, "An extrinsic evaluation for question-biased text summarization on QA tasks," in *Proceedings of the NAACL Workshop on Automatic Summarization*, 2001.

[4] X. Wan and J. Zhang, "CTSUM: extracting more certain summaries for news articles," in *Proceedings of the 37th International ACM SIGIR Conference on Research and Development in Information Retrieval (SIGIR '14)*, pp. 787–796, Queensland, Australia, July 2014.

[5] B. Chen, S.-H. Lin, Y.-M. Chang, and J.-W. Liu, "Extractive speech summarization using evaluation metric-related training criteria," *Information Processing & Management*, vol. 49, no. 1, pp. 1–12, 2013.

[6] D. R. Radev, E. Hovy, and K. McKeown, "Introduction to the special issue on summarization," *Computational Linguistics*, vol. 28, no. 4, pp. 399–408, 2002.

[7] E. Baralis, L. Cagliero, N. Mahoto, and A. Fiori, "Graph Sum: discovering correlations among multiple terms for graph-based summarization," *Information Sciences*, vol. 249, no. 16, pp. 96–109, 2013.

[8] X. Li, S. Zhu, H. Xie et al., "Document summarization via self-present sentence relevance model," in *Database Systems for Advanced Applications*, pp. 309–323, Springer, Berlin, Germany, 2013.

[9] P. Goyal, L. Behera, and T. M. McGinnity, "A context-based word indexing model for document summarization," *IEEE Transactions on Knowledge & Data Engineering*, vol. 25, no. 8, pp. 1693–1705, 2013.

[10] D. R. Radev, H. Jing, M. Styś, and D. Tam, "Centroid-based summarization of multiple documents," *Information Processing & Management*, vol. 40, no. 6, pp. 919–938, 2004.

[11] D. Wang, T. Li, S. Zhu, and C. Ding, "Multi-document summarization via sentence-level semantic analysis and symmetric matrix factorization," in *Proceedings of the 31st Annual International ACM SIGIR Conference on Research and Development in Information Retrieval*, pp. 307–314, ACM, July 2008.

[12] J.-P. Mei and L. Chen, "SumCR: a new subtopic-based extractive approach for text summarization," *Knowledge & Information Systems*, vol. 31, no. 3, pp. 527–545, 2012.

[13] Y. Gong and X. Liu, "Generic text summarization using relevance measure and latent semantic analysis," in *Proceedings of the 24th ACM Annual International ACM SIGIR Conference on Research and Development in Information Retrieval (SIGIR '01)*, pp. 19–25, New Orleans, La, USA, September 2001.

[14] D. Wang, S. Zhu, T. Li et al., "Comparative document summarization via discriminative sentence selection," *ACM Transactions on Knowledge Discovery from Data*, vol. 6, no. 3, pp. 1963–1966, 2009.

[15] R. He, J. Tang, P. Gong, Q. Hu, and B. Wang, "Multi-document summarization via group sparse learning," *Information Sciences*, vol. 349-350, pp. 12–24, 2016.

[16] T. Li, "A general model for clustering binary data," in *Proceedings of the 11th ACM SIGKDD International Conference on Knowledge Discovery and Data Mining*, pp. 188–197, August 2005.

[17] S. Park, J.-H. Lee, D.-H. Kim, and C.-M. Ahn, "Multi-document summarization based on cluster using non-negative matrix factorization," in *SOFSEM 2007: Theory and Practice of Computer Science: 33rd Conference on Current Trends in Theory and Practice of Computer Science, Harrachov, Czech Republic, January 20–26, 2007. Proceedings*, vol. 4362 of *Lecture Notes in Computer Science*, pp. 761–770, Springer, Berlin, Germany, 2007.

[18] I. S. Dhillon, "Co-clustering documents and words using bipartite spectral graph partitioning," in *Proceedings of the 7th ACM SIGKDD International Conference on Knowledge Discovery and Data Mining (KDD '01)*, pp. 269–274, San Francisco, Calif, USA, August 2001.

[19] R. Katragadda, P. Pingali, and V. Varma, "Sentence position revisited: a robust light-weight update summarization 'Baseline' algorithm," in *Proceedings of the 3rd International Workshop Cross Lingual Information Access: Addressing the Information Need of Multilingual Societies (CLIAWS3 '09)*, pp. 46–52, Boulder, Colo, USA, June 2009.

[20] C.-Y. Lin and E. Hovy, "Identifying topics by position," in *Proceedings of the 5th conference on Applied Natural Language Processing*, pp. 283–290, Washington, DC, USA, April 1997.

[21] C.-Y. Lin and E. Hovy, "The automated acquisition of topic signatures for text summarization," in *Proceedings of the 18th Conference on Computational Linguistics (COLING '00)*, pp. 495–501, Saarbrücken, Germany, August 2000.

[22] R. Barzilay and M. Elhadad, "Using lexical chains for text summarization," in *Proceedings of the ACL Workshop Intelligent Scalable Text Summarization*, pp. 10–17, Madrid, Spain, July 1997.

[23] M. H. Haggag, "Semantic text summarization based on syntactic patterns," *International Journal of Information Retrieval Research*, vol. 3, no. 4, pp. 18–34, 2013.

[24] Y. Ko and J. Seo, "An effective sentence-extraction technique using contextual information and statistical approaches for text summarization," *Pattern Recognition Letters*, vol. 29, no. 9, pp. 1366–1371, 2008.

[25] E. Canhasi and I. Kononenko, "Multi-document summarization via Archetypal Analysis of the content-graph joint model," *Knowledge & Information Systems*, vol. 41, no. 3, pp. 821–842, 2014.

[26] F. Wei, W. Li, Q. Lu, and Y. He, "A document-sensitive graph model for multi-document summarization," *Knowledge and Information Systems*, vol. 22, no. 2, pp. 245–259, 2010.

[27] P. Goyal, L. Behera, and T. M. McGinnity, "A context-based word indexing model for document summarization," *IEEE Transactions on Knowledge and Data Engineering*, vol. 25, no. 8, pp. 1693–1705, 2013.

[28] S. Harabagiu and F. Lacatusu, "Topic themes for multi-document summarization," in *Proceedings of the 28th Annual International ACM SIGIR Conference on Research and Development in Information Retrieval (SIGIR '05)*, pp. 202–209, August 2005.

[29] R. Mihalcea, "Graph-based ranking algorithms for sentence extraction, applied to text summarization," in *Proceedings of the ACL on Interactive Poster and Demonstration Sessions*, p. 20, Association for Computational Linguistics, 2004.

[30] R. Ferreira, F. Freitas, L. De Souza Cabral et al., "A four dimension graph model for automatic text summarization," in *Proceedings of the IEEE/WIC/ACM International Joint Conferences on Web Intelligence and Intelligent Agent Technologies (IAT '13)*, vol. 1, pp. 389–396, November 2013.

[31] R. Ferreira, R. D. Lins, F. Freitas, S. J. Simske, and M. Riss, "A new sentence similarity assessment measure based on a three-layer sentence representation," in *Proceedings of the ACM Symposium on Document Engineering (DocEng '14)*, pp. 25–34, Fort Collins, Colo, USA, September 2014.

[32] Y. Bengio, R. Ducharme, P. Vincent, and C. Jauvin, "A neural probabilistic language model," *Journal of Machine Learning Research*, vol. 3, no. 6, pp. 1137–1155, 2003.

[33] G. E. Hinton, "Learning distributed representations of concepts," in *Proceedings of the 8th Annual Conference of the Cognitive Science Society*, vol. 1, pp. 1–12, Amherst, Mass, USA, 1986.

[34] M. J. Kusner, Y. Sun, N. I. Kolkin et al., "From word embeddings to document distances," in *Proceedings of the 32nd International Conference on Machine Learning (ICML '15)*, pp. 957–966, Lille, France, 2015.

[35] K. Sarkar, "Automatic single document text summarization using key concepts in documents," *Journal of Information Processing Systems*, vol. 9, no. 4, pp. 602–620, 2013.

[36] Y. Sankarasubramaniam, K. Ramanathan, and S. Ghosh, "Text summarization using Wikipedia," *Information Processing & Management*, vol. 50, no. 3, pp. 443–461, 2014.

[37] J.-U. Heu, I. Qasim, and D.-H. Lee, "FoDoSu: multi-document summarization exploiting semantic analysis based on social Folksonomy," *Information Processing & Management*, vol. 51, no. 1, pp. 212–225, 2015.

[38] Y.-S. Lin, J.-Y. Jiang, and S.-J. Lee, "A similarity measure for text classification and clustering," *IEEE Transactions on Knowledge & Data Engineering*, vol. 26, no. 7, pp. 1575–1590, 2014.

8

A Robust Text Classifier Based on Denoising Deep Neural Network in the Analysis of Big Data

Wulamu Aziguli,[1,2] Yuanyu Zhang,[1,2] Yonghong Xie,[1,2] Dezheng Zhang,[1,2] Xiong Luo,[1,2,3] Chunmiao Li,[1,2] and Yao Zhang[4]

[1]*School of Computer and Communication Engineering, University of Science and Technology Beijing (USTB), Beijing 100083, China*
[2]*Beijing Engineering Research Center of Industrial Spectrum Imaging, Beijing 100083, China*
[3]*Key Laboratory of Geological Information Technology, Ministry of Land and Resources, Beijing 100037, China*
[4]*Tandon School of Engineering, New York University, Brooklyn, NY 11201, USA*

Correspondence should be addressed to Yonghong Xie; xieyh@ustb.edu.cn, Dezheng Zhang; zdzchina@ustb.edu.cn, and Xiong Luo; xluo@ustb.edu.cn

Academic Editor: Anfeng Liu

Text classification has always been an interesting issue in the research area of natural language processing (NLP). While entering the era of big data, a good text classifier is critical to achieving NLP for scientific big data analytics. With the ever-increasing size of text data, it has posed important challenges in developing effective algorithm for text classification. Given the success of deep neural network (DNN) in analyzing big data, this article proposes a novel text classifier using DNN, in an effort to improve the computational performance of addressing big text data with hybrid outliers. Specifically, through the use of denoising autoencoder (DAE) and restricted Boltzmann machine (RBM), our proposed method, named denoising deep neural network (DDNN), is able to achieve significant improvement with better performance of antinoise and feature extraction, compared to the traditional text classification algorithms. The simulations on benchmark datasets verify the effectiveness and robustness of our proposed text classifier.

1. Introduction

While entering the era of big data with the development of information technology and the Internet, the amount of data is getting geometric growth. We are entering information overload era. The issue that people are facing is no longer how to get information, but how to extract useful information quickly and efficiently from massive amount of data. Therefore, how to effectively manage and filter information has always been an important research area in engineering and science fields.

With the rapid increase of the amount of data, information representation is also diversified, mainly including text, sound, and image. Compared with sound and image, text data uses less network resources and is easier to be uploaded and downloaded. Since other forms of information can be also expressed by text, text has become the main carrier of information and always occupies a leading position in the network resources.

Traditionally, it is time-consuming and difficult to achieve the desired results of text processing, and it can not adapt to the demand of information society for explosive growth of digital information. Hence, effectively obtaining information in accordance with the user feedback can help users to get the information quickly and accurately. Then, text classification becomes a critical technology to achieve free human-machine interaction and contribute to artificial intelligence. It can address the messy information issue to a large extent, so that users can locate the information accurately.

1.1. Text Classification. The purpose of text classification is to assign large amounts of text to one or more categories based on the subject, content, or attributes of the document. The methods of text classification are divided into two categories, including rules-based and statistical classification methods

[1, 2]. Among them, the rules-based classification methods need more knowledge and rules base in this field. However, the development of rules and the difficulties of updating them make the application of this method relatively narrow and suitable for only a specific field. Statistical learning methods are usually based on a statistic or some kinds of statistical knowledge; these methods establish learning parameters of the corresponding data model through the sample statistics and calculation on the train set and then conduct the training of the classifier. In the test stage, the categories of the samples could be predicted according to these parameters.

Recently, a large number of statistical machine learning methods are applied to the text classification system. The application of the earliest machine learning method is naive Bayes (NB) [3, 4]. Subsequently, almost all the important machine learning algorithms have been applied to the field of text classification, for example, K nearest neighbor (KNN), neural network (NN), support vector machine (SVM), decision tree, kernel learning, and some others [5–10]. SVM uses the shallow linear model to separate the objective. In low dimensional space, when different types of data vectors can not be divided, SVM will map it to a high dimensional space through kernel function and finds the optimal hyperplane. In addition, NB, linear classification, decision tree, KNN, and other methods are relatively weak, but their models are simple and efficient; then those methods are accordingly improved.

But these models are shallow machine learning methods. Although they have also been proven to be able to efficiently address some of the issues in the case of simple or multiple restrictions, when facing complex practical problems, for example, biomedical multiclass text classification, the data is noisy and dataset distribution is uneven classification and shallow machine learning model and generalization ability of integrated classifier method will be unsatisfactory. Therefore, the exploration of some other new methods, for example, deep learning method, is necessary.

1.2. Deep Learning.
With the success of deep learning methods [11, 12], some other improvement for NN, for example, deep belief network (DBN) [13], has been developed. Here, DBN is designed on the basis of the cascaded restricted Boltzmann machine (RBM) [14] learning algorithm, through unsupervised greedy layer pretraining strategy combining the supervision of fine-tuning training methods. It can tackle the problem of complex deep learning model optimization, so that the deep neural network (DNN) has witnessed the rapid advancements.

Meanwhile, DNN has been applied to many learning tasks, for example, voice and image recognitions [15]. For example, since 2011, Microsoft and Google's speech recognition research team achieved a voice recognition error rate reduction of 20%–30% using DNN model, stepping forward in the field of speech recognition in the past decades. In 2012, DNN technology in the ImageNet [15] evaluation task (image recognition field) improved the error rate from 26% to 15% [16].

Moreover, the automatic encoder (AE) as a DNN reproduces the input signal [17, 18]. Its main principle is that there is a given input; it first encodes the input signal using an encoder and then decodes the encoded signal using a decoder, while achieving the minimum reconstruction error by constantly adjusting the parameters of encoder and decoder [19]. Additionally, there are some improvements to AE, for example, sparse AE and denoising AE [17, 18]. The performance of some machine learning algorithms could be further improved through the use of those AEs [20].

Recently, deep learning methods have a significant impact on the field of natural language processing (NLP) [11, 21].

1.3. Status Analysis.
Due to the complex feature of large text data, and different effects of noise, the performance is not satisfactory when dealing with large dataset using traditional text classification algorithms.

More recently, deep learning has been applied to a series of classification issues with multiple modes successfully. Then, the user can effectively extract the complex semantic relations of the text by using deep learning-based methods [11, 22]. With the popularity of deep learning algorithms, DNN has some advantages in dealing with large-scale dataset. In this article, motivated by DNN, the denoising deep neural network (DDNN) is designed and the feature extraction is conducted by using this model.

For the shallow text representation (feature selection), there is a problem of missing semantics. For the deep text representation of the model based on the linear calculation, the selection of the threshold is added to the classifier training, which actually destroys the self-taught learning ability of the text. Meanwhile, for text classification of multilabel and multicategory, there is also a problem of ignoring label dependencies and lack of generalizing ability. To cope with the above problems, some improvements are achieved through deep learning methods. For example, a two-layer replicated softmax model (RSM) was proposed in [23], which is better than latent Dirichlet allocation (LDA), that is, a semantically consistent topic model [24]. However, the model is designed using weighted sharing technique and there are only two layers. In the process of dimension reduction, the missing information of documents is relatively larger, and the ability of noise handling is poor, resulting in little difference between different documents using the model.

In order to avoid such limitations and develop a better approach, this article proposes a DDNN model through the combination of some state-of-the-art deep learning methods. Specifically, in our model, the data is denoised with the help of denoising autoencoder (DAE), and then the feature of the text is extracted effectively using RBM. Compared with those traditional text classification algorithms, our proposed algorithm can achieve significant improvement with better performance of antinoise and feature extraction, due to the efficient learning ability of hybrid deep learning methods used in this model.

The reminder of this article is organized as follows. In Section 2, we give a technique analysis for DAE [25] and RBM [26]. Then, our proposed text classifier is presented in Section 3, where more attention is paid for the implementation of DDNN. Section 4 provides some simulation results and discussions. Finally, the conclusion is given in Section 5.

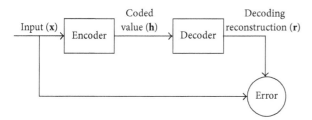

FIGURE 1: Schematic diagram of automatic encoder model.

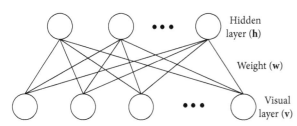

FIGURE 2: Schematic diagram of restricted Boltzmann machine.

2. Background

In this article, we use two kinds of state-of-the-art deep learning models, that is, DAE and RBM [25, 26].

2.1. Denoising Autoencoder (DAE). Generally, the structure of AE [27] is shown in Figure 1. Here, the whole system consists of two networks, that is, encoder and decoder. Its purpose is to make the reconstruction layer output as similar to the input as possible. The coding network will code and calculate the input **x** and then reconstruct the result **h** to **r** by the decoder. And denoising automatic coding is developed according to the automatic coding, it will learn a more robust representation of the input signal and has stronger generalization ability than ordinary encoders by adding noise to the training data.

2.2. Restricted Boltzmann Machine (RBM). As shown in Figure 2, RBM network has two layers [28, 29]. Here, the first layer is the visual layer (**v**), also called the input layer, which consists of m visible nodes. And the second layer is the hidden layer (**h**), that is, the feature extraction layer, and it consists of n hidden nodes. If v is known, then $P(h/v) = P(h_1/v) \cdots P(h_n/v)$ and all hidden nodes are conditional independent. Similarly, all the visible nodes are also conditional independent when the hidden layer **h** is known, the nodes within the layer are not connected, and the nodes from different layers are fully connected.

3. The Proposed Text Classifier

3.1. Denoising Deep Neural Network (DDNN)

3.1.1. Framework. Here, a DDNN is designed using DAE and RBM, which can effectively reduce the noise while extracting the feature.

The input of the DDNN model is a vector with fixed dimension. Firstly, we conduct the training by the denoising module composed of two layers, named DAE1 and DAE2, using unsupervised training methods. Here, only one of them is trained each time, and each training can minimize the reconstruction error for the input data, that is, the output of the previous layer. Because we can calculate the encoder or its potential expression based on the previous layer k, so the $(k + 1)$th layer could be processed directly using the output of the kth layer, until all the denoising layers are trained.

The operation of this model is shown in Figure 3.

After being processed through the denoising layer, the data enters the portion of RBM, which can further extract the feature that is different from the denoising autocoder layer. The feature extracted after this part will be more representative and essential. Figure 4 is the diagram for the RBM feature extraction.

This part is constructed by stacking two layers of RBM. Training can be conducted by training RBM from low to high as follows.

(1) The input of bottom RBM is the output of the denoising layer.

(2) The feature extracted from the bottom RBM is taken as the input of the top RBM.

Because RBM can be trained quickly by contrastive divergence (CD) learning algorithm [30], this training framework avoids the high complexity calculation of directly getting a deep network with one training by dividing it into multiple RBMs training. After this training, the initial parameter values of some pretraining models are obtained. Then, a backpropagation (BP) NN is initialized using these parameters; the network parameters are fine-tuned by the traditional global learning algorithm using the dataset with tags. Thus, the function can converge to the global optimal point.

The reason for choosing DAE here is that, in the process of text classification, data will be inevitably mixed into different types and intensity of noise, which tends to affect the training of the model, resulting in deterioration of the final classification performance. DAE is a preliminary extraction of the original features, and its learning criteria is noise reduction. In the pretraining stage, adding a variety of different strength and different types of noise signals to the original input signal can make the encoding process obtain better stability and robustness. It is shown in Figure 5.

Moreover, the reason for choosing RBM is that RBM is characterized by the fact that it can simulate the discrete distribution of arbitrary samples and it is very suitable for feature expression when the number of hidden layer units is sufficient.

3.1.2. Implementation. The DDNN model consists of four layers, that is, DAE1, DAE2, RBM1, and RBM2. The layer **v** is both visual layer and the input layer of the DDNN model. Each document in this article is represented by a fixed dimension vector, where W_1, W_2, W_3, and W_4 represent the connection weight between the layers, respectively. In addition, h_1, h_2, h_3, and h_4 represent each hidden layer corresponding to the output layers DAE1, DAE2, RBM1, and

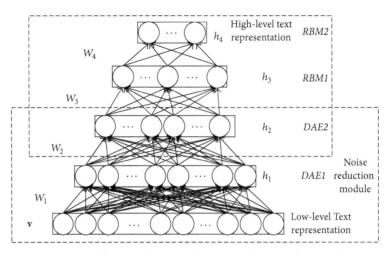

FIGURE 3: Schematic diagram of denoising deep neural network.

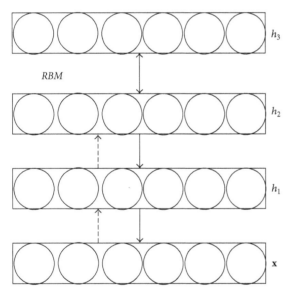

FIGURE 4: Illustration of feature extraction in RBM.

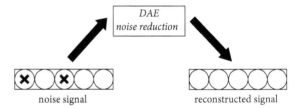

FIGURE 5: Noise reduction with DAE.

training the model parameters. Here, RBM energy function is defined as

$$E(v, h) = -\sum_{i=1}^{n}\sum_{j=1}^{m} w_{ij} h_i v_j - \sum_{j=1}^{m} b_j v_j - \sum_{i=1}^{n} c_i h_i. \qquad (1)$$

Here, (1) represents the energy function of each visible node and hidden node connection structure. Among them, n is the number of hidden nodes, m is the number of visible layer nodes, and b and c are the bias of visual layer and hidden layer, respectively. The objective function of the RBM model is to accumulate the energy of all the visible nodes and the hidden nodes. Therefore, it is necessary for each sample to count the value of all the hidden nodes corresponding to it, so that the total energy can be calculated. The calculation is complex. An effective solution is to convert the problem into probabilistic computing. The joint probability of the visible and the hidden node is

$$P(v, h) = \frac{e^{-E(v,h)}}{\sum_{v,h} e^{-E(v,h)}}. \qquad (2)$$

By introducing this probability, the energy function can be simplified, and the objective of the solution is to minimize the energy value. There is a theory in statistical learning that the state of low energy has higher probability than high energy, so we maximize this probability and introduce the

RBM2, respectively. DAE2 layer is the output layer of the denoising module, and also the input layer of the two-layer RBM module. RBM2 is the output layer of the DDNN model which represents the feature of the document, and it will be compared with the visual layer **v**. This layer is the high-level feature representation of the text data. The subsequent text classification task is also addressed on the basis of this vector. For all nodes, there is no connection between the same layer nodes, but the nodes between those two layers are fully connected.

Specifically, the introduction of the energy model is to capture the correlation between variables, while optimizing the model parameters. Therefore, it is important to embed the optimal solution problem into the energy function when

FIGURE 6: The architecture of a classifier.

free energy function. The definition of free energy function is as follows:

$$\text{FreeEnergy}(v) = -\ln \sum_h e^{-E(v,h)}. \tag{3}$$

Therefore,

$$P(v) = \frac{e^{\text{FreeEnergy}(v)}}{Z}, \quad Z = \sum_{v,h} e^{-E(v,h)}, \tag{4}$$

where Z is the normalization factor. Then, the joint probability $P(v)$ can be transformed into

$$\ln P(v) = -\text{FreeEnergy}(v) - \ln Z. \tag{5}$$

The first term on the right side of (5) is the negative value of the sum of the free energy functions of the whole network, and the left is the likelihood function. As we described in the model description, the model parameters can be solved using maximum likelihood function estimation.

Here, we first construct a denoising function module for the original features. It is mainly composed of a DAE. The two-layer DAE is placed at the bottom of the model so as to make full use of the character of denoising. The input signal can be denoised by reconstructing the input signal through unsupervised learning, so that the signal entering the network is purer after being processed by the encoder. Then the impact of noise data on the subsequent construction of the classifier will be reduced.

The second module is developed using DBN. It is generated through RBM; then the ability of feature extraction in this model will be improved. Furthermore, the model can obtain the complex rules in the data, and the high-level features extracted are more representative. In order to achieve better sorting results, we use the extracted representative feature as an input for the final classifier after further extraction using RBM.

Considering the complexity of the training and the efficiency of the model, a two-layer DAE and a two-layer RBM will be used.

3.2. Text Classification Using DDNN. Here, the final DDNN-based text classifier is developed. And there are three key modules in its architecture, as shown in Figure 6.

3.2.1. Text Preprocessing Module. First, the feature words processed here are mapped into the vocabulary form [31–33]. Then, the weights are counted using TF-IDF (term frequency, inverse document frequency) algorithm [34]. In addition, using vector to represent the text is implemented. Meanwhile, it is also normalized.

3.2.2. Feature Learning Module. The DDNN mentioned in Section 3.1 is used to implement feature learning.

3.2.3. Classification Identification Module. In this module, we use Softmax classifier in classification, and its input is the feature which is learned from the feature learning module. In the classifier, the hypothetical text dataset has n texts from k categories, where the training set is expressed as $\{(x^{(1)}, y^{(1)}), (x^{(2)}, y^{(2)}), \ldots, (x^{(n-1)}, y^{(n-1)}), (x^{(n)}, y^{(n)})\}$ and $x^{(i)}$ represents the ith training text, and y represents different categories ($y^{(i)} \in \{1, 2, \ldots, k-1, k\}$). The main purpose of the algorithm is to calculate the probability of x belonging to the tag category, for the given training set x. Here, that function is as shown in

$$
h_\theta\left(x^{(i)}\right) =
\begin{bmatrix}
P\left(y^{(i)} = 1 \mid x^{(i)}; \theta\right) \\
P\left(y^{(i)} = 2 \mid x^{(i)}; \theta\right) \\
\vdots \\
P\left(y^{(i)} = k \mid x^{(i)}; \theta\right)
\end{bmatrix}
$$

$$
= \frac{1}{\sum_{j=1}^{k} e^{\theta_j^T x^{(i)}}}
\begin{bmatrix}
e^{\theta_1^T x^i} \\
e^{\theta_2^T x^{(i)}} \\
\vdots \\
e^{\theta_k^T x^{(i)}}
\end{bmatrix}. \tag{6}
$$

Each subvector of vector $h_\theta(x^{(i)})$ is the probability value that x belongs to different tag categories, and the probability value is required to be normalized, so that the sum of probability value of all the subvectors is 1. And $\theta_1, \theta_2, \ldots, \theta_{k-1}, \theta_k \in \mathbb{R}^{n+1}$ represents the parameter vectors, respectively.

After getting θ, we can obtain the previously assumed function $h_\theta(x)$. It can be used to calculate the probability value that text x belongs to each category. The category which has the biggest probability value is the final classified result by the classifier algorithm.

4. Simulation Results and Discussions

In this article, simulations are conducted in two steps. First, we analyze the key parameters that affect the performance of the DAE and the RBM models (the basic components of DDNN model) and implement the simulation with appropriate parameters. Second, we compare the DDNN with NB, KNN, SVM, and DBN using the data with noise and the data without noise and verify the effectiveness of the proposed DDNN.

4.1. Evaluation Criterion of Text Classification Results. For the text classification results, we mainly use the accuracy as a classification criterion. This index is widely used to evaluate the performance in the field of information retrieval and statistical classification.

If there are two categories of information in the original sample, there are a total of P samples which belong to category 1, and category 1 is positive. And there are a total of N samples which belong to category 0, and category 0 is negative.

After the classification, TP samples that belong to category 1 are divided into category 1 correctly, and FN samples are divided into category 0 incorrectly. And TN samples that belong to category 0 are divided into category 0 correctly, FP samples are divided into category 1 incorrectly.

Then, the accuracy is defined as

$$\text{Accuracy} = \frac{\text{TP}}{\text{TP} + \text{FP}}. \tag{7}$$

Here, the accuracy can reflect the performance of the classifier.

The recall is defined as

$$\text{Recall} = \frac{\text{TP}}{\text{TP} + \text{FN}} = 1 - \frac{\text{FN}}{P}. \tag{8}$$

It can reflect the proportion of the positive samples classified correctly.

The F-score is defined as

$$F\text{-score} = \frac{2 \times \text{Recall} \times \text{Accuracy}}{\text{Recall} + \text{Accuracy}}. \tag{9}$$

It is a comprehensive reflection of the classification of data.

4.2. Dataset Description. In our simulations, we test the algorithm performance using two news datasets, namely, 20-Newsgroups and BBC news datasets.

The 20-Newsgroups dataset consists of 20 different news comment groups in which each group represents a news topic. There are three versions in the website (http://qwone .com/~jason/20Newsgroups/). And we select the second version, that is, a total of 18846 documents, and the dataset has been divided into two parts, where there are 11314 documents for the train set and 7532 documents for the test set. The distribution of the 20 sample details can be found in that website. Note that, in our simulations, the serial number of those 20 labels varies from 0 to 19.

The dataset of BBC news consists of several news documents on the BBC website (http://www.bbc.co.uk/news/business/market_data/overview/). The dataset includes a total of 2225 documents corresponding to five topics, that is, business, entertainment, politics, sports, and technology. Similarly, we randomly select 1559 documents for train set, and 666 documents for a test set.

4.3. Simulation Results. All the simulations are conducted according to the following. The operating system is Ubuntu 16.04. The hardware environment is NVIDIA Corporation GM204GL [Tesla M60]. The software environment is Cuda V8.0.61 and cuDNN 5.1. Deep learning framework is Keras, while using sklearn and nltk toolkits.

4.3.1. Impact of Parameters. For all deep learning algorithms, the parameter tuning greatly affects the performance of simulation results. For the DDNN, the parameters which we

mainly adjust include the plus noise ratio of the data, the number of hidden layer nodes, and the learning rate.

In order to test the robustness of the DDNN, we set the plus noise ratio of the training set to 0.01, 0.001, and 0.0001. The result are shown in the Table 1.

As shown in Table 1, the stability of the model can be guaranteed within the range of plus noise ratio (0.01, 0.001), but when the plus noise ratio is too high, that is, higher than 0.1, the data will be damaged especially for the sparse data, and it will affect the classification performance. Moreover, the performance of the classifier to robust feature extraction will be weakened if the plus noise ratio is too low. Hence, we set the plus noise ratio finally to 0.001. After we conduct the simulation, we set the noise factor as 0.01, 0.02, 0.03, 0.04, and 0.05 to verify the denoising performance of the proposed model.

The number of the input layer nodes is fixed according to the result of the weight using TF-IDF algorithm. Since the main purpose of DAE is to reconstruct original data, we set the numbers of the input layer nodes and output layer nodes to the same value. Because the number of the hidden layer nodes is unknown, we set the numbers of the two hidden-layer nodes in DAE to 1600 and 1500, 1700 and 1500, and 1800 and 1500, respectively. In addition, the numbers of the two hidden-layer nodes in RBM are set as 600 and 100, 700 and 100, and 800 and 100, respectively. Then, we conduct the simulation. And we set the learning rate to 0.1, 0.01, and 0.001. The results are shown in Table 2.

As shown in Table 2, the performance of the DDNN model will be better when the numbers of two hidden-layer nodes are set to 1700 and 1500 for DAE and 700 and 100 for RBM, respectively. And the learning rate should be set to 0.01.

4.3.2. Comparisons and Analysis. In this article, we compare our DDNN model with NB, KNN, SVM, and DBN models.

In text preprocessing, we select the frequency of the first 2000 words to simulation and set batch size with 350. Compared with the DDNN model (two-layer DAE and two-layer RBM) proposed in this article, the DBN model is also set to four layers. The number of iterations in the pretraining phase is 100, and the model updating parameter is 0.01.

Here, we take the BBC news dataset for an example to show the process of training. From Figures 7 and 8, we can see that, with the increase of epoch, the loss of training is decreasing and the accuracy is increasing towards test datasets, which shows that the effect of training is well.

Table 3 compares the results of DDNN with other models using the BBC news dataset and Table 4 compares them using the 20-Newsgroups dataset. Moreover, we compare these models in consideration of different types of data, including the data without noise and the data with a noise factor of 0.01, 0.02, 0.03, 0.04, and 0.05. Here, it is noted that, for each vector of text extracted, the standard normal distribution of noise factor multiplication is added. If a dimension is less than 0, it is directly set to 0. In this article, the accuracy rate (Accuracy), recall rate (Recall), and F-Score are observed to evaluate the performance of classifier. Take the calculation of Accuracy, for example. Towards each classifier, we firstly calculate the accuracy of each category according to the metric (7) and

TABLE 1: Text classification performance of DDNN with different plus noise ratio.

Plus noise ratio	Noise factor					
	0.00	0.01	0.02	0.03	0.04	0.05
0.001	0.7530	0.7529	0.7479	0.7450	0.7349	0.7287
0.01	0.7536	0.7561	0.7550	0.7542	0.7443	0.7378
0.1	0.5379	0.5310	0.5270	0.5179	0.5027	0.4978

TABLE 2: Text classification performance of DDNN with different parameters.

Learning rate	DAE		RBM		Accuracy
	1600	1500	600	100	0.9640
0.01	1700	1500	700	100	0.9700
	1800	1500	800	100	0.9686
	1600	1500	600	100	0.9655
0.02	1700	1500	700	100	0.9654
	1800	1500	800	100	0.9670
	1600	1500	600	100	0.9625
0.03	1700	1500	700	100	0.9627
	1800	1500	800	100	0.9491

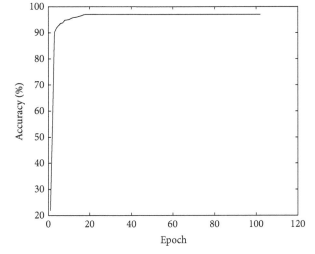

FIGURE 7: The test accuracy in the training process for BBC news dataset.

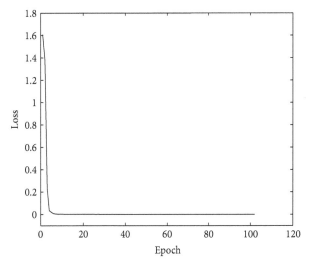

FIGURE 8: The test loss in the training process for BBC news dataset.

then compute the average of these subaccuracies as the result. The simulation data is the optimal classification result after running many times.

After comparing DDNN model with shallow submodel, including KNN and SVM, from those analysis results in Tables 3 and 4, DDNN achieves a better performance. The reason is that when the training set is sufficient, the DDNN can be fully trained, so that the parameters of the network itself can reach the optimal value as much as possible to fit the distribution of training data, and the high-level features extracted from the underlying features are more discriminative for the final classification function.

Compared with the DBN model, DDNN first uses the DAE model to train the classification results more accurately in the case that the two layers of the model are the same (they

are all four layers). This is because the first two layers in the DDNN model are with DAE, which can effectively reduce the impact of noise data, and the DDNN model can be more flexible to adjust the parameters. On the other hand, due to the use of DAE as the initial layer, the dimension of data can also be reduced preliminary.

As shown in Tables 3 and 4, the classification performance of NB, KNN, and SVM is obviously decreased when the dataset is adjusted with noise factor, and the DNNN has better antinoise effect for only about 1% decline.

Furthermore, Table 5 shows the running time of different models. We can easily find that, for each sample, the NB classifier holds the shortest running time and SVM classifier holds the longest running time. Meanwhile, it can be seen that

TABLE 3: Text classification performance with different models using BBC news dataset.

	Classifier	Plus ratio noise					
		0.00	0.01	0.02	0.03	0.04	0.05
Accuracy	NB	0.9659	0.9560	0.9339	0.8736	0.8186	0.7852
	KNN	0.9375	0.9325	0.9284	0.9373	0.9119	0.9260
	SVM	0.9715	0.9701	0.9672	0.9583	0.9340	0.9075
	DBN	0.9462	0.9434	0.9268	0.9076	0.8789	0.8479
	DDNN	0.9700	0.9685	0.9582	0.9541	0.9381	0.9286
Recall	NB	0.9655	0.9550	0.9294	0.8453	0.7387	0.6652
	KNN	0.9354	0.9324	0.9279	0.9369	0.9114	0.9249
	SVM	0.9715	0.9700	0.9670	0.9580	0.9309	0.8964
	DBN	0.9459	0.9429	0.9249	0.9039	0.8769	0.8393
	DDNN	0.9700	0.9685	0.9580	0.9535	0.9399	0.9249
F-score	NB	0.9657	0.9555	0.9316	0.8592	0.7766	0.7202
	KNN	0.9364	0.9324	0.9281	0.9371	0.9116	0.9254
	SVM	0.9715	0.9700	0.9671	0.9581	0.9324	0.9019
	DBN	0.9460	0.9431	0.9258	0.9057	0.8779	0.8436
	DDNN	0.9700	0.9685	0.9581	0.9538	0.9390	0.9267

TABLE 4: Text classification performance with different models using 20-Newsgroup dataset.

	Classifier	Noise factor					
		0.00	0.01	0.02	0.03	0.04	0.05
Accuracy	NB	0.7506	0.7274	0.6895	0.6678	0.5887	0.4633
	KNN	0.6136	0.6161	0.6213	0.6142	0.6043	0.5978
	SVM	0.7598	0.7527	0.7294	0.6968	0.6652	0.6453
	DBN	0.7235	0.7207	0.7041	0.6849	0.6562	0.6252
	DDNN	0.7536	0.7561	0.7550	0.7542	0.7443	0.7378
Recall	NB	0.7483	0.6693	0.5053	0.3526	0.2613	0.2027
	KNN	0.5959	0.6000	0.6070	0.6034	0.5939	0.5820
	SVM	0.7525	0.7415	0.6966	0.6094	0.4891	0.3833
	DBN	0.7149	0.7120	0.6990	0.6826	0.6439	0.6250
	DDNN	0.7459	0.7500	0.7549	0.7534	0.7439	0.7320
F-score	NB	0.7494	0.6971	0.5832	0.4615	0.3619	0.2820
	KNN	0.6046	0.6079	0.6141	0.6088	0.5991	0.5898
	SVM	0.7561	0.7471	0.7126	0.6502	0.5637	0.4809
	DBN	0.7192	0.7163	0.7015	0.6837	0.6500	0.6251
	DDNN	0.7497	0.7530	0.7549	0.7538	0.7441	0.7349

TABLE 5: The running time of different models (ms).

Classifier	Dataset	
	BBC news	20-Newsgroups
NB	0.005	0.006
KNN	0.150	0.870
SVM	1.660	12.060
DBN	0.110	0.180
DDNN	0.120	0.210

the DDNN classifier can keep good classification speed while achieving good classification performance.

5. Conclusion

This article combines the DAE and RBM to design a novel DNN model, named DDNN. The model first denoises the data based on the DAE and then extracts feature of the text effectively based on RBM. Specifically, we conduct the simulations on the 20-Newsgroups and BBC news datasets and compare the proposed model with other traditional classification algorithms, for example, NB, KNN, SVM, and DBN models, considering the impact of noise. It is verified that the DDNN proposed in this article achieves better antinoise performance, which can extract more robust and deeper features while improving the classification performance.

Although the proposed model DDNN has achieved satisfactory performance in text classification, the text used in the simulations is long-type data. However, considering that there are also some short text data in text classification task, we should address this issue using the model DDNN. Moreover, to further improve the computational performance in the implementation of deep learning methods, in the future we can also design some hybrid learning algorithms by incorporating some advanced optimization techniques, for example, kernel learning and reinforcement learning, into the framework of DDNN, while applying it in some other fields.

Conflicts of Interest

The authors declare that there are no conflicts of interest regarding the publication of this paper.

Acknowledgments

This research is funded by the Fundamental Research Funds for the China Central Universities of USTB under Grant FRF-BD-16-005A, the National Natural Science Foundation of China under Grant 61174103, the National Key Research and Development Program of China under Grants 2017YFB1002304 and 2017YFB0702300, the Key Laboratory of Geological Information Technology of Ministry of Land and Resources under Grant 2017320, and the University of Science and Technology Beijing-National Taipei University of Technology Joint Research Program under Grant TW201705.

References

[1] A. M. Rinaldi, "A content-based approach for document representation and retrieval," in *Proceedings of the 8th ACM Symposium on Document Engineering (DocEng '08)*, pp. 106–109, ACM, São Paulo, Brazil, September 2008.

[2] E. Baykan, M. Henzinger, L. Marian, and I. Weber, "A comprehensive study of features and algorithms for URL-based topic classification," *ACM Transactions on the Web*, vol. 5, no. 3, article 15, 2011.

[3] P. Langley, W. Iba, and K. Thompson, "An analysis of bayesian classifiers," in *Proceedings of the 10th National Conference on Artificial Intelligence*, pp. 223–228, San Jose, Calif, USA, 1992.

[4] A. McCallum and K. Nigam, "A comparison of event models for naive bayes text classification," in *Proceedings of the 15th National Conference on Artificial Intelligence—Workshop on Learning for Text Categorization*, pp. 41–48, Madison, Wis, USA, 1998.

[5] Y. Yang and X. Liu, "A re-examination of text categorization methods," in *Proceedings of the 22nd ACM SIGIR Conference on Research and Development in Information Retrieval (SIGIR '99)*, pp. 42–49, Berkeley, Calif, USA, August 1999.

[6] S. Godbole, S. Sarawagi, and S. Chakrabarti, "Scaling multi-class support vector machines using inter-class confusion," in *Proceedings of the 8th ACM SIGKDD International Conference on Knowledge Discovery and Data Mining*, pp. 513–518, Edmonton, Canada, July 2002.

[7] S. L. Y. Lam and D. L. Lee, "Feature reduction for neural network based text categorization," in *Proceedings of the 6th International Conference on Database Systems for Advanced Applications*, pp. 195–202, Hsinchu, Taiwan, 1999.

[8] M. E. Ruiz and P. Srinivasan, "Hierarchical neural networks for text categorization," in *Proceedings of the 22nd Annual International ACM SIGIR Conference on Research and Development in Information Retrieval*, pp. 281-282, Berkeley, Calif, USA, August 1999.

[9] L. E. Peterson, "K-nearest neighbor," *Scholarpedia*, vol. 4, no. 2, article 1883, 2009.

[10] X. Luo, J. Deng, J. Liu, W. Wang, X. Ban, and J. Wang, "A quantized kernel least mean square scheme with entropy-guided learning for intelligent data analysis," *China Communications*, vol. 14, no. 7, pp. 127–136, 2017.

[11] Y. LeCun, Y. Bengio, and G. Hinton, "Deep learning," *Nature*, vol. 521, no. 7553, pp. 436–444, 2015.

[12] D. Silver, A. Huang, C. J. Maddison et al., "Mastering the game of Go with deep neural networks and tree search," *Nature*, vol. 529, no. 7587, pp. 484–489, 2016.

[13] G. E. Hinton, "Deep belief networks," *Scholarpedia*, vol. 4, no. 5, article 5947, 2009.

[14] P. Smolensky, "Information processing in dynamical systems: foundations of harmony theory," in *Parallel Distributed Processing: Explorations in the Microstructure of Cognition, Volume 1: Foundations*, D. E. Rumelhart and J. L. McLelland, Eds., pp. 194–281, MIT Press, 1986.

[15] J. Deng, W. Dong, R. Socher, L. J. Li, K. Li, and F. F. Li, "ImageNet: a large-scale hierarchical image database," in *Proceedings of the IEEE Computer Society Conference on Computer Vision and Pattern Recognition (CVPR '09)*, pp. 248–255, Miami, Fla, USA, June 2009.

[16] A. Krizhevsky, I. Sutskever, and G. E. Hinton, "ImageNet classification with deep convolutional neural networks," *Communications of the ACM*, vol. 60, no. 6, pp. 84–90, 2017.

[17] P. Vincent, H. Larochelle, and Y. Bengio, "Extracting and composing robust features with denoising autoencoders," in *Proceedings of the 25th International Conference on Machine Learning*, pp. 1096–1103, ACM, Helsinki, Finland, July 2008.

[18] P. Vincent, H. Larochelle, and I. Lajoie, "Stacked denoising autoencoders: learning useful representations in a deep network with a local denoising criterion," *Journal of Machine Learning Research*, vol. 11, pp. 3371–3408, 2010.

[19] G. E. Hinton, "Training products of experts by minimizing contrastive divergence," *Neural Computation*, vol. 14, no. 8, pp. 1771–1800, 2002.

[20] X. Luo, Y. Xu, W. Wang et al., "Towards enhancing stacked extreme learning machine with sparse autoencoder by correntropy," *Journal of the Franklin Institute*, 2017.

[21] R. Collobert, J. Weston, and L. Bottou, "Natural language processing (almost) from scratch," *Journal of Machine Learning Research*, vol. 12, pp. 2493–2537, 2011.

[22] I. Arel, D. C. Rose, and T. P. Karnowski, "Deep machine learning—a new frontier in artificial intelligence research," *IEEE Computational Intelligence Magazine*, vol. 5, no. 4, pp. 13–18, 2010.

[23] G. E. Hinton, S. Osindero, and Y.-W. Teh, "A fast learning algorithm for deep belief nets," *Neural Computation*, vol. 18, no. 7, pp. 1527–1554, 2006.

[24] X. Wei and W. B. Croft, "LDA-based document models for ad-hoc retrieval," in *Proceedings of the 29th Annual International ACM SIGIR Conference on Research and Development in Information Retrieval*, pp. 178–185, Seattle, Wash, USA, August 2006.

[25] X. Lu, Y. Tsao, S. Matsuda, and C. Hori, "Speech enhancement based on deep denoising autoencoder," in *Proceedings of the 14th*

Annual Conference of the International Speech Communication Association, pp. 436–440, Lyon, France, August 2013.

[26] N. Le Roux and Y. Bengio, "Representational power of restricted Boltzmann machines and deep belief networks," *Neural Computation*, vol. 20, no. 6, pp. 1631–1649, 2008.

[27] Y. Bengio, "Learning deep architectures for AI," *Foundations and Trends in Machine Learning*, vol. 2, no. 1, pp. 1–27, 2009.

[28] A. Fischer and C. Igel, "An introduction to restricted Boltzmann machines," in *Proceedings of the 17th Iberoamerican Congress on Progress in Pattern Recognition, Image Analysis, Computer Vision, and Applications*, pp. 14–36, Buenos Aires, Argentina, 2012.

[29] L. F. Polana and K. E. Barner, "Exploiting restricted Boltzmann machines and deep belief networks in compressed sensing," *IEEE Transactions on Signal Processing*, vol. 65, no. 17, pp. 4538–4550, 2017.

[30] R. Karakida, M. Okada, and S.-I. Amari, "Dynamical analysis of contrastive divergence learning: Restricted Boltzmann machines with Gaussian visible units," *Neural Networks*, vol. 79, pp. 78–87, 2016.

[31] T. Mikolov, I. Sutskever, K. Chen, G. Corrado, and J. Dean, "Distributed representations of words and phrases and their compositionality," in *Proceedings of the International Conference on Neural Information Processing Systems*, pp. 3111–3119, Lake Tahoe, Calif, USA, 2013.

[32] I. Sutskever, O. Vinyals, and Q. V. Le, "Sequence to sequence learning with neural networks," in *Proceedings of the 28th Annual Conference on Neural Information Processing Systems*, pp. 3104–3112, Montreal, Canada, 2014.

[33] M. Zhong, H. Liu, and L. Liu, "Method of semantic relevance relation measurement between words," *Journal of Chinese Information Processing*, vol. 23, no. 2, pp. 115–122, 2009.

[34] L. P. Jing, H. K. Huang, and H. B. Shi, "Improved feature selection approach TFIDF in text mining," in *Proceedings of the International Conference on Machine Learning and Cybernetics*, vol. 2, pp. 944–946, Beijing, China, 2002.

9

Big Data in Cloud Computing: A Resource Management Perspective

Saeed Ullah ⓘ, M. Daud Awan, and M. Sikander Hayat Khiyal

Faculty of Computer Science, Preston University, Islamabad, Pakistan

Correspondence should be addressed to Saeed Ullah; saeedullah@gmail.com

Academic Editor: Sungyong Park

The modern day advancement is increasingly digitizing our lives which has led to a rapid growth of data. Such multidimensional datasets are precious due to the potential of unearthing new knowledge and developing decision-making insights from them. Analyzing this huge amount of data from multiple sources can help organizations to plan for the future and anticipate changing market trends and customer requirements. While the Hadoop framework is a popular platform for processing larger datasets, there are a number of other computing infrastructures, available to use in various application domains. The primary focus of the study is how to classify major big data resource management systems in the context of cloud computing environment. We identify some key features which characterize big data frameworks as well as their associated challenges and issues. We use various evaluation metrics from different aspects to identify usage scenarios of these platforms. The study came up with some interesting findings which are in contradiction with the available literature on the Internet.

1. Introduction

We live in the information age, and an important measurement of present times is the amount of data that is generated anywhere around us. Data is becoming increasingly valuable. Enterprises are aiming at unlocking data's hidden potential and deliver competitive advantage [1]. Stratistics MRC projected that the data analytics and Hadoop market, which accounted for $8.48 billion in 2015, is expected to reach at $99.31 billion by 2022 [2]. The global big data market has estimated that it will jump from $14.87 billion in 2013 to $46.34 billion in 2018 [3]. Gartner has predicted that data will grow by 800 percent over the next five years and 80 percent of the data will be unstructured (e-mails, documents, audio, video, and social media content) and 20 percent will be structured (e-commerce transactions and contact information) [1].

Today's largest scientific institution, CERN, produces over 200 PB of data per year in the Large Hadron Collider project (as of 2017). The amount of generated data on the Internet has already exceeded 2.5 exabytes per day. Within one minute, 400 hours of videos are uploaded on YouTube, 3.6 million Google searches are conducted worldwide each minute of every day, more than 656 million tweets are shared on Twitter, and more than 6.5 million pictures are shared on Instagram each day. When a dataset becomes so large that its storage and processing become challenging due to the constraints of existing tools and resources, the dataset is referred to as big data [4, 5]. It is the first part of the journey towards delivering decision-making insights. But instead of focusing on people, this process utilizes a much more powerful and evolving technology, given the latest breakthroughs in this field, to quickly analyze huge streams of data, from a variety of sources, and to produce one single stream of useful knowledge [6].

Big data applications might be viewed as the advancement of parallel computing, but with the important exception of the scale. The scale is the necessity arising from the nature of the target issues: data dimensions largely exceed conventional storage units, the level of parallelism needed to perform computation within a strict deadline is high, and obtaining final results requires the aggregation of large numbers of partial results. The scale factor, in this case, does not only have the same effect that it has in classical parallel computing, but it surges towards a dimension in which automated resource management and its exploitation are of significant value [7].

An important factor for the success in big data analytical projects is the management of resources: these platforms use a substantial amount of virtualized hardware resources to optimize the tradeoff between costs and results. Managing such resources is definitely a challenge. Complexity is rooted in their architecture: the first level of complexity stems from their performance requirements of computing nodes: typical big data applications utilize massively parallel computing resources, storage subsystems, and networking infrastructure because of the fact that results are required within a certain time frame, or they can lose their value over time. Heterogeneity is a technological need: evolvability, extensibility, and maintainability of the hardware layer imply that the system will be partially integrated, replaced, or extended by means of new parts, according to the availability on the market and the evolution of technology [7]. Another important consideration of modern applications is the massive amount of data that need to be processed. Such data usually originate from different sets of devices (e.g., public web, business applications, satellites, or sensors) and procedures (e.g., case studies, observational studies, or simulations). Therefore, it is imperative to develop computational architectures with even better performance to support current and future application needs. Historically, this need for computational resources was provided by high-performance computing (HPC) environments such as computer clusters, supercomputers, and grids. In traditional owner-centric HPC environments, internal resources are handled by a single administrative domain [19]. Cluster computing is the leading architecture for this environment. In distributed HPC environments, such as grid computing, virtual organizations manage the provisioning of resources, both internal and external, to meet application needs [20]. However, the paradigm shift towards cloud computing has been widely discussed in more recent researches [19, 21], targeting the execution of HPC workloads on cloud computing environments. Although organizations usually prefer to store their most sensitive data internally (on-premises), huge volumes of big data (owned by the enterprises or generated by third parties) may be stored externally; some of it may already be on a cloud. Retaining all data sources behind the firewall may result in a significant waste of resources. Analyzing the data where it resides either internally or in a public cloud data center makes more sense [1, 22].

Even if cloud computing has to be an enabler to the growth of big data applications, common cloud computing solutions are rather different from big data applications. Typically, cloud computing solutions offer fine-grained, loosely coupled applications, run to serve large numbers of users that operate independently, from multiple locations, possibly on own, private, nonshared data, with a significant amount of interactions, rather than being mainly batch-oriented, and generally fit to be relocated with highly dynamic resource needs. Despite such differences, cloud computing and big data architectures share a number of common requirements, such as automated (or autonomic) fine-grained resource management and scaling related issues [7].

As cloud computing begins to mature, a large number of enterprises are building efficient and agile cloud environments, and cloud providers continue to expand service offerings [1]. Microsoft's cloud Hadoop offering includes Azure Marketplace, which runs Cloudera Enterprise, MapR, and Hortonworks Data Platform (HDP) in a virtual machine, and Azure Data Lake, which includes Azure HDInsight, Data Lake Analytics, and Data Lake Store as managed services. The platform offers rich productivity suites for database, data warehouse, cloud, spreadsheet, collaboration, business intelligence, OLAP, and development tools, delivering a growing Hadoop stack to Microsoft community. Amazon Web Services reigns among the leaders of cloud computing and big data solutions. Amazon EMR is available across 14 regions worldwide. AWS offers versions of Hadoop, Spark, Tez, and Presto that can work off data stored in Amazon S3 and Amazon Glacier. Cloud Dataproc is Google's managed Hadoop and Spark cluster to use fully managed cloud services such as Google BigQuery and Bigtable. IBM differentiates BigInsights with end-to-end advanced analytics. IBM BigInsights runs on top of IBM's SoftLayer cloud infrastructure and can be deployed on more than 30 global data centers. IBM is making significant investments in Spark, BigQuality, BigIntegrate, and IBM InfoSphere Big Match that run natively with YARN to handle the toughest Hadoop use cases [23].

In this paper, we give an overview of some of the most popular and widely used big data frameworks, in the context of cloud computing environment, which are designed to cope with the above-mentioned resource management and scaling problems. The primary object of the study is how to classify different big data resource management systems. We use various evaluation metrics for popular big data frameworks from different aspects. We also identify some key features which characterize big data frameworks as well as their associated challenges and issues. We restricted our study selection criteria to empirical studies from existing literature with reported evidence on performance evaluation of big data resource management frameworks. To the best of our knowledge, thus far there has been no empirical based performance evaluation report on major resource management frameworks. We investigated the validity of existing research by performing a confirmatory study. For this purpose, the standard performance evaluation tests as well as custom load test cases were performed on a 10+1 nodes t2.2xlarge Amazon AWS cluster. For experimentation and benchmarking, we followed the same process as outlined in our earlier study [24].

The study came up with some interesting findings which are in contradiction with the available literature on the Internet. The novelty of the study includes the categorization of cloud-based big data resource management frameworks according to their key features, comparative evaluation of the popular big data frameworks, and the best practices related to the use of big data frameworks in the cloud.

The inclusion and exclusion criteria for relevant research studies are as follows:

(i) We selected only those resource management frameworks for which we found empirical evidence of being offered by various cloud providers.

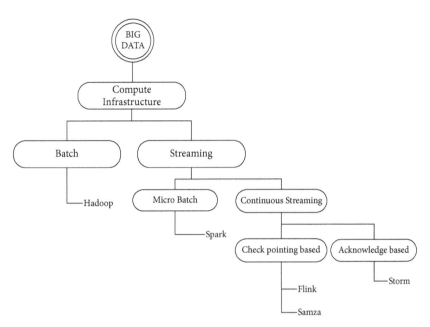

FIGURE 1: Classification of big data resource management frameworks.

(ii) Several vendors offer their proprietary solutions for big data analysis which could be the potential candidate for comparative analysis being conducted in this study. However, these frameworks were not selected based on two reasons. Firstly, most of these solutions are the extension of open-source solution and hence these exhibit the identical perform results in most of the cases. Secondly, for our empirical studies, researchers mostly prefer open-source solutions as the documentation, usage scenarios, source code, and other relevant details are freely available. Hence, we selected open-source solutions for the performance evaluation.

(iii) We did not include the frameworks which are now deprecated or discounted, such as Apache S4, in favor of other resource management systems.

This paper is organized as follows. Section 2 reviews the popular resource management frameworks. The comparison of big data frameworks is presented in Section 3. Based on the comparative evaluation, we categorize these systems in Section 4. Related work is presented in Section 5 and, finally, we present conclusion and possible future directions in Section 6.

2. Big Data Resource Management Frameworks

Big data is offering new emerging trends and opportunities to unearth operational insight towards data management. The most challenging issues for organizations are often that the amount of data is massive which needs to be processed at an optimal speed to synthesize relevant results. Analyzing such huge amount of data from multiple sources can help organizations plan for the future and anticipate changing market trends and customer requirements. In many of the cases, big data is analyzed in batch mode. However, in many situations, we may need to react to the current state of data or analyze the data that is in motion (data that is constantly coming in and needs to be processed immediately). These applications require a continuous stream of often unstructured data to be processed. Therefore, data is continuously analyzed and cached in memory before it is stored on secondary storage devices. Processing streams of data works by filtering in-memory tables of data across a cluster of servers. Any delay in the data analysis can seriously impact customer satisfaction or may result in project failure [25].

While the Hadoop framework is a popular platform for processing huge datasets in parallel batch mode using commodity computational resources, there are a number of other computing infrastructures that can be used in various application domains. The primary focus of this study is to investigate popular big data resource management frameworks which are commonly used in cloud computing environment. Most of the popular big data tools available for cloud computing platform, including the Hadoop ecosystem, are available under open-source licenses. One of the key appeals of Hadoop and other open-source solutions is the low total cost of ownership. While proprietary solutions have expensive license fees and may require more costly specialized hardware, these open-source solutions have no licensing fees and can run on industry-standard hardware [14]. Figure 1 demonstrates the classification of various styles of processing architectures of open-source big data resource management frameworks.

In the subsequent section, we discuss various open-source big data resource management frameworks that are widely used in conjunction with cloud computing environment.

2.1. Hadoop. Hadoop [26] is a distributed programming and storage infrastructure based on the open-source implementation of the MapReduce model [27]. MapReduce is the first and current de facto programming environment for developing data-centric parallel applications for parsing and processing large datasets. The MapReduce is inspired by Map and Reduce primitives used in functional programming. In MapReduce programming, users only have to write the logic of Mapper and Reducer while the process of shuffling, partitioning, and sorting is automatically handled by the execution engine [14, 27, 28]. The data can either be saved in the Hadoop file system as unstructured data or in a database as structured data [14]. Hadoop Distributed File System (HDFS) is responsible for breaking large data files into smaller pieces known as blocks. The blocks are placed on different data nodes, and it is the job of the NameNode to notice what blocks on which data nodes make up the complete file. The NameNode also works as a traffic cop, handling all access to the files, including reads, writes, creates, deletes, and replication of data blocks on the data nodes. A pipeline is a link between multiple data nodes that exists to handle the transfer of data across the servers. A user application pushes a block to the first data node in the pipeline. The data node takes over and forwards the block to the next node in the pipeline; this continues until all the data, and all the data replicas, are saved to disk. Afterwards, the client repeats the process by writing the next block in the file [25].

The two major components of Hadoop MapReduce are job scheduling and tracking. The early versions of Hadoop supported limited job and task tracking system. In particular, the earlier scheduler could not manage non-MapReduce tasks and it was not capable of optimizing cluster utilization. So, a new capability was aimed at addressing these shortcomings which may offer more flexibility, scaling, efficiency, and performance. Because of these issues, Hadoop 2.0 was introduced. Alongside earlier HDFS, resource management, and MapReduce model, it introduced a new resource management layer called Yet Another Resource Negotiator (YARN) that takes care of better resource utilization [25].

YARN is the core Hadoop service to provide two major functionalities: global resource management (ResourceManager) and per-application management (ApplicationMaster). The ResourceManager is a master service which controls NodeManager in each of the nodes of a Hadoop cluster. It includes a scheduler, whose main task is to allocate system resources to specific running applications. All the required system information is tracked by a Resource Container which monitors CPU, storage, network, and other important resource attributes necessary for executing applications in the cluster. The ResourceManager has a slave NodeManager service to monitor application usage statistics. Each deployed application is handled by a corresponding ApplicationMaster service. If more resources are required to support the running application, the ApplicationMaster requests the NodeManager and the NodeManager negotiates with the

ResourceManager (scheduler) for the additional capacity on behalf of the application [26].

2.2. Spark. Apache Spark [29], originally developed as Berkeley Spark, was proposed as an alternative to Hadoop. It can perform faster parallel computing operations by using in-memory primitives. A job can load data in either local memory or a cluster-wide shared memory and query it iteratively with much great speed as compared to disk-based systems such as Hadoop MapReduce [27]. Spark has been developed for two applications where keeping data in memory may significantly improve performance: iterative machine learning algorithms and interactive data mining. Spark is also intended to unify the current processing stack, where batch processing is performed using MapReduce, interactive queries are performed using HBase, and the processing of streams for real-time analytics is performed using other frameworks such Twitter's Storm. Spark offers programmers a functional programming paradigm with data-centric programming interfaces built on top of a new data model called Resilient Distributed Dataset (RDD) which is a collection of objects spread across a cluster stored in memory or disk [28]. Applications in Spark can load these RDDs into the memory of a cluster of nodes and let the Spark engine automatically manage the partitioning of the data and its locality during runtime. This versatile iterative model makes it possible to control the persistence and manage the partitioning of data. A stream of incoming data can be partitioned into a series of batches and is processed as a sequence of small-batch jobs. The Spark framework allows this seamless combination of streaming and batch processing in a unified system. To provide rapid application development, Spark provides clean, concise APIs in Scala, Java, and Python. Spark can be used interactively from the Scala and Python shells to rapidly query big datasets.

Spark is also the engine behind Shark, a complete Apache Hive-compatible data warehousing system that can run much faster than Hive. Spark also supports data access from Hadoop. Spark fits in seamlessly with the Hadoop 2.0 ecosystem (Figure 2) as an alternative to MapReduce, while using the same underlying infrastructure such as YARN and the HDFS. Spark is also an integral part of the SMACK stack to provide the most popular cloud-native PaaS such as IoT, predictive analytics, and real-time personalization for big data. In SMACK, Apache Mesos cluster manager (instead of YARN) is used for dynamic allocation of cluster resources, not only for running Hadoop applications but also for handling heterogeneous workloads.

The GraphX and MLlib libraries include state-of-the-art graph and machine learning algorithms that can be executed in real time. BlinkDB is a novel parallel, sampling-based approximate query engine for running interactive SQL queries that trade off query accuracy for response time, with results annotated by meaningful error bars. BlinkDB has been proven to run 200 times faster than Hive within an error rate of 2–10%. Moreover, Spark provides an interactive tool called Spark Shell which allows exploiting the Spark cluster in real time. Once interactive applications are created, they may subsequently be executed interactively in the cluster.

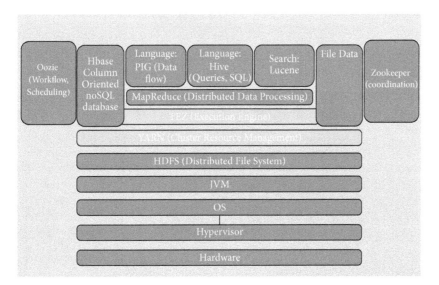

FIGURE 2: Hadoop 2.0 ecosystem, source: [14].

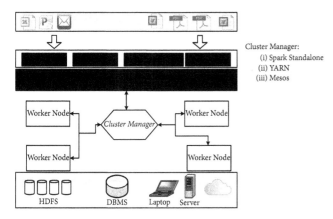

FIGURE 3: Spark architecture, source: [15].

In Figure 3, we present the general Spark system architecture.

2.3. Flink. Apache Flink is an emerging competitor of Spark which offers functional programming interfaces, much similar to Spark. It shares many programming primitives and transformations in the same way as what Spark does for iterative development, predictive analysis, and graph stream processing. Flink is developed to fill the gap left by Spark, which uses minibatch streaming processing instead of a pure streaming approach. Flink ensures high processing performance when dealing with complex big data structures such as graphs. Flink programs are regular applications which are written with a rich set of transformation operations (such as mapping, filtering, grouping, aggregating, and joining) to the input datasets. The Flink dataset uses a table-based model; therefore application developers can use index numbers to specify a particular field of a dataset [27, 28].

Flink is able to achieve high throughput and a low latency, thereby processing a bundle of data very quickly. Flink is designed to run on large-scale clusters with thousands of nodes, and in addition to a standalone cluster mode, Flink provides support for YARN. For distributed environment, Flink chains operator subtasks together into tasks. Each task is executed by one thread [16]. Flink runtime consists of two types of processes: there is at least one JobManager (also called masters) which coordinates the distributed execution. It schedules tasks, coordinates checkpoints, and coordinates recovery on failures. A high-availability setup may involve multiple JobManagers, one of which one is always the leader, and the others are standby. The TaskManagers (also called workers) execute the tasks (or, more specifically, the subtasks) of a dataflow/buffer and exchange the data streams. There must always be at least one TaskManager. The JobManagers and TaskManagers can be started in various ways: directly on the machines as a standalone cluster, in containers, or managed by resource frameworks like YARN or Mesos. TaskManagers connect to JobManagers, announcing themselves as available, and are assigned work. Figure 4 demonstrates the main components of Flink framework.

2.4. Storm. Storm [17] is a free open-source distributed stream processing computation framework. It takes several characteristics from the popular actor model and can be used with practically any kind of programming language for developing applications such as real-time streaming analytics, critical work flow systems, and data delivery services. The engine may process billions of tuples each day in a fault-tolerant way. It can be integrated with popular resource management frameworks such as YARN, Mesos, and Docker. Apache Storm cluster is made up of two types of processing actors: spouts and bolts.

  (i) Spout is connected to the external data source of a stream and is continuously emitting or collecting new data for further processing.

  (ii) Bolt is a processing logic unit within a streaming processing topology; each bolt is responsible for a

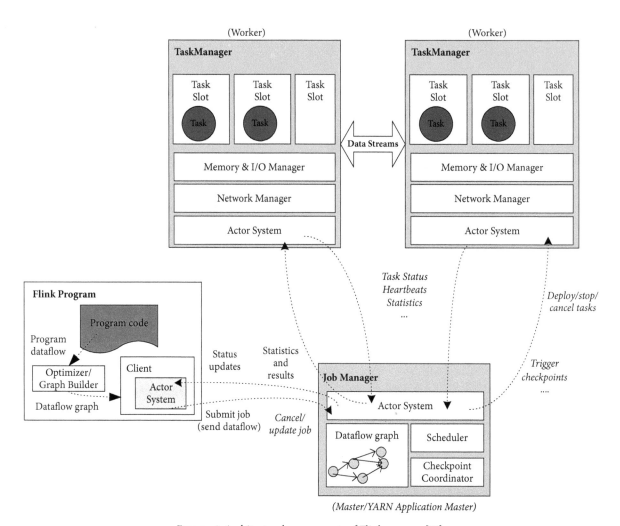

FIGURE 4: Architectural components of Flink, source: [16].

certain processing task such as transformation, filtering, aggregating, and partitioning.

Storm defines workflow as directed acyclic graphs (DAGs), called topologies with connected spouts and bolts as vertices. Edges in the graph define the link between the bolts and the data stream. Unlike batch jobs being only executed once, Storm jobs run forever until they are killed. There are two types of nodes in a Storm cluster: nimbus (master node) and supervisor (worker node). Nimbus, similar to Hadoop JobTracker, is the core component of Apache Storm and is responsible for distributing load across the cluster, queuing and assigning tasks to different processing units, and monitoring execution status. Each worker node executes a process known as the supervisor which may have one or more worker processes. Supervisor delegates the tasks to worker processes. Worker process then creates a subset of topology to run the task. Apache Storm does rely on an internal distributed messaging system, called Netty, for the communication between nimbus and supervisors. Zookeeper manages the communication between real-time job trackers (nimbus) and supervisors (Storm workers). Figure 5 outlines the high-level view of Storm cluster.

2.5. Apache Samza. Apache Samza [18] is a distributed stream processing framework, mainly written in Scala and Java. Overall, it has a relatively high throughput as well as somewhat increased latency when compared to Storm [8]. It uses Apache Kafka, which was originally developed for LinkedIn, for messaging and streaming, while Apache Hadoop YARN/Mesos is utilized as an execution platform for overall resource management. Samza relies on Kafka's semantics to define the way streams are handled. Its main objective is to collect and deliver massively large volumes of event data, in particular, log data with a low latency. A Kafka system's architecture is comparatively simple as it only consists of a set of brokers which are individual nodes that make up a Kafka cluster. Data streams are defined by topics, which is a stream of related information that consumers can subscribe to. Topics are divided into partitions that are distributed over the broker instances for retrieving the corresponding messages using a pull mechanism. The basic flow of job execution is presented in Figure 6.

Tables 1 and 2 present a brief comparative analysis of these frameworks based on some common attributes. As shown in the tables, MapReduce computation data flow follows chain of stages with no loop. At each stage, the program

TABLE 1: Comparison of big data frameworks.

Attribute	Framework				
	Hadoop	Spark	Storm	Samza	Flink
Current stable version	2.8.1	2.2.0	1.1.1	0.13.0	1.3.2
Batch processing	Yes	Yes	Yes	No	Yes
Computational model	MapReduce	Streaming (microbatches)	Streaming (microbatches)	Streaming	Supports continuous flow streaming, microbatch, and batch
Data flow	Chain of stages	Directed acyclic graph	Directed acyclic graphs (DAGs) with spouts and bolts	Streams (acyclic graph)	Controlled cyclic dependency graph through machine learning
Resource management	YARN	YARN/Mesos	HDFS (YARN)/Mesos	YARN/Mesos	Zookeeper/YARN/Mesos
Language support	All major languages	Java, Scala, Python, and R	Any programming language	JVM languages	Java, Scala, Python, and R
Job management/optimization	MapReduce approach	Catalyst extension	Storm-YARN/3rd-party tools like Ganglia	Internal JobRunner	Internal optimizer
Interactive mode	None (3rd-party tools like Impala can be integrated)	Interactive shell	None	Limited API of Kafka streams	Scala shell
Machine learning libraries	Apache Mahout/H2O	Spark ML and MLlib	Trident-ML/Apache SAMOA	Apache SAMOA	Flink-ML
Maximum reported nodes (scalability)	Yahoo Hadoop cluster with 42,000 nodes	8000	300	LinkedIn with around a hundred node clusters	Alibaba customized Flink cluster with thousands of nodes

TABLE 2: Comparative analysis of big data resource frameworks ($s = 5$).

	Hadoop	Spark	Flink	Storm	Samza
Processing speed	★★★	★★★★	★★★★★	★★★★	★★★★
Fault tolerance	★★★★	★★	★★★★	★★★	★★★★
Scalability	★★★★★	★★★★	★★★	★★★	★★★
Machine learning	★★	★★★★★	★★★★	★★★	★★★★
Low latency	★★	★★★	★★★	★★★★	★★★★
Security	★★★★	★★★★★	★★★★	★★★★	✘
Dataset size	★★★★★	★★★	★★★★	★★★	★★★

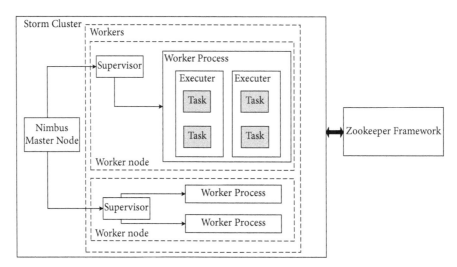

FIGURE 5: Architecture of Storm Cluster, source: [17].

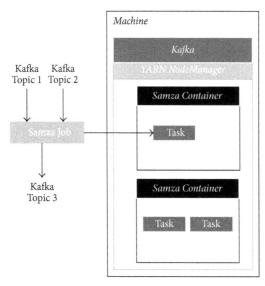

FIGURE 6: Samza architecture, source: [18].

Hadoop and Storm do not provide any default interactive environment. Apache Spark has a command-line interactive shell to use the application features. Flink provides a Scala shell to configure standalone as well as cluster setup. Apache Hadoop is highly scalable and it has been used in the Yahoo production consisting of 42000 nodes in 20 YARN clusters. The largest known cluster size for Spark is of 8000 computing nodes while Storm has been tested on a maximum of 300 node clusters. Apache Samza cluster, with around a hundred nodes, has been used in LinkedIn data flow and application messaging system. Apache Flink has been customized for Alibaba search engine with a deployment capacity of thousands of processing nodes.

3. Comparative Evaluation of Big Data Frameworks

Big data in cloud computing, a popular research trend, is posing significant influence on current enterprises, IT industries, and research communities. There are a number of disruptive and transformative big data technologies and solutions that are rapidly emanating and evolving in order to provide data-driven insight and innovation. Furthermore, modern cloud computing services are offering all kinds of big data analytic tools, technologies, and computing infrastructures to speed up the data analysis process at an affordable cost. Although many distributed resource management frameworks are available nowadays, the main issue is how to

proceeds with the output from the previous stage and generates an input for the next stage. Although machine learning algorithms are mostly designed in the form of cyclic data flow, Spark, Storm, and Samza represent it as directed acyclic graph to optimize the execution plan. Flink supports controlled cyclic dependency graph in runtime to represent the machine learning algorithms in a very efficient way.

select a suitable big data framework. The selection of one big data platform over the others will come down to the specific application requirements and constraints that may involve several tradeoffs and application usage scenarios. However, we can identify some key factors that need to be fulfilled before deploying a big data application in the cloud. In this section, based on some empirical evidence from the available literature, we discuss the advantages and disadvantages of each resource management framework.

3.1. Processing Speed. Processing speed is an important performance measurement that may be used to evaluate the effectiveness of different resource management frameworks. It is a common metric for the maximum number of I/O operations to disk or memory or the data transfer rate between the computational units of the cluster over a specific amount of time. Based on the context of big data, the average processing speed represented as $\overline{m}$, calculated after n iterations run, is the maximum amount of memory/disk intensive operations that can be performed over a time interval t_i:

$$\overline{m} = \frac{\sum_{i=1}^{n} m_i}{\sum_{i=1}^{n} t_i}. \tag{1}$$

Veiga et al. [30] conducted a series of experiments on a multicore cluster setup to demonstrate performance results of Apache Hadoop, Spark, and Flink. Apache Spark and Flink resulted to be much efficient execution platforms over Hadoop while performing nonsort benchmarks. It was further noted that Spark showed better performance results for operations such as WordCount and K-Means (CPU-bound in nature) while Flink achieved better results in PageRank algorithm (memory bound in nature). Mavridis and Karatza [31] experimentally compared performance statistics of Apache Hadoop and Spark on Okeanos IaaS cloud platform. For each set of experiments, necessary statistics related to execution time, working nodes, and the dataset size were recorded. Spark performance was found optimal as compared to Hadoop for most of the cases. Furthermore, Spark on YARN platform showed suboptimal results as compared to the case when it was executed in standalone mode. Some similar results were also observed by Zaharia et al. [32] on a 100 GB dataset record. Vellaipandiyan and Raja [33] demonstrated performance evaluation and comparison of Hadoop and Spark frameworks on resident's record dataset ranging from 100 GB to 900 GB of size. Spark scale of performance was relatively better when the dataset size was between small and medium size (100 GB–750 GB); afterwards, its performance declined as compared to Hadoop. The primary reason for the performance decline was evident as Spark cache size could not fit into the memory for the larger dataset. Taran et al. [34] quantified performance differences of Hadoop and Spark using WordCount dataset which was ranging from 100 KB to 1 GB. It was observed that Hadoop framework was five times faster than Spark when the evaluation was performed using a larger set of data sources. However, for the smaller tasks, Spark showed better performance results. However, the speed-up ratio was decreased for both databases with the growth of input dataset.

Gopalani and Arora [35] used K-Means algorithm on some small, medium, and large location datasets to compare Hadoop and Spark frameworks. The study results showed that Spark performed up to three times better than MapReduce for most of the cases. Bertoni et al. [36] performed the experimental evaluation of Apache Flink and Storm using large genomic dataset data on Amazon EC2 cloud. Apache Flink was superior to Storm while performing histogram and map operations while Storm outperformed Flink while genomic join application was deployed.

3.2. Fault Tolerance. Fault tolerance is the characteristic that enables a system to continue functioning in case of the failure of one or more components. High-performance computing applications involve hundreds of nodes that are interconnected to perform a specific task; failing a node should have zero or minimal effect on overall computation. The tolerance of a system, represented as $\mathrm{Tol_{FT}}$, to meet its requirements after a disruption is the ratio of the time to complete tasks without observing any fault events to the overall execution time where some fault events were detected and the system state is reverted back to consistent state:

$$\mathrm{Tol_{FT}} = \frac{T_x}{T_x + \sigma^2}, \tag{2}$$

where T_x is the estimated correct execution time obtained from a program run that is presumed to be fault-free, or by averaging the execution time from several application runs that produce a known correct output, and σ^2 represents the variance in a program's execution time due to the occurrence of fault events. For an HPC application that consists of a set of computationally intensive tasks $\Gamma = \{\tau_1, \tau_2, \ldots, \tau_n\}$ and since $\mathrm{Tol_{FT}}$ for each individual task is computed as Tol_{τ_i}, then the overall application resilience, Tol, may be calculated as [37]

$$\mathrm{Tol} = \sqrt[n]{\mathrm{Tol}_{\tau_1} \cdot \mathrm{Tol}_{\tau_2} \cdot \ldots \cdot \mathrm{Tol}_{\tau_n}}. \tag{3}$$

Lu et al. [38] used StreamBench toolkit to evaluate performance and fault tolerance ability of Apache Spark, Storm, Spark, and Samza. It was found that, with the increased data size, Spark is much stable and fault-tolerant as compared to Storm but may be less efficient when compared to Samza. Furthermore, when compared in terms of handling large capacity of data, both Samza and Spark outperformed Storm. Gu and Li [39] used PageRank algorithm to perform a comparative experiment on Hadoop and Spark frameworks. It was observed that, for smaller datasets such as wiki-Vote and soc-Slashdot0902, Spark outperformed Hadoop with a much better margin. However, this speed-up result degraded with the growth of dataset, and for large datasets, Hadoop easily outperformed Spark. Furthermore, for massively large datasets, Spark was reported to be crashed with JVM heap exception while Hadoop still performed its task. Lopez et al. [40] evaluated throughput and fault tolerance mechanism of Apache Storm and Flink. The experiments were based on a threat detection system where Apache Storm demonstrated better throughput as compared to Flink. For fault tolerance, different virtual machines were manually turned off to analyze the impact of node failures. Apache Flink used its internal subsystem to detect and migrate the failed tasks to other machines and hence resulted in very few message losses. On the other hand, Storm took more time as Zookeeper, involving some performance overhead, was responsible for reporting the state of nimbus and thereafter processing the failed task on other nodes.

3.3. Scalability. Scalability refers to the ability to accommodate large loads or change in size/workload by provisioning of resources at runtime. This can be further categorized as scale-up (by making hardware stronger) or scale-down (by adding additional nodes). One of the critical requirements of enterprises is to process large volumes of data in a timely manner to address high-value business problems. Dynamic resource scalability allows business entities to perform massive computation in parallel, thus reducing overall time, complexity, and effort. The definition of scalability comes from Amdahl's and Gustafson's laws [41]. Let W be the size of workload before the improvement of the system resources; the fraction of the execution workload that benefits from the improvement of system resources is α and the fraction concerning the part that would not benefit from improvement in the resources is $1 - \alpha$. When using an n-processor system, user workload is scaled to

$$\acute{W} = \alpha W + (1 - \alpha) nW. \tag{4}$$

The parallel execution time of a scaled workload $\acute{W}$ on n-processors is defined as scaled-workload speed-up $\acute{S}$ as shown in

$$\acute{S} = \frac{\acute{W}}{W} = \frac{\alpha W + (1 - \alpha) nW}{W}. \tag{5}$$

García-Gil et al. [42] performed scalability and performance comparison of Apache Spark and Flink using feature selection framework to assemble multiple information theoretic criteria into a single greedy algorithm. The ECBDL14 dataset was used to measure scalability factor for the frameworks. It was observed that Spark scalability performance was 4–10 times faster than Flink. Jakovits and Srirama [43] analyzed four MapReduce based frameworks including Hadoop and Spark for benchmarking partitioning around Medoids, Clustering Large Applications, and Conjugate Gradient linear system solver algorithms using MPI. All experiments were performed on 33 Amazon EC2 large instances cloud. For all algorithms, Spark performed much better as compared to Hadoop, in terms of both performance and scalability. Boden et al. [44] aimed to investigate the scalability with respect to both data size and dimensionality in order to demonstrate a fair and insightful benchmark that reflects the requirements of real-world machine learning applications. The benchmark was comprised of distributed optimization algorithms for supervised learning as well as algorithms for unsupervised learning. For supervised learning, they implemented machine learning algorithms by using Breeze library, while for unsupervised learning they chose the popular k-Means clustering algorithm in order to assess the scalability

of the two resource management frameworks. The overall execution time of Flink was relatively low on the resource-constrained settings with a limited number of nodes, while Spark had a clear edge once enough main memory was available due to the addition of new computing nodes.

3.4. Machine Learning and Iterative Tasks Support. Big data applications are inherently complex in nature and usually involve tasks and algorithms that are iterative in nature. These applications have distinct cyclic nature to achieve the desired result by continually repeating a set of tasks until these cannot be substantially reduced further.

Spangenberg et al. [45] used real-world datasets, consisting of four algorithms, that is, WordCount, K-Means, PageRank, and relational query, to benchmark Apache Flink and Storm. It was observed that Apache Storm performs better in batch mode as compared to Flink. However, with the increasing complexity, Apache Flink had a performance advantage over Storm and thus it was better suited for iterative data or graph processing. Shi et al. [46] focused on analyzing Apache MapReduce and Spark for batch and iterative jobs. For smaller datasets, Spark resulted to be a better choice, but when experiments were performed on larger datasets, MapReduce turned out to be several times faster than Spark. For iterative operations such as K-Means, Spark turned out to be 1.5 times faster as compared to MapReduce in its first iteration, while Spark was more than 5 times faster in subsequent operations.

Kang and Lee [47] examined five resource management frameworks including Apache Hadoop and Spark with respect to performance overheads (disk input/output, network communication, scheduling, etc.) in supporting iterative computation. The PageRank algorithm was used to evaluate these performance issues. Since static data processing tends to be a more frequent operation than dynamic data as it is used in every iteration of MapReduce, it may cause significant performance overhead in case of MapReduce. On the other hand, Apache Spark uses read-only cached version of objects (resilient distributed dataset) which can be reused in parallel operations, thus reducing the performance overhead during iterative computation. Lee et al. [48] evaluated five systems including Hadoop and Spark over various workloads to compare against four iterative algorithms. The experimentation was performed on Amazon EC2 cloud. Overall, Spark showed the best performance when iterative operations were performed in main memory. In contrast, the performance of Hadoop was significantly poor as compared to other resource management systems.

3.5. Latency. Big data and low latency are strongly linked. Big data applications provide true value to businesses, but these are mostly time critical. If cloud computing has to be the successful platform for big data implementation, one of the key requirements will be the provisioning of high-speed network to reduce communication latency. Furthermore, big data frameworks usually involve centralized design where the scheduler assigns all tasks through a single node which may significantly impact the latency when the size of data is huge.

Let T_{elapsed} be the elapsed time between the start and finish time of a program in a distributed architecture, T_i be the effective execution time, and λ_i be the sum of total idle units of ith processor from a set of N processors. Then, the average latency, represented as $\lambda(W, N)$, for the size of workload W, is defined as the average amount of overhead time needed for each processor to complete the task:

$$\lambda(W, N) = \frac{\sum_{i=1}^{N} \left(T_{\mathrm{elapsed}} - T_i + \lambda_i \right)}{N}. \quad (6)$$

Chintapalli et al. [49] conducted a detailed analysis of Apache Storm, Flink, and Spark streaming engines for latency and throughput. The study results indicated that, for high throughput, Flink and Storm have significantly lower latency as compared to Spark. However, Spark was able to handle high throughput as compared to other streaming engines. Lu et al. [38] proposed StreamBench benchmark framework to evaluate modern distributed stream processing frameworks. The framework includes dataset selection, data generation methodologies, program set description, workload suites design, and metric proposition. Two real-world datasets, AOL Search Data and CAIDA Anonymized Internet Traces Dataset, were used to assess performance, scalability, and fault tolerance aspects of streaming frameworks. It was observed that Storm's latency in most cases was far less than Spark's except in the case when the scales of the workload and dataset were massive in nature.

3.6. Security. Instead of the classical HPC environment, where information is stored in-house, many big data applications are now increasingly deployed on the cloud where privacy-sensitive information may be accessed or recorded by different data users with ease. Although data privacy and security issues are not a new topic in the area of distributed computing, their importance is amplified by the wide adoption of cloud computing services for big data platform. The dataset may be exposed to multiple users for different purposes which may lead to security and privacy risks.

Let N be a list of security categories that may be provided for security mechanism. For instance, a framework may use encryption mechanism to provide data security and access control list for authentication and authorization services. Let $\max(W_i)$ be the maximum weight that is assigned to the ith security category from a list of N categories and W_i be the reputation score of a particular resource management framework. Then, the framework security ranking score can be represented as

$$\mathrm{Sec}_{\mathrm{score}} = \frac{\sum_{i=1}^{N} W_i}{\sum_{i=1}^{N} \max(W_i)}. \quad (7)$$

Hadoop and Storm use Kerberos authentication protocol for computing nodes to provide their identity [50]. Spark adopts a password based shared secret configuration as well as Access Control Lists (ACLs) to control the authentication and authorization mechanisms. In Flink, stream brokers are responsible for providing authentication mechanism across multiple services. Apache Samza/Kafka provides no built-in security at the system level.

3.7. Dataset Size Support. Many scientific applications scale up to hundreds of nodes to process massive amount of data that may exceed over hundreds of terabytes. Unless big data applications are properly optimized for larger datasets, this may result in performance degradation with the growth of the data. Furthermore, in many cases, this may result in a crash of software, resulting in loss of time and money. We used the same methodology to collect big data support statistics as presented in earlier sections.

4. Discussion on Big Data Framework

Every big data framework has been evolved for its unique design characteristics and application-specific requirements. Based on the key factors and their empirical evidence to evaluate big data frameworks, as discussed in Section 3, we produce the summary of results of seven evaluation factors in the form of star ranking, $\mathrm{Ranking}_{\mathrm{RF}} \in [0, s]$, where s represents the maximum evaluation score. The general equation to produce the ranking, for each resource framework (RF), is given as

$$\mathrm{Ranking}_{\mathrm{RF}} = \left\| \frac{s}{\sum_{i=1}^{7} \sum_{j=1}^{N} \max(W_{ij})} * \sum_{i=1}^{7} \sum_{j=1}^{N} W_{ij} \right\|, \quad (8)$$

where N is the total number of research studies for a particular set of evaluation metrics, $\max(W_{ij}) \in [0, 1]$ is the relative normalized weight assigned to each literature study based on the number of experiments performed, and W_{ij} is the framework test-bed score calculated from the experimentation results from each study.

Hadoop MapReduce has a clear edge on large-scale deployment and larger dataset processing. Hadoop is highly compatible and interoperable with other frameworks. It also offers a reliable fault tolerance mechanism to provide a failure-free mechanism over a long period of time. Hadoop can operate on a low-cost configuration. However, Hadoop is not suitable for real-time applications. It has a significant disadvantage when latency, throughput, and iterative job support for machine learning are the key considerations of application requirements.

Apache Spark is designed to be a replacement for batch-oriented Hadoop ecosystem to run-over static and real-time datasets. It is highly suitable for high throughput streaming applications where latency is not a major issue. Spark is memory intensive and all operations take place in memory. As a result, it may crash if enough memory is not available for further operations (before the release of Spark version 1.5, it was not capable of handling datasets larger than the size of RAM and the problem of handling larger dataset still persists in the newer releases with different performance overheads). Few research efforts, such as Project Tungsten, are aimed at addressing the efficiency of memory and CPU for Spark applications. Spark also lacks its own storage system so its integration with HDFS through YARN or Cassandra using Mesos is an extra overhead for cluster configuration.

Apache Flink is a true streaming engine. Flink supports both batch and real-time operations over a common runtime to fulfill the requirements of Lambda architecture. However, it may also work in batch mode by stopping the streaming source. Like Spark, Flink performs all operations in memory, but in case of memory hog, it may also use disk storage to avoid application failure. Flink has some major advantages over Hadoop and Spark by providing better support for iterative processing with high throughput at the cost of low latency.

Apache Storm was designed to provide a scalable, fault tolerance, real-time streaming engine for data analysis, which Hadoop did for batch processing. However, the empirical evidence suggests that Apache Storm proved to be inefficient to meet the scale-up/scale-down requirements for real-time big data applications. Furthermore, since it uses microbath stream processing, it is not very efficient where continuous stream process is a major concern, nor does it provide a mechanism for simple batch processing. For fault tolerance, Storm uses Zookeeper to store the state of the processes which may involve some extra overhead and may also result in message loss. On the other hand, Storm is an ideal solution for near-real-time application processing where workload could be processed with a minimal delay with strict latency requirements.

Apache Samza, in integration Kafka, provides some unique features that are not offered by other stream processing engines. Samza provides a powerful check-pointing based fault tolerance mechanism with minimal data loss. Samza jobs can have high throughput with low latency when integrated with Kafka. However, Samza lacks some important features as data processing engine. Furthermore, it offers no built-in security mechanism for data access control.

To categorize the selection of best resource engine based on a particular set of requirements, we use the framework proposed by Chung et al. [51]. The framework provides a layout for matching, ranking, and selecting a system based on some particular requirements. The matching criterion is based on user goals which are categorized as soft and hard goals. Soft goals represent the nonfunctional requirements of the system (such as security, fault tolerance, and scalability) while hard goals represent the functional aspects of the system (such as machine learning and data size support). The relationship between the system components and the goals can be ranked as very positive (++), positive (+), negative (−), and very negative (−−). Based on the evidence provided from the literature, the categorization of major resource management frameworks is presented in Figure 7.

5. Related Work

Our research work differs from other efforts because the subject goal and object of study are not identical, as we provide an in-depth comparison of popular resource engines based on empirical evidence from existing literature. Hesse and Lorenz [8] conducted a conceptual survey on stream processing systems. However, their discussion was focused on some basic differences related to real-time data processing engines. Singh and Reddy [9] provided a thorough analysis of big data analytic platforms that included peer-to-peer networks, field programmable gate arrays (FPGA), Apache Hadoop ecosystem, high-performance computing (HPC)

clusters, multicore CPU, and graphics processing unit (GPU). Our case is different here as we are particularly interested in big data processing engines. Finally, Landset et al. [10] focused on machine learning libraries and their evaluation based on ease of use, scalability, and extensibility. However, our work differs from their work as the primary focuses of both studies are not identical.

Chen and Zhang [11] discussed big data problems, challenges, and associated techniques and technologies to address these issues. Several potential techniques including cloud computing, quantum computing, granular computing, and biological computing were investigated and the possible opportunities to explore these domains were demonstrated. However, the performance evaluation was discussed only on theoretical grounds. A taxonomy and detailed analysis of the state of the art in big data 2.0 processing systems were presented in [12]. The focus of the study was to identify current research challenges and highlight opportunities for new innovations and optimization for future research and development. Assunção et al. [13] reviewed multiple generations of data stream processing frameworks that provide mechanisms for resource elasticity to match the demands of stream processing services. The study examined the challenges associated with efficient resource management decisions and suggested solutions derived from the existing research studies. However, the study metrics are restricted to the elasticity/scalability aspect of big data streaming frameworks.

As shown in Table 3, our work differs from the previous studies which focused on the classification of resource management frameworks on theoretical grounds. In contrast to the earlier approaches, we classify and categorize big data resource management frameworks based on empirical grounds, derived from multiple evaluation/experimentation studies. Furthermore, our evaluation/ranking methodology is based on a comprehensive list of study variables which were not addressed in the studies conducted earlier.

6. Conclusions and Future Work

There are a number of disruptive and transformative big data technologies and solutions that are rapidly emanating and evolving in order to provide data-driven insight and innovation. The primary object of the study was how to classify popular big data resource management systems. This study was also aimed at addressing the selection of candidate resource provider based on specific big data application requirements. We surveyed different big data resource management frameworks and investigated the advantages and disadvantages for each of them. We carried out the performance evaluation of resource management engines based on seven key factors and each one of the frameworks was ranked based on the empirical evidence from the literature.

6.1. Observations and Findings. Some key findings of the study are as follows:

(i) In terms of processing speed, Apache Flink outperforms other resource management frameworks for small, medium, and large datasets [30, 36]. However, during our own set of experiments on Amazon EC2

TABLE 3: Comparison and application areas of related research studies.

Study reference	Data model	Resource frameworks	Study features	Evaluation/ranking methodology
[8]	Data stream processing systems	Storm, Flink, Spark, Samza	A brief comparison of resource frameworks	✗
[9]	Batch and stream processing systems	Horizontal scaling systems, such as peer-to-peer, MapReduce/MPI, and Spark, and vertical scaling systems, such as CUDA and HDL	Comparison of horizontal and vertical scaling systems	Theoretical comparison of resource frameworks
[10]	Batch and stream processing engines	MapReduce, Spark, Flink, and Storm as well as machine learning libraries	Machine learning libraries and their evaluation mechanism	Performance comparison with respect to machine learning toolkits
[11]	Batch and stream processing frameworks	Hadoop, Storm, and other big data frameworks	In-depth analysis of big data opportunities and challenges	✗
[12]	Batch and stream processing frameworks	Hadoop, Spark, Storm, Flink, and Tez as well as SQL, Graph, and bulk synchronous parallel model	Analysis of current open research challenges in the field of big data and the promising directions for future research	✗
[13]	Stream processing engines	Apache Storm, S4, Flink, Samza, Spark Streaming, and Twitter Heron	Classification of elasticity metrics for resource allocation strategies that meet the demands of stream processing services	Evaluation of elasticity/scaling metrics for stream processing systems

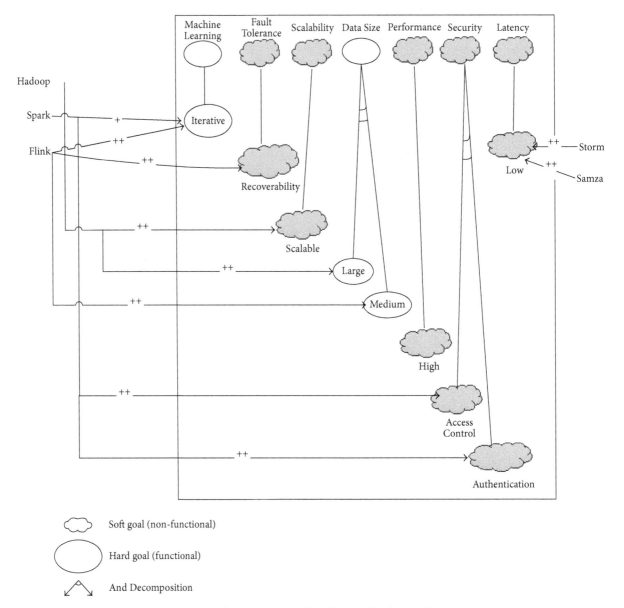

FIGURE 7: Categorization of resource engines based on key big data application requirements.

cluster with varied task managers settings (1–4 task managers per node), Flink failed to complete custom smaller size JVM dataset jobs due to inefficient memory management of Flink memory manager. We could not find any reported evidence of this particular use case in these relevant literature studies. It seems that most of the performance evaluation studies employed standard benchmarking test sets where dataset size was relatively large and hence this particular use case was not reported in these studies. Further research effort is required to elucidate the underlying specific of factors under this particular case.

(ii) Big data applications usually involve massive amount of data. Apache Spark supports necessary strategies for fault tolerance mechanism, but it has been reported to crash on larger datasets. Even during

our experimentations, Apache Spark version 1.6 (selected due to the compatibility reasons with earlier researches) crashed on several occasions when the dataset was larger than 500 GB. Although Spark has been ranked higher in terms of fault tolerance with the increase of data scale in several studies [38, 52], it has limitations in handling larger typical big data dataset applications and hence such studies cannot be generalized.

(iii) Spark MLlib and Flink-ML offer a variety of machine learning algorithms and utilities to exploit distributed and scalable big data applications. Spark MLlib outperforms Flink-ML in most of the machine learning use cases [42], except in the case when repeated passes are performed on unchanged data. However, this performance evaluation may further be investigated as research studies such as [53], reported differently where Flink outperformed Spark on sufficiently large cases.

(iv) For graph processing algorithms such as PageRank, Flink uses Gelly library that provides native closed-loop iteration operators, making it a suitable platform for large-scale graph analytics. Spark, on the other hand, uses GraphX library that has much longer pre-processing time to build graph and other data structures, making its performance worse as compared to Apache Flink. Apache Flink has been reported to obtain the best results for graph processing datasets (3x–5x in [54] and 2x-3x in [45]) as compared to Spark. However, some studies such as [55] reported Spark to be 1.7x faster than Flink for large graph processing. Such inconsistent behavior may be further investigated in the future research studies.

6.2. Future Work. In the area of big data, there is still a clear gap that requires more effort from the research community to build in-depth understanding of performance characteristics of big data resource management frameworks. We consider this study a step towards enlarging our knowledge to understand the big data world and provide an effort towards the direction of improving the state of the art and achieving the big vision on the big data domain. In earlier studies, a clear ranking cannot be established as the study parameters were mostly limited to a few issues such as throughput, latency, and machine learning. Furthermore, further investigation is required on resource engines such as Apache Samza in comparison with other frameworks. In addition, research effort needs to be carried out in several areas such as data organization, platform specific tools, and technological issues in big data domain in order to create next-generation big data infrastructures. The performance evaluation factors might also vary among systems depending on the used algorithms. As future work, we plan to benchmark these popular resource engines for meeting resource demands and requirements for different scientific applications. Moreover, a scalability analysis could be done. Particularly, the performance evaluation of adding dynamic worker nodes and the resulting performance analysis is of peculiar interest. Additionally, further research can be carried out in order to evaluate performance aspects with respect to resource competition between jobs (on different research schedulers such as YARN and Mesos) and the fluctuation of available computing resources. Finally, most of the experimentations in earlier studies were performed using standard parameter configurations; however, each resource management framework offers domain specific tweaks and configuration optimization mechanisms for meeting application-specific requirements. The development of a benchmark suite that aims to find maximum throughput based on configuration optimization would be an interesting direction of future research.

Conflicts of Interest

The authors declare that they have no conflicts of interest.

References

[1] "Big Data in the Cloud: Converging Technologies, (August 11)," https://www.intel.com/content/dam/www/public/emea/de/de/documents/product-briefs/big-data-cloud-technologies-brief.pdf.

[2] Q. He, J. Yan, R. Kowalczyk, H. Jin, and Y. Yang, "Lifetime service level agreement management with autonomous agents for services provision," *Information Sciences*, vol. 179, no. 15, pp. 2591–2605, 2009.

[3] O. Rana, M. Warnier, T. B. Quillinan, and F. Brazier, "Monitoring and reputation mechanisms for service level agreements," in *5th International Workshop on Grid Economics and Business Models, GECON '08*, vol. 5206 of *Lecture Notes in Computer Science (including subseries Lecture Notes in Artificial Intelligence and Lecture Notes in Bioinformatics): Preface*, pp. 125–139, 2008.

[4] N. Yuhanna and M. Gualtieri, "The Forrester Wave™: Big Data Hadoop Cloud Solutions, Q2 2016 Elasticity, Automation, and Pay-As-You-Go Compel Enterprise Adoption of Hadoop in the Cloud, (June 20)," https://ncmedia.azureedge.net/ncmedia/2016/05/The_Forrester_Wave__Big_D.pdf.

[5] R. Arora, "An introduction to big data, high performance computing, high-throughput computing, and Hadoop," *Conquering Big Data with High Performance Computing*, pp. 1–12, 2016.

[6] F. Pop, J. Kołodziej, and B. D. Martino, *Resource Management for Big Data Platforms Algorithms, Modelling, and High-Performance Computing Techniques*, Springer, 2016.

[7] M. Gribaudo, M. Iacono, and F. Palmieri, "Performance modeling of big data-oriented architectures," in *Resource Management for Big Data Platforms*, Computer Communications and Networks, pp. 3–34, Springer International Publishing, Cham, 2016.

[8] G. Hesse and M. Lorenz, "Conceptual survey on data stream processing systems," in *Proceedings of the 2015 IEEE 21st International Conference on Parallel and Distributed Systems (ICPADS)*, pp. 797–802, Melbourne, Australia, December 2015.

[9] D. Singh and C. K. Reddy, "A survey on platforms for big data analytics," *Journal of Big Data*, vol. 2, Article ID 8, 2014.

[10] S. Landset, T. M. Khoshgoftaar, A. N. Richter, and T. Hasanin, "A survey of open source tools for machine learning with big data in the Hadoop ecosystem," *Journal of Big Data*, vol. 2, no. 1, Article ID 24, 2015.

[11] C. L. P. Chen and C. Y. Zhang, "Data-intensive applications, challenges, techniques and technologies: a survey on Big Data," *Information Sciences*, vol. 275, pp. 314–347, 2014.

[12] F. Bajaber, R. Elshawi, O. Batarfi, A. Altalhi, A. Barnawi, and S. Sakr, "Big data 2.0 processing systems: taxonomy and open challenges," *Journal of Grid Computing*, vol. 14, no. 3, pp. 379–405, 2016.

[13] M. D. d. Assunção, A. d. S. Veith, and R. Buyya, "Distributed data stream processing and edge computing: a survey on resource elasticity and future directions," *Journal of Network and Computer Applications*, vol. 103, pp. 1–17, 2018.

[14] "Big data working group big data taxonomy, 2014".

[15] W. Inoubli, S. Aridhi, H. Mezni, M. Maddouri, and E. M. Nguifo, "An experimental survey on big data frameworks," *Future Generation Computer Systems*, 2018.

[16] H.-K. Kwon and K.-K. Seo, "A fuzzy AHP based multi-criteria decision-making model to select a cloud service," *International Journal of Smart Home*, vol. 8, no. 3, pp. 175–180, 2014.

[17] A. Rezgui and S. Rezgui, "A stochastic approach for virtual machine placement in volunteer cloud federations," in *Proceedings of the 2nd IEEE International Conference on Cloud Engineering, IC2E 2014*, pp. 277–282, Boston, MA, USA, March 2014.

[18] M. Salama, A. Zeid, A. Shawish, and X. Jiang, "A novel QoS-based framework for cloud computing service provider selection," *International Journal of Cloud Applications and Computing*, vol. 4, no. 2, pp. 48–72, 2014.

[19] G. Mateescu, W. Gentzsch, and C. J. Ribbens, "Hybrid computing-where hpc meets grid and cloud computing," *Future Generation Computer Systems*, vol. 27, no. 5, pp. 440–453, 2011.

[20] I. Foster, C. Kesselman, and S. Tuecke, "The anatomy of the grid: enabling scalable virtual organizations," *International Journal of High Performance Computing Applications*, vol. 15, no. 3, pp. 200–222, 2001.

[21] S. Benedict, "Performance issues and performance analysis tools for HPC cloud applications: a survey," *Computing*, vol. 95, no. 2, pp. 89–108, 2013.

[22] E. C. Inacio and M. A. R. Dantas, "A survey into performance and energy efficiency in HPC, cloud and big data environments," *International Journal of Networking and Virtual Organisations*, vol. 14, no. 4, pp. 299–318, 2014.

[23] N. Yuhanna and M. Gualtieri, "Elasticity, Automation, and Pay-As-You-Go Compel Enterprise Adoption Of Hadoop in the Cloud, Q2, 2016".

[24] S. Ullah, M. D. Awan, and M. S. Khiyal, "A price-performance analysis of EC2, google compute and rackspace cloud providers for scientific computing," *Journal of Mathematics and Computer Science*, vol. 16, no. 02, pp. 178–192, 2016.

[25] J. Hurwitz, A. Nugent, F. Halper, and M. Kaufman, *Big Data for Dummies*, John Wiley Sons, 2013.

[26] S. K. Garg, S. Versteeg, and R. Buyya, "A framework for ranking of cloud computing services," *Future Generation Computer Systems*, vol. 29, no. 4, pp. 1012–1023, 2013.

[27] D. Wu, S. Sakr, and L. Zhu, "Big data programming models," in *Handbook of Big Data Technologies*, pp. 31–63, 2017.

[28] S. García, S. Ramírez-Gallego, J. Luengo, J. M. Benítez, and F. Herrera, "Big data preprocessing: methods and prospects," *Big Data Analytics*, vol. 1, no. 1, 2016.

[29] A. Li, X. Yang, S. Kandula, and M. Zhang, "CloudCmp: comparing public cloud providers," in *Proceedings of the 10th ACM SIGCOMM Conference on Internet Measurement (IMC '10)*, pp. 1–14, ACM, Melbourne, Australia, November 2010.

[30] J. Veiga, R. R. Exposito, X. C. Pardo, G. L. Taboada, and J. Tourifio, "Performance evaluation of big data frameworks for large-scale data analytics," in *Proceedings of the 4th IEEE International Conference on Big Data, Big Data 2016*, pp. 424–431, December 2016.

[31] I. Mavridis and H. Karatza, "Log file analysis in cloud with Apache Hadoop and Apache Spark," in *Proceedings of the Second International Workshop on Sustainable Ultrascale Computing Systems (NESUS 2015)*, Poland, 2015.

[32] M. Zaharia, M. Chowdhury, and T. Das, "Fast and interactive analytics over Hadoop data with Spark," *USENIX Login*, vol. 37, no. 4, pp. 45–51, 2012.

[33] S. Vellaipandiyan and P. V. Raja, "Performance evaluation of distributed framework over YARN cluster manager," in *Proceedings of the 2016 IEEE International Conference on Computational Intelligence and Computing Research, ICCIC 2016*, December 2016.

[34] V. Taran, O. Alienin, S. Stirenko, Y. Gordienko, and A. Rojbi, "Performance evaluation of distributed computing environments with Hadoop and Spark frameworks," in *Proceedings of the 2017 IEEE International Young Scientists' Forum on Applied Physics and Engineering (YSF)*, pp. 80–83, Lviv, Ukraine, October 2017.

[35] S. Gopalani and R. Arora, "Comparing Apache Spark and Map Reduce with performance analysis using *K*-means," *International Journal of Computer Applications*, vol. 113, no. 1, pp. 8–11, 2015.

[36] M. Bertoni, S. Ceri, A. Kaitoua, and P. Pinoli, "Evaluating cloud frameworks on genomic applications," in *Proceedings of the 3rd IEEE International Conference on Big Data, IEEE Big Data 2015*, pp. 193–202, November 2015.

[37] S. Hukerikar, R. A. Ashraf, and C. Engelmann, "Towards new metrics for high-performance computing resilience," in *Proceedings of the 7th Fault Tolerance for HPC at eXtreme Scale Workshop, FTXS 2017*, pp. 23–30, June 2017.

[38] R. Lu, G. Wu, B. Xie, and J. Hu, "Stream bench: towards benchmarking modern distributed stream computing frameworks," in *Proceedings of the 7th IEEE/ACM International Conference on Utility and Cloud Computing, UCC 2014*, pp. 69–78, December 2014.

[39] L. Gu and H. Li, "Memory or time: performance evaluation for iterative operation on Hadoop and Spark," in *Proceedings of the 15th IEEE International Conference on High Performance Computing and Communications, HPCC 2013 and 11th IEEE/IFIP International Conference on Embedded and Ubiquitous Computing, EUC 2013*, pp. 721–727, November 2013.

[40] M. A. Lopez, A. G. P. Lobato, and O. C. M. B. Duarte, "A performance comparison of open-source stream processing platforms," in *Proceedings of the 59th IEEE Global Communications Conference, GLOBECOM 2016*, December 2016.

[41] J. L. Gustafson, "Reevaluating Amdahl's law," *Communications of the ACM*, vol. 31, no. 5, pp. 532–533, 1988.

[42] D. García-Gil, S. Ramírez-Gallego, S. García, and F. Herrera, "A comparison on scalability for batch big data processing on Apache Spark and Apache Flink," *Big Data Analytics*, vol. 2, no. 1, 2017.

[43] P. Jakovits and S. N. Srirama, "Evaluating Mapreduce frameworks for iterative scientific computing applications," in *Proceedings of the 2014 International Conference on High Performance Computing and Simulation, HPCS 2014*, pp. 226–233, July 2014.

[44] C. Boden, A. Spina, T. Rabl, and V. Markl, "Benchmarking data flow systems for scalable machine learning," in *Proceedings of the 4th ACM SIGMOD Workshop on Algorithms and Systems for MapReduce and Beyond, BeyondMR 2017*, May 2017.

[45] N. Spangenberg, M. Roth, and B. Franczyk, *Evaluating New Approaches of Big Data Analytics Frameworks*, vol. 208 of *Lecture Notes in Business Information Processing*, Publisher Name Springer, Cham, 2015.

[46] J. Shi, Y. Qiu, U. F. Minhas et al., "Clash of the titans: MapReduce vs. Spark for large scale data analytics," in *Proceedings of the 41st International Conference on Very Large Data Bases*, pp. 2110–2121, Kohala Coast, HI, USA, 2015.

[47] M. Kang and J. Lee, "A comparative analysis of iterative MapReduce systems," in *Proceedings of the the Sixth International Conference*, pp. 61–64, Jeju, Repblic of Korea, October 2016.

[48] H. Lee, M. Kang, S.-B. Youn, J.-G. Lee, and Y. Kwon, "An experimental comparison of iterative MapReduce frameworks,"

in *Proceedings of the 25th ACM International Conference on Information and Knowledge Management, CIKM 2016*, pp. 2089–2094, October 2016.

[49] S. Chintapalli, D. Dagit, B. Evans et al., "Benchmarking streaming computation engines: Storm, Flink and Spark streaming," in *Proceedings of the 30th IEEE International Parallel and Distributed Processing Symposium Workshops, IPDPSW 2016*, pp. 1789–1792, May 2016.

[50] X. Zhang, C. Liu, S. Nepal, W. Dou, and J. Chen, "Privacy-preserving layer over MapReduce on cloud," in *Proceedings of the 2nd International Conference on Cloud and Green Computing, CGC 2012, Held Jointly with the 2nd International Conference on Social Computing and Its Applications, SCA 2012*, pp. 304–310, chn, November 2012.

[51] L. Chung, B. A. Nixon, and E. Yu, "Using nonfunctional requirements to systematically select among alternatives in architectural design," in *Proceedings of the 1st International Workshop on Architectures for Software Systems*, pp. 31–43, 1995.

[52] S. Qian, G. Wu, J. Huang, and T. Das, "Benchmarking modern distributed streaming platforms," in *Proceedings of the 2016 IEEE International Conference on Industrial Technology (ICIT)*, pp. 592–598, Taipei, Taiwan, March 2016.

[53] F. Dambreville and A. Toumi, "Generic and massively concurrent computation of belief combination rules," in *Proceedings of the the International Conference on Big Data and Advanced Wireless Technologies*, pp. 1–6, Blagoevgrad, Bulgaria, November 2016.

[54] R. W. Techentin, M. W. Markland, R. J. Poole, D. R. H. C. R. Haider, and B. K. Gilbert, "Page rank performance evaluation of cluster computing frameworks on Cray Urika-GX supercomputer," *Computer Science and Engineering*, vol. 6, pp. 33–38, 2016.

[55] O.-C. Marcu, A. Costan, G. Antoniu, and M. S. Pérez-Hernández, "Spark versus flink: understanding performance in big data analytics frameworks," in *Proceedings of the 2016 IEEE International Conference on Cluster Computing, CLUSTER 2016*, pp. 433–442, Taipei, Taiwan, September 2016.

10

Cultural Distance-Aware Service Recommendation Approach in Mobile Edge Computing

Yan Li[1] **and Yan Guo** ⓘ [2]

[1]*School of Business and Management, Shanghai International Studies University, Shanghai, China*
[2]*State Key Laboratory of Networking and Switching Technology, Beijing University of Posts and Telecommunications, Beijing, China*

Correspondence should be addressed to Yan Guo; guoyan@bupt.edu.cn

Academic Editor: Youngjae Kim

In the era of big data, traditional computing systems and paradigms are not efficient and even difficult to use. For high performance big data processing, mobile edge computing is emerging as a complement framework of cloud computing. In this new computing architecture, services are provided within a close proximity of mobile users by servers at the edge of network. Traditional collaborative filtering recommendation approach only focuses on the similarity extracted from the rating data, which may lead to an inaccuracy expression of user preference. In this paper, we propose a cultural distance-aware service recommendation approach which focuses on not only the similarity but also the local characteristics and preference of users. Our approach employs the cultural distance to express the user preference and combines it with similarity to predict the user ratings and recommend the services with higher rating. In addition, considering the extreme sparsity of the rating data, missing rating prediction based on collaboration filtering is introduced in our approach. The experimental results based on real-world datasets show that our approach outperforms the traditional recommendation approaches in terms of the reliability of recommendation.

1. Introduction

With the rapid development of Internet of Things and 5G network, a large number of distributed data and computation tasks are generated, which makes traditional centralized computing paradigm suffer large processing pressure. Mobile edge computing is emerging to process the data at the edge of network for high performance big data processing [1].

In mobile edge computing, services are provided within a close proximity of mobile users by servers at the edge of network [2]. With the increasing number of edge services, there are too much choices for users to meet their requirements [3, 4]; therefore, the service recommendation technology is needed to help people find the optimal edge services from a huge mass of services. Because of the ubiquitous services, service recommendation is playing an increasingly significant role in our diary life [5, 6]; for example, Amazon has deployed its recommending system to help recommending books and other products to its users [7].

Although there is a significant research in mobile edge computing, there has been little attention paid to services recommendation in mobile edge computing. Traditional service recommendation system is to dig up service users' preferences based on user's history records and scores and then recommend similar users' services which have never been used by the service user [8, 9]. It can be reduced to a problem of estimating ratings for the services that have not been used by a user. Intuitively, this estimation is usually based on the ratings given by the user to other services. Once the ratings for the yet unrated services can be estimated, we can recommend to the service user the service with the highest estimated rating.

Much research over the past decade has focused on developing service recommendation systems, and they are usually classified based on recommendation approach as content-based recommendation [10], collaborative filtering-based recommendation [11], and model-based collaborative filtering recommendation [12].

Collaborative filtering is one of the most successful recommendation technologies in many recommended systems [13]. The basic idea is to predict the ratings of the services that have not been used by the service user according to the users who have the common experience and the same interest or the services which are similar to the services that have been rated by the service user [14]. However, the efficiency and accuracy of collaborative filtering are not high in practical applications [15].

Traditional collaborative filtering recommendation approach only focuses on the similarity extracted from the rating data in the calculation of similarity, the selection of the nearest neighbor, and recommendation. Specifically, the recommendation is according to the weighted average of evaluation from the nearest neighbor, and the weight is the similarity between the user and the nearest neighbors. However, the similarity is not the only decision factor; there are many other factors having an important role. The preference of users only depends on the similarity, which may lead to an inaccuracy expression of user preference and low reliability of recommendation results.

In addition, traditional service recommendation approaches perform poorly when facing sparse user rating data. There are some approaches that have been proposed to solve the sparsity of ratings data, and it can be divided into three categories. The first is attribution and dimension reduction; however, attribution may lead to the missing of user's personal characteristics data, and dimension reduction may delete useful data. The second effective way to solve the sparse data problem is to introduce the trust into the recommendation system [16, 17]. The third way is to predict the missing ratings by adopting the approach in the similarity calculation [18]. This approach can exploit the effective data while also enlarging the influence of the erroneous data.

Considering that there is a close relationship between the user preference and their cultural background, we introduce cultural distance which can express the user preference to reduce the decision-making power of similarity. For example, in mobile edge computing, users in different edge clouds may have different preference, and users in the same edge clouds may have the same preference.

Responding to the above problems, we propose a new collaborative filtering recommendation approach based on cultural distance in which we combine the cultural distance and similarity to represent the user preference. In the approach, we combine the user-based collaborative filtering and the service-based collaborative filtering approach to take full advantage of the information of the similar users and similar services, and then we recommend service to users based on a cultural distance-aware collaborative filtering recommendation approach. In addition, we predict the missing ratings based on the cultural distance-aware collaborative filtering approach to improve the sparsity of user rating data.

The remainder of the paper is organized as follows: Section 2 introduces the background of service recommendation; Section 3 describes our cultural distance-aware hybrid collaborative filtering recommendation approach; Section 4 presents the experiment results and Section 5 concludes this paper.

2. Background

2.1. Related Concept. The main idea of our approach is the introduction of cultural distance; therefore, we introduce a related concept: cultural distance before the introduction of our approach.

Cultural distance is an important concept to study cultural differences, which is widely used in cross-culture study and cross-culture practice, such as enterprise internationalization [19]. Culture directly impacts on people's beliefs, thoughts, and social behaviors. While some people may not know this impact, culture and values have been rooted in people's minds and are the decisive factor in people's social behavior and their preferences. All computations of cultural distance are based on cultural dimensions.

The most famous cultural dimension research is Hofstede's cultural dimension theory, which first realizes the quantitative description of the abstract complicated concept of culture [20]. This cultural dimension theory enables researchers to compute cultures as data in a more intuitive way to compare differences between different cultures and various behaviors.

The Hofstede's cultural dimension theory consists of six dimensions. The six dimensions are as follows: Power Distance Index, Individualism versus Collectivism, Masculinity versus Femininity, Uncertainty Avoidance Index, Long Term Orientation versus Short Term Normative Orientation, and Indulgence versus Restraint. Based on Hofstede's cultural dimension theory, [21] first uses a simple mathematical formula to define the cultural distance and describes the cultural differences more simply. The formula is as follows:

$$\mathrm{CD}_j = \sum_{i=1}^{m} \frac{\left\{ \left(I_{ij} - I_{ik} \right)^2 / V_i \right\}}{m}, \tag{1}$$

where CD_j is the cultural distance for the jth country, I_{ij} is Hofstede's ith cultural dimension score of the jth country, the kth country is the host country, V_i is the variance of the ith cultural dimension scores, and m is the number of cultural dimensions.

2.2. Related Work. A large number of service recommendation approaches have been proposed in the literature, and we only review some notable approaches here.

Among the numerous service recommendation approaches, collaborative filtering is one of the most successful recommendation technologies. And it includes user-based collaborative filtering [14, 22, 23], service-based collaborative filtering [24–28], and its fusion [18]. User-based collaborative filtering is to predict the rating of users based on the ratings of their similar users, and service-based collaborative filtering is to predict the rating of users based on the ratings of services which are similar to the services chosen by the users. The basic steps of collaborative filtering are rating collection, similarity computation, neighbor selection, rating prediction, and recommendation, and the similarity computation is always based on Person Correlation Coefficient [29]. Besides, [18] proposes a fusion approach which combines user-based and service-based collaborative filtering approaches. Different from [18], our approach considers the cultural factor in rating prediction, and the similarity is not the only weigh factor of neighbors.

However, there are some problems in collaborative filtering approaches, such as the sparse rating data, cold start, malicious attack, and bad system scalability. To solve these problem, many trust-based recommendation approaches are proposed [16, 17, 30, 31]. The paper [30] proposes a TPCF model which joins trust propagation into the collaborative recommendation system and combines the trust in trust propagation model and the similarity in traditional collaborative filtering algorithm by a mixing index to obtain the final user similarity. The paper [17] put forward a random walk algorithm which combines collaborative recommendation based on the item and the recommendation algorithm based on trust to predict the rating of a single item, and the principle is that the ratings of similar projects by highly trusted neighbors are more reliable than the ratings of the target project by lowly trusted neighbors. Besides, some recommendation approach is based on missing rating prediction [18] to improve the sparsity of rating data.

3. Our Approach

Aiming at the more reliable recommendation, we propose a cultural distance-aware service recommendation approach based on missing ratings prediction. Actually, the missing ratings prediction of training data is the same as the ratings prediction of active user in service collaborative filtering recommendation; therefore, we use the same cultural distance-aware collaborative filtering approach to solve them. The first step of our approach is the missing ratings prediction of training data which contains the similarity computation based on initial ratings, neighbor selection, and missing ratings prediction based on cultural distance; the second step is service recommendation which contains the similarity computation based on prediction rating data, neighbor selection, and ratings prediction based on cultural distance and recommendation.

3.1. Ratings Prediction. The foundation of the collaborative filtering recommendation approach is the user-service ratings matrix; however, these matrices are always sparse in practical applications. In our approach, we predict the missing rating values before recommendation to obtain a denser user-service ratings matrix. The main idea of prediction is similar to the collaborative filtering, and it can be divided into three phases: similarity computation, neighbor selection, and ratings prediction.

3.1.1. Similarity Computation. Assume that the original user-service ratings matrix R which expresses users preferences contains n users and m services; the element in this two-dimensional matrix r_{ui} is a vector of QoS values which is obtained by the user u on the service i. In general, a user only invokes a small part of the services and rates less services; as a result, many elements r_{ui} in R are missing.

To predict the missing ratings, we adopt two collaborative filtering prediction approaches: the user-based prediction

approach and the service-based prediction approach. The former is to first match the user's other ratings against other users, compute the similarity between them, and find users with the most similar preferences. The latter is to first match the service's other ratings against other services, compute the similarity between them, and find the most similar services. No matter in user-based or service-based prediction approaches, the similarity computation is based on Pearson correlation coefficient.

The Pearson correlation coefficient is a measure of the linear correlation between two variables. In user-based prediction approach, the similarities between user u and other users can be represented as follows:

$$\text{Sim}_u = \{\text{sim}_{au} \mid a \in C, \ a \neq u\}, \tag{2}$$

where C represents the set of users, sim_{au} represents the similarity between user a and user u, and it is computed as follows:

$$\text{sim}_{au} = \frac{\sum_{i \in I} (r_{ai} - \bar{r}_{Ia})(r_{ui} - \bar{r}_{Iu})}{\sqrt{\sum_{i \in I} (r_{ai} - \bar{r}_{Ia})^2} \sqrt{\sum_{i \in I} (r_{ui} - \bar{r}_{Iu})^2}}, \tag{3}$$

where I represents the subset of services which are rated by both user a and user u, $\bar{r}_{Ia}$ represents the average of ratings obtained by the user a on services in I, and $\bar{r}_{Iu}$ represents the average of ratings obtained by the user u on the services in I. The value of sim_{au} is between -1 and 1, where -1 represents total negative linear correlation, 0 represents no correlation, and 1 represents total positive linear correlation. The larger value of sim_{au} indicates the higher similarity between user a and user u. Note that when I is an empty set, sim_{au} is -1.

In service-based prediction approach, the similarities between service i and other services can be represented as follows:

$$\text{Sim}_i = \{\text{sim}_{ij} \mid j \in S, \ j \neq i\}, \tag{4}$$

where S represents the set of services, sim_{ij} represents the similarity between service i and service j, and it is computed as follows:

$$\text{sim}_{ij} = \frac{\sum_{u \in U} (r_{ui} - \bar{r}_{Ui})(r_{uj} - \bar{r}_{Uj})}{\sqrt{\sum_{u \in U} (r_{ui} - \bar{r}_{Ui})^2} \sqrt{\sum_{u \in U} (r_{uj} - \bar{r}_{Uj})^2}}, \tag{5}$$

where U is the subset of users who rate both service i and service j, $\bar{r}_{Ui}$ represents the average of ratings of service i obtained by the users in U, $\bar{r}_{Uj}$ represents the average of ratings of service j obtained by the users in U. Similar to sim_{au}, the value of sim_{ij} is between -1 and 1, and the larger value of sim_{ij} indicates the higher similarity between service i and service j. Note that when U is an empty set, sim_{ij} is -1.

3.1.2. Neighbor Selection. The main idea of collaborative filtering is to harness the collective intelligence and learn from the opinions of correlative populations; therefore, it is important to select the neighbors which are similar users or similar services. Before ratings prediction, neighbor selection

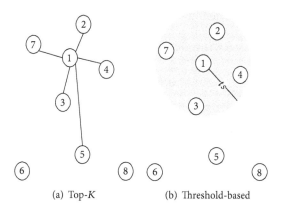

(a) Top-K (b) Threshold-based

FIGURE 1: The traditional neighbor selection approaches.

according to similarities is needed to find users with the most similar preferences or the most similar services.

There are two common ways to identify neighbors in traditional collaborative filtering approaches: Top-K approach and threshold-based approach. Top-K approach is to select the most similar K users or services as neighbors, no matter how similar the neighbors are. As shown in Figure 1(a), to select the 5 neighbors of Point 1, we take the recent five points: Points 2, 3, 4, 7, and 5 according to the distance between the points. However, we can see clearly that this approach has a bad performance on the calculation of isolated points, because the number of neighbors is fixed, and we have to take some points which are not very similar as neighbors when there are not enough similar points nearby. For example, in Figure 1(a), Point 5 is selected as a neighbor of Point 1, but it is not very similar to Point 1. Different from the principle of Top-K approach, threshold-based approach is to select the users or services of which similarity is smaller than threshold as the neighbors. As shown in Figure 1(b) where ts represents the value of threshold, to select the neighbors of Point 1 based on threshold, we consider the circular region with center Point 1, and a radius of ts, and take the points within the circular region as neighbors. In this example, Points 2, 3, 4, and 7 are selected as neighbors. This approach can improve the performance on the calculation of isolated points; however, this approach is very sensitive to the value of threshold; the neighbors selected are few when ts is too small, and when ts is too large. Therefore, how to set the value of threshold is very difficult.

To ensure the similarity of neighbors, we propose a novel neighbor selection approach which combines the Top-K approach and the threshold-based approach. We first set a loose threshold to filter the users or services with low similarity and then select the remaining users or services which are the top K most similar users or services as neighbors.

In user-based prediction approach, the selected neighbors of user u can be described as follows:

$$N_u = \{a \mid \text{sim}_{au} < ts, \ r_{au} < K\}, \tag{6}$$

where N_u represents the neighbors of user u and r_{au} represents the ranking of sim_{au} among Sim_u. The formulation means that user a is a neighbor of user u if user a belongs to

the top K similar users of user u, and sim_{au} is less than the threshold.

In service-based prediction approach, the selected neighbors can be described as follows:

$$N_i = \{j \mid \text{sim}_{ij} < ts, \ r_{ij} < K\}, \tag{7}$$

where N_i represents the neighbors of service i and r_{ij} represents the ranking of sim_{ij} among Sim_i. The formulation means that service j is a neighbor of service i if service j belongs to the top K similar users of service i, and sim_{ij} is less than the threshold.

3.1.3. Ratings Prediction. In traditional collaborative filtering approaches, the similarity between users or services is the only factor to determine the accuracy of prediction results. However, there are other factors having an important role in prediction. Therefore, we adopt the cultural distance in our collaborative filtering approach to improve the accuracy of prediction.

In this paper, we design a cultural factor to represent the preference of users to their neighbors. The cultural factor between user u and its neighbor a is as follows:

$$c_{au} = \left(1 - \frac{|cd_a - cd_u|}{\max_{cdu} - \min_{cdu}}\right), \tag{8}$$

where c_{au} represents the cultural factor of user u to user a, cd_a represents the cultural distance value of user a, cd_u represents the cultural distance value of user u, $\max_{cdu}$ represents the maximum value among the cultural distance values of neighbors of user u, and $\min_{cdu}$ represents the minimum value among the cultural distance values of neighbors of user u.

Similarly, the cultural factor between service i and its neighbor j is as follows:

$$c_{ij} = \left(1 - \frac{|cd_i - cd_j|}{\max_{cdi} - \min_{cdi}}\right), \tag{9}$$

where c_{ij} represents the cultural factor of service i to service j, cd_i represents the cultural distance value of service i, cd_j represents the cultural distance value of service j, $\max_{cdi}$

represents the maximum value among the cultural distance values of neighbors of service i, $\min_{cdi}$ represents the minimum value among the cultural distance values of neighbors of service i.

In our missing ratings prediction approach, we design a hybrid weight which can consider not only the similarity of neighbors but also the cultural factor. In our user-based prediction approach, the compound weight between user u and its neighbor a is

$$w_{au} = \beta \, \text{sim}_{au} + (1 - \beta) \, c_{au}, \tag{10}$$

where β represents the degree of the emphasis on the similarity. And then the prediction value of missing ratings can be computed based on the ratings of neighbors as follows:

$$p_u(r_{u,i}) = \bar{r}_u + \frac{\sum_{a \in N_u} w_{au}(r_{a,i} - \bar{r}_a)}{\sum_{a \in N_u} w_{au}}, \tag{11}$$

where $p_u(r_{u,i})$ represents the prediction value of the missing rating $r_{u,i}$ based on the neighbor users, $\bar{r}_u$ represents the basic prediction value of $r_{u,i}$, and it is the average of ratings obtained by the user u; similarly, $\bar{r}_a$ is the average of ratings obtained by the user a on the services besides service i.

Similarly, in our service-based prediction approach, the compound weight between service i and its neighbor j is

$$w_{ij} = \beta \, \text{sim}_{ij} + (1 - \beta) \, c_{ij}. \tag{12}$$

And then the prediction value of missing ratings can be computed based on the ratings of similar services as follows:

$$p_s(r_{u,i}) = \bar{r}_i + \frac{\sum_{j \in N_i} w_{ij}(r_{u,j} - \bar{r}_j)}{\sum_{j \in N_i} w_{ij}}, \tag{13}$$

where $p_s(r_{u,i})$ represents the prediction value of the missing rating $r_{u,i}$ based on the similar neighbor services, $\bar{r}_i$ represents the average of ratings of service i, and $\bar{r}_j$ represents the average of ratings of service j besides the rating obtained by user u.

In order to take full advantage of the information of the similar users and similar services and ensure the diversity of the recommendation results, our prediction approach combines the two collaborative filtering prediction approaches. Therefore, the prediction value of the missing rating $r_{u,i}$ in our prediction approach is as follows:

$$p(r_{u,i}) = \lambda p_u(r_{u,i}) + (1 - \lambda) p_s(r_{u,i}), \tag{14}$$

where λ represents the weight of the user-based prediction approach.

3.2. Service Recommendation. After the missing ratings prediction, we can recommend services for the active users who require service recommendations based on the prediction rating data of the training users whose ratings have been obtained. Similar to our missing ratings prediction approach, our service recommendation approach can be divided into three phases: similarity computation, neighbor selection, ratings prediction, and recommendation.

The first phase is similar to the last section. The similarities between the active user and the training users and the similarities between the candidate services and other services are computed by Formula (3) and Formula (5). The second phase is to select neighbors for the active users and the candidate services by Formula (6) and Formula (7). The third phase is to predict the ratings of the candidate services from the active users by Formula (14), and the final phase is to recommend service according to the prediction ratings.

4. Experiment

In this section, we implement our cultural distance-based collaborative filtering recommendation approach (named CDCF) to verify the performance and comparatively evaluate CDCF against several service recommendation approaches in terms of the prediction failure rate under the training rating data with different density and the active rating data with different density. The experimental evaluation results show that CDCF can improve the accuracy of recommendation.

4.1. Experiment Setup. To evaluate the performance of CDCF, we implement it by adopting two real-world datasets: WS-Dream dataset [32] and Hofstede's cultural dimension dataset [33].

The WS-Dream dataset contains the real-world QoS evaluation results from 339 users on 5,825 Web services and the location information (e.g., IP address, country, region, latitude, and longitude) of these users and services. Specifically, the QoS evaluation results are the user-service matrices on response time and throughout which can be used as the rating matrix in our approach.

Hofstede's cultural dimension dataset has been published in [33] and it contains the scores for the six cultural dimensions. These scores are obtained according to the items in the IBM database plus extensions and the items in the World Values Survey.

Based on the two datasets, we compare CDCF with other recommendation approaches.

(i) User-Based Collaborative Filtering Recommendation Approach (UCF). This approach is to predict the missing ratings using the traditional user-based prediction approach without adopting the cultural distance firstly and then recommend services for active users by employing the traditional user-based collaborative filtering approach based on the prediction ratings data.

(ii) Service-Based Collaborative Filtering Recommendation Approach (SCF). This approach is to predict the missing ratings using the prediction approach without adopting the cultural distance firstly and then recommend services for active users by employing the traditional service-based collaborative filtering approach based on the prediction ratings data.

(iii) Traditional Hybrid Collaborative Filtering Recommendation Approach (TCF). This approach is to predict the missing ratings by combining the traditional user-based

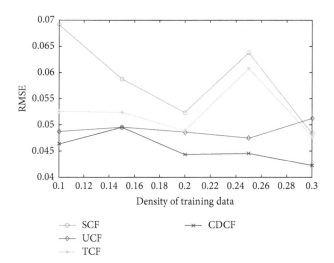

FIGURE 2: Comparison result in terms of RMSE with respect to the density of training data.

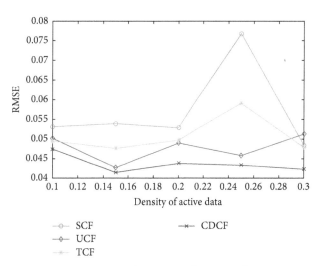

FIGURE 3: Comparison result in terms of RMSE with respect to the density of active data.

prediction approach and traditional service-based prediction approach and then recommend services for active users by combining the traditional user-based approach and service-based prediction approach. Compared with CDCF, both of the prediction and recommendation approaches only depend on the similarity of neighbors.

We select 150 users from the WS-Dream dataset randomly and then divide them into training users and the active users; the rate of training users is 0.75 in our experiments. To evaluate the performance of CDCF in data with different density, we randomly remove some ratings in training rating matrix or active rating matrix and employ different approaches to verify the reliability of CDCF.

The evaluation index used in this paper is Root Mean Square Error (RMSE) to measure the recommendation reliability of CDCF in comparison with other collaborative filtering approaches. RMSE is defined as follows:

$$\text{RMSE} = \sqrt{\frac{\sum (r_{u,i} - \hat{r}_{u,i})^2}{N}}, \quad (15)$$

where $r_{u,i}$ represents the removed rating of active user u, $\hat{r}_{u,i}$ represents the prediction value, and N represents the number of the removed ratings.

4.2. Performance Comparison. Figure 2 shows the comparison results in terms of RMSE with different density of training data ranging from 0.1 to 0.3, while the density of active data is 0.3. As shown in Figure 2, our approach CDCF is much better than other approaches, and its RMSE is 22.2%, 7.5%, and 13.4% lower than SCF, UCF, and TCF on average. In addition, there is no obvious relationship between the recommendation reliability and the density of training data in SCF, UCF, TCF, and CDCF.

Figure 3 shows the comparison results in terms of RMSE with different density of active data ranging from 0.1 to 0.3, while the density of training data is 0.3. As shown in Figure 2, our approach CDCF is much better than other approaches,

and its RMSE is 23.4%, 8.6%, and 13.9% lower than SCF, UCF, and TCF on average. In addition, there is no obvious relationship between the recommendation reliability and the density of training data in SCF, UCF, TCF, and CDCF.

In a word, as shown in Figures 2 and 3, although TCF takes full advantage of the information of the similar users and similar services and ensures the diversity of the recommendation results, its accuracy is lower than SCF with the low accuracy of UCF. Our approach CDCF can ensure not only the diversity of the recommendation results, but also the high recommendation reliability.

5. Conclusion

In this paper, we propose a cultural distance-aware service recommendation approach based on missing rating prediction. The main idea is to adopt the cultural distance to represent the user preference and combine the cultural factor with similarity to improve the reliability of recommendation. In addition, we predict the missing ratings by cultural distance-aware collaborative filtering approach to improve the sparsity of rating data. Experimental results show that compared to previous approaches, our approach can significantly improve the accuracy of the recommendation results. However, the cultural factor is at the regional/national level in this paper. A narrower grouping is required to improve the reliability of recommendation. Consequently, the next study in this area could focus on the presentation of the user cultural factor in a narrower group.

Conflicts of Interest

The authors declare that there are no conflicts of interest regarding the publication of this paper.

Acknowledgments

The work presented in this study was supported by the National Natural Science Foundation of China (Grant no.

71402097), Major Project supported by the National Social Science Foundation of China (Grant no. 15ZDA063), and Youth Foundation Program in Shanghai International Studies University (Grant no. Kx181102).

References

[1] A. Ahmed and E. Ahmed, "A survey on mobile edge computing," in *Proceedings of the 10th International Conference on Intelligent Systems and Control, ISCO 2016*, January 2016.

[2] M. Satyanarayanan, P. Simoens, Y. Xiao et al., "Edge analytics in the internet of things," *IEEE Pervasive Computing*, vol. 14, no. 2, pp. 24–31, 2015.

[3] S. Wang, L. Huang, L. Sun, C.-H. Hsu, and F. Yang, "Efficient and reliable service selection for heterogeneous distributed software systems," *Future Generation Computer Systems*, vol. 74, pp. 158–167, 2017.

[4] S. Wang, T. Lei, L. Zhang, C.-H. Hsu, and F. Yang, "Offloading mobile data traffic for QoS-aware service provision in vehicular cyber-physical systems," *Future Generation Computer Systems*, vol. 61, pp. 118–127, 2016.

[5] M. You, X. Xin, W. Shangguang, L. Jinglin, S. Qibo, and Y. Fangchun, "QoS evaluation for web service recommendation," *China Communications*, vol. 12, no. 4, pp. 151–160, 2015.

[6] S. Wang, Y. Ma, B. Cheng, F. Yang, and R. Chang, "Multi-dimensional QoS prediction for service recommendations," *IEEE Transaction on Services Computing*, 2016.

[7] X. Su and T. M. Khoshgoftaar, "A survey of collaborative filtering techniques," *Advances in Artificial Intelligence*, vol. 2009, Article ID 421425, 19 pages, 2009.

[8] F. Ricci, L. Rokach, B. Shapira, and P. B. Kantor, Eds., *Recommender Systems Handbook*, Springer, 2011.

[9] S. Wang, Z. Zheng, Z. Wu, M. R. Lyu, and F. Yang, "Reputation measurement and malicious feedback rating prevention in web service recommendation systems," *IEEE Transactions on Services Computing*, vol. 8, no. 5, pp. 755–767, 2015.

[10] Q. Zhu, M.-L. Shyu, and H. Wang, "VideoTopic: Content-based video recommendation using a topic model," in *Proceedings of the 15th IEEE International Symposium on Multimedia, ISM 2013*, pp. 219–222, December 2013.

[11] H. N. Kim., A. T. Ji, I. Ha, and G. S. Jo, "Collaborative filtering based on collaborative tagging for enhancing the quality of recommendation," *Electronic Commerce Research & Applications*, vol. 9, no. 1, pp. 73–83, 2010.

[12] G.-R. Xue, C. Lin, Q. Yang et al., "Scalable collaborative filtering using cluster-based smoothing," in *Proceedings of the 28th Annual International ACM SIGIR Conference on Research and Development in Information Retrieval (SIGIR '05)*, pp. 114–121, ACM, Salvador, Brazil, 2005.

[13] G. Kang, J. Liu, M. Tang, X. Liu, B. Cao, and Y. Xu, "AWSR: Active web service recommendation based on usage history," in *Proceedings of the 2012 IEEE 19th International Conference on Web Services, ICWS 2012*, pp. 186–193, June 2012.

[14] J. S. Breese, D. Heckerman, and C. Kadie, "Empirical analysis of predictive algorithms for collaborative filtering," in *Proceedings of the Fourteenth Conference on Uncertainty in Artificial Intelligence*, pp. 43–52, 1998.

[15] B. Sarwar, G. Karypis, J. Konstan, and J. Riedl, "Analysis of recommendation algorithms for e-commerce," in *Proceedings of the 2nd ACM Conference on Electronic Commerce (EC '00)*, pp. 158–167, 2000.

[16] A. Zarghami, S. Fazeli, N. Dokoohaki, and M. Matskin, "Social trust-aware recommendation system: A T-index approach," in *Proceedings of the 2009 IEEE/WIC/ACM International Conference on Web Intelligence and Intelligent Agent Technology - Workshops, WI-IAT Workshops 2009*, pp. 85–90, September 2009.

[17] M. Jamali and M. Ester, "TrustWalker: a random walk model for combining trust-based and item-based recommendation," in *Proceedings of the 15th ACM SIGKDD International Conference on Knowledge Discovery and Data Mining (KDD '09)*, pp. 397–405, July 2009.

[18] Z. Zheng, H. Ma, M. R. Lyu, and I. King, "QoS-aware web service recommendation by collaborative filtering," *IEEE Transactions on Services Computing*, vol. 4, no. 2, pp. 140–152, 2011.

[19] L. Tihanyi, D. A. Griffith, and C. J. Russell, "The effect of cultural distance on entry mode choice, international diversification, and MNE performance: A meta-analysis," *Journal of International Business Studies*, vol. 36, no. 3, pp. 270–283, 2005.

[20] M. Reformat, L. DengMing, and L. Cuong, "Approximate reasoning and Semantic Web services," in *Proceedings of the NAFIPS 2004 - Annual Meeting of the North American Fuzzy Information Processing Society: Fuzzy Sets in the Heart of the Canadian Rockies*, vol. 1, pp. 413–418, June 2004.

[21] B. Kogut and H. Singh, "The Effect of National Culture on the Choice of Entry Mode," *Journal of International Business Studies*, vol. 19, no. 3, pp. 411–432, 1988.

[22] J. L. Herlocker, J. Konstan, A. Borchers, and J. Riedl, "An algorithmic framework for performing collaborative filtering," in *Proceedings of the 22nd Annual International ACM SIGIR Conference on Research and Development in Information Retrieval (SIGIR '99)*, pp. 230–237, Berkeley, Calif, USA, August 1999.

[23] R. Jin, J. Y. Chai, and L. Si, "An automatic weighting scheme for collaborative filtering," in *Proceedings of Sheffield SIGIR - Twenty-Seventh Annual International ACM SIGIR Conference on Research and Development in Information Retrieval*, pp. 337–344, July 2004.

[24] M. Deshpande and G. Karypis, "Item-based top-N recommendation algorithms," *ACM Transactions on Information and System Security*, vol. 22, no. 1, pp. 143–177, 2004.

[25] G. Linden, B. Smith, and J. York, "Amazon.com recommendations: item-to-item collaborative filtering," *IEEE Internet Computing*, vol. 7, no. 1, pp. 76–80, 2003.

[26] B. Sarwar, G. Karypis, J. Konstan, and J. Riedl, "Item-based collaborative filtering recommendation algorithms," in *Proceedings of the 10th International Conference on World Wide Web (WWW '01)*, pp. 285–295, 2001.

[27] S. Wang, Y. Zhao, L. Huang, J. Xu, and C. Hsu, "QoS prediction for service recommendations in mobile edge computing," *Journal of Parallel and Distributed Computing*, 2017.

[28] S. Wang, Y. Ma, B. Cheng, F. Yang, and R. N. Chang, "Multi-Dimensional QoS Prediction for Service Recommendations," *IEEE Transaction on Services Computing*, 2016.

[29] P. Resnick, N. Iacovou, M. Suchak, P. Bergstrom, and J. Riedl, "GroupLens: an open architecture for collaborative filteringof netnews," in *Proceedings of the ACM Conference on Computer Supported Cooperative Work*, pp. 175–186, Chapel Hill, NC, USA, October 1994.

[30] X. C. Chen, R. J. Liu, and H. Y. Chang, "Research of collaborative filtering recommendation algorithm based on trust propagation model," in *Proceedings of the 2010 International Conference on Computer Application and System Modeling, ICCASM 2010*, vol. 4, pp. 177–183, October 2010.

[31] S. Wang, L. Huang, C.-H. Hsu, and F. Yang, "Collaboration reputation for trustworthy Web service selection in social networks," *Journal of Computer and System Sciences*, vol. 82, no. 1, part B, pp. 130–143, 2016.

[32] Z. Zheng, Y. Zhang, and M. R. Lyu, "Investigating QoS of real-world web services," *IEEE Transactions on Services Computing*, vol. 7, no. 1, pp. 32–39, 2014.

[33] G. Hofstede, *Cultures and Organizations: Software of the Mind, Third Edition - Software for the Mind*, Business Expert Press, 3rd edition, 2010.

11

Implementation of Secondary Index on Cloud Computing NoSQL Database in Big Data Environment

Bao Rong Chang,[1] **Hsiu-Fen Tsai,**[2] **Chia-Yen Chen,**[1]
Chien-Feng Huang,[1] **and Hung-Ta Hsu**[1]

[1]*Department of Computer Science and Information Engineering, National University of Kaohsiung, Kaohsiung 81148, Taiwan*
[2]*Department of Marketing Management, Shu-Te University, Kaohsiung 82445, Taiwan*

Correspondence should be addressed to Chien-Feng Huang; cfhuang15@nuk.edu.tw

Academic Editor: Gianluigi Greco

This paper introduces the combination of NoSQL database HBase and enterprise search platform Solr so as to tackle the problem of the secondary index function with fast query. In order to verify the effectiveness and efficiency of the proposed approach, the assessment using Cost-Performance ratio has been done for several competitive benchmark databases and the proposed one. As a result, our proposed approach outperforms the other databases and fulfills secondary index function with fast query in NoSQL database. Moreover, according to the cross-sectional analysis, the proposed combination of HBase and Solr database is capable of performing an excellent query/response in a big data environment.

1. Introduction

Regarding big data storage [1, 2], the way of fast and easy data query is a concerned issue in NoSQL database. In general, NoSQL scheme [3, 4] is capable of supporting various data format to process the storage; yet it sacrifices the index searching function. HBase is of a NoSQL database as part of Hadoop ecosystem. It is known as the scheme of key value and usually stores the results coming out of MapReduce execution. HBase features high scalability and high flexibility, delivering a high IO performance of big data. Solr is of a blazing fast open source enterprise search engine that can quickly create index and proceed with powerful full-text search. In this paper, we are able to combine HBase and Solr to enhance the secondary index function for HBase. After the success of this combination, we go for a series of stress tests using several testing items and then make the performance comparison between the proposed one and the other benchmark databases. Finally, a cost effectiveness evaluation called Cost-Performance ratio (C-P ratio) [5] has been done for a variety of databases. As a result, the assessment about C-P ratio will be analyzed and discussed for all of databases

mentioned in this paper. Based on the cross-sectional data analysis [6], it will explore the performance of data access in NoSQL database in a big data environment as well.

For key-value database, it allows the application to store its data in a schema-less way. The data could be stored in a data type of a programming language or an object. There is no need for a fixed data model. Key-value storing divides many categories, like eventually consistent (always keeps the newest result if there is no update), hierarchical (can use the parent's attributes), cache in RAM (key value stored in memory, hash stored in cache, and hash used to present key-value index; time complexity is $O(1)$), solid state or rotating disk (like Google Bigtable which is used in solid state disk to enhance IO access speed), and ordered (with key-value pairs which can sort keys or values). For tabular database, it is a database that is structured in a tabular form. It arranges data elements in vertical columns and horizontal rows. Each cell is formed by the intersection of a column and row. Each row and column are uniquely numbered to make it orderly and efficient. This type of database has a virtually infinite range for mass data storage. Structuring data in tabular form may be the oldest method used. It is also simple. Tabular

TABLE 1: NoSQL database benchmark on 5 criteria.

Database	Performance	Scalability	Flexibility	Complexity	Functionality
Key-value store	High	High	High	Low	Variable
Column store	High	High	Moderate	Low	Minimum
Document store	High	Variable	High	Low	Variable
Graph database	Variable	Variable	High	High	Graph theory
Relational database	Variable	Variable	Low	Moderate	Relational algebra

database has several properties. They share the same set of properties per record. This means that every row has the same set of column titles. They access records through identifiers. Each table in a tabular database contains a particular set of related information that is connected with the database subject through key fields, which describe each record (row) so that, in the event of a query, the system can quickly locate the record. There are several famous databases of this type, like Google Bigtable, Apache Accumulo, Apache HBase, and Hypertable. For column store database, it stores data tables as sections of columns of data rather than rows of data. For RDBMS, rows are commonly used; the column store database has the advantage of aggregating computed data over large numbers of similar data items. Column store is used in data warehouse and CRM system. Using column store database, the system can evaluate which columns are being accessed and retrieved only if values are requested from the specific columns. For NoSQL database, each mechanism has different uses, and a famous database can have many properties, like Google Bigtable. It owns solid state disk key-value type and tabular type. For this study, HBase is a column-store database. It has an easy method to use, and its performance as well as the scalability is better than the others. Table 1 explains the performance of each type of database over 5 criteria.

The following paragraphs of this paper are arranged as follows. In Section 2, combination of NoSQL database and enterprise search platform will be described. The way to system assessment is given in Section 3. The experimental results and discussion will be obtained in Section 4. Finally, we drew a brief conclusion in Section 5.

2. Combination of NoSQL Database and Enterprise Search Platform

This paper studies how the combination of HBase and Solr runs in big data environment based on cloud computing platform. All of application programs were installed in a Linux-based operating system. HBase is placed over Hadoop HDFS system. Thus, HBase can be attached to Hadoop after the core parts of Hadoop have been installed in a physical machine such as MapReduce and HDFS. Solr can operate independently without any support from any other applications. With the corporation with Solr, HBase can easily create index. On the other hand, Solr is able to provide GUI interface for user's operation. The procedure to establish the combination of two applications can be listed as follows.

(1) Install Linux O/S on every host, connect them together via SSH, and deploy JVM to every host to achieve a Linux cluster environment.

(2) Establish master and slave nodes and start them up. Master node shall deploy Hadoop to slave nodes. This has Hadoop done in every host in a cluster environment [7–9].

(3) After deploying Hadoop and ZooKeeper to cluster, we need to confirm the start-up of Hadoop and ZooKeeper services. We are able to give jps instruction at terminal to check whether or not the services are running normally. After that, we establish HBase service [10–13] within Hadoop.

(4) When procedure #3 has been done, web browser is used to view the start-up of Hadoop and HBase services. Key in http://localhost:50030/, 50040, 50070, and 60010 is used to check each node if operating normally.

(5) Before we get Solr started, we need to modify the execution parameters in solrconfig.xml, which is a configuration file within ./solr-version/examples/solr/collection1/conf/. We have to determine the Solr whether or not setting input word string to act as an index, content storage, and data format. Apache Solr needed http web container to get it started, for example, either Apache Tomcat or Apache Jetty. Here, we chose Jetty because of the default setting. After setting up, we key in "java –jar start, jar" to start up Solr in terminal. Finally, we got Solr's address, which is http://localhost:8983/.

(6) Since HBase cannot support automatically generated row key, several big data files shall be modified in advance. We need to design a unique and complex rowkey which corresponds to a large number of rows (up to ten million rows). In this study, we chose the American Yellow Page as data source. Our data combination is "rowkey-category-shop name-telephone-province-address" with a total of 6 columns. These data files have to translate into CSV format, and "," symbols are used to separate each column.

(7) The CSV file is uploaded to Hadoop file system, and these files are imported to HBase as full-text input via the special tool, "bulk load tool" [14]. We need to check the data integrity in HBase after data importing.

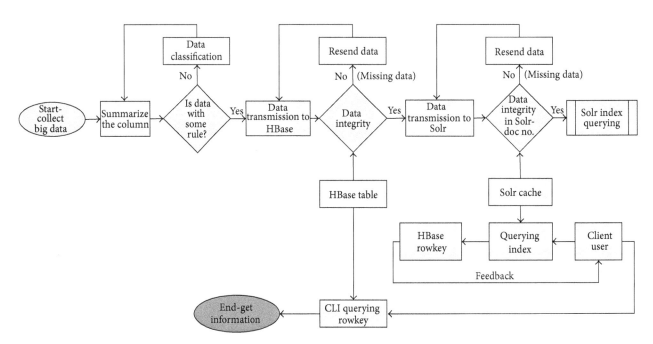

```
by nature
1.1: multiValued attribute introduced, false by default
1.2: omitTermFreqAndPositions attribute introduced, true by default
     except for text fields.
1.3: removed optional field compress feature
1.4: autoGeneratePhraseQueries attribute introduced to drive QueryParser
     behavior when a single string produces multiple tokens.  Defaults
     to off for version >= 1.4
1.5: omitNorms defaults to true for primitive field types
     (int, float, boolean, string...)
-->

<fields>
  <field name="_version_" type="long" indexed="true" stored="true"/>
  <field name="rowkey" type="text_general" indexed="true" stored="true" required="true" multiValued="false" />
  <field name="address" type="text_general" indexed="false" stored="true" multiValued="true"/>
  <field name="category" type="text_general" indexed="true" stored="true" multiValued="false"/>
  <field name="shopname" type="text_general" indexed="true" stored="true" multiValued="false"/>
  <field name="province" type="text_general" indexed="true" stored="true" multiValued="false"/>
  <field name="tel" type="text_general" indexed="true" stored="true" multiValued="false"/>
</fields>

<!-- Field to use to determine and enforce document uniqueness.
     Unless this field is marked with required="false", it will be a required field
-->
<uniqueKey>rowkey</uniqueKey>
```

FIGURE 1: Apache Solr configuring file for indexing.

FIGURE 2: Flowchart of HBase together with Solr to implement secondary index operation.

(8) Then, we use HBase output API and Apache HTTP API to transfer the document to Solr from HBase [15–17]. After the transmission, the indexes are created and the content is saved in memory in Solr, that is, the schema as defined and shown in Figure 1. We can use web browser to check the amount of documents in Solr. Data in a row represent a document. We can use query function to search our keyword (Secondary index or more) and reversely to search the primary index in Solr. We may be able to apply filter function to improve the precision of search results.

(9) After finishing the setup of the proposed system, we chose some other benchmarks to compare with the proposed one in the experiment. After the experiment, we are able to give a kind of assessment on those, for instance a cost effectiveness evaluation.

In Figure 2, a flowchart represents HBase together with Solr to implement secondary index operation.

3. System Assessment

In terms of the performance evaluation, we have initially tested the time for data read/write to a variety of databases, such as Apache HBase, Cassandra, Huawei HBase, Solandra, and Lily Project. Next, the time for data transfer to Solr from the databases mentioned above has to be recorded. Finally, the response time for the query function performed in Solr needed to be measured as well. According to four tests on data write, data read, document transfer, and query/response to any of databases as mentioned above, first of all we have to measure a single datum access time taking a number of different data size as shown in (1), where $t_{s_{ijk}}$ represents a single datum access time, for a single run t_{ijk} stands for

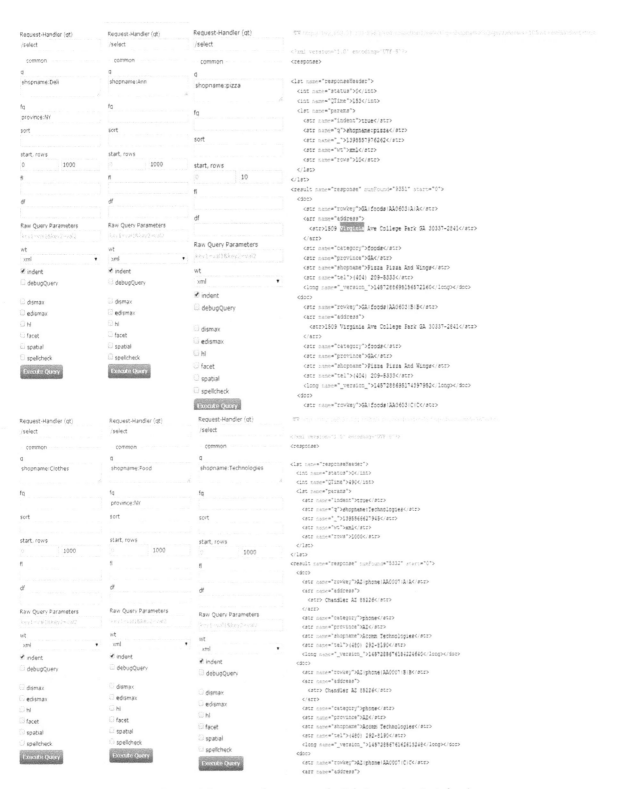

FIGURE 3: Latency under stress test for Solr (presenting 6 windows).

measured total time for a specific data size at a certain database, and N_{ik} means a specific data size. In (2), $\bar{t}_{s_{ijk}}$ represents average time of a single datum access and w_i stands for the respective weight factor for $t_{s_{ijk}}$. A normalized performance index for a specific database at a certain test can be obtained as shown in (3), where $\overline{PI}_{jk}$ represents a normalized performance index. After that, we have evaluated the weighted average of normalized performance index and it turned out to be the performance index [18] for each database as shown in (4), where PI_j represents performance index, SF_1 stands for scale factor #1, W_k is the respective weight, and $\overline{PI}_{jk}$ means a normalized performance index. In order to assess the cost effectiveness evaluation, we need to calculate total cost of ownership [19] in (5), showing the expenditure of money in the implementation of secondary index function for NoSQL database, where HC_a presents hardware cost, S_b stands for software cost, $RCAW_c$ means repairing cost after the warranty, DTC_d is downtime cost, and EUC_e explains extra upgrade cost. The monetary value of total cost of ownership may vary with location, market, and tax. Thus, a higher cost, for example, might be obtained in US and a lower cost in Taiwan. In the system assessment, a typical cost effectiveness evaluation called C-P ratio has been introduced here to do the assessment in (6), where CP_{jg} is C-P ratio, SF_2 stands for scale factor #2, and TCO_{jg} means total cost of ownership as well as subscript j that represents various data center and g that stands for a certain period of time. Consider the following:

$$t_{s_{ijk}} = \frac{t_{ijk}}{N_{ik}}, \tag{1}$$

where $i = 1, 2, \ldots, l$, $j = 1, 2, \ldots, m$, and $k = 1, 2, \ldots, n$,

$$\bar{t}_{s_{jk}} = \sum_{i=1}^{l} w_i \cdot t_{s_{ijk}}, \tag{2}$$

where $j = 1, 2, \ldots, m$, $k = 1, 2, \ldots, n$, and $\sum_{i=1}^{l} w_i = 1$,

$$\overline{PI}_{jk} = \frac{1/\bar{t}_{s_{jk}}}{\text{Max}_{h=1,2,\ldots,m} \left(1/\bar{t}_{s_{hk}} \right)}, \tag{3}$$

where $j = 1, 2, \ldots, m$ and $k = 1, 2, \ldots, n$,

$$PI_j = SF_1 \cdot \left(\sum_{k=1}^{n} W_k \cdot \overline{PI}_{jk} \right), \tag{4}$$

where $j = 1, 2, \ldots, m$, $k = 1, 2, \ldots, n$, $SF_1 = 10^2$, and $\sum_{k=1}^{n} W_k = 1$,

$$TCO_{jg} = \sum_a HC_a + \sum_b S_b + \sum_c RCAW_c + \sum_d DTC_d + \sum_e EUC_e, \tag{5}$$

where $j = 1, 2, \ldots, m$ and $g = 1, 2, \ldots, o$,

$$CP_{jg} = SF_2 \cdot \frac{PI_j}{TCO_{jg}}, \tag{6}$$

where $j = 1, 2, \ldots, m$, $g = 1, 2, \ldots, o$, and $SF_2 = 10^4$.

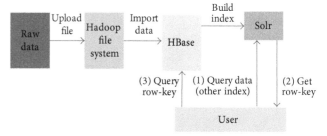

FIGURE 4: Implementation procedure.

FIGURE 5: Scanning a table in HBase using CLI.

In order to examine the stability and reliability of NoSQL database secondary index function, a stress test of data retrieval in Solr has been taken in a big data environment. Technically speaking, this test generated up to 20 threads (20 windows) to respond to 10 to 1000 queries and we had checked the latency (time interval) simultaneously. The key index in every query was different as shown in Figure 3. Clearly, the result would indicate the response time for the query in Solr and explain what correlation between the amount of windows and the latency was found.

4. Experimental Results and Discussion

There are a few experiments and a discussion presented in the following subsections.

4.1. Data Transfer and Data Integrity Checking. In regard to implementation procedure as shown in Figure 4, which indicated data transfer from HDFS to HBase and/or from HBase to Solr, there are risks of losing data during the transition. We have to verify the data integrity in HBase inner table and the amount of input documents in Solr. For examining HBase, we checked inner table using the command "scan table-name" in CLI as shown in Figure 5. In Figure 6, the document transfer from HBase to Solr has been done using the command in CLI. For examining Solr, we checked our input document amount in Solr using web interface as shown in Figure 6. Furthermore, in terms of the performance evaluation, the time for data writing/reading in every database has been measured as listed in Tables 2 and 3.

TABLE 2: Time for writing data to database (unit: sec.).

Data size	HBase + Solr	Cassandra	Huawei HBase	Solandra	Lily Project
10^4	23	110.4	23	120	23
10^5	23.2	1109.2	23	1215	24
10^6	123.4	11211.3	125	11253	137
10^7	388.5	113157.7	390	113189	412

TABLE 3: Time for reading data from database (unit: sec.).

Data size	HBase + Solr	Cassandra	Huawei HBase	Solandra	Lily Project
10^4	27.2	27.6	30	29	27
10^5	266.5	270.7	269	288.5	273
10^6	2572.2	2614.2	2589.7	2735	2566
10^7	24312	24701	24479	24988	24385

FIGURE 6: Importing data to Solr from HBase.

FIGURE 7: Presentation of Imported data in Solr using GUI.

Time for data transfer to Solr from every database has been recorded as listed in Table 4.

Speaking of data import to HBase, we adopted a bulk-load tool with MapReduce computing to transfer the original file into HBase because this tool is capable of handling a large amount of data in the way of fast and smoothly transferring. For Solr, a program with specific port at Solr and designated HBase API has activated to quickly transfer documents to Solr from HBase where a java client to access Solr called Solrj has logged into the http server, that is Solr, to respond swiftly to the connection and deliver the on-line document to http server. This also demonstrates an efficient way to realize a fast document transfer based on a client-server model for a huge amount of data. Alternatively, the other choice is that HBase coprocessor may launch a process to do the batch update frequently. However, HBase coprocessor is not stable because it is still in the developing phase.

4.2. Querying Function and Performance Index. Once the document transfer from HBase to Solr has been done completely, the data are available in Solr and we could check the

amount of document in Solr as shown in Figure 7. In order to verify the secondary index function in the combination of HBase and Solr, we launched the query test in Solr as shown in Figure 8, where we can check the information about the related operations on the web. Solr provides normal search, filtering search, spatial search, and other more search functions. For example, we did a search using the shop-name field that included "Food" as its keyword, and 1000 results appeared filtering the province tag with "NY." We keyed in "shopname:Food" in "q" field, inputted "province:NY" in "fq" field, and gave 1000 in rows field. Figure 8 has shown the operation of query. In Table 5, the response time for the query function performed in Solr has also been marked. Besides, average time-consuming on data read/write, document transfer, and query function is eventually obtained as listed in Table 6. After that, according to (4), we are able to evaluate the performance index for each database over a 5-year period of time as shown in Table 7.

4.3. Assessment. In the system assessment, we first analyze total cost of ownership (TCO) according to several items such as hardware cost, staff cost, software cost, repair cost

FIGURE 8: Response to a query in Solr using GUI.

after warranty, downtime cost, and extra upgrade cost. A summary of TCO has been shown in Table 7. Here we estimated that hardware cost for two computers is $2666. Then, we assumed that the maintenance bill is $13000 every year for Hadoop together with HBase, Solr maintenance cost is approximately $300 per year, and for Cassandra it would be $10300 every year. Accordingly, we do the same maintenance estimation as the above-mentioned applications for Solandra and Lily Project because they are just the combination of the above applications. All of software cost is totally free due to open source. For hardware maintenance after warranty, we assumed that all the devices had the same risk of breakdown, and thus the chance of device breakdown in the 4th year

was about 25%, while in the 5th year it will be 50% chance. For the software upgrade cost, there is no charge because of open source. Regarding downtime cost, we assumed that one application will cost $20 per year and the total cost would depend on the amount of software. Table 8 gives a summary of the total cost of ownership for this study. As for the system assessment, C-P ratio evaluation according to (6) for all of databases will yield a summary of those over a 5-year period of time as listed in Table 9.

4.4. Stress Test and Discussion. The issue about the stability and reliability of NoSQL database secondary index function has been concerned and hence a stress test of data retrieval

TABLE 4: Document transfer time from database to Solr (unit: sec.).

Data size	HBase + Solr	Cassandra	Huawei HBase	Solandra	Lily Project
10^4	109	120	115	123	115
10^5	1121	1130	1125	1154	1130
10^6	11105	11286	11173	11330	11186
10^7	108055	112806	112347	113105	112395

TABLE 5: Response time for querying function performed in Solr (unit: sec.).

Data size	HBase + Solr	Cassandra	Huawei HBase	Solandra	Lily Project
10^4	0.15	0.91	45	2	1
10^5	0.5	11.12	288	7	5
10^6	2	143.1	547	15	10
10^7	10	2011.13	1867	60	45

TABLE 6: Average time of a single datum access (unit: sec.).

Operation	HBase + Solr	Cassandra	Huawei HBase	Solandra	Lily Project
Data write	0.000673563	0.011164768	0.0006735	0.011680475	0.00067955
Data read	0.0025971	0.002637825	0.0026819	0.0027547	0.002608625
Document transfer	0.011005125	0.01146665	0.011289425	0.011620125	0.011306375
Query/response	0.00000575	0.000136603	0.002028425	0.00007275	0.000041125

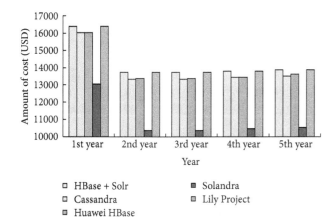

FIGURE 9: Total cost of ownership among various databases over a 5-year period.

TABLE 7: Performance index.

Database	Performance index
HBase + Solr	99
Cassandra	51
Huawei HBase	73
Solandra	50
Lily Project	77

TABLE 8: Total cost of ownership over a 5-year period (unit: USD).

Database	1st year	2nd year	3rd year	4th year	5th year
HBase + Solr	16393.3	13726.7	13726.7	13804.1	13877.9
Cassandra	16020	13353.3	13353.3	13430.8	13504.6
Huawei	16040	13373.3	13373.3	13450.8	13629.9
Solandra	13040	10373.3	10373.3	10450.8	10524.6
Lily Project	16393.3	13726.7	13726.7	13804.1	13877.9

TABLE 9: C-P ratio over a 5-year period.

Database	1st year	2nd year	3rd year	4th year	5th year
HBase + Solr	61.00	72.85	72.85	72.44	72.06
Cassandra	31.94	38.32	38.32	38.10	37.89
Huawei	45.92	55.07	55.07	54.76	54.04
Solandra	38.85	48.84	48.84	48.48	48.14
Lily Project	47.27	56.46	56.46	56.14	55.84

in Solr has been taken in a big data environment. In this test, there are up to 20 threads (20 windows) used to accept the number of queries from 10 to 1000 and in the meantime the latency (time interval) has been counted. The key index in every query was different as shown in Figure 3. Table 10 has listed the summary of latency and we have examined the results afterward. In the test from the statistics point of view, the amount of opening windows obviously did not affect the length of latency occurring in the query in Solr. The stability and reliability of NoSQL database secondary index function have been verified because all of queries had responded in 5 seconds during the stress test.

It noted that performance indexes for five databases have been listed in Table 7 and they are time-invariant. In Figure 9,

the total cost of ownership for our proposed approach has varied from year to year where it goes down dramatically and goes up slowly over a 5-year period. Accordingly, C-P ratio of the proposed approach goes up abruptly and almost

TABLE 10: Latency under stress test (unit: sec) (Win.: window).

Query	Win. #1	Win. #2	Win. #3	Win. #4	Win. #5	Win. #6	Win. #7	Win. #8	Win. #9	Win. #10
10	0.15	0.1	0.2	0.2	0.1	0.15	0.16	0.15	0.2	0.2
100	1	1	0.8	1	1	0.8	1	1	1	1
1000	3	4	3	4	3	4	3	4	5	4
	Win. #11	Win. #12	Win. #13	Win. #14	Win. #15	Win. #16	Win. #17	Win. #18	Win. #19	Win. #20
10	0.15	0.15	0.15	0.15	0.2	0.2	0.16	0.15	0.2	0.2
100	1.2	0.8	1.1	1	1.1	1	1.2	1	1.1	1.2
1000	3	4	3	4	5	4	4	4	5	5

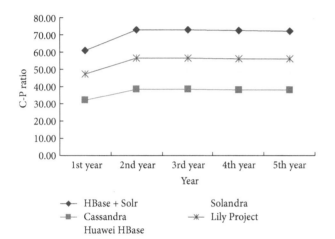

FIGURE 10: C-P ratio among various databases over a 5-year period.

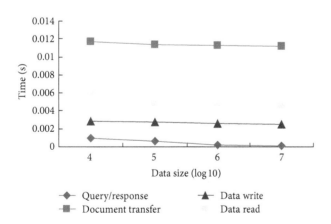

FIGURE 11: Average time of a single datum access in a certain database.

maintains the same level afterward as shown in Figure 10. Consequently, according to C-P ratio, our proposed approach outperforms the others during this period, as listed in Table 9. This has verified that our proposed approach has been realized successfully and performed significantly for a NoSQL secondary index function and fast query.

There are four tests about the function of data read, data write, document transfer, and query/response, as mentioned above in this paper to measure the average time of a single datum access in a certain database as listed in Tables 2 to 4. What we are interested in is to figure out whether the average time of a single datum access may be varied with data size or not for these functions. As shown in Figure 11, the cross-sectional data analysis [6] gave that it takes least time on the function of query/response when comparing with the other functions. The average time reduces dramatically as data size increases because the hit rate of data retrieval goes up rapidly in memory cache and concurrently the response time shrinks sharply. This figure illustrates that NoSQL database with secondary index function can achieve an excellent performance in query/response of a certain database, especially in a big data environment.

5. Conclusion

This paper introduces the combination of NoSQL database HBase and enterprise search platform Solr to realize the secondary index function with fast query. In the assessment, a cost effectiveness evaluation called C-P ratio has been done among several competitive benchmark databases and the proposed one. As a result, our proposed approach outperforms the other databases and fulfills secondary index function with fast query in NoSQL database. Besides, a stress test has been taken to verify the stability and reliability of the proposed approach. Finally, according to the cross-sectional analysis, the proposed combination of HBase and Solr database is capable of performing an excellent query/response in a big data environment.

Conflict of Interests

The authors declare that there is no conflict of interests regarding the publication of this paper.

Acknowledgment

This work is supported by the Ministry of Science and Technology, Taiwan, Republic of China, under Grant no. MOST 103-2221-E-390-011.

References

[1] D. Howe, M. Costanzo, P. Fey et al., "Big data: the future of biocuration," *Nature*, vol. 455, no. 7209, pp. 47–50, 2008.

[2] A. Jacobs, "The pathologies of big data," *Communications of the ACM—A Blind Person's Interaction with Technology*, vol. 52, no. 8, pp. 36–44, 2009.

[3] R. Cattell, "Scalable SQL and NoSQL data stores," *ACM SIGMOD Record*, vol. 39, no. 4, pp. 12–27, 2010.

[4] J. Pokorny, "NoSQL databases: a step to database scalability in web environment," *International Journal of Web Information Systems*, vol. 9, no. 1, pp. 69–82, 2013.

[5] B. R. Chang, H.-F. Tsai, C.-M. Chen, and C.-F. Huang, "Analysis of virtualized cloud server together with shared storage and estimation of consolidation ratio and TCO/ROI," *Engineering Computations*, vol. 31, no. 8, pp. 1746–1760, 2014.

[6] C.-C. Lee and C.-P. Chang, "Energy consumption and economic growth in Asian economies: a more comprehensive analysis using panel data," *Resource and Energy Economics*, vol. 30, no. 1, pp. 50–65, 2008.

[7] P. Zhou, J. Lei, and W. Ye, "Large-scale data sets clustering based on MapReduce and Hadoop," *Journal of Computational Information Systems*, vol. 7, no. 16, pp. 5956–5963, 2011.

[8] J. K. Chiang, "Authentication, authorization and file synchronization for hybrid cloud—the development centric to google apps, hadoop and linux local hosts," *Journal of Internet Technology*, vol. 14, no. 7, pp. 1141–1148, 2013.

[9] J. Leverich and C. Kozyrakis, "On the energy (in) efficiency of Hadoop clusters," *ACM SIGOPS Operating Systems Review*, vol. 44, no. 1, pp. 61–65, 2010.

[10] T. White, *Hadoop: The Definitive Guide*, O'Reilly Media, Sebastopol, Calif, USA, 2009.

[11] N. Dimiduk, *HBase in Action*, Manning Publications, Greenwich, UK, 2012.

[12] Y. Jiang, *HBase Administration Cookbook*, Packt Publishing, Birmingham, UK, 2012.

[13] C. Boja, A. Pocovnicu, and L. Batagan, "Distributed parallel architecture for big data," *Informatica Economica*, vol. 16, no. 2, pp. 116–127, 2012.

[14] J. Dean and S. Ghemawat, "MapReduce: simplified data processing on large clusters," *Communications of the ACM*, vol. 51, no. 1, pp. 107–113, 2008.

[15] M. Hausenblas and J. Nadeau, "Apache drill: interactive ad-hoc analysis at scale," *Big Data*, vol. 1, no. 2, pp. 100–104, 2013.

[16] R. Kuc, *Apache Solr 4 Cookbook*, Packt Publishing, Birmingham, UK, 2013.

[17] T. Grainger and T. Potter, *Solr in Action*, Manning Publications, Greenwich, UK, 2014.

[18] B. R. Chang, H.-F. Tsai, and C.-M. Chen, "High-performed virtualization services for in-cloud enterprise resource planning system," *Journal of Information Hiding and Multimedia Signal Processing*, vol. 5, no. 4, pp. 614–624, 2014.

[19] B. R. Chang, H.-F. Tsai, and C.-M. Chen, "Evaluation of virtual machine performance and virtualized consolidation ratio in cloud computing system," *Journal of Information Hiding and Multimedia Signal Processing*, vol. 4, no. 3, pp. 192–200, 2013.

12

Incremental Graph Pattern Matching Algorithm for Big Graph Data

Lixia Zhang[1] **and Jianliang Gao** ⓘ[2]

[1]*College of Mathematics and Computer Science, Key Laboratory of High Performance Computing and Stochastic Information Processing, Ministry of Education of China, Hunan Normal University, Changsha 410081, China*
[2]*School of Information Science and Engineering, Central South University, Changsha 410083, China*

Correspondence should be addressed to Jianliang Gao; gaojianliang@csu.edu.cn

Academic Editor: Longxiang Gao

Graph pattern matching is widely used in big data applications. However, real-world graphs are usually huge and dynamic. A small change in the data graph or pattern graph could cause serious computing cost. Incremental graph matching algorithms can avoid recomputing on the whole graph and reduce the computing cost when the data graph or the pattern graph is updated. The existing incremental algorithm PGC_IncGPM can effectively reduce matching time when no more than half edges of the pattern graph are updated. However, as the number of changed edges increases, the improvement of PGC_IncGPM gradually decreases. To solve this problem, an improved algorithm iDeltaP_IncGPM is developed in this paper. For multiple insertions (resp., deletions) on pattern graphs, iDeltaP_IncGPM determines the nodes' matching state detection sequence and processes them together. Experimental results show that iDeltaP_IncGPM has higher efficiency and wider application range than PGC_IncGPM.

1. Introduction

Graph pattern matching is to find all the subgraphs that are the same or similar to a given pattern graph P in a data graph G. It is widely used in a number of applications, for example, web document classification, software plagiarism detection, and protein structure detection [1–3].

With the rapid development of Internet, huge amounts of graph data emerge every day. For example, the Linked Open Data Project, which aims to connect data across the Web, has published 149 billion triples until 2017 [4]. In addition, real-world graphs are dynamic [5]. It is often cost-prohibitive to recompute matches starting from scratch when G or P is updated. An incremental matching algorithm is needed, which aims to minimize unnecessary recomputation by analyzing and computing the changes of matching result in response to updates ΔG (resp., ΔP) to G (resp., P).

For example, Figure 1(a) is a pattern graph P and Figure 1(b) is a data graph G. The subgraph which is composed of A_1, B_1, C_1, D_1, E_1, and the edges between them (for simplicity, denoted as $\{A_1, B_1, C_1, D_1, E_1\}$) is the only matching subgraph. Assuming that (B, E) and (C, D) are

removed from the pattern graph, the traditional recomputing algorithm will compute the matches for the new pattern graph on the whole data graph. It is time consuming. The incremental algorithm will just check a part of nodes in G, that is, B_2, B_3, C_2, C_3, A_2, and A_3, and add new matching subgraphs ($\{A_2, B_2, C_2, D_2, E_2\}$, $\{A_3, B_3, C_3, D_3, E_3\}$) to the original matching result.

At present, the study of incremental graph pattern matching is still in its infancy and existing work [6–12] mainly focuses on the updates of data graphs. In our previous study, we proposed an incremental graph matching algorithm named PGC_IncGPM, which can be used in scenarios where data graphs are constant and pattern graphs are updated [13]. PGC_IncGPM can effectively reduce the runtime of graph matching as long as the number of changed edges is less than the number of unchanged edges in P. However, the improvement effect of PGC_IncGPM gradually decreases as the number of changed edges increases. In this paper, the bottleneck of PGC_IncGPM is further analyzed. An optimization method of nodes' matching state detection sequence is proposed, and a more efficient algorithm called iDeltaP_IncGPM is designed and implemented.

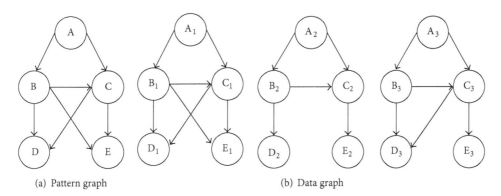

(a) Pattern graph   (b) Data graph

FIGURE 1: An example of incremental graph pattern matching.

Using Figure 1 as an example, suppose (B, E) and (C, D) are deleted from the pattern graph. PGC_IncGPM algorithm will first consider the deletion of (B, E), that is, checking B_2, A_2, B_3, and A_3, and then consider the deletion of (C, D), that is, checking C_2, B_2, A_2, C_3, B_3, and A_3. Thus B_2, A_2, B_3, and A_3 are all checked twice. iDeltaP_IncGPM considers the two deletions together; C_2, B_2, A_2, C_3, B_3, and A_3 are all checked only once.

The remainder of this paper is organized as follows. In Section 2, related work is reviewed. The model and definition are described in Section 3. In Section 4, our algorithm is presented. Section 5 is experimental results and comparison, and Section 6 presents the conclusion.

2. Related Work

We surveyed related work in two categories: graph pattern matching models and incremental algorithms for graph matching on massive graphs.

Graph pattern matching is typically defined in terms of subgraph isomorphism [14, 15]. However, subgraph isomorphism is an NP-complete problem [16]. In addition, subgraph isomorphism is often too restrictive because it requires that the matching subgraphs have exactly the same topology as the pattern graph. These hinder its applicability in emerging applications such as social networks and crime detection. Thus, graph simulation [17] and its extensions [18–22] are adopted for pattern matching. Graph simulation preserves the labels and the child relationship of a graph pattern in its match. In practical applications, graph simulation is so loosely that it may produce a large number of useless matches, which can flood useful information. Dual simulation [18] enhances graph simulation by imposing an additional condition, to preserve both child and parent relationships (downward and upward mappings). Due to the good balance and high practical value of dual simulation in response time and effectiveness, graph pattern matching is defined as dual simulation in this paper.

At present, the study of incremental graph pattern matching is still in its infancy; existing work [6–12] mainly focuses on the updates of data graphs. Fan et al. proposed the incremental graph simulation algorithm IncMatch [6, 7]. Sun et al. studied the Maximal Clique Enumeration problem on

dynamic graph [8]. Stotz et al. studied incremental inexact subgraph isomorphic problem [9]. Wang and Chen proposed an incremental approximation graph matching algorithm, which transformed the approximate subgraph search into vector space relation detection [10]. When inserting or deleting on the data graph, the vectors of relevant nodes are modified and whether the new vectors still contain the vector of the pattern graph is rechecked. Choudhury et al. developed a fast matching system StreamWorks for dynamic graphs [11]. The system can real-time detect suspicious pattern graphs and early warn high-risk data transfer modes on constantly updated network graphs. Semertzidis and Pitoura proposed an approach to find the most durable matches of an input graph pattern on graphs that evolve over time [12]. In [13], an incremental graph matching algorithm was proposed for updates of pattern graphs.

In big data era [23], graph computing is widely used in different fields such as social networks [24], sensor networks [25, 26], internet-of-things [27, 28], and cellular networks [29]. Therefore, there is urgent demand for improving the performance of big graph processing, especially graph pattern matching.

3. Model and Definition

For graph pattern matching, pattern graphs and data graphs are directed graphs with labels. Each node in graphs has a unique label, which defines the attitude of the node (such as keywords, skills, class, name, and company).

Definition 1 (graph). A node-labeled directed graph (or simply a graph) is defined as $G = (V, E, L)$, where V is a finite set of nodes, $E \subseteq V \times V$ is a finite set of edges, and L is a function that map each node u in V to a label $L(u)$; that is, $L(u)$ is the attribute of u.

Definition 2 (graph pattern matching). Given a pattern graph $P = (V_p, E_p, L_p)$ and a data graph $G = (V, E, L)$, P matches Q if there is a binary relation $R \subseteq V_p \times V$, such that

(1) if $(u, v) \in R$, then $L_p(u) = L(v)$;

(2) $\forall u \in V_p$, there exists a node v in G such that $(u, v) \in R$ and (a) $\forall (u, u') \in E_p$, there exists an edge $(v, v') \in E$

such that $(u', v') \in R$; (b) $\forall (u'', u) \in E_p$, there exists an edge $(v'', v) \in E$ such that $(u'', v'') \in R$.

Condition (2)(a) ensures that the matching node v keeps the child relationship of u; condition (2)(b) ensures that v maintains the parent relationship of u.

For any P and G, there exists a unique maximum matching relation R_M. Graph pattern matching is to find R_M, and the result graph G_r is a subgraph of G that can represent R_M.

Considering a real-life example, a recruiter wants to find a professional software development team from social network. Figure 2(a) is the basic organization graph of a software development team. The team consists of the following staffs with identity: project manager (PM), database engineer (DB), software architecture (SA), business process analyst (BA), user interface designers (UD), software developer (SD), and software tester (ST). Each node in the graph represents a person, and the label of node means the identity of person. The edge from node A to node B means that B works well under the supervision of A. A social network is shown in Figure 2(b). In this example, R_M is {(DB, DB$_1$), (PM, PM$_1$), (SA, SA$_1$), (BA, BA$_1$), (UD, UD$_1$), (SD, SD$_1$), (SD, SD$_2$), (ST, ST$_1$), (ST, ST$_2$)}. Because BA$_2$ does not have a child matching UD and SA$_2$ does not have a parent matching DB, PM$_2$ does not keep the child relationship of PM. For the same reason, SD$_3$ (resp. ST$_3$) does not match SD (resp. ST).

Definition 3 (incremental graph pattern matching for pattern graph changing). Given a data graph G and a pattern graph P, the matching result in G for P is $M(P,G)$. Assuming that P changes ΔP, the new pattern graph is expressed as $P \oplus \Delta P$. As opposed to batch algorithms that recompute matches starting from scratch, an incremental graph matching algorithm aims to find changes of ΔM to $M(P,G)$ in response to ΔP such that $M(P \oplus \Delta P, G) = M(P,G) \oplus \Delta M$.

When ΔP is small, ΔM is usually small as well, and it is much less costly to compute than to recompute the entire set of matches. In other words, this suggests that we compute matches once on the entire graph via a batch-matching algorithm and then incrementally identify new matches in response to ΔP without paying the cost of the high complexity of graph pattern matching.

In order to get ΔM quickly, indexes can be prebuilt based on the selected data features of graphs to reduce the search space during incremental matching. The more indexes, the shorter the time to get ΔM and the larger the space to store indexes. For large-scale data graphs, both response time and storage cost are needed to be reduced. Considering the balance of storage cost and response time, in this paper, three kinds of sets generated in the process of graph matching are used as index. (1) First are candidate matching sets $cand(\cdot)$; for each node u in P, $cand(u)$ includes all the nodes in G which only have the same label with u. The nodes in $cand(\cdot)$ are called c-nodes. (2) The second are child matching sets $sim(\cdot)$; for each node u in P, $sim(u)$ includes all the nodes in G which preserve the child relationship of u. The nodes in $sim(\cdot)$ are called s-nodes. (3) The third are complete matching sets $mat(\cdot)$; for each node u in P, $mat(u)$ includes all the nodes in G which preserve both the child and parent relationship of u. The nodes in $mat(\cdot)$ are called m-nodes.

The symbols used in this paper are shown in Notions Section.

4. iDeltaP_IncGPM Algorithm

In this section, we propose the improved incremental graph pattern matching algorithm for pattern graph changing (ΔP).

4.1. The Idea of PGC_IncGPM Algorithm. The basic framework of PGC_IncGPM [13] is shown in Figure 3.

The graph pattern matching algorithm (GPMS) is first performed on the entire data graph G for the pattern graph P. It computes the matching result graph G_r and creates the index needed for subsequent incremental matching. ΔP may include edge insertions (E^+) and edge deletions (E^-). Incremental graph pattern matching algorithm PGC_IncGPM first calls the subalgorithm AddEdges for E^+ to get G_r' and $index'$ and then calls the subalgorithm SubEdges for E^- to get G_r'' and $index''$. G_r'' is the new matching result $M(P \oplus \Delta P, G)$, and $index''$ is the new index that can be used for subsequent incremental matching if the pattern graph changes again.

Edge insertions (resp., edge deletions) in ΔP are processed one by one by AddEdges (resp., SubEdges). For example, when deleting multiple edges from P, the processing of PGC_IncGPM is as follows.

In the first step, the following operations are performed for each deleted edge (u, u'): for each $v \in cand(u)$, whether v keeps the child relationship of u in $P \oplus \Delta P$ is checked. If v keeps the child relationship of u, then v is removed from $cand(u)$ to $sim(u)$ and the parents of v in $cand(\cdot)$ are also processed.

In the second step, each node in $sim(\cdot)$ is repeatedly filtered according to its parents and children; the new generated m-nodes are added to $mat(\cdot)$.

In the first step, when deleting (u, u') from P, some nodes in $cand(u)$ and $cand(u'')$ (u'' is an ancestor of u) may change from c-nodes to s-nodes. So when a c-node becomes an s-node, a bottom-up approach is used to find its parents and ancestors from $cand(\cdot)$. If (u_1, u_1') and (u_2, u_2') are deleted, and u_1 and u_2 have a common ancestor u', then $cand(u')$ will be visited twice. In summary, there is a bottleneck of PGC_IncGPM for multiple deleted edges. There is the same problem for multiple inserted edges.

4.2. Optimization for Matching State Detection Sequence. Since PGC_IncGPM deals with edge insertions (resp., deletions) one by one, the efficiency of it gradually decreases as the number of changed edges increases. To overcome the bottleneck of PGC_IncGPM, multiple edge insertions (resp., deletions) should be considered together. In this paper, the optimization method for nodes' matching state detection sequence is proposed. The optimization can be applied to both insertions and deletions on P.

Taking SubEdges as an example, the optimization method is as follows.

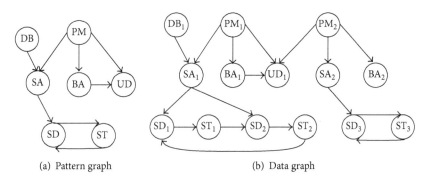

FIGURE 2: An example of graph pattern matching.

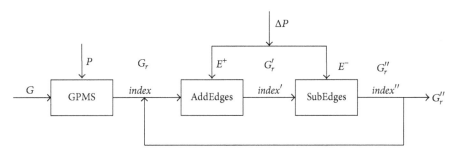

FIGURE 3: Basic framework of PGC_IncGPM algorithm.

First, analyze all edges deleted from P to determine which nodes' candidate matching sets may change. If $cand(u)$ may change, then u is added to $filtorder^-$ set.

Secondly, $filtorder^-$ is sorted by the inverse topological sequence of P. There may be some strong connected components in P. In this case, we first find out all the strong connected components in P and, then, converge each strong connected component into a node to get a directed acyclic graph P' and find the inverse topological sequence of P'; finally, we replace the strong connected component convergence node with the original node set. Thus, the approximate inverse topological sequence of P is obtained.

Finally, for each u in $filtorder^-$, $cand(u)$ is processed in turn. Depending on whether there is a deleted edge from u, two different filtering methods are used: (1) if u has at least one out-edge to be deleted, then each node in $cand(u)$ is likely to keep the child relationship of u now. So whether they keep the child relationship of u should be checked; (2) if u does not have an out-edge be deleted, then only part of the nodes in $cand(u)$ are needed to be checked. That is, a node in $cand(u)$ will be checked only if it has at least one child which changes from c-node to s-node.

The visited times of some candidate matching sets can be reduced through the above optimization.

4.3. iDeltaP_IncGPM Algorithm. Based on the optimization method proposed in Section 4.2, iDeltaP_IncGPM is proposed. It uses the optimized method for both multiple inserted edges and multiple deleted edges. The optimization algorithm for edge deletions is shown in Algorithm 1. In Algorithm 1, $nodes^-$ contains all the nodes which have out-edge deleted. For a node u in P, if the changes of P may

result in some nodes in $cand(u)$ becoming s-nodes, then $u \in filtorder^-$. $Filtorder^-$ is sorted by the inverse topological sequence of P (lines (1)–(5)). If u has an out-edge removed, that is, $u \in nodes^-$, then all the nodes in $cand(u)$ need to be checked whether they keep the child relationship of u (lines (7)–(12)). If $u \in filtorder^-$ and u is not in $nodes^-$, then only part of nodes in $cand(u)$ are checked. That is, if w has a child w' and w' is moved from $cand(u')$ to $sim(u')$ ($w' \in snew(u')$), then whether w is still an s-node will be checked (lines (14)–(20)).

Here we use an example to illustrate the implementation process of PGC_IncGPM and iDeltaP_IncGPM. The pattern graph P is shown in Figure 4, assuming that (E, H), (G, I), and (C, G) are deleted from P.

The process of PGC_IncGPM is as follows. (1) the deletion of (E, H) is processed, and each w in $cand(E)$ is checked whether it keeps the child relationship of u in $P \oplus \Delta P$. If w keeps the child relationship of u, then its parents founded from $cand(B)$ (resp., $cand(C)$) are checked. If these nodes keep the child relationship of B (resp., C), then they are removed to $sim(B)$ (resp., $sim(C)$). After that, their parents founded from $cand(A)$ are checked; (2) the deletion of (G, I) is processed, and the nodes in $cand(G)$, $cand(C)$, $cand(D)$, and $cand(A)$ are checked in turn; (3) the deletion of (C, G) is processed, and the nodes in $cand(C)$ and $cand(A)$ are checked in turn. From the above steps, it can be seen that $cand(C)$ and $cand(A)$ are visited three times, $cand(G)$, $cand(D)$, $cand(E)$, and $cand(B)$ are visited once.

The process of iDeltaP_IncGPM is as follows: because of the deletion of (E, H), (G, I), and (C, G), some nodes in $cand(E)$, $cand(G)$, $cand(C)$, $cand(B)$, $cand(D)$, and $cand(A)$ may become s-nodes. The nodes in $cand(\cdot)$ are checked by

(1) $nodes^- = \Phi$; $filtorder^- = \Phi$;
(2)   **for** each deleted edge $e = (u, u')$ **do**
(3) $nodes^- = nodes^- \cup \{u\}$;
(4) $filtorder^- = filtorder^- \cup \{u$ and all ancestor nodes of $u\}$;
(5)   sort $filtorder^-$ according to the inverse topological of P;
(6)   **for** each node u in $filtorder^-$ **do**
(7)   **if** $u \in nodes^-$ **then**
(8)   **for** each $w \in cand(u)$ **do**
(9)   check if w keeps the child relationship of u;
(10)   **if** w keeps the child relationship of u **then**
(11) $sim(u) = sim(u) \cup \{w\}$; $cand(u) = cand(u)\backslash\{w\}$;
(12) $snew(u) = snew(u) \cup \{w\}$;
(13)   **else**
(14)   **for** each $w \in cand(u)$ **do**
(15)   **if** there exist w' which is a child of w such that $(u, u') \in E_p$, $w' \in snew(u')$ **then**
(16)   check if w keeps the child relationship of u;
(17)   **if** w keeps the child relationship of u **then**
(18) $sim(u) = sim(u) \cup \{w\}$;
(19) $cand(u) = cand(u)\backslash\{w\}$;
(20) $snew(u) = snew(u) \cup \{w\}$;
(21) repeatly filter $sim(\cdot)$ according to the parent and child relationships of nodes in the
      subgraph constructed by $sim(\cdot)$ to get added $mat(\cdot)$ and updated $sim(\cdot)$ and $cand(\cdot)$;

ALGORITHM 1: iDeltaP_IncGPM for edge deletions.

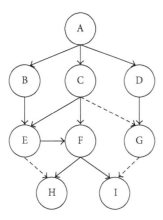

FIGURE 4: An example for pattern graph changing.

the order $\{G, E, D, C, B, A\}$. That is, the nodes in $cand(G)$ are checked first, and the nodes in $cand(A)$ are checked at last. E, G, and C all have out-edges deleted, so all the nodes in their candidate matching sets are checked. For the nodes in $cand(B)$, $cand(D)$, and $cand(A)$, only if they have a child changing from c-node to s-node, they will be checked. Therefore, $cand(C)$, $cand(D)$, $cand(A)$, $cand(G)$, $cand(E)$, and $cand(B)$ are only visited once. In other words, the optimized scheme reduces the visited times of $cand(\cdot)$.

For multiple edges inserted to the pattern graph, the similar optimization method is adopted. $nodes^+$ contains all the source nodes of inserted edges. If some nodes in $sim(u)$ may become c-nodes because of edge insertions, then u is in $filtorder^+$. $filtorder^+$ is ordered by the reverse topological sequence of the pattern graph. $nodes^+$ and $filtorder^+$ are used to reduce the visited times of $sim(\cdot)$ and $mat(\cdot)$.

5. Experiments and Results Analysis

The following experiments evaluate our proposed algorithm. Runtime is used as a key assessment of algorithms. In addition, in order to show the effectiveness of incremental algorithms visually, improvement ratio (IR) is proposed, which is the ratio of runtime saved by incremental matching algorithms to the runtime of ReComputing algorithm. Two real data sets (Epinions and Slashdot [30]) are used for experiments. The former is a trust network with 75879 nodes and 508837 edges. The latter is a social network with 82168 nodes and 948464 edges. In previous work, we experimented with normal size and large size pattern graphs, respectively, and the results show that the complexity and effectiveness of incremental matching algorithm are not affected by the size of pattern graph. Therefore, in this paper, by default, the number of nodes in P ($|V_p|$) is 9, the original number of edges in P ($|E_p|$) is 8 (resp., 16) for insertions (resp., deletions) and 9 for both insertions and deletions.

In order to evaluate the improvement of our proposed algorithm, iDeltaP_IncGPM, PGC_IncGPM, and ReComputing are all performed on Epinions and Slashdot under different settings. Each experiment was performed 5 times with different pattern graphs, and the average results are reported here. The experimental results are shown in Figure 5. The histogram represents the runtime of algorithm, and the line chart represents the improvement ratio of iDeltaP_IncGPM and PGC_IncGPM to ReComputing.

Figure 5(a) (resp., Figure 5(b)) shows the runtime of three algorithms over Epinions (resp., Slashdot) for insertions on pattern graphs. The X-axis represents the number of insertions on P, "+2" represents that two edges are inserted to P, "+4" represents four edges are inserted

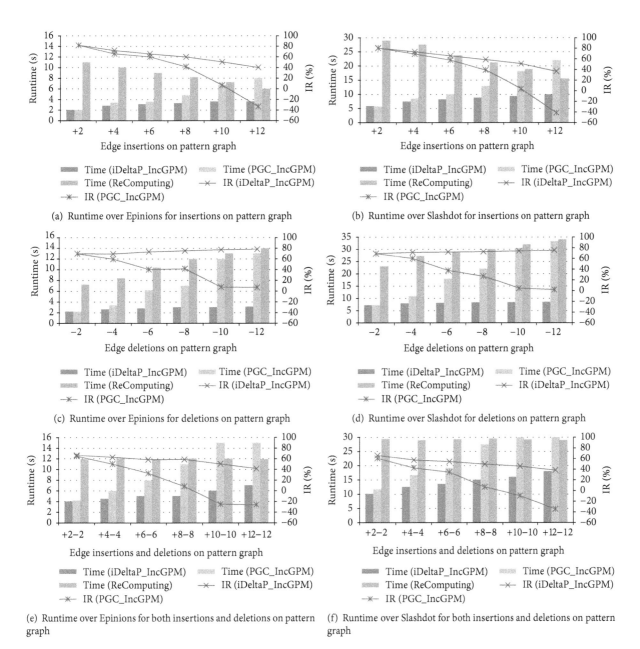

FIGURE 5: The runtime of different algorithms when pattern graph changed.

to P, and so on. The figure tells us the following: (a) when insertions are no more than 10, the runtime of PGC_IncGPM and iDeltaP_IncGPM is significantly shorter than that of ReComputing, and iDeltaP_IncGPM has the shortest runtime; (b) when insertions are 12 (new inserted edges account for 60% of the edges in $P \oplus \Delta P$), the runtime of PGC_IncGPM is longer than that of ReComputing, while iDeltaP_IncGPM still gets the shortest runtime; (c) the improvement ratio of iDeltaP_IncGPM and PGC_IncGPM decreases with the increase of edge insertion, but the decrease of iDeltaP_IncGPM is smaller. The more inserted edges, the better iDeltaP_IncGPM than PGC_IncGPM. When 12 edges are inserted to P, the IR of iDeltaP_IncGPM is 40% on average, and the IR of PGC_IncGPM is 33% on average. Therefore, iDeltaP_IncGPM is better than PGC_IncGPM. The

reason is that PGC_IncGPM processes the inserted edges one by one. Therefore, as insertion increases, its runtime grows almost linearly. However, iDeltaP_IncGPM integrates all the inserted edges, analyzes which matching sets are affected, and processes them in the appropriate order. This will prevent some matching sets to be processed repeatedly, which will shorten the running time.

Figure 5(c) (resp., Figure 5(d)) shows the runtime of three algorithms over Epionions (resp., Slashdot) for deletions on pattern graph. The X-axis represents the number of deletions on P, "−2" represents that two edges are deleted from P, "−4" represents four edges are deleted from P, and so on. It can be seen that (a) when deletion changes from 2 to 12, the runtime of all three algorithms increases, and iDeltaP_IncGPM always has the shortest runtime; (b) as the deletion increases, the IR of PGC_IncGPM decreases and the IR of iDeltaP_IncGPM slowly increases. For 12 deletions, the IR of PGC_IncGPM decreases to 7% on average, while the IR of iDeltaP_IncGPM increases to 78% on average. The reason is that as the deletion increases, the runtime of ReComputing increases dramatically, while the runtime of iDeltaP_IncGPM increases a little. iDeltaP_IncGPM is better than PGC_IncGPM because it compositely processes deleted edges and its runtime does not increase linearly as the number of deleted edges increases.

Figure 5(e) (resp., Figure 5(f)) shows the runtime of three algorithms over Epionions (resp., Slashdot) for both insertions and deletions on pattern graph. The X-axis represents the number of insertions and deletions on P, "+2−2" means that two edges are inserted to P and the other two edges are removed from P, and so on. As shown in the figure, iDeltaP_IncGPM always has shorter runtime than others do.

In conclusion, iDeltaP_IncGPM effectively improves the efficiency of PGC_IncGPM through the optimization strategy. For the same ΔP, the runtime of iDeltaP_IncGPM is shorter, and as $|\Delta P|$ increases, the runtime increases less; the decrease of IR is also more moderate. Therefore, iDeltaP_IncGPM can be applied to larger changes of the pattern graph, and it has a wider range of applications.

6. Conclusion

In this paper, we analyze PGC_IncGPM to find its efficiency bottleneck and propose a more efficient incremental matching algorithm iDeltaP_IncGPM. Multiple insertions (resp., deletions) are considered together and the optimization method for nodes' matching state detection sequence is used. Experimental results on real data sets show that iDeltaP_IncGPM has higher efficiency and wider application range than PGC_IncGPM.

Next, we will study the distributed incremental graph matching algorithm. Real-life graphs grow rapidly in size and hyper-massive data graphs cannot be centrally stored in one data center and need to be distributed across multiple data centers. It is very worthy studying how to make efficient incremental matching on distributed large graphs.

Notations

P/G: Pattern graph/data graph
u/u': Nodes in P
v/v': Nodes in G
ΔP: Changes of P
ΔG: Changes of G
$P \oplus \Delta P$: New pattern graph
$cand(u)$: Nodes in G that have same label with u but do not keep child relationship of u
$sim(u)$: Nodes in G that only keep child relationship of u
$mat(u)$: Nodes in G that keep child and parent relationships of u
index: The sets including $cand(u)$, $sim(u)$ and $mat(u)$

$c/s/m$-node: v in G such that
$v \in cand(u)/sim(u)/mat(u)$
$M(P, G)$: The maximum match in G for P
Gr: The result graph, a subgraph represents $M(P, G)$.

Conflicts of Interest

The authors declare that there are no conflicts of interest regarding the publication of this paper.

References

[1] X. Ren and J. Wang, "Multi-query optimization for subgraph isomorphism search," *Proceedings of the VLDB Endowment*, vol. 10, no. 3, pp. 121–132, 2016.

[2] Z. Yang, A. W.-C. Fu, and R. Liu, "Diversified top-k subgraph querying in a large graph," in *Proceedings of the 2016 ACM SIGMOD International Conference on Management of Data, SIGMOD 2016*, pp. 1167–1182, USA, July 2016.

[3] J. Gao, B. Song, W. Ke, and X. Hu, "BalanceAli: Multiple PPI Network Alignment With Balanced High Coverage and Consistency," *IEEE Transactions on NanoBioscience*, vol. 16, no. 5, pp. 333–340, 2017.

[4] A. Jentzsch, "Linked Open Data Cloud," in *Linked Enterprise Data*, X.media.press, pp. 209–219, Springer Berlin Heidelberg, Berlin, Heidelberg, 2014.

[5] Y. Hao, G. Li, P. Yuan, H. Jin, and X. Ding, "An Association-Oriented Partitioning Approach for Streaming Graph Query," *Scientific Programming*, vol. 2017, pp. 1–11, 2017.

[6] W. Fan, J. Li, J. Luo, Z. Tan, X. Wang, and Y. Wu, "Incremental graph pattern matching," in *Proceedings of ACM SIGMOD and 30th PODS 2011 Conference*, pp. 925–936, Greece, June 2011.

[7] W. Fan, C. Hu, and C. Tian, "Incremental Graph Computations," in *Proceedings of ACM International Conference*, pp. 155–169, Chicago, Illinois, USA, May 2017.

[8] S. Sun, Y. Wang, W. Liao, and W. Wang, "Mining Maximal Cliques on Dynamic Graphs Efficiently by Local Strategies," in *Proceedings of IEEE 33rd International Conference on Data Engineering (ICDE)*, pp. 115–118, San Diego, CA, USA, April 2017.

[9] A. Stotz, R. Nagi, and M. Sudit, "Incremental graph matching for situation awareness," in *Proceedings of 12th International Conference on Information Fusion, FUSION 2009*, pp. 452–459, usa, July 2009.

[10] C. Wang and L. Chen, "Continuous subgraph pattern search over graph streams," in *Proceedings of the 25th IEEE International Conference on Data Engineering, ICDE 2009*, pp. 393–404, China, April 2009.

[11] S. Choudhury, L. Holder, G. Chin, A. Ray, S. Beus, and J. Feo, "Streamworks - A system for dynamic graph search," in *Proceedings of ACM SIGMOD Conference on Management of Data, SIGMOD 2013*, pp. 1101–1104, USA, June 2013.

[12] K. Semertzidis and E. Pitoura, "Durable Graph Pattern Queries on Historical Graphs," in *Proceedings of International Conference on Data Engineering*, pp. 541–552, October 2016.

[13] L. X. Zhang, W. P. Wang, J. L. Gao, and J. X. Wang, "Pattern graph change oriented incremental graph pattern matching," *Journal of Software. Ruanjian Xuebao*, vol. 26, no. 11, pp. 2964–2980, 2015.

[14] X. Ren and J. Wang, "Exploiting Vertex Relationships in Speeding up Subgraph Isomorphism over Large Graphs," in *Proceedings of the 3rd Workshop on Spatio-Temporal Database Management, Co-located with the 32nd International Conference on Very Large Data Bases, VLDB 2006*, pp. 617–628, kor, September 2006.

[15] F. Bi, L. Chang, X. Lin, L. Qin, and W. Zhang, "Efficient subgraph matching by postponing Cartesian products," in *Proceedings of ACM SIGMOD International Conference on Management of Data*, pp. 1199–1214, USA, July 2016.

[16] J. R. Ullmann, "An algorithm for subgraph isomorphism," *Journal of the ACM*, vol. 23, no. 1, pp. 31–42, 1976.

[17] W. Fan, J. Li, S. Ma, N. Tang, Y. Wu, and Y. Wu, "Graph pattern matching," *Proceedings of the VLDB Endowment*, vol. 3, no. 1-2, pp. 264–275, 2010.

[18] W. Fan, "Graph pattern matching revised for social network analysis," in *Proceedings of the 15th International Conference on Database Theory, ICDT 2012*, pp. 8–21, deu, March 2012.

[19] J. Gao, Q. Ping, and J. Wang, "Resisting re-identification mining on social graph data," *World Wide Web-Internet and Web Information Systems*, 2017.

[20] S. Ma, Y. Cao, W. Fan, J. Huai, and T. Wo, "Capturing topology in graph pattern matching," *Proceedings of the VLDB Endowment*, vol. 5, no. 4, pp. 310–321, 2011.

[21] A. Fard, M. U. Nisar, L. Ramaswamy, J. A. Miller, and M. Saltz, "A distributed vertex-centric approach for pattern matching in massive graphs," in *Proceedings of IEEE International Conference on Big Data, Big Data 2013*, pp. 403–411, USA, October 2013.

[22] Y. Liang and P. Zhao, "Similarity Search in Graph Databases: A Multi-Layered Indexing Approach," in *Proceedings of IEEE 33rd International Conference on Data Engineering (ICDE)*, pp. 783–794, San Diego, CA, USA, April 2017.

[23] X. Liu, Y. Liu, H. Song, and A. Liu, "Big Data Orchestration as a Service Network," *IEEE Communications Magazine*, vol. 55, no. 9, pp. 94–101, 2017.

[24] J. Gao, J. Wang, J. He, and F. Yan, "Against Signed Graph Deanonymization Attacks on Social Networks," *International Journal of Parallel Programming*.

[25] Q. Zhang and A. Liu, "An unequal redundancy level-based mechanism for reliable data collection in wireless sensor networks," *EURASIP Journal on Wireless Communications and Networking*, vol. 2016, article 258, 2016.

[26] J. Gao, J. Wang, P. Zhong, and H. Wang, "On Threshold-Free Error Detection for Industrial Wireless Sensor Networks," *IEEE Transactions on Industrial Informatics*, pp. 1–11.

[27] Y. Xu, A. Liu, and C. Changqin, "Delay-aware program codes dissemination scheme in internet of everything, mobile information systems," *Mobile Information Systems*, vol. 2016, Article ID 2436074, 18 pages, 2016.

[28] X. Liu, S. Zhao, A. Liu, N. Xiong, and A. V. Vasilakos, "Knowledge-aware Proactive Nodes Selection approach for energy management in Internet of Things," *Future Generation Computer Systems*, 2017.

[29] K. Zhou, J. Gui, and N. Xiong, "Improving cellular downlink throughput by multi-hop relay-assisted outband D2D communications," *EURASIP Journal on Wireless Communications and Networking*, vol. 2017, no. 1, 2017.

[30] Stanford Large Network Dataset Collection, http://snap.stanford.edu/data/index.html.

13

Feature Reduction Based on Hybrid Efficient Weighted Gene Genetic Algorithms with Artificial Neural Network for Machine Learning Problems in the Big Data

Tareq Abed Mohammed [ID],[1,2] Shaymaa Alhayali [ID],[1] Oguz Bayat,[1] and Osman N. Uçan[1]

[1]Altinbas University, College of Engineering, Istanbul, Turkey
[2]Kirkuk University, College of Science, Kirkuk, Iraq

Correspondence should be addressed to Tareq Abed Mohammed; tareq.mohammed@altinbas.edu.tr

Academic Editor: Marco Aldinucci

A large amount of data being generated from different sources and the analyzing and extracting of useful information from these data becomes a very complex task. The difficulty of dealing with big data arises from many factors such as the high number of features, existence of lost data, and variety of data. One of the most effective solutions that used to overcome the huge amount of big data is the feature reduction process. In this paper, a set of hybrid and efficient algorithms are proposed to classify the datasets that have large feature size by merging the genetic algorithms with the artificial neural networks. The genetic algorithms are used as a prestep to significantly reduce the feature size of the analyzed data before handling that data using machine learning techniques. Reducing the number of features simplifies the task of classifying the analyzed data and enhances the performance of the machine learning algorithms that are used to extract valuable information from big data. The proposed algorithms use a new gene-weight mechanism that can significantly enhance the performance and decrease the required search time. The proposed algorithms are applied on different datasets to pick the most relative and important features before applying the artificial neural networks algorithm, and the results show that our proposed algorithms can effectively enhance the classifying performance over the tested datasets.

1. Introduction

In recent years, the major increase in the amount of generated data makes it very important to develop new robust and scalable tools that are able to extract the hidden knowledge and information from the big datasets [1]. When the dataset that we are dealing with has a massive volume of data and includes both structured and unstructured data, it is called a big data [2, 3]. The big data becomes a specific and separated field in computer engineering society since it is difficult to be processed using the traditional database and software techniques. Big data has other different specific properties, such as the velocity which refers to the speed at which data are being generated, the variety which means the existence of structured and unstructured data, and the variability which means the inconsistencies of the data. The main objective of big data is to help people and companies to improve their operations and make faster and more intelligent decisions. Recently, the big data technologies have received increasing attention from researchers and companies, and many conferences and journal special sessions are established to discuss their issues and characteristics [4, 5].

One of the most critical problems of big data is the degrading of the performance of the machine learning and data mining algorithms when dealing with such large amount of data [6]. This can happen because of many factors such as the existence of a large number of features, the existence of lost data, and the high computations of traditional machine learning and data mining algorithms which makes them unsuitable to efficiently deal with large datasets. Several new classification techniques are proposed to overcome the challenges of big data which can classify the big data according to the data format during the processing and the type of classification required. Most of the proposed classification methods are based on the specific selected applications and may not give good results if it is applied to other big data applications [7]. In order to classify the data efficiently, usually a convenient algorithm is needed to extract the relevant information from a large amount of data as a prestep and then the classification algorithm can be applied [8, 9]. Two main approaches are used to reduce the available data before applying the classification algorithms which are filtering the data and feature reduction. In this paper, we will concentrate on the feature reduction methods which identify the most important features (rather than using all of them) only and use them in next classification steps.

The classification process can be defined as a method for identifying the category or the class (it should be two or more classes) of a certain piece of data based on a system that was trained using data whose class is known. In the real world, there are classification problems everywhere, and we can find hundreds or thousands of real-world classification problems [6, 10]. In the classification of big data problems, the feature selection is very important since it addresses the problem of large dimension by choosing only the most relevant features that can lead to correct classification. The process of eliminating the irrelevant and redundant features is called feature reduction or feature selection, and it has many advantages such as reduced training time, decreased complexity of the learned classifiers, and enhanced performance of the classification results. Although the feature selection algorithms are used before the classification run, it is very important and can significantly affect the results of the classification; this is because the existence of redundant and irrelevant features may cause the build of the incorrect classification system during the training process.

In this paper, three efficient genetic algorithms are proposed to pick the relative and important features before applying the artificial neural networks algorithm. The proposed algorithms use the new mechanism which is the weight-based correction for each feature, which can guide the searching process quickly to optimal solutions. The results show that our proposed algorithms can effectively enhance the classifying performance over the tested datasets.

This paper is organized as follows. Section 2 reviews the related work regarding the methods used to enhance the data mining algorithms when applied on big datasets. In Sections 3, 4, and 5, we present and explain our algorithms to enhance the artificial neural networks to be able to deal with large feature datasets and discussion of datasets. The experiments and the discussions are given in Section 6. Section 7 concludes the paper.

2. Related Work

By reviewing the literature, it can be noted that the feature selection algorithms gain increasing interest, especially in the big data fields. In this section, we will summarize the research work on the feature selection problem and try to list the most important algorithms that are proposed to address this problem. Feature selection can be used with many machine learning algorithms such as regression, clustering, and classification, whereas in this paper, we will concentrate only on the feature selection with classification.

In literature, the feature selection algorithms can be classified into two categories: filter methods and wrapper methods [11, 12]. The wrapper methods usually use the classification algorithm to measure the performance of the tested feature selection method. On the contrary, the filter feature selection algorithms are independent of any classification algorithm and use other scientific methods to measure the goodness of each feature. The filter-based feature selection methods are often less computationally expensive than the wrapper methods, since it does not need the run of the classification algorithm to test the considered method. However, the wrapper methods usually obtain better results and performance than the filter methods [13, 14].

One of the earliest works on feature selection is the usage of the greedy search methods such as sequential forward selection and sequential backward selection. In [15], the authors proposed a method of measurement selection to identify the best subset of features based on a forwarded selection technique. The used evaluation method uses a nonparametric estimation of the error probability given a finite sample set. The main advantage of this method is the direct and nonparametric evaluation of measurement subsets. On the contrary, the sequential backward selection proposed in [16] tried to develop a formal method to measure the effectiveness of a set of features or tests. The authors mainly consider the following question: "what constitutes an effective set of tests, and how is this effectiveness dependent on the correlations among, and the properties of, the individual tests in the set?" [16]. Unfortunately, both of forwarding selection and sequential backward selection methods suffer from a problem called the nesting effect, which happens as a result of removing or selecting a feature once only. This means that if a feature is removed in an early step, it cannot be used in next steps. To overcome this problem, another approach is proposed in [17] to merge the two methods together by applying the forward selection method one time and then follow it with multiple runs of the sequential backward selection method. Much other research works are proposed to enhance the performance of the forwarding selection and sequential backward selection methods by using the floating search methods as in sequential backward floating selection and sequential forward floating selection [18, 19].

In another work, Fan Mina, Qinghua Hub, and William Zhu proposed a feature selection algorithm that includes a test cost constraint problem [20]. The new algorithm uses the backtracking algorithm which is a well-known algorithm used to solve many specific optimization problems. The authors argued that the backtracking algorithm is convenient and efficient to be used to solve the feature selection problem on medium-sized data. In addition, another heuristic algorithm is developed to be used in parallel with the backtracking algorithm to make it more scalable and able to work on large datasets. The experimental results of this algorithm demonstrate that the developed heuristic algorithm can identify the optimal solution of the problem in many cases.

After the development of evolutionary computation algorithms (EC), many researchers tried to use these algorithms to solve the problem of feature selection. For example, in [21], the authors presented a genetic algorithm that is modified to consider the bounds of the generalization error in the support vector machines (SVMs). The proposed algorithm was compared to the other traditional algorithms and approved its validity when solving such feature selection problems. Oh et al. [22] proposed a new genetic algorithm by modifying the existing one to be more suitable for feature selection. The main objective of the new proposed algorithm is the hybridization of the local search operation and the genetic algorithm to make tuning for the search process. According to the authors, the hybridization process can produce a significant improvement in the final performance of the genetic algorithm.

Recently, some hybrid bioinspired heuristic approaches were proposed to reduce the feature size of the input data such as the work of Zawbaa et al. [23], whereas a hybrid algorithm is proposed to handle the large-dimensionality small-instance set feature selection problems. In [24], another algorithm is proposed to handle the feature selection problem using Levy Antlion optimization. The flower pollination algorithm [25] is used also in another research to make an attribute reduction after modifying it using new adaptive techniques to handle such problems.

The multiobjective evolutionary algorithms are also used to reduce the number of selected features. In [26], the authors presented the first research on multiobjective optimization particle swarm optimization to solve the feature selection problem using the particle swarm optimization (PSO). The algorithm works by generating a set of nondominated solutions to be considered as the candidates feature subsets. The authors investigated two multiobjective algorithms based on PSO. The first algorithm uses the nondominated sorting algorithm and PSO to where the second algorithm uses crowding distance, dominance relation, and mutation to search for the best solutions. The results of comparing the two proposed multiobjective algorithms with other feature selection algorithms show that the PSO multiobjective algorithms can significantly outperform the other algorithms and get better results. Recently, there were many other new algorithms that proposed to solve the feature selection problem using multiobjective evolutionary algorithms using different techniques [27–29].

3. Proposed Techniques

Feature selection problems become one of the most important problems in big data society. The main issue of such problems is the existence of large search space, which can be considered as NP-hard problems that cannot be solved until testing all the search space. Another issue in feature selection is the feature interaction problem which leads to the translation of some features from relevant to redundant or weakly features. On the contrary, some features become very important when combined with other features. The evolutionary computation (EC) algorithms have a very useful property that makes them the best choice to solve feature selection problems, which is it

does not require any domain knowledge or assumption about the search space to solve the feature selection problem. Another advantage of the EC algorithms is the process of evolving a set of solutions (called as the population in EC) which speeds up the process of converging to the optimal solutions. Therefore, our proposed algorithm to solve the feature selection problem involves the hybridization of both machine learning algorithms and evolutionary algorithms, as described in the rest of this section.

3.1. Main Steps of the Proposed Algorithm. Our proposed algorithm mainly merges the well-known artificial neural network (ANN) algorithm as a classification algorithm with a new and efficient evolutionary algorithm called the weighted gene genetic algorithm (WGGA). Figure 1 shows the main steps of the proposed algorithm. Firstly, the dataset is read and entered to be used in the process of generating a random set of features. After that, the generated feature sets are used to classify the dataset using the ANN algorithm. According to the results of classification, our proposed WGGA algorithm generates new sets of features that are a candidate to have a better performance. The evolving and optimization process is repeated many times until reaching the stop criteria. If the stop condition is not satisfied, the process of evaluating new feature sets is continuing to search for better solutions. The stop condition can be reaching a maximum number of iterations, reaching a predetermined performance value, or maybe a hybridization of both cases to avoid very long running time.

3.2. The Weighted Gene Genetic Algorithm (WGGA). In literature, there are many evolutionary algorithms proposed to solve several optimization problems. In this paper, a new efficient genetic algorithm is presented which was especially developed to handle the feature selection problem. We called it weighted gene genetic algorithm (WGGA), since it stores weight for each gene in order to enhance the convergence ability of the algorithm. Figure 2 summarizes the steps of the proposed algorithm.

The proposed weighted gene genetic algorithm (WGGA) uses the binary representation to encode the solutions. Therefore, each solution is represented by an array that has a size equal to the number of features in the dataset. Each feature is represented by one variable in the array, and value 1 indicates that this feature will be used in the classification process of the ANN, whereas value 0 indicates that it will not be included. Figure 3 shows an example of the encoding of two solutions when the number of features is equal to 10. In the first row of Figure 3, there are 10 elements in the array where 6 of them have a value of 1 and 4 have a value of 0, which indicates that the first, the third, the fourth, and the eighth features will not be used by this solution. In the second solution, the second and seventh features will only be excluded from the classification process.

In the first step, the WGGA algorithm initializes the population randomly and then the fitness function of each solution in the population is computed using the ANN algorithm. The fitness value of each solution is the

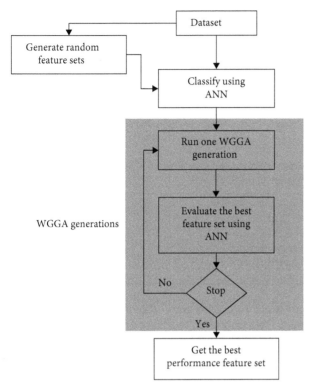

FIGURE 1: The main steps of the proposed algorithms to solve the feature selection problem.

classification accuracy of that feature set using the input dataset. It can be calculated using the following equation:

$$\text{Accuracy of ANN} = \frac{TP + TN}{TP + TN + FP + FN}, \quad (1)$$

where TP, TN, FP, and FN indicate the true positive, true negative, false positive, and false negative of the tested sample. The weight of each gene is also initialized by zero to be used in next steps.

Based on the evaluation of each solution, the best two solutions are selected to be used for the crossover operation. In this work, a one-point binary crossover is selected to be applied on the best two solutions. In this crossover, a point is randomly selected and then the tails of the two parents are swapped to generate the new off springs. Figure 4 shows an example of the one-point crossover.

In the mutation step, simply according to the mutation percent, a fixed number of genes are chosen and flagged for all population solutions. To ensure the validity of solutions, it is not allowed to be a solution with all genes equal to zero in the population. Therefore, in our algorithm after the crossover and mutation processes, the solutions are checked again and if a solution is found that has all genes are zeros then it is translated to become a gene with all genes equal to one.

Finally, another important step is carried out which is the correction of genes according to their weights. In each generation, the selected features for the best solution are used to increase the weights of that features. This process is accomplished by simply adding one for each selected feature of the best solution in each generation. After that, these stored data are used to correct the false change that may occur in the

Begin

Ds = ReadDataSet ()

Pop = InitializePop()   // initialize randomly the population

WghSolutions = Initialize(0)   // initialize the weights by zeros

While termination condition not satisfied **do**

.

Res = EvaluateANN(Pop)   // evaluate all solutions

Perf = ComputePerformance(Res)

Sol1 = FindFirstBestSol(Pop, Perf)

Sol2 = FindSecondBestSol(Pop, Perf)

WghSolutions = UpdateSolutionWeights(WghSolutions,Sol1)

// Crossover

   OnePointCrossover(Sol1,Sol2)

// Mutation

BinaryFlagMutation(Pop)

TestValidity(Pop)

If iteration > CC, **then**

        CorrectGenes(Pop, WghSolutions)

end

end //   while end

end //   Algorithm end

FIGURE 2: The main steps of the proposed weighted gene genetic algorithm (WGGA).

FIGURE 3: Two examples for binary encoding used in the WGGA algorithm.

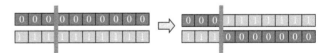

FIGURE 4: One-point crossover example that is used in the WGGA algorithm.

mutation and crossover processes. This process is carried out after the running of suitable number of generations to ensure the reliability and correctness of the collected information regarding the features. Therefore, it is carried out after CC number of generations as described in Figure 2. When this mechanism is applied, at the end of each generation, the witness weight of each feature is computed by dividing its value in the weighted array by the number of iteration that finished at that time, and the resulted value is compared with another two parameters called high parameter (HP) and low parameter (LP). For each gene (represents a feature), if its

TABLE 1: The properties of the selected datasets and their features and samples numbers.

Name of date set	Number of features	Number of samples	Description
Heart	13	270	Heart medical analysis
Lung cancer	56	32	Lung cancer analysis
WBCD	9	699	Breast cancer database
Phishing	30	11055	Phishing websites features
Messidor	19	1151	Messidor image set prediction
Sport articles	59	1000	Sports articles for objectivity analysis data set

weight value is greater than HP then it is directly assigned to a value of 1. On the contrary, if its weight value is less than LP, then it is directly assigned to a value of 0. Using this mechanism, the genetic algorithm can concentrate more on the weak or semiweak features, where the strong features are always selected. This process can significantly improve the performance of the feature selection process and decrease the search time as described in next section.

Regarding the computational cost of our proposed algorithm, it can be seen that it does not add any significant cost to the genetic algorithm. This is because our mechanism mainly depends on gathering information about the current population and storing it. Therefore, only an additional small memory is needed for the storing process, and the other used mechanisms have a very small cost which can be ignored. As all embedded feature selection algorithms, the proposed algorithm needs more time comparing with filter-based feature selection algorithms that are presented in literature.

4. Proposed Algorithms

In this section, the setting and results of the empirical experiments are presented to ensure the performance of the proposed algorithms. As mentioned in the previous section, three genetic algorithms are proposed and incorporated in our experiments as follows.

4.1. Low Weighted Gene Genetic Algorithm (LWGGA). This algorithm uses our proposed weight-based mechanism to exclude the weak features from the selected feature set if they have very low weights. In this case, the flagged features (continuously changing from one to zero or from zero to one) will mostly be out of the selected features after the run of the certain number of generations.

4.2. High Weighted Gene Genetic Algorithm (HWGGA). This algorithm uses our proposed weight-based mechanism to include the strong features always in the selected feature set if they have very high weights. In this case, the strong features (continuously being selected in the best solutions) will mostly be selected after the run of a certain number of generations.

4.3. Weighted Gene Genetic Algorithm (WGGA). This algorithm uses both of the low and high weighted mechanisms described in previous LWGGA and HWGGA algorithms. The merger of these two mechanisms makes the genetic

TABLE 2: The parameters used in the genetic algorithm of our proposed algorithms.

The parameter name	Used value
Size of population	10
Type of crossover	One point (0.7)
Type of mutation	Flagged (0.2)
Parents selection	Best two
Stop criteria	Number of generations

algorithm to concentrate on the important features which enhance the convergence ability of the algorithm and decreases the search time.

Another two algorithms are included in the experiments which are the artificial neural network (ANN) and the normal feature selection genetic algorithm merged with the ANN algorithm denoted as (GA + ANN).

5. Diseases Datasets

To investigate the performance of the proposed algorithms, six datasets from different sources and with different features are selected. Table 1 summarizes the features of the tested datasets. As the table shows, the datasets are selected from different fields and the number of features (attributes) is selected to be in different ranges to test our proposed algorithms using different levels [30].

(1) Heart medical analysis

(2) Lung cancer analysis

(3) Breast cancer database

(4) Phishing websites features

(5) Messidor image set prediction

(6) Sport articles

6. Results and Discussions of Experiments

We used the ANN algorithm with two hidden layers. In addition, validation and training techniques are used to ensure more efficient results. For all datasets, the percent of training is selected to be 40%, the validation percent is 30%, and the testing ratio is also 30%. The parameters that we used in the genetic algorithm in all algorithms are presented in Table 2. In the first experiment, we compared the performance of the five explained algorithms using the six datasets. In this experiment, a population size of 10 and iteration number of 40 are used for all algorithms. The results of this experiment are computed using Equation (1) and presented in Table 3.

TABLE 3: Classification performance comparison between the different proposed algorithms.

P = 10, it = 40	Heart	Lung cancer	WBCD	Phishing	Messidor	Sport articles
Num of features	13	56	9	30	19	59
ANN	0.837	0.250	0.969	0.919	0.686	0.823
GA + ANN	0.859	0.935	0.974	0.927	0.735	0.849
LWGGA + ANN	0.859	0.935	0.974	0.927	0.749	0.854
HWGGA + ANN	0.859	0.968	0.975	0.927	0.748	0.854
WGGA + ANN	0.8667	0.969	0.976	0.927	0.752	0.854

TABLE 4: The performance of the WGGA + ANN algorithm using different number of generations.

# of generations	Heart	Lung cancer	WBCD	Phishing	Messidor	Sport articles
1	0.837	0.250	0.969	0.919	0.686	0.635
10	0.866	0.912	0.972	0.927	0.735	0.826
20	0.867	0.937	0.972	0.927	0.738	0.849
40	0.870	0.969	0.976	0.927	0.752	0.849
60	0.870	0.969	0.976	0.927	0.752	0.851
80	0.870	0.969	0.976	0.927	0.752	0.854

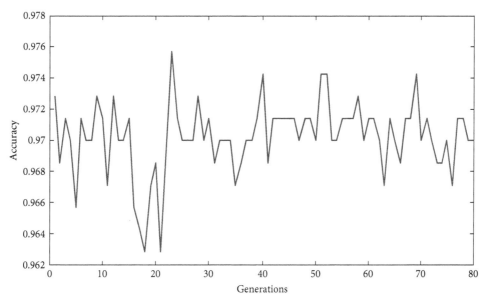

FIGURE 5: The accuracy of the WGGA algorithm for the WBCD dataset by running 80.

As the table shows, the proposed three algorithms significantly enhance the performance of the ANN algorithm. The best algorithm in all results is the WGGA, since it outperforms all other algorithms in four datasets and gets the same performance with other algorithms in one dataset. The second-best algorithm is the HWGGA algorithm which gets acceptable results in more than two datasets. The results of this table ensure the performance of our proposed weight-based genes mechanism which makes the genetic algorithm concentrates on the flagged features during the search and depends slightly on changing the strong features (which is included in all best solutions).

On the contrary, the other comparing algorithms try to find a better set of features by only randomly selecting different set of features, which get good results but needs long time. The proposed algorithms take some experiences from the first generations of the genetic algorithm, and then it uses these experiences to distinguish between the features that should be always included in the best feature set, the features that should always be excluded from the best feature set, and the feature that are not checked yet. According to this, the proposed algorithm can quickly converge to the best feature set by saving the efforts of searching on the already checked good and bad features and check the other features that are not known yet.

Moreover, the results show that the WGGA algorithm benefits from merging the two mechanisms of LWGGA and HWGGA algorithms which makes it the best algorithm. It is also important to note that the enhancement ratio is varying from one dataset to other; for example, in the Lung cancer dataset, the performance is enhanced very well (from 0.25 to

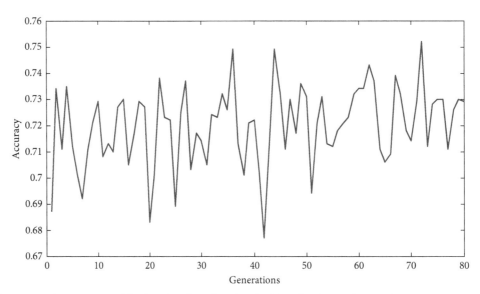

FIGURE 6: The accuracy of the WGGA algorithm for the Messidor dataset by running 80 generations.

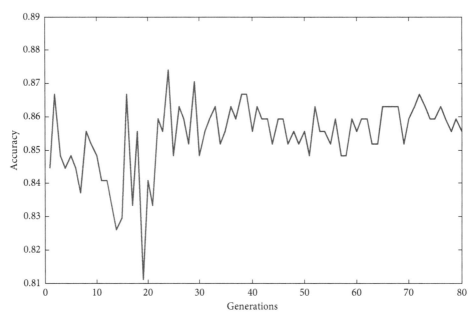

FIGURE 7: The accuracy of the WGGA algorithm for the WBCD dataset by running 80 generations.

0.969), whereas in the Phishing dataset, it only enhances by a small value (from 0.919 to 0.927).

In the second experiment, we will investigate the effect of increasing the number of generations on the performance of the WGGA algorithm. Five different generation numbers are used from 10 to 80, and the six datasets are tested again; the accuracy is computed using Equation (1). As the results of Table 4 show, the performance of the proposed algorithm can convergence fast, and the accuracy does not enhance significantly after 40 generations in most of the tested datasets. These results again ensure that the incorporated new mechanisms make the optimization process of the genetic algorithm very effective and reach the optimal solution quickly.

Figures 5–10 show the accuracy of the proposed algorithm WGGA for the six datasets when using 80 generations.

The figures show the best accuracy in each generation as computed from Equation (1). The figures again ensure the quick convergence of our proposed algorithm which is clear since the best value occurs usually before the 40th generation. We can also note that the algorithms can fluctuate between good and bad values during the evolving process. This means that the best solution in later steps may become worse than the best solution of earlier steps which first seems not good, where in fact it is a good aspect, since it gives the algorithm the ability to search in worst solution to get better solutions. Therefore, we can see from figures that the accuracy becomes bad and then it can get a solution better than all previous solutions as in Figure 1 in the 21 through 25 generations. In addition, we can see that the average of accuracies in last generations is much better than the values

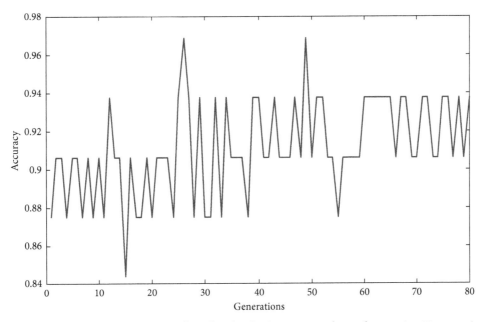

FIGURE 8: The accuracy of the WGGA algorithm for the Lung cancer dataset by running 80 generations.

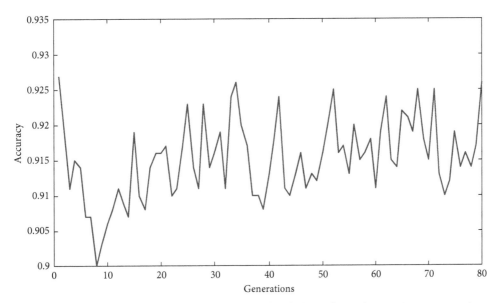

FIGURE 9: The accuracy of the WGGA algorithm for the Phishing dataset by running 80 generations.

of earlier generations which more emphasize the effectiveness of our proposed algorithm.

As in any algorithm, there are some few drawbacks of the proposed algorithm. Firstly, since our algorithm needs to gather some information regarding the features, it starts activating its weighted gene mechanism after number of generations (after collecting the needed data). This process takes some time but it can be neglected when the number of generations is big. Secondly, in dynamic environment, the proposed algorithm may not work efficiently especially in very fast changing environments. This is because the proposed algorithm depends on previous static experience, whereas in dynamic environments, this experience becomes unimportant because of frequent changing.

7. Conclusion and Future Work

To overcome the big data complexity problem, the feature reduction becomes one of the most effective solutions that are used nowadays. In this paper, a set of hybrid and efficient algorithms are proposed to classify the datasets that have large feature size by merging genetic algorithms with the artificial neural networks. The genetic algorithms are used as a prestep to significantly remove the irrelevant features from the datasets before handling that data using machine learning techniques. Three new genetic algorithms are proposed and incorporated in the ANN algorithm which is low weighted gene genetic algorithm (LWGGA), high weighted gene genetic algorithm (HWGGA), and weighted gene genetic

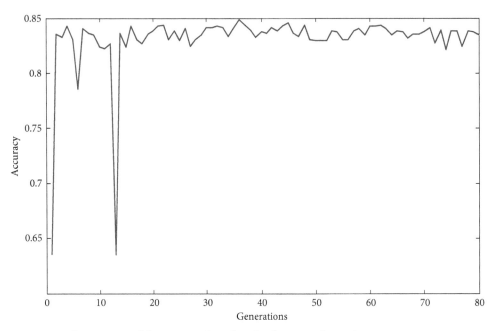

FIGURE 10: The accuracy of the WGGA algorithm for the Sport dataset by running 80 generations.

algorithm (WGGA). The proposed algorithms use a new gene-weight mechanism that can significantly enhance the performance and decrease the required search time. The proposed algorithms are applied on six datasets to pick the most relative and important features before applying the artificial neural networks algorithm, and the results show that our proposed algorithms can effectively enhance the classifying performance over the tested datasets.

In future work, we are planning to compare our proposed algorithms against more evolutionary algorithms such as PSO and ACO. At the same time, the new proposed weight-gene mechanism can be merged with other algorithms. We expect that this mechanism may get better results if it is checked using other evolutionary algorithms.

Conflicts of Interest

The authors declare that they have no conflicts of interest.

References

[1] S. J. Walker, "Big data: a revolution that will transform how we live, work, and think," *International Journal of Advertising*, vol. 33, no. 1, pp. 181–183, 2014.

[2] J. Manyika, M. Chui, B. Brown et al., *Big Data: The Next Frontier for Innovation, Competition, and Productivity*, McKinsey, New York, NY, USA, 2011.

[3] P. Zikopoulos and C. Eaton, *Understanding Big Data: Analytics for Enterprise Class Hadoop and Streaming Data*, McGraw-Hill Osborne Media, New York, NY, USA, 2011.

[4] A. Katal, M. Wazid, and R. H. Goudar, "Big data: issues, challenges, tools and good practices," in *Proceedings of 2013 Sixth International Conference on Contemporary Computing (IC3)*, pp. 404–409, IEEE, Noida, India, August 2013.

[5] C. P. Chen and C. Y. Zhang, "Data-intensive applications, challenges, techniques and technologies: a survey on Big Data," *Information Sciences*, vol. 275, pp. 314–347, 2014.

[6] X. Wu, X. Zhu, G. Q. Wu, and W. Ding, "Data mining with big data," *IEEE Transactions on Knowledge and Data Engineering*, vol. 26, no. 1, pp. 97–107, 2014.

[7] Z. Obermeyer and E. J. Emanuel, "Predicting the future—big data, machine learning, and clinical medicine," *New England Journal of Medicine*, vol. 375, no. 13, pp. 1216–1219, 2016.

[8] R. Ho, *Big Data Machine Learning*, 2012.

[9] I. H. Witten, E. Frank, M. A. Hall, and C. J. Pal, *Data Mining: Practical Machine Learning Tools and Techniques*, Morgan Kaufmann, Burlington, MA, USA, 2016.

[10] G. George, M. R. Haas, and A. Pentland, "Big data and management," *Academy of Management Journal*, vol. 57, no. 2, pp. 321–326, 2014.

[11] M. Dash and H. Liu, "Feature selection for classification," *Intelligent Data Analysis*, vol. 1, no. 1–4, pp. 131–156, 1997.

[12] I. Guyon and A. Elisseeff, "An introduction to variable and feature selection," *Journal of Machine Learning Research*, vol. 3, pp. 1157–1182, 2003.

[13] H. Liu and Z. Zhao, "Manipulating data and dimension reduction methods: feature selection," in *Encyclopedia of Complexity and Systems Science*, pp. 5348–5359, Springer, Berlin, Germany, 2009.

[14] H. Liu, H. Motoda, R. Setiono, and Z. Zhao, "Feature selection: an ever evolving frontier in data mining," in *Proceedings of Fourth International Workshop on JMLR Feature Selection in Data Mining*, vol. 10, pp. 4–13, Hyderabad, India, June 2010.

[15] A. W. Whitney, "A direct method of nonparametric measurement selection," *IEEE Transactions on Computers*, vol. C-20, no. 9, pp. 1100–1103, 1971.

[16] T. Marill and D. M. Green, "On the effectiveness of receptors in recognition systems," *IEEE Transactions on Information Theory*, vol. 9, no. 1, pp. 11–17, 1963.

[17] S. D. Stearns, "On selecting features for pattern classifier," in *Proceedings of 3rd International Conference on Pattern Recognition*, pp. 71–75, Coronado, CA, USA, November 1976.

[18] P. Pudil, J. Novovičová, and J. V. Kittler, "Floating search methods in feature selection," *Pattern Recognition Letters*, vol. 15, no. 11, pp. 1119–1125, 1994.

[19] Q. Mao and I. W.-H. Tsang, "A feature selection method for multivariate performance measures," *IEEE Transactions on Pattern Analysis and Machine Intelligence*, vol. 35, no. 9, pp. 2051–2063, 2013.

[20] F. Min, Q. Hu, and W. Zhu, "Feature selection with test cost constraint," *International Journal of Approximate Reasoning*, vol. 55, no. 1, pp. 167–179, 2014.

[21] H. Frohlich, O. Chapelle, and B. Scholkopf, "Feature selection for support vector machines by means of genetic algorithm," in *Proceedings of 15th IEEE International Conference on Tools with Artificial Intelligence, 2003*, pp. 142–148, Sacramento, CA, USA, November 2003.

[22] I. S. Oh, J. S. Lee, and B. R. Moon, "Hybrid genetic algorithms for feature selection," *IEEE Transactions on Pattern Analysis and Machine Intelligence*, vol. 26, no. 11, pp. 1424–1437, 2004.

[23] H. M. Zawbaa, E. Emary, C. Grosan, and V. Snasel, "Large-dimensionality small-instance set feature selection: a hybrid bioinspired heuristic approach," *Swarm and Evolutionary Computation*, vol. 42, pp. 29–42, 2018.

[24] E. Emary and H. M. Zawbaa, "Feature selection via Levy Antlion optimization," *Pattern Analysis and Applications*, pp. 1–20, 2018.

[25] W. Yamany, H. M. Zawbaa, E. Emary, and A. E. Hassanien, "Attribute reduction approach based on modified flower pollination algorithm," in *Proceedings of International Conference on Fuzzy Systems (FUZZ-IEEE)*, pp. 1–7, Istanbul, Turkey, August 2015.

[26] B. Xue, M. Zhang, and W. N. Browne, "Particle swarm optimization for feature selection in classification: a multi-objective approach," *IEEE Transactions on Cybernetics*, vol. 43, no. 6, pp. 1656–1671, 2013.

[27] T. M. Hamdani, J. M. Won, A. M. Alimi, and F. Karray, "Multi-objective feature selection with NSGA II," in *Proceedings of International Conference on Adaptive and Natural Computing Algorithms*, pp. 240–247, Springer, Berlin, Heidelberg, April 2007.

[28] L. S. Oliveira, R. Sabourin, F. Bortolozzi, and C. Y. Suen, "Feature selection using multi-objective genetic algorithms for handwritten digit recognition," in *Proceedings of 16th International Conference on Pattern Recognition, 2002*, vol. 1, pp. 568–571, IEEE, Quebec City, Canada, August 2002.

[29] M. Morita, R. Sabourin, F. Bortolozzi, and C. Y. Suen, "Unsupervised feature selection using multi-objective genetic algorithms for handwritten word recognition," in *Proceedings of Seventh International Conference on Document Analysis and Recognition, 2003*, pp. 666–670, IEEE, Edinburgh, UK, August 2003.

[30] D. Dua and E. K. Taniskidou, *UCI Machine Learning Repository*, University of California, School of Information and Computer Science, Irvine, CA, USA, 2017, http://archive.ics.uci.edu/ml.

14

Big Data Management for Cloud-Enabled Geological Information Services

Yueqin Zhu ⓘ,[1,2] Yongjie Tan ⓘ,[1,2] Xiong Luo ⓘ,[3,4] and Zhijie He ⓘ[3,4]

[1]Development and Research Center, China Geological Survey, Beijing 100037, China
[2]Key Laboratory of Geological Information Technology, Ministry of Land and Resources, Beijing 100037, China
[3]School of Computer and Communication Engineering, University of Science and Technology Beijing (USTB), Beijing 100083, China
[4]Beijing Key Laboratory of Knowledge Engineering for Materials Science, Beijing 100083, China

Correspondence should be addressed to Yueqin Zhu; yueqin_zhu@126.com and Xiong Luo; xluo@ustb.edu.cn

Academic Editor: Anfeng Liu

Cloud computing as a powerful technology of performing massive-scale and complex computing plays an important role in implementing geological information services. In the era of big data, data are being collected at an unprecedented scale. Therefore, to ensure successful data processing and analysis in cloud-enabled geological information services (CEGIS), we must address the challenging and time-demanding task of big data processing. This review starts by elaborating the system architecture and the requirements for big data management. This is followed by the analysis of the application requirements and technical challenges of big data management for CEGIS in China. This review also presents the application development opportunities and technical trends of big data management in CEGIS, including collection and preprocessing, storage and management, analysis and mining, parallel computing based cloud platform, and technology applications.

1. Introduction

In the era of big data, the data-driven modeling method enables us to exploit the potential of massive amount of geological data easily [1–3]. In particular, by mining the data scientifically, one can offer new services that bring higher values to customers. Furthermore, it is now possible to implement the transition from digital geology to intelligent geology by integrating multiple systems in geological research through the use of big data and other technologies [4].

The application of geological cloud makes it possible to fully utilize structured and unstructured data, including geology, minerals, geophysics, geochemistry, remote sensing, terrain, topography, vegetation, architecture, hydrology, disasters, and other digitally geological data distributed in every place on the surface of the earth [4, 5]. Moreover, the geological cloud will enable the integration of data collection, resource integration, data transmission, information extraction, and knowledge mining, which will pave the way for the transition from data to information, from

information to knowledge, and from knowledge to wisdom. In addition, it provides data analysis, mining, organization, and management services for the scientific management of land resources, prospecting breakthrough strategic action and social services, while conducting multilevel, multiangle, and multiobjective demonstration applications on geological data for government decision-making, scientific research, and public services [5].

Big data technologies are bringing unprecedented opportunities and challenges to various application areas, especially to geological information processing [2, 6, 7]. Under these circumstances, there are some advancements achieved in the development of this area [8, 9]. Furthermore, from various disciplines of science and engineering, there has been a growing interest in this research field related to geological data generated in the geological information services (GIS). We analyze the number of those documents indexed in "Web of Science" [10]. In Figures 1 and 2, we can easily find that, in the past ten years, the number of those documents in which "geological data" is in the "Title" and in the "Topic" are both increasing, respectively. Hence, the analysis for geological

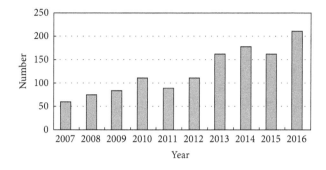

FIGURE 1: The trend of the number of documents in which "geological data" is in the "Title" from 2007 to 2016.

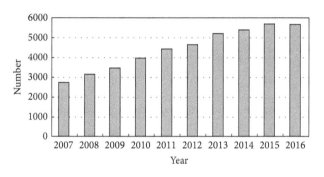

FIGURE 2: The trend of the number of documents in which "geological data" is in the "Topic" from 2007 to 2016.

data in GIS is an interesting and important research topic currently.

Considering the development status of cloud-enabled geological information services (CEGIS) and the application requirements of big data management analysis, this article describes the significant impact and revolution on GIS brought by the advancement of big data technologies. Furthermore, this article outlines the future application development and technology development trend of big data management analysis in CEGIS.

The remainder of this article is organized as follows. In Section 2, we provide a review on CEGIS, with an emphasis on the descriptions for the system architecture and those requirements from big data management. Then, the challenges for big data management in CEGIS are presented in Section 3. Furthermore, the key technologies and trends on big data management in CEGIS are analyzed in Section 4. Finally, conclusion is drawn in Section 5.

2. Review on Cloud-Enabled Geological Information Services

The construction of geological cloud differs from the current big data analysis based on Internet and Internet of Things (IoT). Having a deep understanding of data characteristics is necessary to collect, process, analyze, and interpret data in different fields, because the nature and types of data vary in different fields and in different problems. Geology is a data intensive science and geological data are characterized with multisource heterogeneity, spatiotemporal variation, correlation, uncertainty, fuzziness, and nonlinearity. Therefore, the geological cloud has a certain degree of confidentiality and it is highly domain-specific; meanwhile, it is developed on the basis of a large amount of geological data accumulated over a long period of time [5, 11]. There are many real-time data generated from some issues like geological disasters and geological environment. The geological cloud includes core basic data, which can be divided into three parts: existing structured database, some unstructured data, and public application data. Therefore, it is important to take good advantage of the existing traditional structured data, use the big data technologies to deal with the relevant unstructured data, and also consider the peripheral public data.

Geological big data are multidimensional, and they consist of both structured and unstructured data [12]. The technical methods of big data analysis differ greatly from those of professional databases. Long-term geological survey, geological study, and years of geological information accumulation have formed a rich and professional database, which is an important fundamental assurance for land and resources science management, geological survey, and geological information public service [13]. This "professional cloud" objectively requires the technology research and development, such as construction of professional local area network, data sharing platform, and geological big data visualization services. Hence, the construction of geological cloud is closely related to land resource management, deployment decision, and the application demand of public service. The key technologies of research and development include the following: unstructured data extraction and mining analysis, structured and unstructured data mixed storage and management, big data sharing platform, data transmission, and visualization [11].

Generally, the construction of geological cloud is a long-term systematic project. This means that it is required to follow the basic principles of "standing on the reality, focusing on the future" and "focusing on the long-term and overall situation, embarking on the current and local situation," in order to achieve the analysis and application of geological cloud public data and core data gradually in accordance with the technical route of big data analysis; thus the construction of geological cloud will be implemented eventually. For the earth, the land and resources management should cover many respects, including human behavior, climate change, development and utilization of various resources, natural disasters, environmental pollution, and the ecosystem cycle. Then, the introduction of big data technologies can integrate this type of resource information to provide the ability of uniformly dealing with the problems related to the entire earth information resources, which has a significant effect on the strategic planning of land and resources management [3].

The geological cloud is an important part in the science system for geological data research. The ultimate goal for developing geological cloud is to better describe and understand the complex earth system and geological framework,

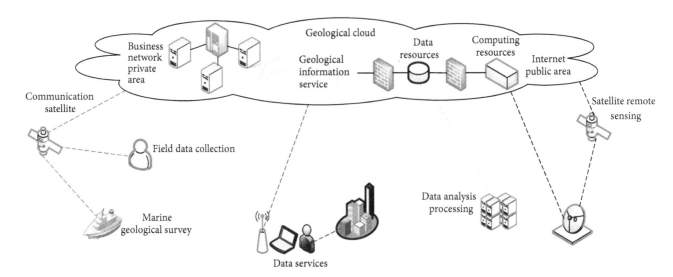

FIGURE 3: The system architecture of geological cloud.

provide the scientific basis for the description of the land surface and the biodiversity characteristics of the earth, and improve the ability to deal with complex social problems.

2.1. System Architecture. Because the business service functions of each country are different, the system architecture of the geological cloud would vary. In the following, we present a system architecture in Figure 3 [14], using China as an example.

The geological cloud combines the geological survey Intranet and the geological survey Extranet. It enables the sharing and management of computing resources, storage resources, network resources, software resources, and geological data resources [15].

Geological cloud can be summarized with the following characteristics [14].

(i) *"One Platform: The Geological Cloud Management Platform."* It uniformly manages computing resources, storage resources, network resources, software resources, and geological data resources.

(ii) *"Two Networks: The Geological Survey Intranet and the Geological Survey Extranet."* Here, the Intranet is constructed by creating a network that is physically isolated from the Internet. The Intranet is developed on the basis of the existing geological survey network and each node is linked through a dedicated line or bare fiber. All of the internal business management systems, software systems, and data are deployed on the Internet, providing services to 28 local units and those users of more than 350 geological survey projects. Facilitated by the public geological survey network, the geological survey business management system, geological data information service system, and public geological data can be deployed on the Extranet accessed by the general public. The communication between the Intranet and the Extranet,

including data exchange and audit, can be carried out by single-directional light gate.

(iii) *"One Main Node and Three Domain-Specific Nodes."* One main node is constructed in China Geological Survey Development Research Center. In addition, three domain-specific nodes—namely, marine node, geological environment node, and aviation geophysical exploration and remote sensing node—are constructed, respectively. Each node is configured with the corresponding servers, storage equipment, network equipment, management platform, large-scale specialized data processing software system and various customized applications. Each node would store huge amounts of geological data and conform to current data security standards. The master node and the domain-specific nodes are linked via optical fibers. The master node will consist of 200 computing nodes with 3 PB storage capacity and will be equipped with some geological data processing software system. The master node will be hosted in a medium-sized supercomputing center and it will provide support for the three-dimensional seismic exploration data processing and other large-scale computing. The three domain-specific nodes are to maintain their scale in the near future to facilitate reasonable scheduling and efficient utilization of information resources and data resources.

On the Extranet, it deploys a system for geological survey business management and auxiliary decision-making. The system provides a real-time tracking and management function for geological survey projects and various resources.

Main users of the geological cloud include institutional users, geological survey project users, and the general public users. The institutional users can store the current geological database and newly collected data in the geological cloud through the geological survey business network and can

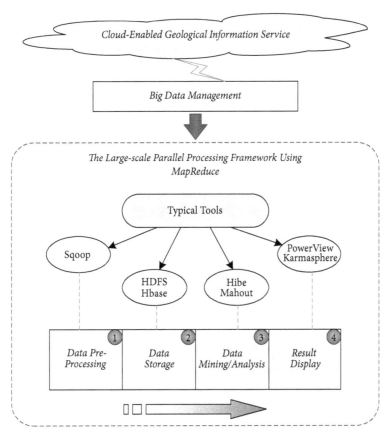

FIGURE 4: Schematic diagram of big data analysis.

obtain the geological data of other institutions from the cloud as needed. The geological survey project users can access the cloud geological background data through 4G or satellite lines and can collect data through data the collection system.

2.2. Requirement from Big Data Management. The construction of geological cloud must meet customer demand. Big data technologies are then used as the means to implement the geological cloud.

The types and quantity of geological data have been continuously growing over the years. Geological data include all kinds of electronic documents, structured, semistructured, and unstructured data, such as various databases (map database, spatial database, and attribute database), pictures, tables, video, and audio. Generally speaking, those important data may be buried in the massive data without the guidance for requirements. Hence, the first step is to understand the user requirements and then gain the capability of large-scale data processing. This is followed by data mining, algorithm, and analysis, which will ultimately generate value. Big data technologies in the field of geography must meet different needs from people at different levels, including the public demand of the geologic data services and professional data demand for geological research institutions, as well as related enterprises and government departments [16].

On the basis of big data analysis technologies, a complete data link is formed connecting data, information, knowledge,

and service, through the use of advanced cloud computing system, IoT, and big data processing flow. It is shown in Figure 4 [5].

3. Challenges for Big Data Management in Cloud-Enabled Geological Information Services

Geological big data are generated regarding various layers of the earth, the history of the conformation and evolution of the earth, and the material composition of the earth and its changes. It also involves the exploration and utilization of mineral resources. In the current geological work, the collection, mining, processing, analysis, and utilization of various complex type data are closely related to those general big data. The "4V" characteristics of big data—namely, Volume, Velocity, Variety, and Veracity—also apply to geological big data.

3.1. Volume. Currently, there is no consensus on the size of geological data. Geological big data are a collection of data, including geology, minerals, remote sensing, geophysical exploration, geochemical exploration, surveying, and mapping, which are interconnected and integrated. In terms of the number of mines, there are at least 70000 in China, and some official documents and popular science books indicate that there are more than 200000 deposits and minerals that have been found. The information is huge and cannot be processed using conventional tools. For example, an Excel spreadsheet cannot contain all the information of 70000 mining areas. Then, it is difficult to classify and rank the 200000 mines, so it is necessary to rely on the concepts and technologies of big data [17].

Especially in recent years, images, video, and other types of data have emerged on a large scale. With the application of 3D scanning and other devices, the data volume has been increasing exponentially. The ability to describe the data is more and more powerful, and the data are gradually approximated to the real world. In addition, the large amount of data is also reflected in the aspect that the methods and ideas used by people to deal with data have undergone a fundamental change. In the early days, people used the sampling method to process and analyze data in order to approximate the objective with a small number of subsample data. With the development of technologies, the number of samples gradually approaches the overall data. Using all the data can lead to a higher accuracy, which can explain things in more detail [18].

Recently, the China geological survey system has built databases including regional geological database (covering the 1 : 2500000, 1 : 1000000, 1 : 500000, 1 : 250000, and 1 : 200000 regional geological map; the national 1 : 200000 natural sand; the isotope geological dating; and the lithostratigraphic unit database), basic geological database (covering the national rock property database and national geological working degree database), mineral resources database (covering the national mineral resources, the national mineral resources utilization survey mining resources reserves verification results, the national survey of large and medium-sized mines, the prospect of mineral resources, the survey of the resources potential of major solid mineral resources in China, and the geological and mineral resources database), oil and gas energy database (covering the oil and gas basins in China, the geological survey results of the national oil and gas resources, the national petroleum and geophysical exploration, national shale gas, national coal bed methane, national natural gas hydrate, and other databases), geophysical database (covering 1 : 1 million, 1 : 500000, 1 : 250000, 1 : 200000, and 1 : 50000 gravity, national regional gravity, national aeromagnetism, national ground magnetism, national electrical survey, seismic survey, national aviation radioactivity, and national logging database), geochemical database (covering the databases of national 1 : 250000 and 1 : 20 geochemical exploration, national multiobjective geochemical and national land quality evaluation results), remote sensing survey database (covering national aeronautical remote sensing image, China resources satellite data, space remote sensing image, national mine environmental remote sensing monitoring, national high score satellite, and other databases), drilling database (covering the national geological borehole information, the national important geological borehole, the Chinese mainland scientific drilling core scanning image library, and so on), hydraulic cycle hazards database, data literature database, special subject database (covering the national mineral resources potential evaluation database, the important mineral "three-rate" investigation and evaluation database), work management database (covering the national exploration right, mining right, mining right verification, geological information metadata database, and many others) [17].

For those databases, they are still expanding and consummating, and their practical values have not yet been fully reflected. However, the vast majority of researchers are virtually impossible to have all of the above data, at most, using their own accumulated data. Anyway, even if their accumulated data, both on the quantity and on type, is incomparable by 10 years and 20 years ago, they are, in fact, in the era of the "relatively big data." From 1999 to 2004, for example, in "the Chinese mineralization system and regional metalorganic evaluation" project, although there are 202 national academic experts that participated in it, they only master data of 4500 properties (all kinds of minerals). From 2006 to 2013, the study of "national important mineral and regional mineralization laws" was conducted; meanwhile, the mining area covered only by the mineral resources research institute was 30600. Therefore, the increase of information and the amount of data are unprecedented in the last ten years.

3.2. Variety. From the formal point of view, the geological big data have many characteristics, including multidimensionality, multiscale, and multitenses. And they contain structured, semistructured, and unstructured data and usually are stored in forms of text, graphics, images, databases (including image database, spatial database, and attribute database), tables, videos, and audios in a fragmented state. For example, a large number of field outcrop description data, borehole core description data, and all kinds of geological survey, exploration report, and a large number of geological maps, drawings, and photos were stored and managed in the form of paper for a long time; even the numerous relational databases and spatial databases were primarily used to store and manage structured data that are tabulated and vectorized, while the text descriptions, records, and summaries were directly stored. Very few standardized processing and structural transformations were performed. Furthermore, there is no tool available to effectively integrate storage and manage structured, semistructured, and unstructured data.

3.3. Velocity. The increase of geological data is very fast, especially in remote sensing geology, aviation geophysical exploration, regional geochemical exploration, and other fields, due to the introduction of new technologies and new methods. Meanwhile, high speed processing is also a characteristic of big data. In addition to the need of analyzing data in real time, people also need to describe the results of data mining and processing through the use of several data processing techniques, such as image and video, while requiring effective and efficient handling skills. For example, the detection of the deep earth information not only needs to obtain parameters of the seismic wave reflection and refraction but also needs to conduct quick processing, so as to timely predict whether earthquake will occur and forecast the time, location, and intensity. In this way, we can avoid the disaster effectively. When applying a variety of data to a particular mountain, one should learn which ones have spatial limitations and which are not related to spatiality, so that one deduces the metallogenic law and guides the prospecting better [17].

3.4. Veracity. For the understanding of the value of big data, most people consider it low value density. It means that the real useful information in the vast amount of data is very little. Taking video as an example, the useful data may be only a second or two in the continuous monitoring process. While big data is high value, it does not need to be invested too much; just collecting information from the Internet can bring business value. Therefore, big data has the characteristics of low value density and high business value. The same is true for geological big data. So far, there has been a lot of information about geophysical prospecting, but only a few have been confirmed, and the discovered mines were less. But once a breakthrough was made, its socioeconomic value was enormous, such as the lithium polymetallic deposit in Tibet and the newly discovered Jima copper polymetallic deposit in the outskirts of Sichuan [17].

In addition, the spatial attribute and temporal attribute of geological data also bring a big challenge to data accuracy. Any geological data have spatial attribute, and their values are reflected in the spatial law of distribution of mineral resources. For this reason, in the process of establishing the metallogenic series, exploring the metallogenic law, and constructing the mathematical model, the spatial attribute of the metallogenic model should be considered. Obviously, every metallogenic series has its spatial attribute. Geological data also has the time attribute, which is very different from physical, chemical, and other natural sciences. One of the fundamental pillars of geology is the geological time scale. The rocks, strata, and deposits of different geological periods have different distribution characteristics and regularity, so those data have their own time attribute.

It is obvious that those characteristics of geological big data mentioned above impose very challenging obstacles to the data management in CEGIS. The challenges related to geological big data management can be summarized as follows:

(i) It is quite difficult to describe and model geological big data, since there are few effective characteristics description mechanisms and object modeling approaches under the cloud computing environment.

(ii) There remain many technical issues that must be addressed to fully manage, mine, analyze, integrate, and share those geological big data, in consideration of those complex characteristics, including multisource heterogeneous data, highly spatiotemporal variation, high-volume and high-correlation data, and many others.

(iii) Many issues appear in achieving decision support, such as data incompleteness, data uncertainty, and high-dimensionality of data.

The broad range of challenges described here make good topics for research within the field of big data management in CEGIS. They are analyzed in the next section.

4. Key Technologies and Trends on Big Data Management in Cloud-Enabled Geological Information Service (CEGIS)

With the rapid advancement of big data technologies, some key technologies are accordingly developed for big data management in CEGIS. Specifically, a schematic diagram of those key technologies is shown in Figure 5. Then, in this section we present an analysis on those key technologies. Meanwhile, the trends along this direction are also discussed.

4.1. Geological Big Data Collection and Preprocessing. Geological big data collection and preprocessing aim to categorize those geological big data obtained from geological data, geological information, and geological literature.

4.1.1. Geological Data Collection Access. In addition to the traditional collection ways, it is also required to carry out large-scale network information access and provide realtime, high concurrency, and fast web content acquisition, combining with the application characteristics in the cloud environment. Currently, considering that the growth rate of geological information generated from the network is very fast, the big data analysis system should obtain relevant data quickly.

4.1.2. Quality and Usability Characteristics of Geological Data. It needs to distinguish and identify valuable information through intelligent discovery and management technologies. Because the information value density contained in different data sources differs from each other, filtering out the useless or low-value data source can effectively reduce the data storage and processing costs. Then, it can also further improve the efficiency and accuracy of analysis.

4.1.3. Geological Data Entity Recognition Model. According to the subject domain of geology, the distributed data are extracted to form a data warehouse, after conducting the operation of processing and integration. When extracting data in the field of geology, it needs to use entity modeling method to abstract entities from the vast numbers of data, so as to find out the relationship between those entities. This approach ensures that the data used in warehouse data can be consistent and relevant in accordance with the data model [19]. These recognized data are directly input into the system, stored as metadata, which could be used for data management and analysis.

4.1.4. Aggregation of Geological Big Data. Generally, different data sources and even the same data source may generate data with different formats. As mentioned above, because these structural, semistructured, and unstructured multimodal geological big data are integrated together, the data heterogeneity is obvious in big data analysis. Then, data aggregation as the key technology in achieving data extraction and transformation [20] enables data sharing and data fusion between heterogeneous data sources. Through

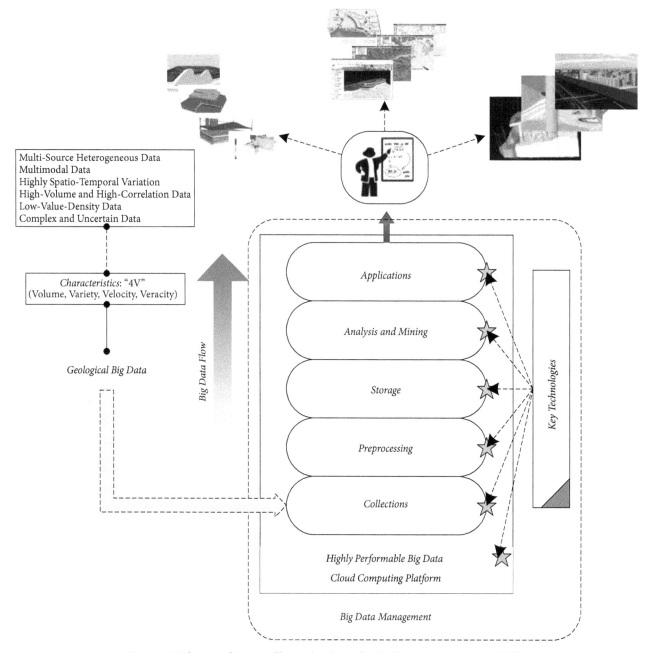

FIGURE 5: Schematic diagram of key technologies for big data management in CEGIS.

the use of heterogeneous information aggregation technologies, the unified data retrieval and data presentation could be achieved. On the basis of it, after aggregating those distributed heterogeneous data sources, they are extracted and converted to achieve the functions of automatically constructing subject domain database and data warehouse [21].

4.1.5. Management of Geological Big Data Evolution Tracking Records. In order to effectively utilize geological big data, it needs to track the evolution of big data during the whole life cycle of GIS, with the purpose of achieving the traceable big data management.

Here, we provide an example of aggregating and collecting geological big data in CEGIS. Figure 6 illustrates this process. While developing CEGIS, all kinds of geological data should be processed. Through the use of geological cloud, big data are collected, and then they are aggregated to achieve some key functions in geological information service platform, including catalog sharing, intelligent searching, data products release, and collaborative service.

4.2. Geological Big Data Storage and Management. From the data collection perspective, geological data can be divided into field survey data, drilling and engineering exploration data, remote detection data, analytical test data, and

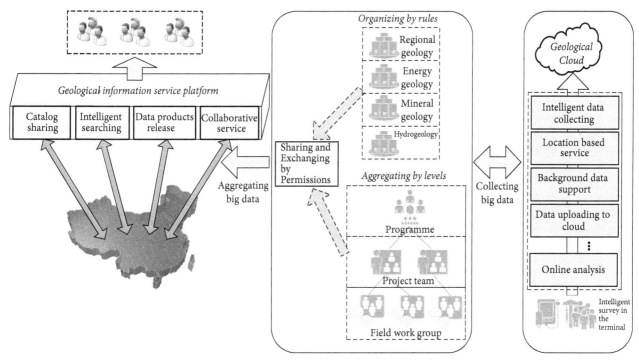

FIGURE 6: An example of aggregating and collecting geological big data in CEGIS.

comprehensive study data. From the angle of comprehensive application fields, they can be also divided into regionally geological survey data, energy and mineral resources evaluation and exploration survey results data, geological disaster monitoring and early warning data, geological environment survey and evaluation results data, and marine geological survey and evaluation data. From the data formality point of view, they can be divided into picture data, text report data, tabular data, and image data. These data are collected by different units.

Facing these complex geological big data mentioned above, the traditional relational database will be difficult to handle them, while the distributed storage system can be used to store such huge amounts of data and manage them. Then, the data system places the massive data in many machines, which avoids such limitation of storage capacity, and also brings many problems that have not occurred before in stand-alone systems. Hence, some distributed data storage solutions have accordingly emerged, including Hadoop, Spark, and other nonrelational database systems (like HBase, MongoDB, and many others) [22]. These different solutions satisfy the specific requirements from different applications. When applying to the analysis of big data, different solutions can be employed according to the specific needs of different intelligence analysis. Furthermore, different solutions can be combined to meet specific needs. Actually, there have been some attempts to develop combination strategies for distributed storage model, varying in the big data management performance requirement, and the complexity of collected big data that are supported by the distributed storage system [23]. Hence, there is still a room for improvement and optimization of geological big data storage, while designing

a hybrid distributed storage model through the use of cloud advantages of flexibly scalable deployment, to meet the users' requirement for geological big data resource management with satisfactory data durability and high availability [23].

Here, the hot research topics include the following:

(i) For geological applications, the load optimization storage should be implemented to achieve the coupling for data storage and application and the coupling for distributed file system and the new storage system.

(ii) Based on the application characteristics of distributed databases, more studies could be conducted on the application of new databases NoSQL and NewSQL in geological survey work.

With the development of big data technologies, more and more mature distributed data storage solutions will emerge and will be applied to big data analysis [24, 25].

Specifically, in the management of geological big data, the implementation of data query—for example, spatial query—has been a long-term focus. Generally, considering those advantages with unified modeling language (UML) and computer-aided software engineering (CASE) methodology, the spatial database could be accordingly designed and implemented to characterize and realize the object-oriented spatial vector big data firstly [26]. And then, in the developed spatial database, the function of self-generating codes would be achieved to realize two-way spatial query between graphic-objects and property data [26]. Moreover, in consideration of the complex characteristics of geological big data, the spatial query is achieved finally through the use of Flex technology in ArcGIS Server software platform [27]. Practically speaking, in this technology, the spatial query could be implemented through two functions, including "Query" and "Find" query methods [28].

4.3. Geological Big Data Analysis and Mining.

In terms of geological data analysis and mining, it needs to combine geological data, geological information, and geological literatures, through the analysis of geological application demand of real-time mining, to explore geological big data environment analysis and mining algorithm, in an effort to fully achieve the goal of intelligent mining for geological big data.

Figure 7 shows a schematic diagram of discovering geological knowledge through analyzing and mining geological big data. It can be easily found that geological big data analysis and mining play an important role in achieving the final goal. More relevant research work related to it mainly involves the following aspects.

4.3.1. Geological Big Data Analysis.

Considering the special applications, geological big data technologies would apply big data concepts to analyze the metallogenic rules by making full use of various data related to ore, to recognize deposit metallogenic series, to summarize the metallogenic regularities and express in an appropriate way (like voice, image, and many others), and to establish the scientifically mathematical model. The model then uses new exploration data to predict future data and to guide geological prospecting.

In addition, it is necessary to pay special attention to the analysis of new geological big data information collected from social medium and networks [29]. These include the geological text information flow data from microblog web sites, the geological multimedia data from media sharing web sites, the geology-related user interaction data on social networking web sites, and many others [30]. These multisource data complement traditional big data. Specifically, such data should be addressed with the help of multilingual information processing, multilingual machine translation, and social network cross-language retrieval [31]. Big data analysis of such data is a key to deep use of geological data in a broader dimension. With the maturity of big data analysis technologies, it becomes possible to analyze and extract valuable information from these data [32] and to provide effective solutions for geological big data applications.

4.3.2. Geological Big Data Mining.

Data mining is to extract the unknown and useful knowledge and information from the massive multilevel spatiotemporal data and attribute data, using statistics, pattern recognition, artificial intelligence, set theory, fuzzy mathematics, cloud computing, machine learning, visualization, and relevant techniques and methods. Data mining could reveal the relationship and evolution trend behind the geological big data, achieve the automatic or semiautomatic acquisition of the new knowledge, and provide the decision basis for resource prediction, prospecting, environmental assessment, and disaster prevention and mitigation [33]. Therefore, the knowledge is obtained directly from known geological data to provide relevant decision support [34]. In consideration of the amount of data, it may

deal with terabytes or even petabytes of data, as well as multidimensional data, all kinds of noise data and dynamic data. Because data mining algorithms will directly influence the outcome of the discovered knowledge, selecting the most appropriate algorithms and parallel computing strategy is the key to data mining.

Effective data mining also could reduce manual intervention during information processing and make use of methods and tools of big data intelligent analysis [35, 36]. Recently, there has been a growing interest in the geological big data mining through the use of some novel computational intelligent methods—for example, rough set [37] and fuzzy aggregation [38]. Moreover, with the development of those neural network based machine learning algorithms in recent years, some popular methods, including extreme learning machine [39, 40], approximate dynamic programming [41], and kernel learning [42], could be used to further improve mining effectiveness for geological big data in the future.

4.4. Highly Performable Big Data Cloud Computing Platform.

Highly performable big data cloud computing platform is the foundation for big data analysis. It enables parallel computing for large-scale incremental real-time data and large-scale heterogeneous data [43–46].

With the advent of massive data storage solution, many big data distributed computing frameworks have been proposed. Among them, Hadoop, MapReduce, Spark, and Storm are the most important distributed computing frameworks. These frameworks have different characteristics and solve different problems in applications [47–50]. The Hadoop/MapReduce is often used for offline complex big data processing, the Spark is often employed in offline fast big data processing, and the Storm is often available for real-time online big data processing. Different computing frameworks have their different advantages and disadvantages. Hadoop/MapReduce is easy to program, and it is with satisfactory scalability and fault tolerance. In addition, it is suitable for offline processing of massive data with petabyte level, but it does not support real-time computation and flow calculation. Spark is a memory-based iterative computing framework. By placing intermediate data in memory, Spark can achieve higher iterative calculation performance. The programming model of Spark is more flexible than that of Hadoop/MapReduce, but Spark is not suitable for those applications in which the fine-grained updates are conducted asynchronously. Hence, Spark may be unavailable for those application models that require incremental changes. Storm is suitable for stream data processing. It can be used to handle a stream of incoming messages and can write the processed result to a specified storage device. Another major application of Storm is real-time data processing where data are not necessary to be written into storage devices, which usually results in low time delay. Hence, Storm is particularly suitable for scenarios where real-time online analysis is required to obtain results for big data analysis.

An application example is geological big data aggregation mining framework based on Hadoop [16]. Geological big data aggregation mining platform research is based on the

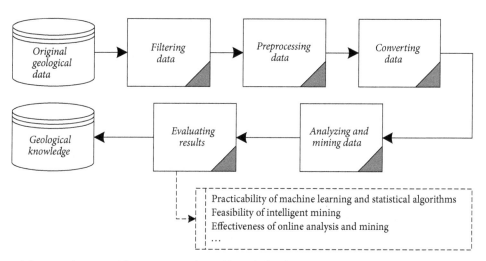

FIGURE 7: Schematic diagram of discovering geological knowledge through analyzing and mining geological big data.

China geological survey data network, and it uses the Hadoop technology to improve and modify existing platform, to make it suitable for big data applications, and to provide a platform for the pilot applications. The geological survey grid platform can be updated in three layers—that is, the virtual layer, the computing layer, and the terminal application layer. The virtual layer is the virtualization of computer resources based on Hadoop distributed file system (HDFS) virtualization technology, which is the foundation of cloud computing and cloud services. The computing layer mainly uses MapReduce method to implement the analysis algorithms for geological big data. Currently, the geological big data technologies mainly use the block calculation strategy to achieve parallel analysis through the utilization of the characteristics of Hadoop, in an effort to speed up the analysis and processing of geological data. The terminal application layer is designed to display the results and receive user feedback to improve system availability.

MapReduce has been used to perform morphological correlation analysis, which involves the analysis of geochemical data processing and the study of the correlation between multielements. Figure 8 shows the pattern correlation between elements. It can be seen from Figure 8 that the elements of Mn, Co, and Be are similar in the distribution of morphology. Therefore, from a qualitative point of view, the correlation is relatively high. Moreover, after testing, the proposed prototype system is running three times more quickly than the existing common computing platform, showing that the geological big data is applicable to the Hadoop platform. Furthermore, some applications of using MapReduce could be found in [51].

4.5. Applications of Geological Big Data Technologies

4.5.1. Exploration of Metallogenic Law. The metallogenic law is the human regular knowledge of the temporal and spatial distribution of mineral resources, and its cognitive level, ability, and scope are all related to the size of data, the type of data, and the way of data processing. Therefore, to deduce

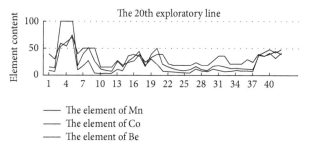

FIGURE 8: Correlation among three element morphologies.

the metallogenic law, it is necessary to fully understand the massive data about spatial distribution, reserves and production in mineral origin, the geological structure of the mineral origin, and related geological survey data. Then, it is to conduct the regular speculation and objectivity expression of these geological big data, so that one can identify the essential reasons for the distribution of mineral origin. Actually, using geological big data technologies could help to translate data into new understanding or knowledge and help to guide the future geological prospecting work.

4.5.2. Smart Prospecting. The types of deposits vary, and the formation of them is related to certain geological backgrounds and geological effects, respectively. The geological backgrounds include tectonic unit and stratigraphic unit, deep upper mantle and lithosphere conditions, and paleogeography and palaeoclimate environment on the surface of the earth. Geological effects include tectonism, magmatism, sedimentation, metamorphism, and weathering. Theses geologic backgrounds and effects in the wide range of space, and in the long geologic history, are a dynamic change and repeated stack, and large deposits can be formed only in a variety of favourable conditions. Long-term scientific research and experience accumulation formed mineral deposit and mineralization prediction subject. Professionals are guided by certain theories and methods to adopt quantitative or qualitative methods to predict prospecting with the existing knowledge and experience.

However, in view of the difficulties of geological data sharing and the limitations of calculation tools and calculation methods, most of the known deposits in the past are independent of each other. In the future, we can use geological data to connect several adjacent deposit exploration data, conduct unified analysis and specialized processing, determine the "digital" characteristics of the distribution of metallogenic materials, find out metallogenic potential, delineate the abnormal area and prospective area, and promote geological prospecting. Furthermore, geological data informatization and standardization could be improved [52].

4.5.3. Service of People's Livelihood Geology. After entering the 21st century, geological work is more closely related to economic development, and geological work plays an important role in every aspect of social and economic life. Agricultural geology, urban geology, environmental geology, tourism geology, disaster geology, and other works have been strengthened, and the service area has also been expanded [53]. Meanwhile, the public demand for geological information is increasingly urgent [54].

In order to meet the social demand for geological data, China Geological Survey carried out the construction of geological cloud, which built cluster geologic data service system with the National Geological Information Center and the Provincial Geological Information Center as the backbone nodes, conducted the integration of data resources, and applied the GIS cloud technology, in order to obtain large-scale computing ability and solve those key problems, such as the distributed storage, processing, query, interoperability, and virtualization of massive spatial data [5, 13]. Recently, in China, Shandong Provincial Bureau of Geology and Mineral Resources also carried out the construction of "the application system of geological business based on e-government cloud platform." It mainly relies on the public service cloud platform of the e-government in Shandong province and constructs the government external network service system and Internet service system to achieve the unified management and information service of the mineral resource. Using technical methods of spatial analysis, big data mining, and three-dimensional geological model, it develops a basic system framework for geological mining services, featured by "a (cloud) platform, a (data) center, and many application systems," to improve the ability of the people's livelihood geological service, promote interaction with the public, realize socialization services, and promote the clustering and industrialization of the mineral resources information services.

4.5.4. Application of Knowledge Visualization Service. With the continuous development of web technology, human beings have experienced the "Web 1.0" era, which is characterized by document interconnection, and "Web 2.0", which is characterized by data interconnection, and are moving towards the new "Web 3.0" era based on the interconnected

knowledge of the entity. Due to the continuous release of user-generated content and linking open data on the Internet, people need to explore knowledge interconnection methods which both conform to the development of the network information resources and meet users' requirements from a new perspective according to the knowledge organization principles in the large data environment, to reveal human cognition on a deeper level [55].

In this context, knowledge graph (KG) was formally put forward by Google in May 2012, and its goal is to improve the search results and describe the various entities and concepts that exist in the real world and the relationship between these entities and concepts. KG is a great choice to select the essence and discard the dross, as well as the sublimation of the present semantic web technology. In recent years, the applications of KG have been increasing rapidly, and there is now a mature method used to draw a KG and conduct intelligent searching research based on KG [34]. However, the function of KG has not been fully implemented at present, especially for the specific object of geological big data; the application aspect still needs to be further strengthened. Along this direction, the visualization service for geological data in the web-based system is attracting more and more attention [56, 57].

5. Conclusion

Big data technologies make it possible to process massive amount of unstructured and semistructured geological data. And the geological cloud enables us to explore the application of demand-driven geological core data and to extract new information from unstructured data, while supporting the decision-making in land resources management. Thus, the geological cloud could effectively organize and use geological big data, to mine the data scientifically, with the purpose of producing higher value and achieving the corresponding service.

In the architecture of geological cloud, this article describes the application background of CEGIS and the demands from big data management. Furthermore, we elaborate the application requirements and challenges faced in big data management technologies. Then, more analyses are provided from four aspects, including data size, data type, data processing speed, and data processing accuracy, respectively. In addition, this article outlines the research status and technology development opportunities of big data related in CEGIS, from the perspectives of big data acquisition and preprocessing, big data storage and management, big data analysis and mining, highly performable big data cloud computing platform, and big data technology applications. With the continuous development of big data technologies in addressing those challenges related to geological big data, such as the difficulties of describing and modeling geological big data with some complex characteristics, CEGIS will move towards a more mature and more intelligent direction in the future.

Conflicts of Interest

The authors declare that there are no conflicts of interest regarding the publication of this article.

Acknowledgments

This work was supported in part by the Key Laboratory of Geological Information Technology of Ministry of Land and Resources under Grant 2017320, the National Key Technologies R&D Program of China under Grant 2015BAK38B01, and the National Key R&D Program of China under Grant 2016YFC0600510.

References

[1] P. Vermeesch and E. Garzanti, "Making geological sense of 'big data' in sedimentary provenance analysis," *Chemical Geology*, vol. 409, pp. 20–27, 2015.

[2] J. Chen, J. Xiang, Q. Hu et al., "Quantitative geoscience and geological big data development: a review," *Acta Geologica Sinica*, vol. 90, no. 4, pp. 1490–1515, 2016.

[3] Y. Zhu, Y. Tan, R. Li, and X. Luo, "Cyber-Physical-Social-Thinking modeling and computing for geological information service system," *International Journal of Distributed Sensor Networks*, vol. 12, no. 11, 2016.

[4] M. M. Song, Z. Li, B. Zhou, and C. L. Li, "Cloud computing model for big geological data processing," *Applied Mechanics and Materials*, vol. 475-476, pp. 306–311, 2014.

[5] J. P. Chen, J. Li, N. Cui, and P. P. Yu, "The construction and application of geological cloud under the big data background," *Geological Bulletin of China*, vol. 34, no. 7, pp. 1260–1265, 2015.

[6] C. Li, "The technical infrastructure of geological survey information grid," in *Proceedings of the 18th International Conference on Geoinformatics*, pp. 1–6, 2010.

[7] L. Wu, L. Xue, C. Li et al., "A geospatial information grid framework for geological survey," *PLoS ONE*, vol. 10, no. 12, Article ID e0145312, 2015.

[8] K. Evangelidis, K. Ntouros, S. Makridis, and C. Papatheodorou, "Geospatial services in the Cloud," *Computers and Geosciences*, vol. 63, no. 2, pp. 116–122, 2014.

[9] M. Huang, A. Liu, T. Wang, and C. Huang, "Green data gathering under delay differentiated services constraint for internet of things," *Wireless Communications and Mobile Computing*, 2018, http://downloads.hindawi.com/journals/wcmc/aip/9715428.pdf.

[10] https://www.webofknowledge.com/.

[11] C. Yang, M. Yu, F. Hu, Y. Jiang, and Y. Li, "Utilizing Cloud Computing to address big geospatial data challenges," *Computers, Environment and Urban Systems*, vol. 61, pp. 120–128, 2017.

[12] L. Wu, L. Xue, C. Li et al., "A knowledge-driven geospatially enabled framework for geological big data," *ISPRS International Journal of Geo-Information*, vol. 6, no. 6, article no. 166, 2017.

[13] Y. Tan, "Architecture and key issues of geological big data and information service project," *Geomatics World*, vol. 23, no. 1, pp. 1–9, 2016.

[14] Y. Tan, "Architecture investigation of the construction of geological big data system," *Geological Survey of China*, vol. 3, no. 3, pp. 1–6, 2016.

[15] W. He and Y. Wang, "Prototype system of geological cloud computing," *Progress in Geophysics*, vol. 29, no. 6, pp. 2886–2896, 2014.

[16] Y. Zhu, Y. Tan, J. Zhang, B. Mao, J. Shen, and C. Ji, "A framework of hadoop based geology big data fusion and mining technologies," *Acta Geodaetica et Cartographica Sinica*, vol. 44, no. S0, pp. 152–159, 2015.

[17] D. Wang, X. Liu, and L. Liu, "Characteristics of big geodata and its application to study of minerogenetic regularity and minerogenetic series," *Mineral Deposits*, vol. 34, no. 6, pp. 1143–1154, 2015.

[18] B. Pan and R. Yang, "Management and utilization of big data for geology," *Surveying and Mapping of Geology and Mineral Resources*, vol. 33, no. 1, pp. 1–3, 2017.

[19] P. Yang and L. J. Lu, "The research on encoding methodology of the character of geological entity based on mass geological data," *Advanced Materials Research*, vol. 962-965, pp. 208–212, 2014.

[20] X. Luo, D. Zhang, L. T. Yang, J. Liu, X. Chang, and H. Ning, "A kernel machine-based secure data sensing and fusion scheme in wireless sensor networks for the cyber-physical systems," *Future Generation Computer Systems*, vol. 61, pp. 85–96, 2016.

[21] C.-L. Kuo and J.-H. Hong, "Interoperable cross-domain semantic and geospatial framework for automatic change detection," *Computers & Geosciences*, vol. 86, pp. 109–119, 2016.

[22] Y.-J. Wang, W.-D. Sun, S. Zhou, X.-Q. Pei, and X.-Y. Li, "Key technologies of distributed storage for cloud computing," *Journal of Software*, vol. 23, no. 4, pp. 962–986, 2012.

[23] M. Armbrust, A. Fox, R. Griffith et al., "Above the clouds: a berkeley view of cloud computing," Tech. Rep. UCB/EECS-2009-28, University of California at Berkeley, California, Calif, USA, 2009.

[24] J. Xia, Z. Bai, B. Wang, J. Chang, and Y. Wu, "Design and implementation of comprehensive management platform for geological data informatization," *Acta Scientiarum Naturalium Universitatis Pekinensis*, vol. 50, no. 2, pp. 295–300, 2014.

[25] W. Hua, J. Liu, and X. Liu, "Data management of object type geological features on control dictionary," *Earth Science - Journal of China University of Geosciences*, vol. 40, no. 3, pp. 425–430, 2015.

[26] B. Jia, C. Wang, C. Liu, and W. W. Sun, "Design and implementation of object-oriented spatial database of coalfield geological hazards -Based on object-oriented data model," in *Proceedings of the 2010 International Conference on Computer Application and System Modeling, ICCASM '10*, pp. V1282–V1286, Taiyuan, China, IEEE, October 2010.

[27] http://server.arcgis.com/.

[28] X. Zhou, X. Li, A. Chen et al., "Design and implementation of the service system of spatial data for geological data," *Journal of Geomatics*, vol. 38, no. 4, pp. 57–60, 2013 (Chinese).

[29] H. Huang, Z. Chao, and C. Feng, "Opportunities and challenges of big data intelligence analysis," *CAAI Transactions on Intelligent Systems*, vol. 11, no. 6, pp. 719–727, 2016.

[30] S. Jin, W. Lin, H. Yin, S. Yang, A. Li, and B. Deng, "Community structure mining in big data social media networks with MapReduce," *Cluster Computing*, vol. 18, no. 3, pp. 999–1010, 2015.

[31] C. C. Yang, C.-P. Wei, and L.-F. Chien, "Managing and mining multilingual documents: Introduction to the special topic issue of information processing management," *Information Processing & Management*, vol. 47, no. 5, pp. 633-634, 2011.

[32] X. Luo, J. Deng, W. Wang, J.-H. Wang, and W. Zhao, "A quantized kernel learning algorithm using a minimum kernel risk-sensitive loss criterion and bilateral gradient technique," *Entropy*, vol. 19, no. 7, article 365, 2017.

[33] C. H. Tse, Y. L. Li, and E. Y. Lam, "Geological applications of machine learning in hyperspectral remote sensing data," in *Proceedings of Conference on Image Processing - Machine Vision Applications VIII*, 2015.

[34] Y. Zhu, W. Zhou, Y. Xu, J. Liu, and Y. Tan, "Intelligent learning for knowledge graph towards geological data," *Scientific Programming*, vol. 2017, Article ID 5072427, 13 pages, 2017.

[35] H. X. Vo and L. J. Durlofsky, "Data assimilation and uncertainty assessment for complex geological models using a new PCA-based parameterization," *Computational Geosciences*, vol. 19, no. 4, pp. 747–767, 2015.

[36] A. Gasmi, C. Gomez, H. Zouari, A. Masse, and D. Ducrot, "PCA and SVM as geo-computational methods for geological mapping in the southern of Tunisia, using ASTER remote sensing data set," *Arabian Journal of Geosciences*, vol. 9, no. 20, article 753, 2016.

[37] Z.-S. Luo and Y.-T. Wei, "Research on Rough set applied in the geological measure data prediction model," *Advanced Materials Research*, vol. 457-458, pp. 792–798, 2012.

[38] M. Farzamian, A. K. Rouhani, A. Yarmohammadi, H. Shahi, H. A. F. Sabokbar, and M. Ziaiie, "A weighted fuzzy aggregation GIS model in the integration of geophysical data with geochemical and geological data for Pb–Zn exploration in Takab area, NW Iran," *Arabian Journal of Geosciences*, vol. 9, no. 2, article no. 104, pp. 1–17, 2016.

[39] Y. Xu, X. Luo, W. Wang, and W. Zhao, "Efficient DV-HOP localization forwireless cyber-physical social sensing system: a correntropy-based neural network learning scheme," *Sensors*, vol. 17, no. 1, article 135, 2017.

[40] X. Luo, Y. Xu, W. Wang et al., "Towards enhancing stacked extreme learning machine with sparse autoencoder by correntropy," *Journal of The Franklin Institute*, 2017.

[41] X. Luo, H. Luo, and X. Chang, "Online optimization of collaborative web service qos prediction based on approximate dynamic programming," *International Journal of Distributed Sensor Networks*, vol. 2015, Article ID 452492, 9 pages, 2015.

[42] X. Luo, J. Deng, J. Liu, W. Wang, X. Ban, and J. Wang, "A quantized kernel least mean square scheme with entropy-guided learning for intelligent data analysis," *China Communications*, vol. 14, no. 7, pp. 127–136, 2017.

[43] J. Passmore, J. Laxton, and M. Sen, "EarthServer for geological applications opening up access to big data using OGC web services," *Advances in Soil Mechanics and Geotechnical Engineering*, vol. 3, pp. 123–129, 2014.

[44] C. Li, M. Song, L. Xia, X. Luo, and J. Li, "The spatial data sharing mechanisms of geological survey information grid in P2P mixed network systems network architecture model," in *Proceedings of the 9th International Conference on Grid and Cloud Computing, GCC '10*, pp. 258–263, November 2010.

[45] S. A. B. Cruz, A. M. V. Monteiro, and R. Santos, "Automated geospatial Web Services composition based on geodata quality requirements," *Computers & Geosciences*, vol. 47, pp. 60–74, 2012.

[46] J. Xia, C. Yang, K. Liu, Z. Li, M. Sun, and M. Yu, "Forming a global monitoring mechanism and a spatiotemporal performance model for geospatial services," *International Journal of Geographical Information Science*, vol. 29, no. 3, pp. 375–396, 2015.

[47] S. Ibrahim, H. Jin, L. Lu, L. Qi, S. Wu, and X. Shi, "Evaluating MapReduce on virtual machines: the hadoop case," in *Proceedings of the First International Conference on Cloud Computing*, pp. 519–528, 2009.

[48] M. H. Iqbal and T. R. Soomro, "Big data analysis: apache Storm perspective," *International Journal of Computer Trends and Technology*, vol. 19, no. 1, pp. 9–14, 2015.

[49] J. L. Reyes-Ortiz, L. Oneto, and D. Anguita, "Big data analytics in the cloud: spark on Hadoop vs MPI/OpenMP on Beowulf," *Procedia Computer Science*, vol. 53, no. 1, pp. 121–130, 2015.

[50] X. Meng, J. Bradley, B. Yavuz et al., "MLlib: machine learning in apache spark," *Journal of Machine Learning Research*, vol. 17, 2016.

[51] R. Giachetta, "A framework for processing large scale geospatial and remote sensing data in MapReduce environment," *Computers and Graphics*, vol. 49, pp. 37–46, 2015.

[52] S. Huang and X. Liu, "Geological data informatization and standardization based on geological big data," *Coal Geology of China*, vol. 28, no. 7, pp. 74–78, 2016.

[53] K. J. A. Kouame, F. Jiang, Y. Feng, and S. Zhu, "The strengthening of geological infrastructure, research and data acquisition - using gis in ivory coast gold mines," *MATEC Web of Conferences*, vol. 95, p. 18001, 2017.

[54] C. S. J. Karlsson, S. Miliutenko, A. Björklund, U. Mörtberg, B. Olofsson, and S. Toller, "Life cycle assessment in road infrastructure planning using spatial geological data," *The International Journal of Life Cycle Assessment*, vol. 22, no. 8, pp. 1302–1317, 2017.

[55] K. Stock, T. Stojanovic, F. Reitsma et al., "To ontologise or not to ontologise: an information model for a geospatial knowledge infrastructure," *Computers & Geosciences*, vol. 45, pp. 98–108, 2012.

[56] J. Hunter, C. Brooking, L. Reading, and S. Vink, "A Web-based system enabling the integration, analysis, and 3D sub-surface visualization of groundwater monitoring data and geological models," *International Journal of Digital Earth*, vol. 9, no. 2, pp. 197–214, 2016.

[57] R. D. Müller, X. Qin, D. T. Sandwell et al., "The GPlates portal: Cloud-based interactive 3D visualization of global geophysical and geological data in a web browser," *PLoS ONE*, vol. 11, no. 3, Article ID e0150883, 2016.

15

NUMA-Aware Thread Scheduling for Big Data Transfers over Terabits Network Infrastructure

Taeuk Kim ⓘ,[1] Awais Khan ⓘ,[1] Youngjae Kim ⓘ,[1] Preethika Kasu ⓘ,[2] and Scott Atchley[3]

[1]Sogang University, Seoul, Republic of Korea
[2]Ajou University, Suwon, Republic of Korea
[3]Oak Ridge National Laboratory, Oak Ridge, TN 37831, USA

Correspondence should be addressed to Youngjae Kim; youkim@sogang.ac.kr

Academic Editor: Basilio B. Fraguela

The evergrowing trend of big data has led scientists to share and transfer the simulation and analytical data across the geodistributed research and computing facilities. However, the existing data transfer frameworks used for data sharing lack the capability to adopt the attributes of the underlying parallel file systems (PFS). LADS (Layout-Aware Data Scheduling) is an end-to-end data transfer tool optimized for terabit network using a layout-aware data scheduling via PFS. However, it does not consider the NUMA (Nonuniform Memory Access) architecture. In this paper, we propose a NUMA-aware thread and resource scheduling for optimized data transfer in terabit network. First, we propose distributed RMA buffers to reduce memory controller contention in CPU sockets and then schedule the threads based on CPU socket and NUMA nodes inside CPU socket to reduce memory access latency. We design and implement the proposed resource and thread scheduling in the existing LADS framework. Experimental results showed from 21.7% to 44% improvement with memory-level optimizations in the LADS framework as compared to the baseline without any optimization.

1. Introduction

The continuous inflation in data generation is raising the sharing and collaboration needs for effective simulations and real-time analysis. Such sharing and collaboration need a massive-scale data transfer across geodispersed data centers [1]. The Brookhaven National Lab (BNL) cooperates with European Large Hadron Collider (LHC) in the ATLAS experiment where more than 3,000 scientists participate and produce petabytes of simulation and analytical data, motivating collaboration ventures [2]. Such large-scale collaboration environments highly motivate us to revisit the architecture of existing end-to-end data transfer tools such as bbcp [3], LADS [1], and GridFTP [4].

In an end-to-end data transfer between geodispersed data centers, there are three significant factors concerning the data transfer performance and throughput, that is, network, storage, and memory. However, in realistic large-scale HPC environments, the network infrastructure delivers a high bandwidth and it is further improving [5], for example, ESnet of DOE [6]. So, we do not consider network as a major bottleneck in limiting the data transfer activities in large-scale HPC environments equipped with high-speed network connectivity [5, 6].

The parallel file system (PFS) [7, 8] based storage-back-ends deployed in the data centers act as a bottleneck when thread count exceeds the service rate of object storage server (OSS) or multiple threads access the same object storage target (OST). LADS [1], high-speed end-to-end data transfer tool between data centers, minimizes this I/O contention by being aware of data chunk's layout and scheduling threads based on it. The memory bottleneck can be incurred in NUMA environment when threads access remote NUMA node's memory. If the buffer which LADS uses to transfer data is allocated in a different NUMA node from I/O threads, I/O threads need to access remote NUMA node during data transfer and it makes memory access consume longer latency. Currently, LADS tool does not offer any solution to overcome this problem. In this paper, we propose MTS (Memory-aware Thread Scheduling) method to solve the memory bottleneck issues with LADS data transfer tool.

The data transfer frameworks such as GridFTP [4], bbcp [3], and LADS [1] have been designed to ensure high-speed data transmission. However, GridFTP and bbcp are designed on file-based data transfer, whereas LADS is optimized for object-based data transfer where multiple threads can work on multiple object chunks simultaneously to improve end-to-end data transfer speed. With the improvement in network infrastructure, the parallel and distributed file systems such as Lustre [8], Gluster [7], and Ceph [9] are improving their storage and computing frameworks in order to derive the maximum bandwidth. GridFTP [4] and bbcp [3] cannot gain high benefits from these file systems since they are designed without considering the underlying file system, whereas LADS [1], due to its layout-aware nature of the data transfer mechanism, can fully utilize the benefits of these underlying parallel file systems. Besides, LADS uses Common Communication Interface (CCI) [5] to exploit the high-speed terabit networks.

In this paper, we emphasize the possible bottlenecks and opportunities such as high-speed network and NUMA architecture in end-to-end data transfer path. An end-to-end data transfer can meet multiple bottlenecks such as (i) storage, (ii) CPU, and (iii) memory. The storage becomes a bottleneck when data transfer software is unaware of the underlying file system architecture; for example, parallel file systems use chunking and striping techniques to store data in a more efficient fashion. So, the data transfer tool can efficiently utilize storage bandwidth by having the knowledge about storage layout, without which storage bandwidth can be underutilized. The CPU bottleneck occurs, if data transfer tool does not take into account the utilization of multicores while transferring data. The underutilization can happen when the threads are less than the CPU cores and some of the cores remain idle. The overutilization can occur, where thread count is very high with respect to available CPU cores.

The memory contention can occur in two conditions. Firstly, when multiple threads or processes are accessing the same shared memory region. Secondly, when threads hosted on CPU sockets access the remote memory of other CPU sockets. Both these contentions can lead to increased memory access latency. LADS framework addresses the storage and CPU bottlenecks by implementing layout-aware multithreaded architecture [1]. However, LADS does not consider the memory bottleneck issues.

In this paper, we address the memory bottleneck issues by proposing memory buffer partitioning at each CPU socket and scheduling threads with being aware of NUMA architecture. Partitioning the memory buffer reduces the shared memory regions and thread scheduling reduces the remote memory access across CPU sockets.

This paper makes the following contributions:

(i) Increase in the number of I/O threads in LADS leads to contention in memory controller. To address this issue, we propose *Multiple Memory Buffers* (MMB),

which distributes the RMA buffer across all the CPU sockets to reduce memory controller congestion.

(ii) The distributed RMA buffer at each CPU socket alone is not sufficient to improve the memory latency problem. In some cases, threads may try to access the remote RMA buffer hosted at different CPU sockets. To avoid such remote memory access, we design and implement *Memory-aware Thread Scheduling* (MTS) to schedule threads to access only the RMA buffer hosted on the same CPU socket. MTS reduces overall memory latency by eliminating all accesses to remote memory.

(iii) We conduct a comprehensive evaluation for our proposed ideas using a file size distribution based on a snapshot of the real peta-scale file system at ORNL [10]. We compare the performance of our proposed MMB and MTS with default settings where it uses single RMA buffer and where it applies NUMA binding to threads. From our experimental results, we have observed that our proposed idea yields up to 44% higher data transfer rate than the default settings.

The rest of this paper is organized as follows. Section 2 describes the LADS architecture and implementation details. Section 3 outlines the design and implementation of the proposed memory-level optimizations. Experimental setup and evaluation results are presented in Section 4. Section 5 describes the related works and we conclude in Section 6.

2. Layout-Aware Data Scheduling

Data sharing and scientific collaborations are advancing in recent years. Tools like GridFTP [4], bbcp [3], and LADS [1] are developed for efficient data transfer across geodistributed data storage facilities. LADS [1], an end-to-end data transfer tool, exploits the underlying storage architecture for optimizing the bulk data movement between data centers connected via high-speed terabit network. LADS uses Common Communication Interface (CCI) to fully utilize the terabit network [5] capabilities. The work proposed in this paper is an extension of LADS data transfer framework. This section describes LADS architecture.

Threads and Work Queues. LADS consists of three different types of threads, that is, Master (MT), Communication (CT), and I/O thread. The Master thread splits the workload in chunks and makes each chunk into a task. These tasks are inserted into the OST queue. In particular, there are as many OST queues as the number of OSTs in the Lustre file system. Master thread schedules I/O threads to OST queues and the I/O threads dequeue the tasks from OST queues to perform I/O operations. On the other hand, Communication thread manages the end-point communication between source and sink. The I/O thread loads the data chunks from storage to RMA buffer at source and stores them from RMA buffer to storage at sink. Both the Master and the Communication thread own work queues which hold the requests to transfer data objects to each other.

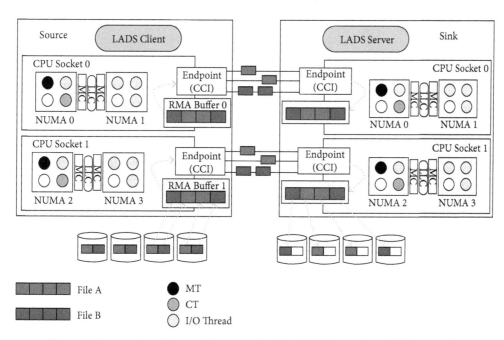

FIGURE 1: An overview of proposed memory-level optimizations in LADS [1] framework.

Communication Protocol. From now, the notation of source-end in the data transmission will be SRC, and the notation of sink-end in the data transmission will be SNK.

Step 1. The SRC MT catches the layout of data chunks for the requested file and adds the request to the SRC Communication Thread Work Queue (CWQ). The SRC CT sends a new file request to the sink-end via CCI end-point connection. Similarly, at the sink-end, SNK CT upon receiving the request forwards it to SNK Master Thread Work Queue (MWQ).

Step 2. The SNK MT upon receiving the request creates a new file with the same name as in the request. The file id corresponding to the newly created file is added to SNK CWQ in the request form and is sent to source-end. After receiving the request at source-end, SRC CT directs the request to SRC MWQ. The SRC MT loads the chunks information into SRC OST queues.

Step 3. Once the SRC MT inserts the data chunk into the SRC OST queue, SRC MT wakes up the SRC I/O threads according to the number of OSTs in the underlying SRC Lustre file system. Every SRC I/O thread at source-end then traverses the OST queues, gets the chunks information, reads the chunks from the physical OST storage, and loads them into the SRC RMA buffer. Then, SRC I/O thread inserts a request into the SRC CWQ to send the data chunk's information. SNK CT receives the request, and it gets the data chunk from SRC RMA buffer via RDMA access.

Step 4. At SNK, after reading the data chunk from SRC RMA buffer, the SNK CT loads the data chunk into the SNK RMA buffer. Then the SNK I/O threads are scheduled to the SNK OST queues by the SNK CT to write the data chunk from the SNK RMA buffer to the SNK physical OST storage. The SNK

CT sends the transfer completion message and repeats Steps 3 and 4, till all the data chunks of all the files are transferred.

3. Design and Implementation

This section describes the proposed optimization methods and its design and implementation details.

3.1. Overview. Figure 1 shows an overview of the proposed memory-level optimizations in LADS software framework [1]. The proposed approach consists of three major elements, (i) distributed RMA buffers at each CPU socket, (ii) Socket-based Memory-aware Thread Scheduling (SMTS), and (iii) NUMA node based Memory-aware Thread Scheduling (NMTS). The proposed optimizations are highly flexible and can be applied to *n* CPU sockets. Each CPU socket consists of cores, shared Last Level Cache (LLC), and one or more memory controllers, whereas the number of cores, LLC, and memory controller depend on the CPU type used. If there are multiple sets of cores and memory controllers in a CPU socket, then there will be more than one NUMA node per CPU socket. As shown in Figure 1, each CPU socket hosts three types of threads, that is, Master (MT), Communication (CT), and I/O thread; each thread performs a specific functionality similar to LADS architecture [1]. Proposed optimization methods are an extension of existing LADS implementation.

The Master thread captures the layout of files to be transferred from Lustre [8] object storage targets (OSTs) and schedules I/O threads to execute I/O operations specific to these OSTs. The I/O threads read the data chunks from the object storage into the RMA buffer and notify the Communication thread, which is responsible for creating an end-point connection via CCI API [5] and sending the data chunks in RMA buffer from source side to sink side.

3.2. MMB: Multiple Memory Buffers. The LADS data transfer framework relies on single RMA buffer, where all the I/O threads load and store the data chunks between RMA buffer [1] and underlying storage system. However, the use of single RMA buffer can cause two problems: (i) memory latency caused by remote CPU socket's memory access and (ii) contention on the memory controller. When threads are created, LADS schedules the threads to random CPU cores. Generally, I/O threads are scattered on all CPU sockets, that is, several I/O threads from different CPU sockets access a specific CPU socket's RMA buffer. This incurs a number of remote memory accesses which have a longer latency than local memory access. Moreover, in LADS the number of I/O threads is configurable and in ideal scenario, it considers the number of OSTs belonging to the target Lustre file system for the number of I/O threads. But, in realistic scenarios, data centers using Lustre may exceed hundreds or thousands of OSTs, so the number of I/O threads will be configured according to the number of CPU cores. If a high number of I/O threads corresponding to the number of cores in a multicore environment access the single RMA buffer, the contention will occur in the memory controller of the CPU socket or NUMA node hosting the RMA buffer. We propose *Multiple Memory Buffer* (MMB) scheme, which distributes the RMA buffer to each CPU socket's memory in the existing LADS framework. Figure 1 shows the RMA buffer distribution to each CPU socket. This partitioning of RMA buffer per CPU socket gives significant benefits. First, it reduces the memory controller contention significantly which is caused by single RMA buffer on increasing the number of I/O threads. Second, it reduces the memory latency due to the less number of remote memory accesses of I/O threads.

3.3. MTS: Memory-Aware Thread Scheduling. This section describes the details about the two levels of *Memory-aware Thread Scheduling* (MTS). First, we discuss the Socket-based Thread Scheduling and second, we present NUMA node based Thread Scheduling when CPU socket has multiple NUMA nodes.

3.3.1. Socket-Based Thread Scheduling. The partitioning of RMA buffer across each CPU socket gives the privilege to reduce the memory controller contention. But the remote memory access is still possible and it can increase memory access latency as compared to local memory access. To solve the remote memory access problem, we propose *Socket-based Memory-aware Thread Scheduling* (SMTS) scheme. SMTS schedules I/O threads between CPU sockets in such a way that all the I/O threads should access RMA buffer residing on the same CPU socket. Also, the RMA buffer is registered by the Communication thread and accessed via RDMA read/write operations through the end-point. So, a single and dedicated Communication thread is required per CPU socket to manage each RMA buffer. In our approach, each CPU socket has only one Master and Communication

thread and configurable number of I/O threads. All threads and connections created per CPU socket are independent of other CPU sockets. The Master thread in each connection controls the chunk-level scheduling and transmits only the assigned files and I/O threads also work against the same objects designated by the Master thread. In this way, all I/O threads are pinned to their local CPU sockets' cores.

3.3.2. NUMA Node Based Thread Scheduling. Here, we discuss the NUMA-aware optimizations required in LADS framework for CPU sockets equipped with multiple NUMA nodes. Considering the fact that it is possible to associate multiple NUMA nodes per CPU socket [11], it is highly necessary to schedule threads onto NUMA nodes at each CPU socket. To address this kind of cases, we propose *NUMA node based Memory-aware Thread Scheduling* (NMTS). NMTS is shown in Figure 1 as threads pinned at each NUMA node in every CPU socket. The motivation behind addressing thread scheduling at NUMA node is to avoid remote memory access inside a CPU socket when the socket is equipped with multiple NUMA nodes. To schedule threads inside a CPU socket, two elements are taken into account, (i) *interaction between threads* and (ii) *fairness of core usage.* In LADS [1] framework, to complete data transfer more efficiently, threads interact with each other at a high extent.

At first, Master and Communication threads interact, when data transfer begins. LADS framework has its own data structures for file metadata and keeps information about the file size, fd, and data chunk layout of the files required to transfer. Both the Master and Communication thread maintain work queues. In the rest of the paper, we will use MWQ to denote Master thread's work queue and CWQ to represent Communication thread's work queue. The Master thread schedules the requested file to CWQ at the start of data transfer. The Communication thread also sends a file request to the MWQ, when a file request is received from the sink side. In case of high transfer traffic, the interaction between Master and Communication threads increases. So, in such scenarios the placement of Master and Communication threads plays a major role. If Master and Communication threads are placed on different NUMA nodes, the performance can degrade due to remote memory access inside CPU socket.

Moreover, Master thread manages the information about OSTs containing data chunks in queue. The number of queues is equivalent to the number of OSTs in target Lustre file system. The I/O threads access these OST queues when loading data chunks from storage to RMA buffer to get information about the chunk. So, placing I/O threads near Master thread is also an important factor in performance optimization. However, due to the high number of I/O threads, it is not possible to keep all the I/O threads in same NUMA node with Master thread. Scheduling all the I/O threads on single NUMA node incurs core contention among I/O threads. Therefore, firstly we suggest scheduling Master and Communication threads on the same NUMA node and then placing I/O threads to NUMA nodes as close as possible to Master thread. We distribute I/O threads across the NUMA nodes to enhance the fairness of per core usage as shown in Figure 1. Figure 1 shows that Master and Communication threads are hosted by same NUMA node and I/O threads are hosted near to the Master thread whereby load is evenly distributed among the NUMA nodes' cores.

4. Evaluation

4.1. Experimental Setup. In this experimental setup, we use a private testbed with eight nodes connected by InfiniBand (IB) EDR (100 Gb/s). The nodes use the IB network to communicate with each other. We use E5-2650 v4 with two CPU sockets (two NUMA nodes for each CPU socket and six cores for each NUMA node), 128 GB DRAM, running with CentOS 7.3, Linux kernel 3.10.0-514.21.1.el7.x86_64. Two of the eight nodes are used as data transfer nodes (DTN) for source and sink hosts. The other six nodes are used as two different storage systems. We built two storage systems for more realistic experiments.

(i) *Testbed-I:* when building a peta-scale storage system with Lustre file system, it uses hundreds of object storage servers with tens of object storage targets in each server. For example, Spider II is a center-wide, Lustre-based system for one of the fastest supercomputer in US, Titan with two namespaces [1]. Each namespace has 144 OSSs, which manage seven OSTs and each OST is configured with 10 HDDs in RAID-10 [1]. That is, the I/O of the PFS used in realistic environment is too fast to use all the available bandwidth of the PFS. In order to emulate such environments, for each source and sink host, we use memory file system mounted on a server node via NFS v4.0 as a high performance file system.

(ii) *Testbed-II:* we experimented with a small-scale testbed equipped with Lustre file system for each source and sink host, which is configured using one OSS, one MDS, and eight OSTs, each mounted over 600 GB 10K RPM 6 Gbps SAS, 2.5″ HotPlug HDD. For each file system, we created 8 logical volume drives on top of the HDDs to make each disk become an OST. We set stripe count to be 1 and stripe size to be 1 MB.

We developed an in-house memory benchmark program in C++ to measure the memory bandwidth between different NUMA nodes of source and sink hosts.

From Table 1, we can notice that in-socket remote NUMA node is 4% slower when compared to in-socket local NUMA node, whereas remote CPU socket NUMA node is 32% slower than in-socket local NUMA node.

We use two representative file distributions to have two file groups appropriate for our small-scale testbed setup: one for small number of big files with 8×3 GB files, referred to as big-file workload, and the other for large number of small files with $6,000 \times 1$ MB files, referred to as small-file workload. HPC file size distribution follows a binomial distribution in terms of file system space occupancy and number of files: larger files occupy most of the file system space, but with fewer numbers of files. On the other hand, small files have

TABLE 1: Memory BW of local and remote NUMA node.

CPU socket & NUMA node locality	BW (MB/s)
In-socket local NUMA node	3160.43
In-socket remote NUMA node	3038.85
Remote socket NUMA node	2131.24

TABLE 2: The evaluation of thread placement across CPU sockets. Total 8 I/O threads are used in this experiment.

Thread placement	Throughput (MB/s)
All threads placed on same CPU socket	2065.21
CT placed on different CPU socket	1914.02
MT placed on different CPU socket	1719.80

a more number of files, but the file system space occupancy is very small [1].

For the convenience of analysis, we define the following schemes:

(i) Baseline: it uses a single RMA buffer. The RMA buffer has a different physical memory location depending on which NUMA node it is placed. Experiment is performed according to the position of RMA buffer and NUMA binding. In the experiment, Ni means that the single RMA buffer is located at NUMA node i, and NBi means that the single RMA buffer is located at NUMA node i with I/O threads bound on same node. If I/O thread count exceeds the number of cores, I/O threads are distributed to NUMA node i and to its nearest node evenly.

(ii) MMB: the RMA buffer is partitioned by CPU socket. In our experiment, a single RMA buffer of baseline is partitioned into two.

(iii) MTS: it applies both Memory-aware Thread Scheduling Algorithms (SMTS and NMTS) to MMB.

For each iteration of memory file system and Lustre experiment, we cleared page caches of the source, sink, and storage servers for a fair evaluation.

4.2. Results

Evaluation of Memory Access Speed by Intimacy of Thread Type. In LADS, threads share data structures; for example, MT and CT share the MWQ and CWQ whereas I/O threads share OST queues with MT. RMA buffer is shared between CT and I/O threads. Thus, increasing the locality between threads and shared data structures (memory variables and queues) benefits to improve the performance.

In this experiment, we perform the evaluation according to the arrangement of MT, CT, and I/O threads on same and different CPU sockets.

Table 2 shows the throughput comparison for various placements of CT and MT on CPU sockets. The experiment was made using small files with Testbed-I. We can clearly see that placing CT and MT on the same NUMA node which has the RMA buffer helps in improving the data transfer rate. The

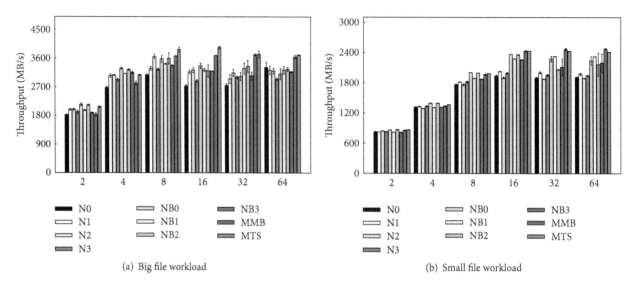

FIGURE 2: Performance comparison for Memory-aware Thread Scheduling using Multiple Memory Buffers per CPU socket. The x-axis shows the I/O thread count. Ni and NBi are for baseline experiments. The error bar depicts min. and max. deviation from the average of 3 iterations.

MTS is aware of thread types and prioritizes to schedule them on the same NUMA nodes. In the following evaluations, we run experiments by fixing the placement of the CT and MT on the same NUMA node with the RMA buffer in cases of NUMA binding.

Evaluating MTS with High-Speed PFS. To verify the effectiveness of the proposed MMB and MTS idea, we compare the data transmission throughput with baseline using a single RMA buffer. Particularly, we experiment by increasing the number of I/O threads to evaluate the performance according to CPU core utilization. Figures 2(a) and 2(b) show the comparison results for big and small file workloads, respectively, with Testbed-I. In order to confirm the performance limitation of the single RMA buffer and the maximum performance achievable by the NUMA binding, we evaluate the baseline by changing the NUMA node position of the single RMA buffer with and without the NUMA binding of threads. The RMA buffer locates on NUMA node i in experiments Ni and NBi, and I/O threads are bounded with considering the location of RMA buffer in NBi.

In Figure 2(a), we first analyze the results with the single RMA buffer (refer to results with labels in Ni and NBi). We can observe about 23% performance improvement on average with NUMA binding over without NUMA binding. As the number of I/O threads increases, overall performance improvement is observed till 8 I/O threads, whereas increasing I/O threads to 16, there is no significant improvement in the performance. This is due to the thread saturation of underlying file system. Moreover, we observe that performance is slightly lower in 16 I/O threads. We suspect the reason of performance degradation to be memory contention and remote memory access by the single RMA buffer.

Second, we compare the baseline results with MMB and MTS. From the results, we can confirm that overall performance improvement by MMB over the baseline varies

from 13.0% to 34.7% and with MTS, its improvement is from 21.7% to 44%. That is, we observe that MTS further increases the performance of MMB by about 10%. Overall, data transfer rate increases as the number of I/O threads increases up to 16, but after that, improvement is not significant. We also see that, up to 2–4 I/O threads, MMB and MTS have little effect. When CPU cores are not fully utilized, single RMA buffer implementation outperforms partitioning the RMA buffer, because where performance storage is not fully exploited due to small number of I/O threads, dividing RMA buffer and binding threads to NUMA node incurs additional overhead. On the other hand, from 8 I/O threads, MMB and MTS show improved performance over the baseline. Particularly, in 16 I/O threads, we observe that the average performance improvements of MMB and MTS are 9.4–15.1% and 16.9–23%, respectively, over the baseline with NUMA binding. This shows that MMB and MTS contribute on the memory-level optimization in data transfer where storage is sufficiently fast.

In Figure 2(b), we have observations similar to the big file workload experiment. Up to 4 I/O threads, there is almost no performance difference. On the other hand, after 8 I/O threads, we can observe that MMB and MTS have on an average higher performance than baseline when we are over 16 threads. We observe little performance impact by MTS over MMB for small file workload, whereas MTS shows higher performance than MMB for big file workload.

Evaluating MTS with Slow PFS. If the storage performance is low, the performance improvement of MMB and MTS can be reduced. Thus, in the next experiment, we test with the source and sink hosts on which the small-scale Lustre file system is mounted (Testbed-II). Figure 3 shows the results of the experiment with big and small file workloads in Testbed-II. First, we observe that the maximum data rate is smaller than the experiment in Testbed-I. We see up to 1363 MB/s transfer rate with 8 I/O threads in big file workload and 435 MB/s

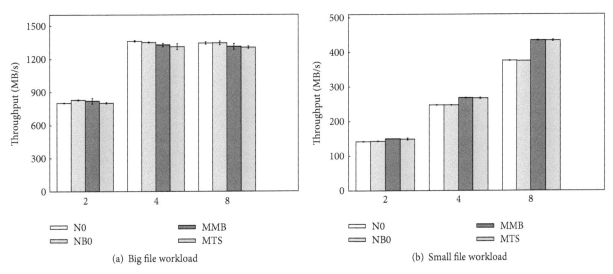

FIGURE 3: Performance comparisons for MMB and MTS with Lustre file systems. The x-axis shows the number of I/O threads. The error bar depicts minimum and maximum deviation from the average of 3 iterations.

rate in small file workload. Unfortunately, in Figure 3(a), we see that MMB and MTS have slight performance impact. In Figure 2(a), MMB and MTS improve the performance on 2000–3000 MB/s range of data transfer rate, but in small-scale Lustre file system which has just 1 OSS and 8 OSTs, MMB and MTS do not show any performance improvement. But, Figure 3(b) shows that in small file workload MMB and MTS depict performance improvement by 9.7% on average and up to 15.7% with 8 I/O threads. Because in baseline, only one pair of MT and CT sends 6,000 files metadata to other work queues sequentially, whereas in MMB and MTS, two pairs of MT and CT work on 3,000 files metadata simultaneously. It is confirmed that if the PFS I/O performance is low, it is difficult to take advantage of the NUMA effect. On the other hand, Testbed-I (memory-based network file system) represents the high-speed PFS environment and confirmed the effects of memory-level optimizations (MMB and MTS). Though the storage is not so fast that makes a bottleneck in end-to-end data transfer, dividing RMA buffer to each CPU socket increases the performance in large number of small files.

5. Related Work

The recent literatures addressing the high-speed data transfer tools include GridFTP [4], bbcp [3], and LADS [1]. bbcp transfers large amount of data efficiently using multiple TCP streams. However, bbcp uses single I/O thread and is unaware of the underlying file system layout. GridFTP [4] supports striping which allows data transmission to multiple peers when data is stored across a set of storage systems. But GridFTP does not consider the existing file system level data chunk layout of the files that are striped on the object-based parallel and distributed file systems. GridFTP and bbcp core design relies on file-based data transfer, whereas LADS [1] is a layout-aware object-based data scheduler which considers the storage layout and uses Common Communication

Interface (CCI) [5] to exploit the high-speed network. Moreover, LADS implements a multithreaded architecture to benefit from parallel file system.

Along the line of advancements in storage and network, the CPU and memory performance is also improving by including the NUMA architecture. Multithreaded applications need to reflect such NUMA-awareness in their design to achieve the highest bandwidth from CPU and memory. Thread and memory locality in NUMA architecture plays a crucial role in performance. With benchmarking with STREAM triad, a research has shown that when benchmark allocates threads on a local NUMA node, the memory access is much higher than placing threads on a remote NUMA node through 1-hop and 2-hop [12]. Another study addressing NUMA-aware Thread Scheduling includes RAMSYS [2]. RAMSYS is a high-speed data transfer tool which uses dedicated threads in asynchronous fashion to incorporate pipelining in each step. But RAMSYS schedules threads without taking into account the underlying storage layout. Also, RAMSYS allocates single task queue on PFS and pushes all I/O requests to single task queue in a similar fashion to single storage device, whereas our approach uses multiple task queues as the number of OSTs in underlying Lustre file system, which enhances the performance on storage level. Our approach is an extension of existing LADS [1] architecture.

6. Conclusion

The advancement in storage, network, and CPU architecture has directed the existing data transfer software to align their design in order to achieve high throughput. Currently, the majority of data transfer tools such as GridFTP [4] and bbcp [3] do not support such design optimizations. LADS [1], a data transfer software designed for high-speed networks, considers the underlying storage architecture. However, LADS ignores the NUMA architecture. In this paper, we propose a NUMA-aware resource and thread scheduling for optimized data transfer in high-speed network. Our approach involves three major sections, (i) distributed RMA buffer to each CPU socket, (ii) high-level Socket-based Thread Scheduling, and (iii) low-level NUMA node based Thread Scheduling. Our approach not only reduces the memory controller contention but also improves the memory access latency. The evaluation has shown improvement up to 44% for high performance file system when compared to baseline.

Disclosure

The portion of this work was presented as work in progress (1-page abstract) in the 2nd Joint International Workshop on Parallel Data Storage and Data-Intensive Scalable Computing Systems (PDSW-DISCS), held in conjunction with SC'17 [13].

Conflicts of Interest

The authors declare that there are no conflicts of interest regarding the publication of this paper.

Acknowledgments

This work was supported by Institute for Information & Communications Technology Promotion (IITP) grant funded by the Korean Government (MSIT) (no. 2015-0-00590, High Performance Big Data Analytic Platform Performance Acceleration Technologies Development). This work also used the resources of the Korea Institute of Science and Technology Information (KISTI), in Daedeok Science Town in Daejeon, South Korea. The authors thank Dr. Sungyong Park for his constructive comments that have significantly improved the paper.

References

[1] Y. Kim, S. Atchley, G. R. Vallée, and G. M. Shipman, "LADS: Optimizing Data Transfers Using Layout-Aware Data Scheduling," in *Proceedings of the 13th USENIX Conference on File and Storage Technologies FAST'15*, 2015.

[2] T. Li, Y. Ren, D. Yu, and S. Jin, "RAMSYS: Resource-aware asynchronous data transfer with multicore systems," *IEEE Transactions on Parallel and Distributed Systems*, vol. 28, no. 5, pp. 1430–1444, 2017.

[3] A. B. Hanushevsky, "Peer-to-Peer Computing for Secure High Performance Data Copying," Tech. Rep. SLAC-PUB-9173, 2002.

[4] I. Foster, "Globus Toolkit Version 4: Software for Service-Oriented Systems," in *Network and Parallel Computing*, vol. 3779 of *Lecture Notes in Computer Science*, pp. 2–13, Springer Berlin Heidelberg, Berlin, Heidelberg, 2005.

[5] S. Atchley, D. Dillow, G. Shipman et al., "The Common Communication Interface (CCI)," in *Proceedings of the 2011 IEEE 19th Annual Symposium on High-Performance Interconnects (HOTI)*, pp. 51–60, Washington, DC, USA, August 2011.

[6] ESnet, "Energy Sciences Network (ESnet)," http://www.es.net.

[7] A. Davies and A. Orsaria, *Scale Out with GlusterFS*, Houston, TX, USA, 2013, http://dl.acm.org/citation.cfm?id=2555789.2555790.

[8] F. Wang, H. S. Oral, G. M. Shipman, O. Drokin, D. Wang, and H. Huang, "Understanding Lustre Filesystem Internals," Tech. Rep. ORNL/TM-2009/117, 2009.

[9] S. A. Weil, S. A. Brandt, E. L. Miller, D. D. Long, and C. Maltzahn, "Ceph: A Scalable, High-Performance Distributed File System," in *Proceedings of the 7th symposium on Operating systems design and implementation. 1em plus 0.5em minus 0*, pp. 307–320, USENIX Association, 2006.

[10] ORNL, "Oak Ridge Leadership Computing Facility," https://www.olcf.ornl.gov/.

[11] Dell, *NUMA Best Practices for Dell PowerEdge 12th Generation Servers*, 2013, http://en.community.dell.com/techcenter/b/techcenter/archive/2013/01/09/.

[12] T. Li, Y. Ren, D. Yu, and S. Jin, "Analysis of NUMA Effects in Modern Multicore Systems for the Design of High-performance Data Transfer Applications," *Future Generation Computer Systems*, vol. 74, pp. 41–50, 2017, http://www.sciencedirect.com/science/article/pii/S0167739X16305799.

[13] T. Kim, A. Khan, Y. Kim, S. Park, and S. Atchley, "NUMA-Aware Thread and Resource Scheduling for Terabit Data Movement," in *Proceedings of the (Work In Progress) PDSW-DISCS'17 (held in conjunction with SC'17)*, p. 1, Denver, CO, USA, 2017.

16

Scalable Parallel Distributed Coprocessor System for Graph Searching Problems with Massive Data

Wanrong Huang, Xiaodong Yi, Yichun Sun, Yingwen Liu, Shuai Ye, and Hengzhu Liu

School of Computer, National University of Defense Technology, Deya Road No. 109, Kaifu District, Changsha, Hunan 410073, China

Correspondence should be addressed to Wanrong Huang; huangwr1990@163.com

Academic Editor: José María Álvarez-Rodríguez

The Internet applications, such as network searching, electronic commerce, and modern medical applications, produce and process massive data. Considerable data parallelism exists in computation processes of data-intensive applications. A traversal algorithm, breadth-first search (BFS), is fundamental in many graph processing applications and metrics when a graph grows in scale. A variety of scientific programming methods have been proposed for accelerating and parallelizing BFS because of the poor temporal and spatial locality caused by inherent irregular memory access patterns. However, new parallel hardware could provide better improvement for scientific methods. To address small-world graph problems, we propose a scalable and novel field-programmable gate array-based heterogeneous multicore system for scientific programming. The core is multithread for streaming processing. And the communication network InfiniBand is adopted for scalability. We design a binary search algorithm to address mapping to unify all processor addresses. Within the limits permitted by the Graph500 test bench after 1D parallel hybrid BFS algorithm testing, our 8-core and 8-thread-per-core system achieved superior performance and efficiency compared with the prior work under the same degree of parallelism. Our system is efficient not as a special acceleration unit but as a processor platform that deals with graph searching applications.

1. Introduction

Information technology, the Internet, and intelligent technology have ushered in the era of big data. Data-intensive applications, as a typical representative of big data applications represented by graph searching, have been receiving increased attention [1]. Many real-world applications could be abstracted as a large graph of millions of vertices, but this procedure is a considerable challenge for processing. These applications represent the connections, relations, and interaction among entities, such as social networks [2], biological interactions [3], and ground transportation [1]. Poor data-driven computation, unstructured organization, irregular memory access, and low computations-to-memory ratio are the prime reasons for parallel large-graph processing inefficiency [4]. To traverse larger graphs caused by data-intensive applications, a variety of scientific programming methods has been proposed [5, 6]. Tithi et al. [5] optimized the programme and used dynamic load balancing with Intel click++ language. Chen et al. [6] proposed a new parallel

model called Codelet model. They all do a good job in speeding up access to memory. However, new parallel computing machines could provide a better platform for software methods. Heterogeneous processing, with reconfigurable logic and field-programmable gate array (FPGAs) as an energy efficient computing systems [7], performs competitively with the multicore CPUs and GPGPUs [4, 8]. The performance of breadth-first search (BFS) on large graphs is bound by the access to high-latency external memory. Thus, we designed considerable parallelism and relatively low clock frequencies to achieve high performance and customized memory architecture to deal with irregular memory access patterns.

The bottleneck of processing graph search is memory. Communication is a primary time overhead in the expansion of processors. In this study, we propose a scalable and novel FPGA-based heterogeneous multicore system for big data applications. The core is multithread for streaming processing, and the communication network is InfiniBand (IB) for scalability. The address mapping is a binary search algorithm mapping, and three levels of hierarchy of memory exist.

The remainder of this paper is organized as follows: Section 2 introduces the details of our 1D decomposition hybrid BFS algorithm. Section 3 shows the details of the proposed parallel system architecture. Section 4 describes the implementation of binary search address mapping. Section 5 provides details of the single processor architecture. Section 6 exhibits the three-level memory hierarchy. Section 7 analyzes the experiment results.

2. Related Works

While parallel computers with millions of cores are already in production, the trend is geared toward higher core densities with deeper memory hierarchies [10] even though other node resources (e.g., memory capacity per core) are not scaling proportionally [11]. Anghel et al. (2014) [12] analyzed node-to-node communications and showed that the application runtime is communication bound and that the communication makeup is as much as 80% of the execution time of each BFS iteration [13].

The Graph500 benchmark is the representative of the graph-based analytic class of applications and is designed to assess the performance of supercomputing systems by solving the BFS graph traversal problem [14, 15].

Fast graph traversal has been approached from a range of architecture methods. Fast graph traversal has been approached from a range of architecture methods. In general-purpose CPU and multicore/supercomputing approaches [16, 17], Agarwal et al. performed locality optimizations on a quad-socket system to reduce memory traffic [18]. A considerable amount of research on parallel BFS implementations on GPUs focuses on level-synchronous or fixed-point methods [19, 20]. The reconfigurable hardware approach in solving graph traversal problems on clusters of FPGAs is limited by graph size and synthesis times [4, 8]. Betkaoui et al. (2012) [4] and Attia et al. (2014) [8] explored highly parallelized processing elements (PEs) and decoupled computation memory. Umuroglu et al. (2015) [11] demonstrated the density, rather than the sparsity, of the treatment of the BFS frontier vector in yielding simpler memory access patterns for BFS, trading redundant computation for DRAM bandwidth utilization, and exploring faster graphs.

3. 1D BFS Algorithm for Testing

In 2013, Beamer et al. [21] proposed a bottom-up algorithm on BFS, which dramatically reduces the number of edges examined, and presented the combination of a conventional top-down algorithm and a novel bottom-up algorithm. The combined algorithm provides a breakthrough for level-synchronized parallel BFS in parallel computation, and this novel bottom-up algorithm is applied in 2D sparse matrix partitioning-based solutions. Today, the 2D bottom-up BFS implementation is a general application in Blue Gene architecture.

Experiments show that with a large number of processors relative to the 1D decomposition, the 2D decomposition can effectively reduce the total communication between processors. In the 2D decomposition, the BFS algorithm has better performance. By contrast, with a small number of processors, the BFS algorithm is suitable in the 1D decomposition. Moreover, our system has eight processors in parallel with unified fine-grained address mapping. Algorithm 1 uses 1D decomposition-optimized BFS algorithm which is proposed by Yasui et al. [22]. In Algorithm 1, V is the set of vertex in graph, while E is the set of edges; that is, $E(u, v) = 1$ means u and v are connected. The parent $[k]$ gives the parent of vertex k in the BFS tree whose source vertex is s; when k is unreachable from s, parent $[k] = -1$. $v \in V$; if v is in the frontier queue, then next $[v] = 1$. The same meaning is given to next (v) (next frontier for each BFS iteration) and visit (v) (when visit $(v) = 1$, v has been visited). Array next, visit, and frontier are stored as bitmap. A new vertex appears in the search; then end $= 0$. When no new vertex appears in the current iteration of BFS, the iteration will end.

4. Massive Parallel Coprocessor System Architecture

Our massive parallel coprocessor system architecture is organized by a single master processing node and large numbers of coprocessing nodes for special computation tasks. The master processing node is an embedded system with ARM processor as its core. The communication architecture of our system is the IB communication network.

The coprocessor is a development board with FPGA (Virtex-7), which is a reconfigurable processor for solving graph problems. Two blocks of DDR3 memory are integrated on each board, and data are transferred by a memory controller (MC). We modified the MC's IP core so that two blocks of DDR3 memory could be accessed in parallel. Any processing node would assign the tasks and transfer data to all coprocessors through the I/O interface and target channel adapter (TCA), which is the communication interface we implement based on the IB protocol. Communications data from the TCA are sent to the IB switch interface through a transmitter (TX) by the IB protocol, and the communication data from IB switch interface are received by TCA through the receiver (RX). The max theoretical line rate is 13.1 Gb/s, and the actual line rate is 10 Gb/s. We have four lines; thus, the communication bandwidth is 40 Gb/s. When the system is initialized, the master node distributes data to the DDR3 memory of each coprocessor via PCI-E bus. After the system has started, each processing node communicates through the IB communication network whose interface is TCA. The program in the master node sends its instructions or data after address mapping (i.e., AM in Figure 1) and each coprocessor communicates after the address mapping. Address mapping is implemented by the FPGA, and the scheme is a functional hardware unit for each node. The architecture is described in Figure 1.

The core is a streaming processor that uses a multi-threading vector. Cross-multithreading is a fine-grained multithreading in which threads are executed alternately. Our massive parallel coprocessor system is a scalable system and a platform for parallel processing of big data applications.

```
         Input: V[1···n], E[1···n][1···n], s (source vertex)
         Output: parent[1···n].
(1)   for ∀v ∈ V do
(2)       visit[v] = 0
(3)        parent[v] = −1
(4)       frontier[v] = 0
(5)       next[v] = 0
(6)   frontier[s] = 1
(7)   level = 0
(8)   end = 0
(9)   while ƒend ≠ 1 do
(10)     end = 1
(11)     if (level < α) or (level > β) then
(12)        for ∀v ∈ V do
(13)           if frontier[v] = 1 then
(14)              for ∀u ∈ E(v) do
(15)                 if visit[u] = 0 then
(16)                    visit[u] = 1
(17)                    next[u] = 1
(18)                    parent[u] = v
(19)                    end = 0
(20)        else
(21)           for ∀v ∈ V do
(22)              if visit[v = 0] then
(23)                 for ∀u ∈ E(v) do
(24)                    if frontier[u] = 1 then
(25)                       visit[v] = 1
(26)                       next[v] = 1
(27)                       parent[v] = u
(28)                       end = 0
(29)                       BREAK
(30)     BARRIER
(31)     for ∀v ∈ V do
(32)        frontier[v] = next[v]
(33)        next[v] = 0
(34)     level = level + 1
(35)
```

ALGORITHM 1: Parallel 1-D BFS algorithm.

5. Binary Search Address Mapping Unit

The architecture of our address mapping is shown in Figure 2. In our scheme, the memory of DDR3 is divided into two areas: the local data blocks and the global translation blocks. The local data blocks store the data that the program needs from I/O requests and TCA. The global translation blocks hold the mapping of all data. Furthermore, the global translation blocks in each node are the same, and they are managed in a fine-grained page.

The basic idea of binary search is as follows: In ascending order of the tables, we take intermediate records as objects of comparison. If the given item is equal to the intermediate records, then the search is done. However, if the given item is smaller than the intermediate records, then we have a binary search in the first half of the ascending table; otherwise, we have a binary search in the bottom half of the ascending table.

The implementation of the binary search address mapping is a pipeline in which the virtual address is the input,

and the output data are the physical address. We divided the registers in the pipeline storage unit into three groups. The first group contains the OMR, DVR, and MTR register, which stores the status of data in RAM. The RAM stores the address mapping of the visited arrays (visited array in the BFS algorithm). The input of the virtual address is the frontier arrays (frontier array in the BFS algorithm). This situation means that we could not find the corresponding mapping in RAM and we would obtain one of the address mappings of the frontier array from the DDR3 memory to be stored in RAMs. This situation is object missing (array missing) where no object is missing in the beginning of a binary search and after the first stack, but the data are missing. The range of virtual address in the array would be entered in the range register (RR). When the input address is not in the range of each RR, a warning that an object is missing is triggered. Then, we would update the data in RR; the order of updating uses the least recently used mechanism. The pipeline then stalls, and we acquire one dataset in the frontier array to continue the

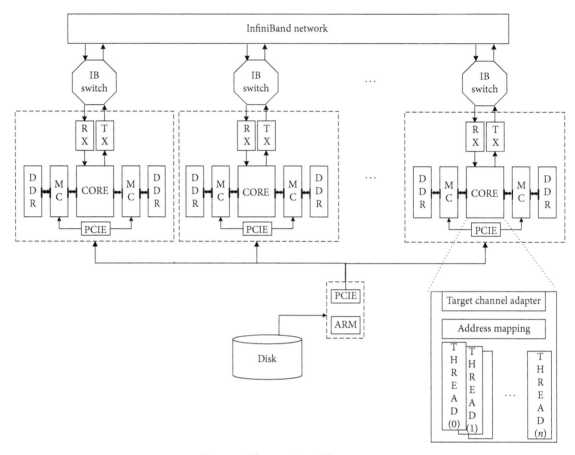

FIGURE 1: The overview of the system.

search. One data item of the frontier array exists in the current stack of RAMs. Thus, when searching the next stack, the next data in RAMs are invalid. We would obtain the address mapping data of the Frontier array from the DDR3 memory to be stored in this RAMs, and the situation is that the data are missing. The ith OMR is the object missing indicator of the ith stack in pipeline. Furthermore, the MTR is the data missing indicator. The 1 bit in DVR indicates the 64 bits of data in the RAMs that are currently stacked. When an object is missing, the DVR is 0. After updating in RAMs, the corresponding bit would be set to 1.

The second group contains the VAR and DVR, which are temporary storage that passes the data to the next stack when the pipeline is running. The third contains the LBR, RBR, and CAR. In the binary search algorithm, in each searching step, the smaller value is in the LBR, and the larger value is in the RBR. The output of the RAMs provides the intermediate element, and CAR records the comparable results in all steps. For instance, in a kth stack, when the virtual address is in the range of LBR and output of RAMs, the kth bit in CAR is 1 and the value of $(k-1)$th to 1 bit is the same as the value in CAR in the $(k-1)$th stack. The number of stacks is equal to the number of processors.

The LRU unit is implemented by a series of shift registers (the number of bits width is the number of shift register minus 1). When RR is updated, we set 1 to the corresponding shift register, and each register shifts left. The register, which is 0, is the least recently used. The LRU unit provides the number, and the corresponding RR is waiting to be updated in the next object missing.

Unlike time complexity $O(n)$ in direct search, the time complexity of binary search is $O(\log n)$. When the value of n increases, the advantages of the method are obvious.

6. Architecture of Streaming Processor

Our streaming processor design is on the basement of the multithreading vector. Cross-multithreading is a fine-grained multithreading, in which threads are executed alternately. This design requires the switching of threads in each clock whether the thread is stalling or not. This mechanism ensures that the pipeline constantly runs. When a stall exists in a thread, the latter would initially have a request. Every time the thread turns to use the pipeline, it would wait until the stall is handled. The execution of the thread using a cycle mode and its architecture is shown in Figure 3.

The architecture of the microprocessor without interlocked piped stages (MIPS) was simplified to efficiently process graph searching problems. The pipeline was divided into Thread Select (TS), Instruction Fetch (IF), Instruction Decode (ID), Execute (EX), and Write Back (WB) sections.

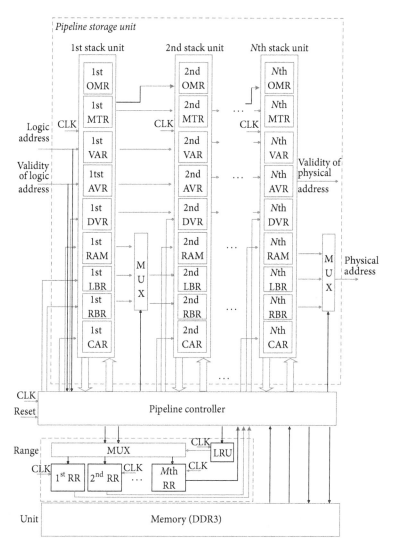

FIGURE 2: Implementation of binary search address mapping.

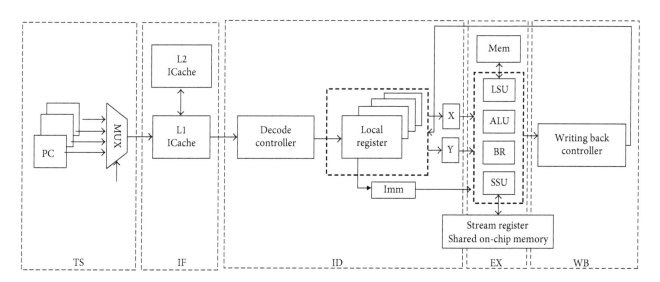

FIGURE 3: The architecture of streaming processor.

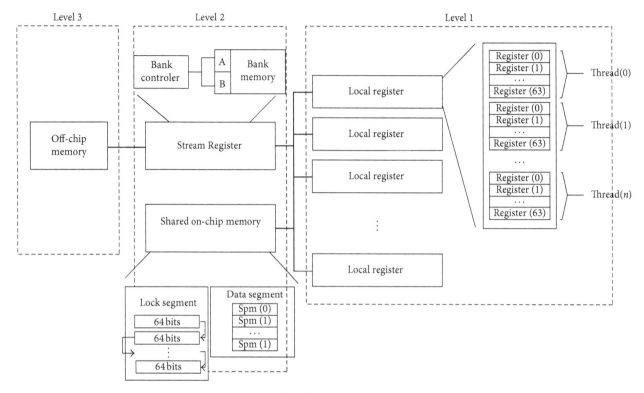

FIGURE 4: Three-level memory hierarchy.

In the Thread Select section, a thread would be selected and the value of the corresponding program counter (PC) register is obtained as the address in the IF section. Each thread has its corresponding PC register and the value in the register is updated according to the Next Program (NPC, in EX section). The update must be done before another thread is selected. Eight threads are implemented and used according to the instruction register in the cycle because of the limitation of the FPGAs resources.

In the Instruction Fetch section, the pipeline obtained the correct instruction according to the corresponding PC value. Two instruction caches exist: L1 and L2 caches. The L1 cache is private for a process, and the L2 cache is shared given more than one process. The L1 cache is 0.5 kB, and it adopts fully associative mapping programs. The L2 cache is 4 kB and adopts direct mapping programs. An instruction register is designed for each thread to store the last instruction. When the thread is blocked, it could take the last instruction from the instruction register.

In the Instruction Decode section, the decode controller matches the instruction and reads the correct data in the data register.

Four types of operation exist in the Execute section: the operation of arithmetic logic, load and store, access in stream register and shared on-chip memory, and branches jump instruction. In the Write Back section, the result in the Execute section is written in the local register. The result could be from LSU (load and store unit), ALU, and SSU (stream register and shared on-chip memory unit). The address is in the instruction.

Load and store unit (LSU) is designed for operation access, which includes vector or scalar access. The load operation is from the memory to the stream register. The store operation is from the stream register to the memory. Shared memory on-chip unit (SSU) is to perform operation accessed stream register or shared on-chip memory. The structures of LSU and SSU are similar.

7. Three-Level Memory Hierarchy

The stored data in the graph search problems has two characteristics: sparsity of the storage and lack of locality in memory accessing. The optimization in cache cannot effectively use the locality of the memory access. By drawing on the experience of the design of stream architecture, a new three-level memory hierarchy is proposed.

Figure 4 shows that the first-level memory is a local register. Our architecture is a multicore and multithread structure. The local register distributes in the inner part of processor. When multithreads exist in the execution in each process, the processor needs to protect the state. A distributed thread registers to create each thread with its own private registers to store their own states. As they have a local register, no access conflicts occurred between the threads. Implement register mapping is unnecessary. Thus, a small access in the address space and low access delay and power exist.

The local register is implemented by a block RAM resource in FPGAs. In the multithread execution, the local register would simultaneously process two requests of reading from decoding and one request of writing from writing back.

Considering that a single block RAM has read-and-write ports, we copy a local register for each thread. When two requests for reading exist, they could be read separately; however, if one request for writing exists, they would be written simultaneously.

The second level is the stream register and the shared memory on the chip. The stream register is a data buffer on the chip that is implemented by block RAM and combined with a bank of stream register to support multirequest from the local register. A bank of stream register contains a bank memory and a controller (as shown in Figure 4). The bank memory provides two read-and-write ports (ports A and B), and they are the interfaces of the local register and the off-chip memory.

The controller of the stream register has three functions. One is handling the data and the request from the local register. Another is handling the data and request from off-chip memory. The last is coordinating the read-and-write ports that consume the data writing or reading in the stream register with a correct sequence.

The shared on-chip memory is a special RAM on a chip. Furthermore, it is controlled through software and is programmable, which is different from cache. The data is accessed by addresses, and it is shared by processors (if we have) and threads. This study's design of a shared on-chip memory is a sharing and communicating interface for the processors and threads. The function of the design is data transaction and synchronization. The shared on-chip memory is divided with the lock and data segments. When more than one processor or thread exists to read and write in the same address, the atomic lock is supported by the lock segment to ensure correct program sequence. A base address exists in the lock segment. The bits begin with the base address, and one bit determines an atomic lock. Each process or thread could read only one bit in a lock segment at a time. The data segment is special shared data in a multithread or multiprocess program execution. Barrier synchronous counter is one of the special shared data items. The data segment is divided into several 64 bits block, and one local register is composed of 64 bits.

Owing to the width in a transaction burst at 512 bits, the width between the interface of the off-chip memory and the stream register is also 512 bits. The data width between the local register and stream register is 64 bits, and it is the same as the data in the local register. The valid data transaction between the stream and local registers is identified by a mask. The mask is given by a program instruction and its range is from 0 to 7.

The third-level memory hierarchy is the off-chip memory. Our off-chip memory is a dual-data rate (DDR3) and is provided by FPGAs.

8. Results and Comparison

The proposed scalable parallel distributed coprocessor system has 8 cores, and each core has 8 threads. We used the 8 Xilinx Virtex-7 FPGA VC709 evaluation board (xc7vx485t-2ffg1761) and a commercial switchboard called Mellanox IS5030, which is based on the IB protocol, to implement the system.

The Xilinx Virtex-7 FPGA VC709 evaluation board has 2 SODIMM DDR3 memory with a storage capacity of 4 GB. Eight channel PCIE interfaces and four line GTH transceivers are included. The communication bandwidth is 40 GB/s, and the memory bandwidth in each core is 10 GB/s in theory. Moreover, two computers that run Linux are used. One of them is responsible for the initialization of the switchboard, and the other is responsible for generating the BFS algorithm, loading data, and receiving returned results. The number of nodes in the system can be expanded as needed. We use the Verilog HDL to achieve a parallel architecture system in Xilinx Vivado 2013.4, which is written to the FPGA chip through the JTAG interface.

In accordance with the Graph500 benchmark, we generated a series of information through a Kronecker graph generator. Then, the information is converted to any type of data structure, which is the input of the BFS algorithm. We verified the results after execution. In the above steps, the creation of the data structure and the design of the BFS algorithm can be customized by the user.

In the Graph500, a fair comparison of the processor with different test bench is obtained using TEPS. According to the performance, which is calculated in Graph500, we proposed a formula to calculate performance P. The details are shown in (1). When the dataset and the root node are determined, E is a constant.

E is the number of edges in the connected region of the root node in the graph. f is the working frequency, which is 200 MHz in our implementation. T_{clk} indicates the number of clock cycles between the beginning and the end of the program. We obtain the T_{clk} through the chip scope. The test dataset in Graph500 is used. Table 1 presents our performance and comparison.

$$P = \frac{E \times f}{T_{clk}}. \tag{1}$$

We run the parallel BFS algorithm described as Algorithm 1 on our prototype system for testing. The scale of graph searching using the BFS is 19 to 23, which means that the scale of graph data is 2^{19} to 2^{23}, and the edge factor of the graph is 16.

In the first experiment step, we use Vivado 2014.1 to load the test data to FPGAs with a computer. The test data is from Graph500. Then we run the BFS programme in Linux which is running in ARM cortex. The ARM cortex is provided by the evaluation board. The ARM cortex initializes the searching and gets the results from FPGAs through PCIE bus. Finally we use ChipScope which is in Vivado 2014.1 to analyze the performance.

As most works targeting high-performance BFS use MTEPS as a metric, comparing raw traversal performance is possible but the available memory bandwidth in the hardware platform sets a hard limit on achievable BFS performance. Our experimental results are from a Virtex-7 platform with much less (utilization of bandwidth is 64%, the theoretical bandwidth is 10 GB/s, the actual bandwidth is 6.4 GB/s) memory bandwidth and work frequency (200 MHz) than platforms in prior work; thus, it is comparatively slow. Our

TABLE 1: Comparison to prior work.

Work	Platform	No. of parallel units	Avg. MTEPS	BW (GB/s)	MTEPS/BW
[4]	Convey HC-2	512	1600	80	20
[4]	Convey HC-2	256	980	80	12.5
[4]	Convey HC-2	128	510	80	6.375
[4]	Convey HC-2	64	350	80	4.375
[4]	Convey HC-2	32	210	80	2.625
[8]	Convey HC-2	64	1900	80	23.75
[9]	Nehalem + Fermi	32	800	128	6.25
This work	Virtex-7 & InfiniBand	8	169	10	16.9
This work	Virtex-7 & InfiniBand	64	763	80	9.54

system has 8 cores and supports 8 threads per core, which is equivalent to 64 threads in parallel. Considering the memory bandwidth, the traversals per unit bandwidth is used as a metric to enable fair comparison with prior work. Table 1 allows the comparison with several related works on the average performance, available memory bandwidth, and traversals per bandwidth over RMAT graphs.

9. Conclusions

We can draw the following conclusions:

(1) Compared with the approach of Betkaoui et al. [4], our system is more efficient. The performance of 64 parallel units is similar to that of approximately 256 parallel units in [4]. Our data of traversals per unit bandwidth in 64 parallel units are between 256 units and 128 parallel units in Betkaoui et al. [4].

(2) Attia et al. [8] is on BFS algorithm optimization, and our system is a scalable general processor platform that performs instruction set decoding and the address mapping. Attia et al. [8] is limited to scale, and it is a special acceleration unit.

(3) Our data of traversals per unit are twice that of Hong et al. [9], and the performance is approximately equal. Moreover, our proposed system has the advantages of power and scalability.

(4) The proposed system can be used as a scalable general processing system for graph application with big data.

Conflicts of Interest

The authors declare that there are no conflicts of interest regarding the publication of this paper.

Acknowledgments

This work was supported by the National Nature Science Foundation of China (no. 61602496).

References

[1] C. Demetrescui, A. Goldberg, and D. Johnson, "The Shortest Path Problem: Ninth DIMACS Implementation Challenge, Proceedings.dimacs Book.ams," in *Proceedings of the The Shortest Path Problem: Ninth DIMACS Implementation Challenge, Proceedings.dimacs Book.ams*, p. 4, 2006.

[2] M. E. J. Newman and M. Girvan, "Finding and evaluating community structure in networks," *Physical Review E: Statistical, Nonlinear, and Soft Matter Physics*, vol. 69, no. 2, Article ID 026113, pp. 1–26113, 2004.

[3] D. Bu, Y. Zhao, L. Cai et al., "Topological structure analysis of the protein-protein interaction network in budding yeast," *Nucleic Acids Research*, vol. 31, no. 9, pp. 2443–2450, 2003.

[4] B. Betkaoui, Y. Wang, D. B. Thomas, and W. Luk, "A reconfigurable computing approach for efficient and scalable parallel graph exploration," in *Proceedings of the 2012 IEEE 23rd International Conference on Application-Specific Systems, Architectures and Processors, ASAP 2012*, pp. 8–15, Netherlands, July 2012.

[5] J. J. Tithi, D. Matani, G. Menghani, and R. A. Chowdhury, "Avoiding locks and atomic instructions in shared-memory parallel BFS using optimistic parallelization," in *Proceedings of the 2013 IEEE 27th International Parallel and Distributed Processing Symposium Workshops and PhD Forum, IPDPSW 2013*, pp. 1628–1637, USA, May 2013.

[6] C. Chen, S. Koliai, and G. Gao, "Exploitation of locality for energy efficiency for breadth first search in fine-grain execution models," *Tsinghua Science and Technology*, vol. 18, no. 6, Article ID 6678909, pp. 636–646, 2013.

[7] A. Putnam, A. M. Caulfield, E. S. Chung et al., "A reconfigurable fabric for accelerating large-scale datacenter services," in *Proceedings of the ACM/IEEE 41st International Symposium on Computer Architecture (ISCA '14)*, pp. 13–24, IEEE, Minneapolis, Minn, USA, June 2014.

[8] O. G. Attia, T. Johnson, K. Townsend, P. Jones, and J. Zambreno, "CyGraph: A reconfigurable architecture for parallel breadth-first search," in *Proceedings of the 28th IEEE International Parallel and Distributed Processing Symposium Workshops, IPDPSW 2014*, pp. 228–235, usa, May 2014.

[9] S. Hong, T. Oguntebi, and K. Olukotun, "Efficient parallel graph exploration on multi-core CPU and GPU," in *Proceedings of the 20th International Conference on Parallel Architectures and Compilation Techniques, PACT 2011*, pp. 78–88, USA, October 2011.

[10] R. Pearce, M. Gokhale, and N. M. Amato, "Scaling techniques for massive scale-free graphs in distributed (external) memory," in *Proceedings of the 27th IEEE International Parallel and Distributed Processing Symposium, IPDPS 2013*, pp. 825–836, USA, May 2013.

[11] Y. Umuroglu, D. Morrison, and M. Jahre, "Hybrid breadth-first search on a single-chip FPGA-CPU heterogeneous platform,"

in *Proceedings of the 25th International Conference on Field Programmable Logic and Applications, FPL 2015*, UK, September 2015.

[12] A. Anghel, G. Rodriguez, and B. Prisacari, "The importance and characteristics of communication in high performance data analytics," in *Proceedings of the 2014 IEEE International Symposium on Workload Characterization, IISWC 2014*, pp. 80-81, USA, October 2014.

[13] A. Amer, H. Lu, P. Balaji, and S. Matsuoka, "Characterizing MPI and hybrid MPI+threads applications at scale: Case study with BFS," in *Proceedings of the 15th IEEE/ACM International Symposium on Cluster, Cloud, and Grid Computing, CCGrid 2015*, pp. 1075–1083, China, May 2015.

[14] M. Anderson, "Better benchmarking for supercomputers: The usual yardstick is not a good metric," *IEEE Spectrum*, vol. 48, no. 1, pp. 12–14, 2011.

[15] A. D. Bader, J. Berry, S. Kahan, and R. Murphy, "The graph 500 list," 2010, http://graph500.org.list.

[16] R. Berrendorf and M. Makulla, "Level-synchronous parallel breadthfirst search algorithms for multicore and multiprocessor systems," in *Proceedings of the the Sixth Intl. Conf. on Future Computational Technologies and Applications*, vol. 26, 2014.

[17] M. Ceriani, G. Palermo, S. Secchi, A. Tumeo, and O. Villa, "Exploring manycore multinode systems for irregular applications with FPGA prototyping," in *Proceedings of the 21st Annual International IEEE Symposium on Field-Programmable Custom Computing Machines, FCCM 2013*, p. 238, USA, April 2013.

[18] V. Agarwal, F. Petrini, D. Pasetto, and D. A. Bader, "Scalable graph exploration on multicore processors," in *Proceedings of the 2010 ACM/IEEE International Conference for High Performance Computing, Networking, Storage and Analysis, SC 2010*, USA, November 2010.

[19] M. Bisson, M. Bernaschi, and E. Mastrostefano, "Parallel distributed breadth first search on the Kepler architecture," *IEEE Transactions on Parallel and Distributed Systems*, vol. 27, no. 7, pp. 2091–2102, 2015.

[20] U. A. Acar, A. Chargueraud, and M. Rainey, *Fast parallel graphsearch with splittable and catenable frontiers*, Inria, 2015.

[21] S. Beamer, K. Asanović, and D. Patterson, "Direction-optimizing breadth-first search," *Scientific Programming*, vol. 21, no. 3-4, pp. 137–148, 2013.

[22] Y. Yasui, K. Fujisawa, and K. Goto, "NUMA-optimized parallel breadth-first search on multicore single-node system," in *Proceedings of the 2013 IEEE International Conference on Big Data, Big Data 2013*, pp. 394–402, USA, October 2013.

17

Development of Multiple Big Data Analytics Platforms with Rapid Response

Bao Rong Chang, Yun-Da Lee, and Po-Hao Liao

Department of Computer Science and Information Engineering, National University of Kaohsiung,
700 Kaohsiung University Rd., Nanzih District, Kaohsiung 811, Taiwan

Correspondence should be addressed to Bao Rong Chang; brchang@nuk.edu.tw

Academic Editor: Wenbing Zhao

The crucial problem of the integration of multiple platforms is how to adapt for their own computing features so as to execute the assignments most efficiently and gain the best outcome. This paper introduced the new approaches to big data platform, RHhadoop and SparkR, and integrated them to form a high-performance big data analytics with multiple platforms as part of business intelligence (BI) to carry out rapid data retrieval and analytics with R programming. This paper aims to develop the optimization for job scheduling using MSHEFT algorithm and implement the optimized platform selection based on computing features for improving the system throughput significantly. In addition, users would simply give R commands rather than run Java or Scala program to perform the data retrieval and analytics in the proposed platforms. As a result, according to performance index calculated for various methods, although the optimized platform selection can reduce the execution time for the data retrieval and analytics significantly, furthermore scheduling optimization definitely increases the system efficiency a lot.

1. Introduction

Big data [1] has been sharply in progress unprecedentedly in recent years and is changing the operation for business as well as the decision-making for the enterprise. The huge amounts of data contain valuable information, such as the growth trend of system application and the correlation among systems. The undisclosed information may contain unknown knowledge and application that are discoverable further. However, big data with the features of high volume, high velocity, and high variety as well as in face of expanding incredible amounts of data, several issues emerging in big data such as storage, backup [2], management, processing, search [3], analytics, practical application, and other abilities to deal with the data also face new challenges. Unfortunately, those cannot be solved with traditional methods and thus it is worthwhile for us to continue exploring how to extract the valuable information from the huge amounts of data. According to the latest survey reported from American CIO magazine, 70% of IT operation has been done by batch processing in the business, which makes it "unable to control processing resources for operation as well as loading" [4]. This becomes one of the biggest challenges for big data application.

Hadoop distributes massive data collections across multiple nodes, enabling big data processing and analytics far more effectively than was possible previously. Spark, on the other hand, does not do distributed storage [5]. It is nothing but a data processing tool, operating on those distributed data collections. Furthermore, Hadoop includes not only a storage component called Hadoop Distributed File System (HDFS), but also a processing component called MapReduce. Spark does not come with its own file management system. Accordingly, it needs to be integrated with Hadoop to share HDFS. Hadoop processing mostly static and batch-mode style can be just fine and originally was designed to handle crawling and searching billions of web pages and collecting their information into a database [6]. If you need to do analytics on streaming data, or to run required multiple operations, Spark is suitable for those. As a matter of fact,

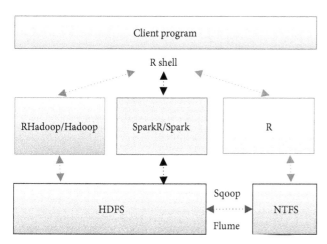

FIGURE 1: Data retrieval and data analytics Stack.

Spark was designed for Hadoop; therefore, data scientists all agree they are better together for a variety of big data applications in the real world.

Through establishing a set of multiple big data analytics platforms with high efficiency, high availability, and high scalability [7], this paper aims to integrate different big data platforms to achieve the compatibility with any existing business intelligence (BI) [8] together with related analytics tools so that the enterprise needs not change large amounts of software for such platforms. Therefore, the goal of this paper is to design the optimization for job scheduling using MSHEFT algorithm as well as to implement optimized platform selection, and established platforms support R command to execute data retrieval and data analytics in big data environment. In such a way the upper-level tools relying on relational database which has stored the original data can run on the introduced platforms through minor modification or even no modification to gain the advantages of high efficiency, high availability, and high scalability. I/O delay time can be shared through reliable distributed file system to speed-up the reading of a large amount of data. Data retrieval and data analytics stack has layered as shown in Figure 1. As a result, according to performance index calculated for various methods, we are able to check out whether or not the proposed approach can reduce the execution time for the data retrieval and analytics significantly.

2. Related Work in Big Data Processing

This paper has introduced data retrieval and data analytics using R programming in conjunction with RHadoop [9]/ Hadoop [10] and SparkR [11]/Spark [12] platforms to build a multiple-platform big data analytics system. Furthermore, the use of distributed file system for fast data analytics and data storage reduces the execution time of processing a huge amount of data. First let us aim to understand the fundamental knowledge of Hadoop and Spark platforms and then build their extended systems RHadoop and SparkR for the purpose of fitting all kinds of relative problems on big data

analytics. This section will introduce their related profiles and key technologies for both platforms accordingly.

2.1. Distributed Computing Framework with Hadoop. Hadoop is a well-known open source distributed computing framework as shown in Figure 2 that provides reliable, scalable, distributed computing, data storage, and cluster computing analytics of big data, including a MapReduce [13] for distributed computing, HDFS [14] distributed file system, and a distributed NoSQL database HBase [15] which can be used to store nonrelational data set. There are some tools that are based on Hadoop applications. First Apache Pig can perform complex MapReduce conversions on a huge amount of data using a simple scripting language called Pig Latin. Next Apache Hive [16] is a data warehousing package that lets you query and manage large datasets in distributed storage using a SQL-style language called HiveQL. Third Apache Sqoop is a tool for transferring large amounts of data between Hadoop and structured data storage as efficiently as possible. Further Apache Flume is a distributed and highly scalable log collection system that can be used for log data collection, log data processing, and log data transmission. Then Apache Zookeeper is a distributed application designed for the coordination of services, it is mainly used to solve the decentralized applications often encountered in some data management issues. Final Apache Avro is a data serialization system designed to support intensive data, the application of huge amounts of data exchange.

Examples of applications using Hadoop are given as follows. Caesars entertainment, a casino gaming company, has built a Hadoop environment [17] that differentiates customer groups and creates exclusive marketing campaign for each group. Healthcare technology company Cerner uses Hadoop to build a set of enterprise data centers [18] to help Cerner and their clients monitor the health of more than one million patients a day. The dating site eHarmony uses Hadoop to upgrade their cloud systems [19], enabling it to send millions of messages for matching friend dating every day.

2.2. Parallel Processing Framework with Spark. Spark is an open source parallel processing framework released by the Apache Software Foundation that supports in-memory processing and dramatically increases the execution speed of big data analytics, as shown in Figure 3. Spark is also designed for fast computing, high availability, and fault tolerance. Using its internal memory capabilities, Spark can be a great choice for machine learning and graph computation, as well as a great choice for big data analytics. Its main functions and positioning are the same as Hadoop MapReduce. Through In-memory cluster computing [20], it hopes to eliminate I/O latency caused by a lot of relay files swapped between memory and disk during MapReduce. Theoretically, the processing speed could be hundreds of times higher than the Hadoop. Spark is written in Scala, but also supports Scala, Java, and Python programming; the underlying storage system can also be directly compatible with HDFS.

Examples of Spark's applications are given as follows. Microsoft launched Spark for Azure HDInsight [21], allowing

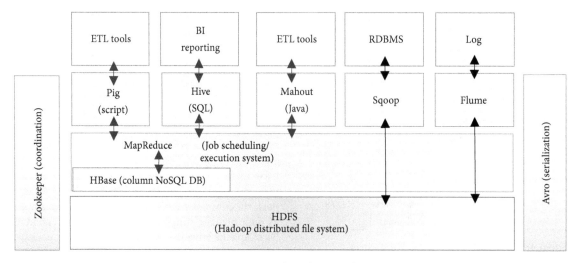

FIGURE 2: Hadoop framework.

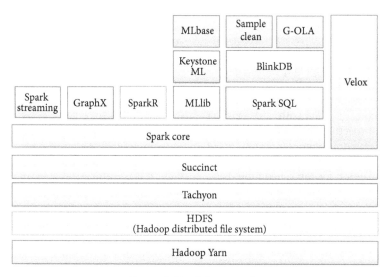

FIGURE 3: Spark framework.

users to use Spark for Azure HDInsight to solve big data challenges in near real-time, such as fraud detection, clickstream analytics, financial alerts, and more. Yahoo used Spark for the development of Audience Expansion in the application of advertising [22] to find the target user. Cloudera develops Spark Streaming's flexibility [23] to enable Cloudera's customers to build complete IoT applications on a unified platform.

2.3. Integrated Development Environment for R. Over the past decade, programming language R has been highly enhanced and greatly upgraded significantly to break the original limit in the past. In academy and industry, R becomes one of the most important tools for the research such as computational statistics, visualization, and data science. Millions of statisticians and data scientists use R to solve problems from counting biology to quantitative marketing. R has become one of the most popular programming language for the analytics of scientific data and finance. R is not only free,

compact, and part of the open source that can run on many platforms, but also integrates data analytics and plotting functions all in one. It may add many additional packages to enhance system's functions, similarly comparable to the functions of commercial software, and can be viewed as one of major tools of contemporary data analytics. R is mainly used to analyze data, and thus the master node in a cluster installs R where big data access through HDFS has been available, or a stay alone computer for centralized processing installs R where small data access through NTFS has achieved. It is noted that data stored in NTFS can be transferred to HDFS via Sqoop [24]/Flume [25] or Hive.

2.4. RHadoop Based on Hadoop. Hadoop is capable of distributed computing and can store large amounts of data, but there is still a lot of information that needs to be analyzed professionally. However, R itself is not able to read the data size more than the size of memory in computer, and hence there is data size limit for processing big data. Therefore, it

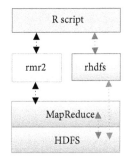

FIGURE 4: RHadoop framework.

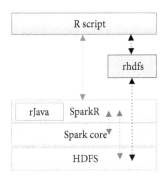

FIGURE 5: SparkR framework.

turns out the integration of Hadoop and R called RHadoop as a sort of data analytics service. In such a way, R will not only handle professional analytics, but it will also allow to easily utilize Hadoop features, such as the ability to access HDFS via rhdfs package and through the rmr2 package [26] to call MapReduce for accomplishing the distributed computing. The framework of RHadoop is shown in Figure 4.

2.5. SparkR Based on Spark. SparkR is an R suite developed by AMPLab that provides Spark with a Resilient Distributed Dataset (RDD) [27] API that allows R to carry out distributed computing using Spark. SparkR was merged into Spark in April 2015 and was released with Spark 1.4 in June 2015, so deploying SparkR requires installing Spark 1.4 or later and installing R related packages, including rJava [28] and rhdfs [29]. rJava lets R call objects, instances, and methods written in Java to make it less difficult for R to call Java-owned resources, such as Spark and Hadoop, and rhdfs, like RHadoop, to access HDFS. The framework of SparkR is shown in Figure 5. Although RHadoop mentioned above can activate distributed computing with R programming, its efficiency is not as good as SparkR. SparkR, adopting in-memory cluster computing, needs more memory resources than RHadoop. In order to avoid shutting down the task due to hardware resources limitation, both RHadoop and SparkR can be installed together for being interchangeably used at same site. In addition, in order to determine the most suitable analytical tools, we also need a matching algorithm to carry out the distributed computing successfully.

TABLE 1: Recipe of compatibility packages.

Software	Version
Hadoop (including RHadoop)	2.6.0
Spark (including SparkR)	1.4.0
R	3.2.2
Oracle Java (JDK)	8u66
Scala	2.10.4
rJava	0.9.7
rhdfs	1.0.8
rmr2	3.3.1

3. System Implementation Method

This paper aims to develop the optimization for job scheduling using MSHEFT algorithm so that system obtains the best throughput. After scheduling all of input queries in a job queue, system is then able to dispatch the job at top of the queue to one of big data analytics platforms through automatic platform selection. Regarding clustering and distributed parallel computing, a cloud computing foundation has been established to implement virtualization architecture because virtual machine has the feature of flexible control in hardware resource and thus it is quite suitable to act as a container provided an environment for the exploration of big data analytics.

3.1. Virtual Machine Deployment. Figure 6 shows a cloud computing [30] with high performance, high availability, and high scalability where server farm at the top layer and storage farm at the bottom layer are built for this study. In order to realize virtualization, an open source virtual machine management (VMM) or hypervisor Proxmox Virtual Environment (PVE) [31] based on KVM is used to implement virtual machine clustering; the status of virtual machine clustering can be effectively monitored through PVE, and the resource configuration of each virtual machine can be dynamically adjusted [32]. Since the platform performance is very closely related to I/O latency, the efficiency of both hard disk and network access should be increased in hardware configuration.

3.2. Recipe of Compatibility Packages. The most difficult aspect of integration of a lot of open source packages in a system is compatibility suite and that is one of the crucial problems of system integration as well. In this paper we proposed a recipe to resolve the challenge of suite compatibility. Several packages will be integrated to establish multiple big data analytics platforms in this paper and all of them are open source software, which are developed and maintained by different open source communities. A lot of software has complex dependency and compatibility problems. The recipe of packages proposed in this paper includes Hadoop, Spark, R, Scala, rJava, rhdfs, and rmr2, which are fully compatible for stable operation in the proposed approach as listed in Table 1.

3.3. Optimized Platform Selection. The program of automatic platform selection assigns a task to an appropriate big data

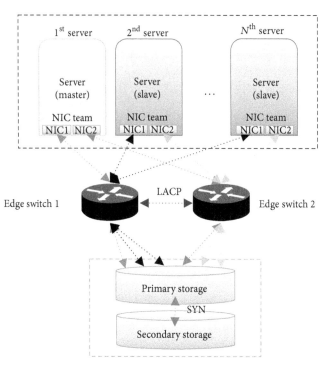

FIGURE 6: Cloud computing with high performance, high availability, and high scalability.

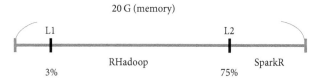

FIGURE 7: Automatic selection of suitable platform.

analytics platform according to the size of remaining amount of memory in a working virtual machine. The function and property for both RHadoop and SparkR are identical in a sense because they can access the same HDFS and support R syntax. Although these two platforms are the same function, they are different in the demand environment and executive manner. The memory size of 20 G for each server in the experiments is given, and it sets the remaining amount of memory size 0.6 G in a virtual machine in cluster denoted Level 1 (roughly 3% of total amount of memory) and 15 G Level 2 (approximately 75% of total amount of memory) as the cut-off points. In Figure 7, the program automatically chooses nothing to carry on the task as the remaining amount of memory is less than 3%; RHadoop would be applied as the remaining amount of memory lies between L1 and L2, and hence SparkR could be employed as the remaining amount of memory is higher than L2.

3.4. Optimization for Job Scheduling. Heterogeneous Earliest Finish Time (HEFT) [33] is an exploratory scheduling algorithm, which is used for scheduling the communication time of previous set of dependent task of heterogeneous network.

HEFT is based on one of list scheduling algorithms, where their characteristics are to establish a priority list in the first step. According to the sorted priority list, HEFT assigns each task to a suitable CPU to make the task completed as soon as possible. The pseudocode of HEFT algorithm is shown in Algorithm 1. HEFT tries to search for local optimization and eventually makes the whole local optimums. In the test of automatic platform selection, the total of 20 GB memory is configured, and it is found that all of analytics platforms can be used when the remaining amount of memory is greater than or equal to L1; in addition, it is better to use RHadoop in case of being less than L2, and SparkR shall be used in case of being greater than L2. Job dispatched to RHadoop platform has run a kind of in-disk computing mode such that it may encounter data swap between disk and memory occasionally. Instead, in-memory computing mode has employed in SparkR platform and thus SparkR needs much more memory allocated for computing. HEFT algorithm is modified to Memory-Sensitive Heterogeneous Earliest Finish Time (MSHEFT) where the priority is considered first; then the size of data file is considered as the second condition, and finally an extra factor is considered, which is "remaining amount

(1) Compute rank$_u$ for all nodes by traversing graph upward, starting from the exit node.
(2) Sort the nodes in a list by nonincreasing order of rank$_u$ values.
(3) while there are unscheduled nodes in the list do
(4) begin
(5)   Select the first task n_i in the list and remove it.
(6)   Assign the task n_i to the processor p_j that minimizes the (EFT) value of n_i.
(7) end

ALGORITHM 1: The HEFT algorithm.

(1) Compute rank$_u$ for all nodes by traversing graph upward, starting from the exit node.
(2) Sort the nodes in a list by nonincreasing order of rank$_u$ values.
(3) while there are unscheduled nodes in the list do
(4) Compare priority.
(5) begin
(6)   Compare job size
(7)   Select the first task n_i in the list and remove it.
(8)   begin
(9)   if the remaining memory size > 0.6 GB
(10)   begin
(11)   what is the value of the remaining memory size?
(12)   Assign the task n_i to the processor p_j that minimizes the (EFT) value of n_i.
(13)   end if
(14)   waiting the remaining memory size and go line 9.
(15)   end
(16) end

ALGORITHM 2: The MSHEFT algorithm.

of memory." In Algorithm 2, the pseudocode of MSHEFT algorithm has been presented. Job processing flow chart is shown in Figure 8.

3.5. Execution Procedure. The execution procedure has been shown in Figure 9. With the user interface, the process is designated to monitor the status of each node in the server farm. MSHEFT algorithm for scheduling optimization together with platform selection has decided to choose an appropriate platform for execution according to the current status monitored through user interface. The proposed approach including MSHEFT algorithm plus platform selection can be denoted MSHEFT-PS in this paper. When the analytics task has finished, the results will be stored back to HDFS and the whole process will be terminated. In addition, job scheduling using first-come-first-serve FCFS will be adopted for each single analytics platform Rhadoop or SparkR, denoted FCFS-SP, in the experiment to check how it performs as a single platform applied. Furthermore, the platform selection mechanism integrated FCFS, denoted FCFS-PS, has also been

employed to test the system performance under the condition of remaining amount of memory in a virtual machine in which a certain node has been resident.

3.6. Performance Evaluation. In order to compare the computation efficiency among the several algorithms, the performance index [2] has been evaluated based on the necessitated equations, which are derived first from measuring access time of data of a single item for a certain dataset on (1), next calculating average access time based on a variety of data size among the datasets on (2), then inducing a normalized performance index among the datasets on (3), and finally resulting in a performance index according to a series of tests on (4). In these equations we denote the subscript i the index of data size, j the index of dataset, and k the index of test condition and the subscript s indicates a single item in a specific dataset. Eq. (1) calculates the average access time (AAT) for each data size. In (1), AAT$_{ijk}$ represents average access time with the same data size, and N_{ik} stands for the current data size. Eq. (2) calculates the average access times overall

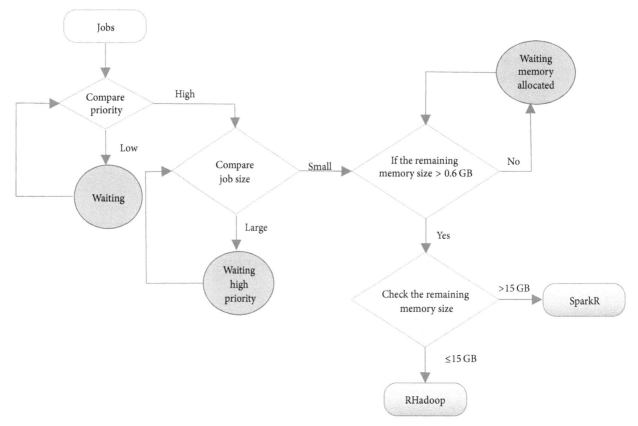

FIGURE 8: Job processing flow chart with MSHEFT algorithm and platform selection.

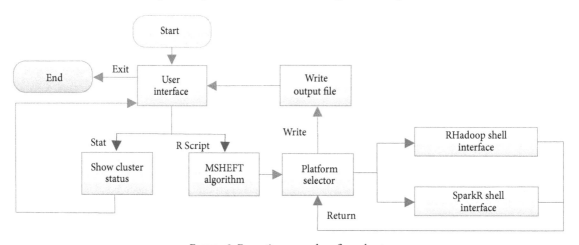

FIGURE 9: Execution procedure flow chart.

$\overline{\text{AAT}_{s_{jk}}}$ for each test (i.e., write, read, and compute) on a specific platform, in which $\text{AAT}_{s_{ijk}}$ represents the average access time of each dataset; please refer back to (1), and ω_i stands for weight for a weighted average. The following formula will evaluate the performance index (PI) [10]. Eq. (3) calculates the normalized performance index for a specific platform. Eq. (4) calculates the performance index overall for a specific platform, SF_1 is a constant value that is used here to quantify the value of performance index in the range 0–100, and W_k stands for weight for a weighted average.

$$\text{AAT}_{s_{ijk}} = \frac{\text{AAT}_{ijk}}{N_{ik}}, \quad \text{where } s = 1, 2, \ldots, d; \; i = 1, 2, \ldots, l; \; j = 1, 2, \ldots, m; \; k = 1, 2, \ldots, n, \tag{1}$$

$$\overline{\text{AAT}_{s_{jk}}} = \sum_{i=1}^{l} \omega_i \cdot \text{AAT}_{s_{ijk}}, \quad \text{where } s = 1, 2, \ldots, d; \; j = 1, 2, \ldots, m; \; k = 1, 2, \ldots, n; \; \sum_{i=1}^{l} \omega_i = 1, \tag{2}$$

$$\overline{\mathrm{PI}_{jk}} = \frac{1/\overline{\mathrm{AAT}_{s_{jk}}}}{\max_{h=1,2,\ldots m}\left(1/\overline{\mathrm{AAT}_{s_{hk}}}\right)}, \quad \text{where } j = 1, 2, \ldots, m; \ k = 1, 2, \ldots, n, \tag{3}$$

$$\mathrm{PI}_j = \left(\sum_{k=1}^{n} W_k \cdot \overline{\mathrm{PI}_{jk}}\right) \cdot \mathrm{SF}_1, \quad \text{where } j = 1, 2, \ldots, m; \ k = 1, 2, \ldots, n; \ \mathrm{SF}_1 = 10^2, \ \sum_{k=1}^{n} W_k = 1. \tag{4}$$

4. Experimental Results and Discussion

This section categories data into simulation data and actual data for test with two cases; the first case (Case 1) uses the test data generated randomly with Java programming; the second case (Case 2) adopts the actual data collected from the Internet. Proxmox Virtual Environment can be used to dynamically adjust the resource allocation to set up the experimental environments according to different memory remaining amounts, as listed in Table 2, so as to implement effect tests on various platforms.

4.1. Generated Data Set and Experimental Environment for Case 1. Case 1 tests each platform with first-come-first-serve algorithm to perform different sizes of test data, R commands having different complexity, and different priorities to all of queries so as to compare the execution time in various environments as is shown in Table 2. R commands for test are as shown in Table 3. In this experiment, there are three methods applied to test. The first approach uses first-come-first-serve algorithm (FCFS) for each single platform RHaoop or SparkR, denoted FCFS-SP. The second one is an optimized platform selection (PS) utilized to choose an appropriate platform for execution according to the remaining amount of memory in a virtual machine but it is still based on FCFS, thus denoted FCFS-PS. The third method introduced the optimization for job scheduling using MSHEFT algorithm employed to reschedule all of input queries in an ascending order in a job queue according to the smallest size of data file first. Once a job has been dequeued and launched, it based on PS will also choose an appropriate platform for execution, thereby denoted MSHEFT-PS. In short, three approaches including FCFS-SP, FCFS-PS, and MSHEFT-PS will be implemented in this paper. The test methods are shown in Table 4. With four fields, test data have been randomly generated with Java programming where the first column is the name of the only key string, the second column is random integer from 0 to 99, the third column is a random integer from 100 to 199, and the fourth column is the generated integer sequence number. Designated data size for test is shown in Table 5.

4.2. Experimental Results in Case 1. As a result, two platforms, RHadoop and SparkR, have performed for several test data sets with different priorities, data sizes, and R commands. As listed in Table 6, the proposed approach MSHEFT-PS has been implemented in the different order of jobs in a queue when comparing with the other methods. Performance comparisons of test are shown in Figures 10, 11, 12, 13, 14, and 15. The average execution time of proposed

approach MSHEFT-PS is faster than the other methods, FCFS-SP and FCFS-PS. The normalized performance index and performance index are listed in Tables 7 and 8. This shows that the proposed approach outperforms the others in Case 1.

4.3. Data Collection and Experimental Environment for Case 2. Case 2 has collected the actual data sets and the designated data size for test as shown in Table 9. The concerned approaches as listed in Table 3 have applied for measuring the average execution time according to different data themes. Similarly, Table 1 has listed two test environments and R command I test is listed in Table 2 as well.

4.4. Experimental Results in Case 2. Executable job list in Case 2 is shown in Table 10. Performance comparisons of test are shown in Figures 16 and 17. The experimental results show that the average execution time of the proposed approach MSHEFT-PS is much lower than the other methods, FCFS-SP and FCFS-PS, over three different conditions. The normalized performance index and performance index are listed in Table 11. Notice that the performance of our proposed approach is superior to the others in Case 2.

4.5. Discussion. There is no specific mechanism so far to estimate job execution time for Rhadoop or SparkR. According to the report in Apache Spark website at https://spark.apache.org/, it noted that run programs up to 100x faster than Hadoop MapReduce in memory, or 10x faster on disk. Technically speaking, SparkR job execution will similarly be up to 100x faster than RHadoop job execution in-memory, or up to 10x on disk as mentioned above. In this paper, the experiments show that run program for a specific job using SparkR is up to 9.7x faster than RHadoop. However, the average in SparkR job execution is nearly 3.9x faster than RHadoop job execution.

5. Conclusion

This paper found that even though the analytics platforms have the same configuration and functions, their performance still has resulted in different efficiency in different experimental conditions when applying scheduling optimization for multiple big data analytics platforms. The performance efficiency can be greatly improved by making the optimization for job scheduling, automatically detecting clustering state, and then choosing an appropriate platform for job processing. According to the experiments in Case 1 with simulation data and Case 2 with actual data, it is found that the remaining amount of memory is less and the scale of

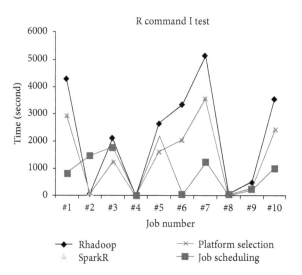

FIGURE 10: Execution time of R command I in test environment I of Case 1.

TABLE 2: Test environment.

Environment	Description
Test environment I	Adjust 10 GB memory space and give it to a virtual machine executing big data processing
Test environment II	Configure 20 GB memory space of a virtual machine executing big data processing

TABLE 3: R command test.

Command	Description
R command I	Only search special field
R command II	Only search special field, and add comparison conditions
R command III	Search special field, add comparison conditions, and execute the commands with while or for

TABLE 4: Test method.

Method	Description
FCFS-SP	Use command of enforced R to execute such platform, and then input R command
FCFS-PS	Directly input R command
MSHEFT-PS	Use command of set to set working quantity, and then input R command

data set is larger, which will much more highlight the importance of scheduling optimization and platform selection. In addition to the job scheduling using MSHEFT algorithm and optimized platform selection proposed in this paper, this system is capable of integrating new analytics platform to it by adding new big data analytics tools with related R shells to system, without any further changes in others.

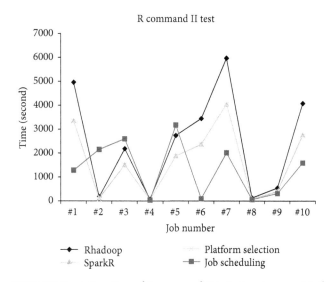

FIGURE 11: Execution time of R command II in test environment I of Case 1.

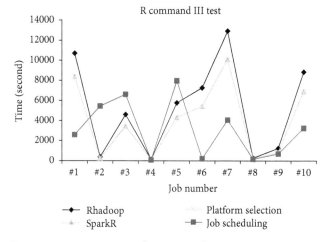

FIGURE 12: Execution time of R command III in test environment I of Case 1.

TABLE 5: Designated data size and its priority in Case 1.

Sequence	Priority	Data size	Code name
1	1	850 G	A
2	3	30 G	B
3	1	400 G	C
4	2	10 G	D
5	5	500 G	E
6	3	630 G	F
7	2	1 T	G
8	4	20 G	H
9	5	100 G	I
10	1	700 G	J

TABLE 6: Executable job list in Case 1.

Method	Job									
	#1	#2	#3	#4	#5	#6	#7	#8	#9	#10
FCFS-SP	A	B	C	D	E	F	G	H	I	J
FCFS-PS	A	B	C	D	E	F	G	H	I	J
MSHEFT-PS	C	J	A	D	G	B	F	H	I	E

TABLE 7: Normalized performance index in Case 1.

Operation	FCFS-SP-RHadoop	FCFS-SP-SparkR	FCFS-PS	MSHEFT-PS
R command I	0.319	0.787	0.799	1.000
R command II	0.441	0.884	0.895	1.000
R command III	0.481	0.880	0.885	1.000

TABLE 8: Average normalized performance index and performance index in Case 1.

Method	Average normalized performance index	Performance index
FCFS-SP-RHadoop	0.413	41.34
FCFS-SP-SparkR	0.850	85.03
FCFS-PS	0.859	85.94
MSHEFT-PS	1.000	100.00

TABLE 9: Designated data size and its priority in Case 2.

Sequence	Priority	Data size	Data theme	Code name
1	4	10 G	World-famous masterpiece	WC
2	1	250 G	Load of production machine: Overlaoding	OD
3	2	250 G	Load of production machine: Underloading	UD
4	3	1 T	Qualified rate of semiconductor products	YR
5	1	750 G	Correlation among temperature and people's power utilization	TE
6	4	750 G	Correlation among rainfall and people's power utilization	RE
7	1	100 G	Flight information in the airport	AP
8	5	500 G	Traffic violation/accidents	TA

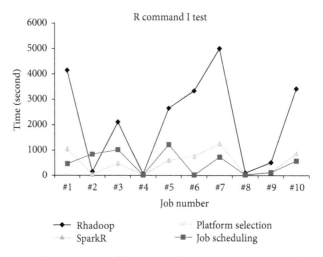

FIGURE 13: Execution time of R command I in test environment II of Case 1.

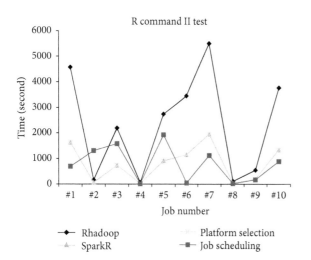

FIGURE 14: Execution time of R command II in test environment II of Case 1.

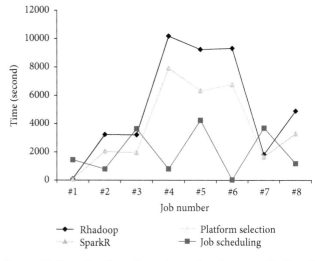

FIGURE 16: Execution time of experimental environment I in Case 2.

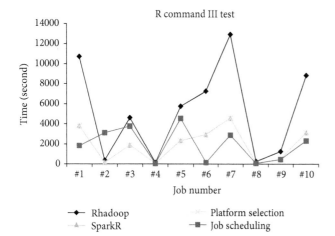

FIGURE 15: Execution time of R command III in test environment II of Case 1.

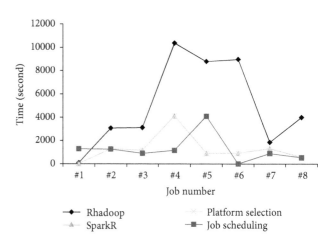

FIGURE 17: Execution time of experimental environment II in Case 2.

TABLE 10: Executable job list in Case 2.

Method	Job							
	#1	#2	#3	#4	#5	#6	#7	#8
FCFS-SP	WC	OD	UD	YR	TE	RE	AP	TA
FCFS-PS	WC	OD	UD	YR	TE	RE	AP	TA
MSHEFT-PS	AP	OD	TE	UD	YR	WC	RE	TA

TABLE 11: Average normalized performance index and performance index in Case 2.

Method	Average normalized performance index	Performance index
FCFS-SP-RHadoop	0.314	31.42
FCFS-SP-SparkR	0.753	75.32
FCFS-PS	0.760	76.02
MSHEFT-PS	1.000	100.00

Conflicts of Interest

The authors declare that they have no conflicts of interest.

Acknowledgments

This work is fully supported by the Ministry of Science and Technology, Taiwan, under Grant nos. MOST 105-2221-E-390-013-MY3 and MOST 104-2622-E-390-006-CC3.

References

[1] H. Chen, R. H. L. Chiang, and V. C. Storey, "Business intelligence and analytics: from big data to big impact," *MIS Quarterly: Management Information Systems*, vol. 36, no. 4, pp. 1165–1188, 2012.

[2] B. R. Chang, H.-F. Tsai, and C.-L. Guo, "High performance remote cloud data center backup using NoSQL database," *Journal of Information Hiding and Multimedia Signal Processing*, vol. 7, no. 5, pp. 993–1005, 2016.

[3] B.-R. Chang, H.-F. Tsai, and H.-T. Hsu, "Secondary index to Big Data NoSQL Database—Incorporating solr to HBase approach," *Journal of Information Hiding and Multimedia Signal Processing*, vol. 7, no. 1, pp. 80–89, 2016.

[4] C. D. Wickens, "Processing resources in attention dual task performance and workload assessment," 1981, Office of Naval Research Engineering Psychology Program, No. N-000-14-79-C-0658.

[5] P. Mika and G. Tummarello, "Web semantics in the clouds," *IEEE Intelligent Systems*, vol. 23, no. 5, pp. 82–87, 2008.

[6] M. Zaharia, M. Chowdhury, M. J. Franklin, S. Shenker, and I. Stoica, "Spark: cluster computing with working sets," in *Proceedings of the 2nd USENIX Workshop on Hot Topics in Cloud Computing*, pp. 95–101, Portland, Ore, USA, 2010.

[7] B.-R. Chang, H.-F. Tsai, Y.-C. Tsai, C.-F. Kuo, and C.-C. Chen, "Integration and optimization of multiple big data processing platforms," *Engineering Computations (Swansea, Wales)*, vol. 33, no. 6, pp. 1680–1704, 2016.

[8] S. Chaudhuri, U. Dayal, and V. Narasayya, "An overview of business intelligence technology," *Communications of the ACM*, vol. 54, no. 8, pp. 88–98, 2011.

[9] D. Harish, M. S. Anusha, and K. V. Daya Sagar, "Big data analytics using RHadoop," *International Journal of Innovative Research in Advanced Engineering*, vol. 2, no. 4, pp. 180–185, 2015.

[10] M. Adnan, M. Afzal, M. Aslam, R. Jan, and A. M. Martinez-Enriquez, "Minimizing big data problems using cloud computing based on Hadoop architecture," in *Proceedings of the 2014 11th Annual High Capacity Optical Networks and Emerging/Enabling Technologies (Photonics for Energy), HONET-PfE 2014*, pp. 99–103, Charlotte, NC, USA, 2014.

[11] X. Yang, S. Liu, K. Feng, S. Zhou, and X.-H. Sun, "Visualization and adaptive subsetting of earth science data in HDFS: a novel data analytics strategy with hadoop and spark," in *Proceedings of the 2016 IEEE International Conferences on Big Data and Cloud Computing, Social Computing and Networking, Sustainable Computing and Communications*, pp. 89–96, Atlanta, Ga, USA, 2016.

[12] Apache Spark, 2017, https://spark.apache.org/.

[13] M. Maurya and S. Mahajan, "Performance analysis of MapReduce programs on Hadoop cluster," in *Proceedings of the 2012 World Congress on Information and Communication Technologies, WICT 2012*, pp. 505–510, Trivandrum, India, 2012.

[14] A. Kala Karun and K. Chitharanjan, "A review on hadoop—HDFS infrastructure extensions," in *Proceedings of the 2013 IEEE Conference on Information and Communication Technologies, ICT 2013*, pp. 132–137, Tamil Nadu, India, 2013.

[15] L. George, *HBase: The Definitive Guide: Random Access to Your Planet-Size Data*, O'Reilly Media, Inc, Sebastopol, Calif, USA.

[16] A. Thusoo, J. S. Sarma, N. Jain et al., "Hive: a warehousing solution over a map-reduce framework," *Proceedings of the VLDB Endowment*, vol. 2, no. 2, pp. 1626–1629, 2009.

[17] Caesars Entertainment, 2017, https://www.cloudera.com/about-cloudera/press-center/press-releases/2015-05-05-cloudera-intel-accelerate-enterprise-hadoop-adoption-industry-partnership.html.

[18] Cerner, 2017, https://www.cloudera.com/customers/cerner.html.

[19] eharmony, 2017, http://www.eharmony.com/engineering/mapping-love-with-hadoop/#.WKCRgTt9600.

[20] J. Heinrich and B. Broeksema, "Big data visual analytics with parallel coordinates," in *Proceedings of the Big Data Visual Analytics, BDVA 2015*, Tasmania, Australia, 2015.

[21] Azure HDInsight, 2017, https://azure.microsoft.com/zh-tw/services/hdinsight/.

[22] G. Li, J. Kim, and A. Feng, "Yahoo audience expansion: migration from hadoop streaming to spark," in *Proceedings of the Spark Summit 2013*, San Francisco, Calif, USA, 2013, Yahoo, 2017, https://spark-summit.org/2013/li-yahoo-audience-expansion-migration-from-hadoop-streaming-to-spark/.

[23] Cloudera Spark Streaming, 2017, https://blog.cloudera.com/blog/2016/05/new-in-cloudera-labs-envelope-for-apache-spark-streaming/.

[24] M. S. Aravinth, M. S. Shanmugapriyaa, M. S. Sowmya, and M. E. Arun, "An efficient hadoop frameworks sqoop and ambari for big data processing," *International Journal for Innovative Research in Science and Technology*, vol. 1, no. 10, pp. 252–255, 2015.

[25] S. Hoffman, *Apache Flume: Distributed Log Collection for Hadoop*, Packt Publishing Ltd, Maharashtra, India, 2013.

[26] A. Gahlawat, "Big data analytics using R and Hadoop," *International Journal of Computational Engineering and Management*, vol. 1, no. 17, pp. 9–14, 2013.

[27] M. Zaharia, M. Chowdhury, T. Das et al., "Fast and interactive analytics over Hadoop data with Spark," *USENIX Login*, vol. 37, no. 4, pp. 45–51, 2012.

[28] S. Urbanek, M. S. Urbanek, and S. J. JDK, "Package 'rJava'," 2017, http://www.rforge.net/rJava/.

[29] S. Salian and D. G. Harisekaran, "Big data analytics predicting risk of readmissions of diabetic patients," *International Journal of Science and Research*, vol. 4, no. 4, pp. 534–538, 2015.

[30] B. R. Chang, H.-F. Tsai, and C.-M. Chen, "Empirical analysis of cloud-mobile computing based VVoIP with intelligent adaptation," *Journal of Internet Technology*, vol. 17, no. 5, pp. 993–1002, 2016.

[31] Proxmox Virtual Environment, 2017, https://pve.proxmox.com/.

[32] B. R. Chang, H.-F. Tsai, and Y.-C. Tsai, "High-performed virtualization services for in-cloud enterprise resource planning system," *Journal of Information Hiding and Multimedia Signal Processing*, vol. 5, no. 4, pp. 614–624, 2014.

[33] H. Topcuoglu, S. Hariri, and M. Wu, "Performance-effective and low-complexity task scheduling for heterogeneous computing," *IEEE Transactions on Parallel and Distributed Systems*, vol. 13, no. 3, pp. 260–274, 2002.

18

Research on Monitoring and Prewarning System of Accident in the Coal Mine Based on Big Data

Xu Xia [ID],[1,2] **Zhigang Chen** [ID],[1] **and Wei Wei** [ID][3]

[1]*School of Software, Central South University, Changsha, China*
[2]*Hunan Vocational Institute of Safety Technology, Changsha, China*
[3]*School of Computer Science and Engineering, Xi'an University of Technology, Xi'an 710048, China*

Correspondence should be addressed to Zhigang Chen; czg@csu.edu.cn

Academic Editor: Wenbing Zhao

More and more big data come from sensor nodes. There are many sensor nodes placed in the monitoring and prewarning system of the coal mine in China for the purpose of monitoring the state of the environment. It works every day and forms the coal mine big data. Traditional coal mine monitoring and prewarning systems are mainly based on mine communication cable, but they are difficult to place at coal working face tunnels. We use WSN to replace mine communication cable and build the monitoring and prewarning system. The sensor nodes in WSN are energy limited and the sensor data are complicated so it is very difficult to use these data directly to prewarn the accident. To solve these problems, in this paper, a new data aggregation strategy and fuzzy comprehensive assessment model are proposed. Simulations compared the energy consumption, delay time, cooperation cost, and prewarning time with our previous work. The result shows our method is reasonable.

1. Introduction

Coal is the main energy source in China. According to 2016 National Economic and Social Development Statistical Bulletin, the coal consumption in 2015 is about 64% of total energy consumption. So the government of China is paying more and more attention to safety production and proposing to use WSN, big data, IOT, and AI technologies to build "digital coal mine" so as to improve the safety level of coal mine industry. In China, most of the coal mining has happened underground, so it is very complicated about the environment in the coal mine. Some gases such as CH4 and CO are easy to gather in the coal mine tunnels; it is the main reason causing explosion accident; many workers lose their life. Since 2010, all of the coal mine industries were asked to install the monitoring system to prevent the happening of the accident. The monitoring system is working 24 hours a day without interruption. It means there are lots of monitoring data produced in the monitoring system every day. These data mainly include the state of equipment, the concertation of gas, the pressure of roof, the speed of the wind, and so on.

These data have the characteristics of big data: large data, many types, high velocity, high value, and complex processing process [1]. Taking the data obtained by monitoring system by the State Administration of Work Safety in 2015 as an example, the cumulative information exceeds 5 million and the space occupied is 10TB [2]. We can use these data to build the suitable prewarning model and decrease the accident. It is meaningful to society.

The traditional communication method of the monitoring system is burying mine communication cable underground, but it is difficult to do at some places such as coal working face because the coal working face always changes with the digging process. With the development of WSN, its characteristics were proved to easily be used in industry [3–5]. For these reasons, many scholars proposed using WSN to replace the mine communication cable of the monitoring system. Obviously, the features of coal mine industry are much different with other fields when we use WSN; the coal mine tunnels are very long and narrow. For example, in the mines of the Nanyang Coal Industry Co., Ltd., Hengyang, China, the main haulage roadway is approximately 12,000 m

FIGURE 1: The main haulage roadway.

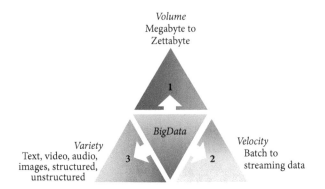

FIGURE 2: Characteristics of big data.

long, and most return airways have lengths of more than 1000 m, but the width is only several meters (Figure 1 shows part of the main haulage roadway). If we want to use WSN in the monitoring system in the coal mine industry, we should solve some problems. The big problem is how to extend the lifetime because it is difficult to change the battery of sensor.

The monitoring system of coal mine almost works every day. So it can produce big data. If we use these data reasonably, we can know the accident in advance and take some measurement to prevent the happening of the accident. Reference [6] proposed if we want to use big data in the coal mine industry with WSN, we should consider how to decrease the energy consumption. Reference [7] proposed that data aggregation can be used in WSN and saved more energy. Based on above research work, this paper will focus on how to use WSN in the monitoring and prewarning system based on big data in coal mine industry.

This paper is organized as follows: Section 2 describes related studies. Section 3 explains the design of the monitoring and prewarning system. Section 4 presents the data aggregation strategy and prewarning model. Section 5 presents the simulation and analyzes the performance. The final section provides the conclusion and future research directions.

2. Related Studies

Big data is not a new concept now. But earlier, the big data was limited to some specific organizations like Google, Microsoft, Yahoo, and so on. However, with the developments of IOT, cloud computing and sensor network, the cost of hardware is decreasing and the storage and processing power is increasing. As a result, many sources such as sensors and applications start to generate more and more data. The organizations tend to store these data easily for a long time because the storage and processing ability are great.

In fact, there is no uniform definition for "big data." The well-known definition is 3V's [8]: volume, variety, and velocity (as shown in Figure 2). EMC [9] has defined big data as any attribute that challenges constraints of a system capability or business need.

More and more big data come from sensor nodes. Reference [10] proposed a greenhouse gas sensor network located throughout California where it collects a large number of real-time data about greenhouse gases and their behavior. The project [11] embedded about 200 sensor nodes on the bridge to monitor the state of the bridge. This monitoring system collects a variety of data including temperature and the pressure of the bridge's concrete reaction to any change. Sensor nodes can collect information in the natural disaster situation in order to optimally utilize the resource and manage supply chains [12]. The challenges in big data mainly include two categories: engineering and semantic [13]. The Jet Propulsion Laboratory (JPL) has identified a number of major challenges in big data [14]; it includes the energy problem especially for the sensor nodes because there are more and more big data coming from sensor nodes in the future.

As to the problem of energy, data aggregation is an efficient method to decrease energy consumption and prolong the lifetime of WSN [15]. To reduce the amount of communication data in WSN, a lot of correlation-based data aggregation methods have been proposed in [7, 16–24]. The traditional data aggregation methods which are used in WSN mainly include two categories, the first type is based on least square method, Bayesian estimation method, D-S evidence theory, and so on; the other is based on artificial intelligence theory of artificial neural network method, fuzzy reasoning method, and rough set method [25]. Reference [26] introduced the data density correlation degree to decrease the amount of data conveyed to sink node, so it can help save more energy.

However, most of the previous studies do not focus on the coal mine. Only a few studies are about coal mining. References [3, 27–30] have studied the energy consumption problem of the coal mine, but all of them did not consider the big data technology and only use single-sink structure. Some novel algorithm is proposed in [31, 32]: in [31] a model for underground mines is generated by adopting a performance-based approach; in [32] a green MAC algorithm is proposed for smart home sensor networks. These strategies

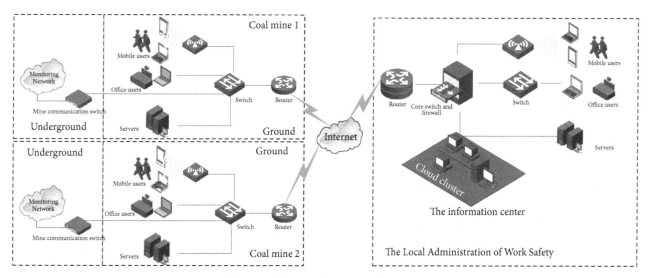

FIGURE 3: The overall structure of system.

effectively extend the network lifetime and improve network performance. Reference [33] introduced IOT and WSN in a mine and described the mine production, monitoring, and prewarning system based on big data technology, but it did not explain how to use sensor nodes and how to build the prewarning model. References [34–44] designed an architecture of monitoring system based on WSN and discussed a data aggregation strategy but did not consider using big data.

Our paper focuses on how to design the monitoring and prewarning system suitable for coal mine industry, how to use data aggregation strategy to decrease energy consumption, and how to build a prewarning model to prevent the accident happening in advance.

3. Design of the Monitoring and Prewarning System

3.1. Overall Structure of System. The Local Administration of Work Safety requires knowing the real-time production state of each coal mine, so all of the monitoring data are sent to the information center of the Local Administration of Work Safety. We design the structure of monitoring and prewarning system based on big data which is shown in Figure 3.

The monitoring data are sent to the cloud cluster and form big data; then we can use furry comprehensive assessment model (explained in Section 4.2) to prewarn the problems of the coal mine in advance. The officers and workers in Local Administration of Work Safety and coal mines can gain the prewarning message through their mobile phone or computer, and then they can make some decisions and measures to solve the problems to avoid the accident in advance [23, 30].

3.2. Structure of Monitoring Network. The monitoring network is located in underground. There are a large number of monitoring data, mainly the data generated by sensors in the WSN, that are generated in the production process, like the values of voltages, the concentration of gas, the speed of the wind, the pressure of roof, and so on [33]. In our study of the monitoring system, we focus on the monitoring of the concentration of CH4; it is the main reason for explosion and fire accident in the coal mine. We can use the same method to monitor and process other gases such as CO.

The Coalmining tunnels in China usually are categorized with their functions, including development tunnels, preparation tunnels, and mining tunnels [23, 30, 35–44]. The development tunnels are served for the whole mine, including the horizontal mining area, such as the main haulage roadways and the main return airways. The preparation tunnels are used for digging tunnels such as upward and downward mining areas. The mining tunnels are used to form the coal working face, such as the return airflow roadway and the haulage roadways of coal working face.

The main haulage roadways are relatively wide conveniently to bury mine communication cable. Along the development tunnels, there are many branches; most of them are coal working face tunnels. The coal working face tunnels are narrow, irregular, and always changing with the development of coal mining, so it is difficult to bury mine communication cables; we use WSN to replace the mine communication cable. For these considerations, in our study, the structure of monitoring network is shown in Figure 4.

The WSN is composed of two types of nodes: sink nodes and sensor nodes. The sink nodes are placed near the junction of haulage roadways and coal working face tunnels; it means the number of sink nodes is equal to the number of branches. The sink nodes connect to each other through the mine communication cable. The sensor nodes are placed at the top and the middle of the roof, because the CH4 is lighter than air and always gather together at the top of the roof. The sensor nodes in each coal working face tunnel have their own ID; the ID number increases along with coal working face tunnel; it means the ID of the first sensor node near the sink node is 1; then its neighbor's ID is 2. In order to gain stable communication performance, we use the Mine Segmenting Wireless Channel Model [31]. The sensor nodes can

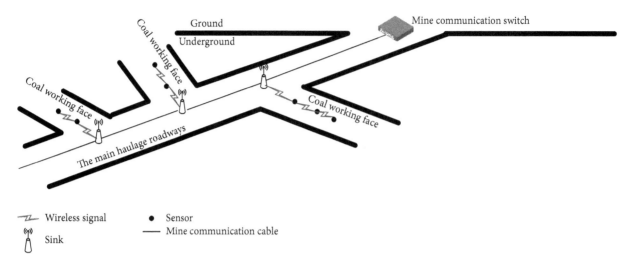

FIGURE 4: The structure of monitoring network.

communicate with neighbor sensor nodes within two hops. The sensor nodes send data to the sink nodes in one or two hops.

In this paper, we suppose that the number of sensor nodes in the network is N, and they are distributed in a long-strip region measuring $L \times W$ with $L \gg W$. As soon as the sink nodes and sensor nodes are deployed, the location is fixed and it no longer changes; the output power of sensor nodes is adjustable according to [31]. The sensor nodes are isomorphic with the same initial energy, and they also have data fusion function and self-sensing of residual energy. Furthermore, the energy of sink nodes is unlimited.

3.3. Working Mode. The monitoring network is always in working state for 24 hours without interruption, so the sensor nodes can collect and transfer data permanently; it means the sensor nodes will consume much energy. As we all know that the sensor nodes are powered by the battery which energy is limited and the consumption of energy mainly comes from the communication process. So in our study, we propose the sensor nodes working in two modes; the first mode is decision mode; the second mode is transferring mode. We describe the two modes as follows.

(1) Decision Mode. According to "coal mine safety regulation" which is issued by State Administration of Work Safety in China, there are three important values in the monitoring system, which are alarm value, power-off value, and power-recovery value; if the concentration is more than the alarm value, the monitoring system will alert to the workers to prevent the concentration from rising and evacuate from their working place; if the concentration is more than the power-off value, all of the electrical equipment will be powered down to prevent the happening of accident; if the concentration is less than the power-recovery value, the monitoring system will give power to the electrical equipment. So it means some data is not important and some data is important. If the sensor nodes only transfer the important data, it will decrease the power consumption largely. So we propose a threshold value

(EV) to help sensor nodes to make a decision; we call this procedure as decision mode. Senor nodes will shut down their communication module, keep collecting environmental parameters, and judge which data should be sent to their neighbor in this mode. When the concentration of CH_4 is larger than E, the sensor nodes will be woken up and enter the transferring mode.

(2) Transferring Mode. In this mode, the sensor nodes will send or receive data. Because the structure of monitoring network is shown in Figure 4, the data will only be sent forward and from the sensor node whose ID is larger than another sensor node. Each sensor node can send its data to next sensor node in two hops; to prolong the network life, we propose the cooperation decision mechanism (explained in Section 4.1.2), to help the sensor node decide which node it will send. After that, the sensor node will send the important data to the selected next sensor node until arriving to the sink node.

4. The Data Aggregation Strategy and Prewarning Model

In our study, we propose a data aggregation strategy and a fuzzy comprehensive assessment model based on big data in the coal mine industry.

The data aggregation strategy is used in the process of data transformation from one sensor node to the next sensor node and eventually arrives to the sink node in underground. The fuzzy comprehensive assessment model is used in the prewarning system on the ground to prevent the happening of the accident.

4.1. Data Aggregation Strategy. We propose this strategy that mainly takes into consideration the limited power capacity of the sensor nodes and tends to extend the lifetime of the WSN. First of all, the sensor node collects the data and estimates the importance of the data locally; thus it prohibits communications corresponding to unimportant or

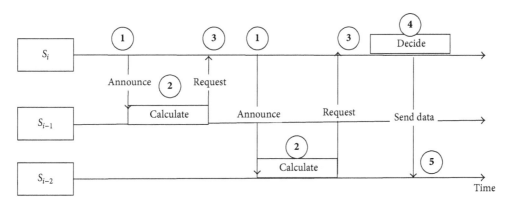

FIGURE 5: Negotiation process among sensor nodes.

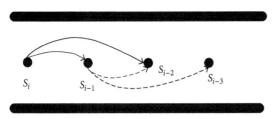

FIGURE 6: Light load rule.

redundant data. When the sensor node s_i (originator node) detects important data, it will send a message to wake up and ask its closest neighbors in two hops (s_{i-1} and s_{i-2}) to cooperate with it. Neighbors decide to cooperate or not, according to their interests, which are defined by a cooperation decision mechanism (explained in Section 4.1.2). The sensor node s_i (originator node) will choose the best neighbor to cooperate and send data to it. Figure 5 shows the overall negotiation process.

4.1.1. Overall Negotiation Process among Sensor Nodes. As Figure 5 shows, the process consists of five steps. s_i is the first sensor node which detects important data; it will send an announcement message to s_{i-1} and s_{i-2} (step 1); the two neighbors will calculate their cooperate relevance (R) according to cooperation decision mechanism (explained in Section 4.1.2). After their calculation, they will send R to s_i (step 3). s_i receives R and selects the larger one as the next cooperation sensor node (step 4). We assume s_{i-2} has the larger R, so s_i will send data to s_{i-2}.

In some special circumstances, the sensor node should send important data to its neighbor node and receive the announcement message to cooperate with other nodes at the same time. It is shown in Figure 6 that the sensor nodes s_{i-1} and s_i detect important data, so s_{i-1} needs not only to send but also receive the announcement message. In this condition, we will have a rule that the data should always be sent to the light load sensor node. It means s_i will send data to s_{i-2} and s_{i-1} will send data to s_{i-3} (along with the bold line).

4.1.2. Cooperation Decision Mechanism. In this section, we explain the mechanism used in the transferring mode to

calculate the cooperate relevance (R) by sensor nodes. When the sensor node wants to send important data to its neighbor nodes, it should choose the better one from them, considered to prolong the lifetime of WSN; we define 4 parameters that may have a large influence on the network. These parameters are as follows: the energy (E), the density (D), the position (P), and the data important degree (I). We use (1) [24] to calculate R. These parameters will be explained in detail later in this section.

$$R = E \times \delta_e + \frac{1}{D} \times \delta_d + P \times \delta_p + I \times \delta_i, \quad (1)$$

where δ_e, δ_d, δ_p, and δ_i are the important factors for the energy, the density, the position, and the data important degree, respectively.

(1) Energy. It is the most important parameter in WSN because the sensor nodes are energy limited. If the sensor node is power exhausted, it will decrease the lifetime of WSN. So we use E to represent the residual energy level. If the sensor node has more residual energy, it is advised to participate in cooperation; another sensor node will save more energy, so it extends the whole lifetime of WSN. We use (2) to calculate E; E_r refers to the residual energy; E_0 refers to the initial energy.

$$E = \frac{E_r}{E_0}. \quad (2)$$

(2) Density. The density is the number of sensor nodes per square meter. We will consider the number of neighbor sensor nodes within its radio range according to [31]. If the sensor node has more neighbors within its radio range, it means the value of D is bigger, the distance between two sensor nodes is shorter, and the energy consumption will be less, so it is advised to participate in cooperation. That is why, in (1), we take the inverse of the density (D) to calculate. We define the density (D) with

$$D = \frac{N_r / (\pi \times r^2)}{N_{\text{ideal}} / (\pi \times r^2)} = \frac{N_r}{N_{\text{ideal}}} \quad (3)$$

where r refers to the radio range of the sensor node, N_r refers to the number of sensor nodes within the radio range, and

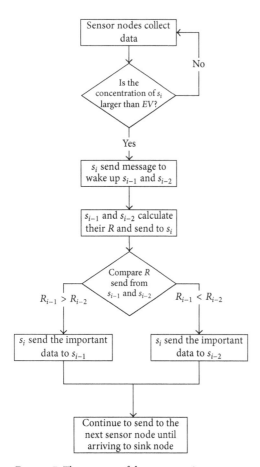

FIGURE 7: The process of data aggregation strategy.

N_{ideal} refers to theoretical number of sensor nodes and it is given from the ideal distribution of sensor nodes according to [31]. In the ideal case, N_r should be equal to N_{ideal}.

(3) Position. There are two types of positions in WSN. The first position is the normal position, where the sensor node has multiple neighbors. The second position is the edge sensor node, which stays at the edge of the network. In fact, only two sensor nodes are belonging to the second position; they are the sensor nodes which have the largest ID and the smallest ID. We define the position as the distance between the sensor node with sink node in the same coal working face.

(4) Data Important Degree. This parameter depends on the running application and the trend of concentration changing of CH4. It is calculated by local processing, where the sensor node estimates the data important degree according to the rule. For example, if the increment of concentration is growing in 6 hours, it indicates some dangerous thing will happen even the concentration is less than the threshold value (*EV*). The data will be estimated as important; otherwise, the data is considered unimportant. Figure 7 describes the process of data aggregation strategy.

4.2. Fuzzy Comprehensive Assessment Model. There are many types of sensor nodes in the coal mine. We focus on the

concentration of CH4 in the monitoring system, but there are numerous factors that may give influence to the safety of coal mine, because the environment underground is very complicated. If we use single-layer evaluation model in the prewarning system, the incorrect divide will happen because some key parameters may be neglected. It is similar with the mode proposed by [45], so we use it as a reference and propose our fuzzy comprehensive assessment model.

According to "coal mine safety regulation," the different place has different requirements. Coal working face and return airway are the most dangerous places; most explosions and roof accidents have happened in this place. The main haulage roadways are relatively safe because the air is fresh and the geological conditions are better than other places. Reference [36] sums up and analyzes the main reasons of gas, roof, transportation, floods, and fire accident, so we propose a fuzzy comprehensive assessment model in this section.

The monitoring system includes environmental monitoring, equipment operation status monitoring, coal mine transportation monitoring, and so on. We take the environmental monitoring system as an example; it mainly includes the concentration of CH_4, CO, O_2, C_2H_2, and so on.

Assuming the state factor set of environmental monitoring in the coal mine is $U = \{u_1, u_2, \ldots, u_n\}$, u_i ($1 \leq i \leq n$) is a certain evaluation factor of the environment. The evaluation set of the safety prewarning model is $X = \{x_1, x_2, \ldots, x_m\}$; x_i ($1 \leq j \leq m$) is the alert level of the coal mine. So the evaluation model is the equal of structuring a mapping rule $f : U \rightarrow X$, making the only sure comments $X_0 = \{x_1', x_2', \ldots, x_m'\}$ that correspond to the facts $U_0 = \{u_1', u_2', \ldots u_n'\}$. So, the safety rewarning evaluation model considers various factors and gets the alert level x_k ($1 \leq k \leq m$).

By using the multilayer comprehensive evaluation model, the state factor set U is divided into h subsets; we call them $U = \{u_1, u_2, \ldots, u_h\}$ and assume the corresponding evaluation weight matrix is $W = \{w_1, w_2, \ldots, w_h\}$, in which W_i ($i = 1, 2, \ldots, h$) is the weight set of each factor subset. Each element is weight set and satisfies the normalization condition $\sum_{i=1}^{h} W_i = 1$. R ($j = 1, 2, \ldots, h$) express the fuzzy constraint relationship between each factor subset and evaluation set.

At the beginning, from the first layer, the level 1 assessment $G_i = W_i \circ R_i$ ($i = 1, 2, \ldots, h$). Then assemble the G_i as the level 2 fuzzy constraint relationship R between factor set and evaluation set. Then step by step evaluate the level set according to the process until arriving to the highest level. The two-layer fuzzy comprehensive evaluation model is shown in Figure 8. The evaluation flow is shown in Figure 9.

5. Performance Evaluation

5.1. Simulations. In order to confirm the performance of data aggregation strategy and fuzzy comprehensive assessment model, we use MATLAB and GlomoSim [37, 43, 44] to do some simulations.

In Table 1, we choose the simulation parameters as close as possible to the reality. For example, the sensor nodes

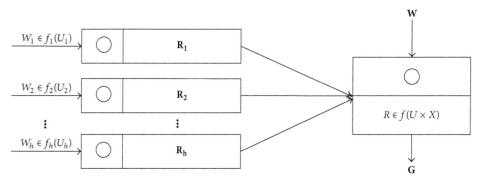

FIGURE 8: Two-layer fuzzy comprehensive evaluation model.

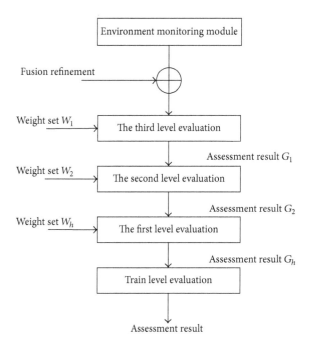

FIGURE 9: The evaluation flow.

TABLE 1: Simulation parameters.

Simulation parameters	Values
Network coverage	(0, 0)–(1000, 20) m
Number of sink nodes	1–6
Number of sensor nodes	0–600
Initial energy of sensor node	0.5 J
Radio range	75 m
Throughput	1 Mbps
Simulation time	48 hours

TABLE 2: Cooperate relevance equation parameters.

Equation parameters	Values
$\delta_e, \delta_p, \delta_i$	0.35
δ_d	0.15

The aim of fuzzy comprehensive assessment model is to decrease the time of prewarn.

In the simulation, we compare the data aggregation strategy with PCEB-MS protocol which is proposed in our previous work [35] and give a simulation to prove the fuzzy comprehensive assessment model can reduce the prewarning time compared with the other methods [33].

(1) Energy Consumption. We define the energy consumption as the average value of the energy consumed by each sensor node during their transmit, receive, and process data. We use the classical energy consumption model [39–41] for simulation. Figure 10 shows the comparison between PCEB-MS and our strategy. The result proves that our strategy is significantly better than our previous work. At the beginning, the average consumption of two methods is similar, but with the increase of sensor nodes, our strategy can save more energy; when the number of sensor nodes is 600, the average energy consumption of PCEB-MS is 15×10^4, but our strategy is only about 10×10^4, so the average energy consumption is reduced by about 34%.

(2) Delay. We define the delay as the average latency needed to send a message from a sensor node which detects important data to the sink; it is including the communication and processing time. At this simulation, we placed 6 sink nodes.

characteristics (transmission, processor, radio range, etc.) are determined according to the specification of [31, 35, 39, 42].

Table 2 resumes the values of importance factor $\delta_e, \delta_p, \delta_i,$ and δ_d. By giving the same value to $\delta_e, \delta_p,$ and $\delta_i,$ it means we give the same importance to the energy, the position, and the data importance degree to calculate the cooperate relevance (R). After we make several simulations, we have found that best values for δ_e and δ_d are 0.35 and δ_d is 0.15. According to the "coal mine safety regulation" and simulations, the threshold value (EV) of CH4 should be between 0.5 and 1.5; for the balance of produce with safety, we choose to fix a threshold of EV to 0.7.

5.2. Performance Analysis. In this section, we will compare and analyze the energy consumption, the delay, the cooperation cost, and the prewarning time. The goal of data aggregation strategy is to reduce the amount of communicated data, increase the valid data in big data, and hence reduce the energy consumption and prolong the lifetime of the network.

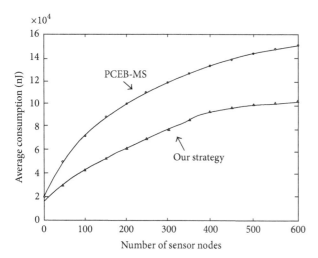

FIGURE 10: Comparison of average energy consumption.

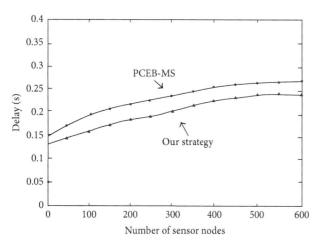

FIGURE 11: Comparison of delay.

Figure 11 shows our strategy needs less time from each sensor node to sink node because relatively the sensor node does not need process complicated data.

(3) Cooperation Cost. When the sensor node needs to send important data, it will wake its neighbor up in two hops and make a decision to choose a neighbor to send data, so it will cause cooperation cost. Figure 12 shows with the increase of the sensor nodes the cooperation cost will decrease and the consumption is very little. It means the cost is valuable.

(4) Prewarning Time. We use the prewarning time to make sure the fuzzy comprehensive assessment model is reasonable. We define it as how long the time is before the accident is prewarned. There are some studies about the prewarning system in China, such as [33, 46, 47], but only [33] has the similar prewarning system structure with our study, so we choose [33] as a comparison. Reference [33] has proposed a data analysis platform to forecast the accident through the IOT and big data technology, but it has not used any prewarning model.

TABLE 3: Comparison result.

Concentration accident	Prewarning time	
	Using our model	Not using our model
CH4	3.5 hours	2.2 hours
CO	2.1 hours	1.5 hours
C_2H^2	2.3 hours	1.8 hours

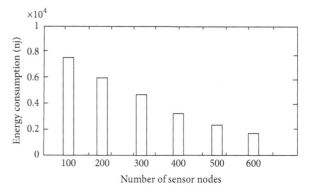

FIGURE 12: Cooperation cost.

In this simulation, we use the fuzzy comprehensive assessment model on the platform. We get the data from the simulated coal mine, which is a project to train the staff for coal mine industry in our college. Table 3 shows the difference between using this model and not using this model to prewarn of the accident. Obviously, the model can increase about 0.5–1.0 hour of prewarning time.

6. Conclusions

In this paper, we focus on the safety problems of coal mine industry in China. We proposed a monitoring and prewarning system based on big data to prevent happening of the accident. We used the WSN network to replace mine communication cable underground at coal working face and designed the data aggregation strategy and fuzzy comprehensive assessment model to help the system prewarn the accident in advance. At last, we use MATLAB and GlomoSim to do some simulations to make sure our strategy and model are reasonable. Results of simulations show that our method can improve the performance of the monitoring network and prewarning system largely.

Conflicts of Interest

The authors declare that there are no conflicts of interest regarding the publication of this paper.

Acknowledgments

This work was supported in part by the National Natural Science Foundation of China (61672540, 61379057), 2015 Prevention of Major Accidents Safety Key Technology Projects (Hunan-0012-2015AQ), and 2017 Hunan Natural Science

Foundation of China (2017JJ5004). This job is supported by the Open Program of Xiamen Key Laboratory of Computer Vision and Pattern Recognition, Huaqiao University (no. 600005-Z17X0001) and the Specialized Research Fund for the Doctoral Program of Higher Education of China (Grant no. 20136118120010).

References

[1] W. Haijun and W. Xianli, "Analysis on application of coal mine big data in age of Internet +," *Coal Science & Technology Magazine*, vol. 44, no. 2, pp. 139–143, 2016.

[2] "Big Data and Safety Production Review," http://aqscjdglj.tjftz .gov.cn/system//02/10/010073245.shtml.

[3] X. Xia, Z. Chen, D. Li, and W. Li, "Proposal for efficient routing protocol for wireless sensor network in coal mine goaf," *Wireless Personal Communications*, vol. 77, no. 3, pp. 1699–1711, 2014.

[4] D. Zhang, Z. Chen, M. K. Awad, N. Zhang, H. Zhou, and X. S. Shen, "Utility-optimal resource management and allocation algorithm for energy harvesting cognitive radio sensor networks," *IEEE Journal on Selected Areas in Communications*, vol. 34, no. 12, pp. 3552–3565, 2016.

[5] D. Zhang, Z. Chen, H. Zhou, L. Chen, and X. Shen, "Energy-balanced cooperative transmission based on relay selection and power control in energy harvesting wireless sensor network," *Computer Networks*, vol. 104, pp. 189–197, 2016.

[6] E. Sun, X. Zhang, and Z. Li, "The internet of things (IOT) and cloud computing (CC) based tailings dam monitoring and pre-alarm system in mines," *Safety Science*, vol. 50, no. 4, pp. 811–815, 2012.

[7] C. M. Chao and T. Y. Hsiao, "Design of structure-free and energy-balanced data aggregation in wireless sensor networks," *Journal of Network & Computer Applications*, vol. 37, no. 1, pp. 229–239, 2014.

[8] W. Zhao, P. M. Melliar-Smith, and L. E. Moser, "Fault tolerance middleware for cloud computing," in *Proceedings of the 3rd IEEE International Conference on Cloud Computing (CLOUD '10)*, pp. 67–74, Miami, FL, USA, July 2010.

[9] R. Lun and W. Zhao, "A survey of applications and human motion recognition with microsoft kinect," *International Journal of Pattern Recognition and Artificial Intelligence*, vol. 29, no. 5, Article ID 1555008, 2015.

[10] "The industry leader in emerging technology research," https:// gigaom.com/archives/energy-environment/.

[11] K. Taylor-Sakyi, "Big Data: Understanding Big Data," 2016.

[12] E. Kinoshita and T. Mizuno, *What Is Big Data Big Data Management*, Springer International Publishing, 2017.

[13] C. Bizer, P. Boncz, M. L. Brodie, and O. Erling, "The meaningful use of big data: four perspectives—four challenges," *ACM SIGMOD Record*, vol. 40, no. 4, pp. 56–60, 2011.

[14] D. L. Jones, K. Wagstaff, D. R. Thompson et al., "Big data challenges for large radio arrays," in *Proceedings of the 2012 IEEE Aerospace Conference*, pp. 1–6, Big Sky, MT, USA, March 2012.

[15] F. Yuan, Y. Zhan, and Y. Wang, "Data density correlation degree clustering method for data aggregation in WSN," *IEEE Sensors Journal*, vol. 14, no. 4, pp. 1089–1098, 2014.

[16] S. Madden, M. J. Franklin, J. M. Hellerstein, and W. Hong, "TAG: a tiny aggregation service for ad-hoc sensor networks," *ACM SIGOPS Operating Systems Review*, vol. 36, no. 1, pp. 131–146, 2002.

[17] J. Zheng, P. Wang, and C. Li, "Distributed data aggregation using slepianwolf coding in cluster-based wireless sensor networks," *IEEE Transactions on Vehicular Technology*, vol. 59, no. 5, pp. 2564–2574, 2010.

[18] M. C. Vuran, Ö. B. Akan, and I. F. Akyildiz, "Spatio-temporal correlation: theory and applications for wireless sensor networks," *Computer Networks*, vol. 45, no. 3, pp. 245–259, 2004.

[19] J. Yuan and H. Chen, "The optimized clustering technique based on spatial-correlation in wireless sensor networks," in *Proceedings of the 2009 IEEE Youth Conference on Information, Computing and Telecommunication (YC-ICT '09)*, pp. 411–414, Beijing, China, September 2009.

[20] A. Rajeswari and P. T. Kalaivaani, "Energy efficient routing protocol for wireless sensor networks using spatial correlation based medium access control protocol compared with IEEE 802.11," in *Proceedings of the 2011 International Conference on Process Automation, Control and Computing (PACC '11)*, pp. 1–6, Coimbatore, India, July 2011.

[21] J. N. Al-Karaki, R. Ul-Mustafa, and A. E. Kamal, "Data aggregation and routing in wireless sensor networks: optimal and heuristic algorithms," *Computer Networks*, vol. 53, no. 7, pp. 945–960, 2009.

[22] C. Hua and T.-S. P. Yum, "Optimal routing and data aggregation for maximizing lifetime of wireless sensor networks," *IEEE/ACM Transactions on Networking*, vol. 16, no. 4, pp. 892–903, 2008.

[23] Z. Sun, H. Song, H. Wang, and X. Fan, "Energy balance-based steerable arguments coverage method in WSNs," *IEEE Access*, p. 99, 2017.

[24] A. Sardouk, M. Mansouri, L. Merghem-Boulahia, D. Gaïti, and R. Rahim-Amoud, "Multi-agent system based wireless sensor network for crisis management," in *Proceedings of the 53rd IEEE Global Communications Conference (GLOBECOM '10)*, pp. 1–6, University of Kansas, January 2011.

[25] M. Zhang and M. Shen, "Research of WSN-based data fusion in water quality monitoring," *Computer Engineering & Applications*, vol. 50, no. 23, pp. 234–238, 2014.

[26] W. Wei, Q. Xu, L. Wang et al., "GI/Geom/1 queue based on communication model for mesh networks," *International Journal of Communication Systems*, vol. 27, no. 11, pp. 3013–3029, 2014.

[27] F. Wang, X. Zhang, M. Wang, and G. Chen, "Energy-efficient routing algorithm for WSNs in underground mining," *Journal of Networks*, vol. 7, no. 11, pp. 1824–1829, 2012.

[28] W. Chen, X. Jiang, X. Li, J. Gao, X. Xu, and S. Ding, "Wireless Sensor Network nodes correlation method in coal mine tunnel based on Bayesian decision," *Measurement*, vol. 46, no. 8, pp. 2335–2340, 2013.

[29] G. Zhou, L. Huang, and Z. Zhu, "A Zoning Strategy for Uniform Deployed Chain-Type Wireless Sensor Network in Underground Coal Mine Tunnel," in *Proceedings of the 2013 IEEE 10th International Conference on High Performance Computing and Communications 2013 IEEE International Conference on Embedded and Ubiquitous Computing (HPCC_EUC)*, pp. 1135–1138, Zhangjiajie, China, November 2013.

[30] W. Wei, X.-L. Yang, P.-Y. Shen, and B. Zhou, "Holes detection in anisotropic sensornets: topological methods," *International Journal of Distributed Sensor Networks*, vol. 2012, Article ID 135054, 9 pages, 2012.

[31] W. Farjow, K. Raahemifar, and X. Fernando, "Novel wireless channels characterization model for underground mines,"

Applied Mathematical Modelling, vol. 39, no. 19, pp. 5997–6007, 2015.

[32] S. Latif and X. Fernando, "A greener MAC layer protocol for smart home wireless sensor networks," in *Proceedings of the 2013 IEEE Online Conference on Green Communications (Online-GreenComm '13)*, pp. 169–174, Piscataway, NJ, USA, October 2013.

[33] C.-M. Li, R. Nie, and X.-Y. Qian, "Forecast and prewarning of coal mining safety risks based on the internet of things technology and the big data technology," *Electronic Journal of Geotechnical Engineering*, vol. 20, no. 20, pp. 11579–11586, 2015.

[34] Y. Zhang, W. Yang, D. Han, and Y.-I. Kim, "An integrated environment monitoring system for underground coal mines-Wireless Sensor Network subsystem with multi-parameter monitoring," *Sensors*, vol. 14, no. 7, pp. 13149–13170, 2014.

[35] X. Xia, Z. Chen, H. Liu, H. Wang, and F. Zeng, "A routing protocol for multisink wireless sensor networks in underground coalmine tunnels," *Sensors*, vol. 16, no. 12, pp. 2032–2054, 2016.

[36] S. Jiping, "Accident analysis and big data and Internet of Things in coal mine," *Industry and Mine Automation*, vol. 41, no. 3, pp. 1–5, 2015.

[37] V. Mishra and S. Jangale, "Analysis and comparison of different network simulators," *International Journal of Application or Innovation in Engineering & Management*, 2014.

[38] Y. Liu, A. Liu, S. Guo, Z. Li, Y. Choi, and H. Sekiya, "Context-aware collect data with energy efficient in Cyber–physical cloud systems," *Future Generation Computer Systems*, 2017.

[39] X. Liu, G. Li, S. Zhang, and A. Liu, "Big program code dissemination scheme for emergency software-define wireless sensor networks," *Peer-to-Peer Networking and Applications*, pp. 1–22, 2017.

[40] X. Chen, M. Ming, and L. Anfeng, "Dynamic Power Management and Adaptive Packet Size Selection for IoT in e-Healthcare," *Computers & Electrical Engineering*, 2017.

[41] X. Fan, H. Song, and X. Fan, "Imperfect information dynamic stackelberg game based resource allocation using hidden markov for cloud computing," *IEEE Transactions on Services Computing*, no. 99, p. 1, 2016.

[42] N. Zhang, H. Chen, X. Chen, and J. Chen, "ELM meets urban computing: ensemble urban data for smart city application," in *Proceedings of the ELM-2015*, vol. 1, pp. 51–63, 2016.

[43] W. Zhao, "A Byzantine Fault Tolerant Distributed Commit Protocol," in *Proceedings of the Third IEEE International Symposium on Dependable, Autonomic and Secure Computing (DASC '07)*, pp. 37–46, Columbia, MD, USA, September 2007.

[44] H. Song, W. Li, and P. Shen, "Gradient-driven parking navigation using a continuous information potential field based on wireless sensor network," *Information Sciences*, vol. 408, pp. 100–114, 2017.

[45] S. Hou, F. Dou, Y. Li, and Z. Long, "Assessment model of the maglev train braking system safety pre-warning and the optimization of Parameters," in *Proceedings of the 28th Chinese Control and Decision Conference (CCDC '16)*, pp. 4915–4920, May 2016.

[46] L. I. Hao-Min, L. U. Jian-Jun, and C. Wei, "Research of coal mine safety monitoring and early warning system based on cloud computing," *Industry and Mine Automation*, vol. 39, no. 3, pp. 46–50, 2013.

[47] C. Qinggui, Z. Jing, S. Qihua, and Y. Kai, "Design and Application of Hidden Danger Management and Early—warning System for Coal Mine Accidents," *Mining Safety & Environmental Protection*, vol. 43, no. 3, pp. 107–114, 2016.

19

SEDC-Based Hardware-Level Fault Tolerance and Fault Secure Checker Design for Big Data and Cloud Computing

Zahid Ali Siddiqui ⓘ,[1] **Jeong-A Lee,**[2] **and Unsang Park** ⓘ[1]

[1]*Department of Computer Science and Engineering, Sogang University, 35 Baekbeom-ro, Mapo-gu, Seoul 04107, Republic of Korea*
[2]*Department of Computer Engineering, Chosun University, 309 Pilmun-daero, Dong-gu, Gwangju 61452, Republic of Korea*

Correspondence should be addressed to Unsang Park; unsangpark@sogang.ac.kr

Academic Editor: Shangguang Wang

Fault tolerance is of great importance for big data systems. Although several software-based application-level techniques exist for fault security in big data systems, there is a potential research space at the hardware level. Big data needs to be processed inexpensively and efficiently, for which traditional hardware architectures are, although adequate, not optimum for this purpose. In this paper, we propose a hardware-level fault tolerance scheme for big data and cloud computing that can be used with the existing software-level fault tolerance for improving the overall performance of the systems. The proposed scheme uses the concurrent error detection (CED) method to detect hardware-level faults, with the help of Scalable Error Detecting Codes (SEDC) and its checker. SEDC is an all unidirectional error detection (AUED) technique capable of detecting multiple unidirectional errors. The SEDC scheme exploits data segmentation and parallel encoding features for assigning code words. Consequently, the SEDC scheme can be scaled to any binary data length "n" with constant latency and less complexity, compared to other AUED schemes, hence making it a perfect candidate for use in big data processing hardware. We also present a novel area, delay, and power efficient, scalable fault secure checker design based on SEDC. In order to show the effectiveness of our scheme, we (1) compared the cost of hardware-based fault tolerance with an existing software-based fault tolerance technique used in HDFS and (2) compared the performance of the proposed checker in terms of area, speed, and power dissipation with the famous Berger code and m-out-of-2m code checkers. The experimental results show that (1) the proposed SEDC-based hardware-level fault tolerance scheme significantly reduces the average cost associated with software-based fault tolerance in a big data application, and (2) the proposed fault secure checker outperforms the state-of-the-art checkers in terms of area, delay, and power dissipation.

1. Introduction

Big data is promising for business applications and is rapidly increasing as an important segment of the IT industry. Big data has also opened doors of significant interest in various fields, including remote healthcare, telebanking, social networking services (SNS), and satellite imaging [1]. Failures in many of these systems may represent significant economic or market share loss and negatively affect an organization's reputation [2]. Hence, it is always intended that whenever a fault occurs, the damage done should be within an acceptable threshold rather than beginning the whole task from scratch, due to which fault tolerance becomes an integral part in cloud computing and big data [3]. Fault tolerance prevents

a computer or network device from failing in the event of an unexpected error [2]. A recent study [4] showed that the cost of fault tolerance in cloud applications with high probability of failure and network latency is around 5% for the range of application sizes, hence providing improved performance at a lower cost.

The fault tolerance schemes in popular big data frameworks like Hadoop and MongoDB are composed of some sort of data replication or redundancy [5, 6]. MongoDB replicates its primary data in secondary devices. In a faulty event, the data is recalled from the secondary or the secondary temporarily acts as a primary. Fault tolerance in Hadoop relies on multiple copies of data stored on different data nodes. Although replication schemes allow complete data recovery, they consume a lot of memory and communication resources. Hence, in recent years, many researchers have proposed fault tolerance algorithms for improved data recovery, effective fault detection, and reduced latency in big data and cloud computing [2, 5–10]. All of which detect fault at the software (SW) level. Even though faults propagated due to transient errors in hardware are also detected by these schemes, and software-based techniques are more flexible, the amount of data required to process to detect a fault costs a lot more than hardware- (HW-) based fault tolerance schemes. A recent study [11] investigated the cause of data corruption in a Hadoop Distributed File System (HDFS) and found that when processing uploaded files, HW errors such as disk failure and bit-flips in processor and memory generate exceptions that are difficult to handle properly. Liu et al. [7] implemented some level of HW-based fault tolerance by modelling CPU temperature to anticipate a deteriorating physical machine. Liu et al. [7] proposed the CPU temperature monitoring as an essential step for preventing machine failure due to overheating as well as for improving the data center's energy efficiency.

Parker [12] discussed how in many cases the faults are a direct consequence of tightly integrating digital and physical components into a single unit at a sensor or field node. In fact, many modern systems rely so heavily on digital technology that the reliability of the system cannot be decomposed and partitioned into physical and SW components due to interactions between them. There is a cost associated with the storage, transmission, and analysis of these higher-dimensional data. Furthermore, many of the SW-based approaches are simulation intensive, which may lead to broad implementation challenges. To overcome some of these challenges, he suggested that onboard, embedded processing will be a practical requirement.

Transient errors in HW, if propagated, may cause chain reaction of errors at the SW layer, causing potential failure at the node/server level. Detection at the HW level requires less computation time (as low as single clock cycle) as compared with detection at the SW level (several machine cycles), while a simple recovery mechanism called recomputation at the HW level can save a lot of data swapping and signaling at the SW level. As discussed in [13], big data has created opportunities for semiconductor companies to develop more sophisticated systems to cover the challenges faced in big data and cloud computing, and a trend towards integration of more functions onto a single piece of silicon is likely to continue. Also, due to advances in semiconductor processing, there has been a reduction in the cost of digital components [12]. For these reasons, we propose the detection of transient faults, as they occur in HW, through a HW-based fault tolerance scheme, while the SW-based fault tolerance stays at the top level as a second check for HW errors and first check for SW errors. As a result, the transient errors that arise in HW are mostly taken care of by lightweight processing at the HW level with little overhead (in terms of area, power, and delay), saving tremendous computation resources at the system level. The potential for catastrophic consequences in big data systems justify the overhead incurred due to HW-based fault tolerance method.

On the other hand, fault tolerance has also become an integral part of very large-scale integration (VLSI) circuits, where downsized, large-scaled, and low-power VLSI systems are prone to transient faults [14]. Transient faults or soft errors are transient-induced events on memory and logic circuits caused by the striking of rays emitted from an IC package and high energy alpha particles from cosmic rays [14–18]. Also, in multilevel cell memories like NAND Flash memories, these errors are mostly caused by cell-to-cell interference and data retention errors [19]. Physical protection such as shielding, temperature control, and grounding circuits are not always feasible; hence, in such cases, concurrent error detecting (CED) methods are employed for protection against these errors. Since CED circuits add to the overall area and delay of the system, the selection of appropriate error detecting, and even error correcting, circuits for a particular application leads to an efficient design [18]. It has been reported that the biggest portion of errors that occur in VLSI circuits and memories are related to unidirectional errors (UE) [19–21] because these errors shift threshold voltage levels to either the positive or negative side [22], causing the circuit node logic from "0" to "1" or from "1" to "0," but not both at the same time.

Many all unidirectional error detection (AUED) schemes have been proposed and implemented, among which the Berger code technique [23] is agreed to be the least redundant. With the ability to detect single- as well as multiple-bit unidirectional errors, this technique provides error detection by simply summing the logic 0's (a B0 scheme) or 1's (a B1 scheme) in the information word, expressing its sum in binary. If the information word contains "n-bits," then a Berger code will require $\lceil \log_2(n + 1) \rceil$-bits. A Berger code checker employs a 0's (or 1's) counter circuitry for reencoding the information word to check bits and then compares it with the preencoded check bits using a two-rail checker [23]. A chain of adders and a tree of two-rail checkers are required to design these checker circuits [23], where area and latency increase drastically as data length increases.

An m-out-of-n code is one in which all valid code words have exactly "m" 1's and "n-m" 0's. These codes can also detect all unidirectional errors when n = 2m. This condition not only increases the code size, but also the checker's area. Cellular realization of an m-out-of-2m code circuit was deemed by Lala [24] as more area- and delay-efficient than the previous implementations.

Given the importance of fault tolerance at the HW level in big data and cloud computing applications, in this paper, we present a fault secure (FS) SEDC checker used with SEDC codes [25]. An FS checker has the ability to safely hide or self-check (detect) its own faults as they occur in its circuitry. The SEDC partitions the input data into smaller segments (2, 3, and 4 bits) and encodes them in parallel. This unique scaling feature makes the system faster and less complex to design for any binary data length. The FS SEDC checker inherits all these features of SEDC codes (i.e., simple scalability, constant latency, and less power dissipation) which suits its implementation in online fault detection in processors, cache memories, and NAND Flash-based memories for big data

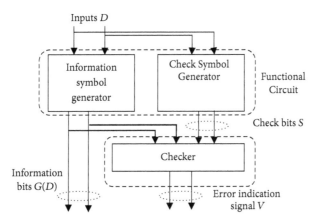

FIGURE 1: Block diagram of the proposed hardware-level fault tolerance system.

applications. The major contributions of this paper are as follows:

(1) We propose HW-level fault tolerance for circuits designed to process big data and cloud computing applications.

(2) In order to show the effectiveness of the proposed HW-level fault tolerance scheme in a big data scenario, we compare the cost associated with and without the proposed fault tolerance scheme and present results that show a significant reduction in the overall cost of fault tolerance in big data when the proposed HW-based fault tolerance scheme is applied.

(3) We also present a novel FS SEDC checker for use with SEDC-based HW-level fault tolerance systems.

(4) In order to prove the superiority of the FS SEDC checker presented in contrast with state-of-the-art AUED checkers, we show that the FS SEDC checker achieves state-of-the-art performance in terms of area, delay, and power dissipation.

The rest of the paper is organized as follows. We present an overall system diagram of the proposed HW-level fault tolerance system in Section 2. We give a brief mathematical foundation of the SEDC scheme and an example to encode logical circuits using SEDC in Section 3. Design details of the FS SEDC checker are described in Section 4. The proposed checker is shown to be FS through the fault testing methods; and its area, delay, and power comparison with state-of-the-art are derived in Section 5. We compute the fault coverage of the proposed SEDC-based fault tolerance system and present the experimental details and results in Section 5. To show the effectiveness of the proposed method in big data and cloud computation applications, we also perform a cost-performance analysis of fault tolerance at the SW level versus HW level in Section 5. Finally, we conclude the paper in Section 6.

2. Introduction to the Overall System

Figure 1 shows the main components of an error detecting codes based HW-level fault tolerance. The functional circuit consists of two subcircuits: an information symbol generator (ISG) and a check symbol generator (CSG). These two circuits do not share any logic. The ISG takes input $\mathbf{D}$ and performs some operation G and produces output $G(\mathbf{D})$. The CSG is a carefully chosen logic function that acts as the encoder and generates check bits $\mathbf{S}$ using the same input $\mathbf{D}$, such that $\mathbf{S} = \phi(G(\mathbf{D}))$, where ϕ denotes the particular coding function. The checker normally contains another encoder that reencodes the information bits $G(\mathbf{D})$ into $\mathbf{S}' = \phi(G(\mathbf{D}))$ and then compares both $\mathbf{S}$ and $\mathbf{S}'$. A mismatch between $\mathbf{S}$ and $\mathbf{S}'$ is treated as an error, which is indicated by the error indication or verification signal $\mathbf{V}$.

The checker shown in Figure 1 plays a vital role in the overall fault tolerance system. The checker must exhibit a self-checking property or failsafe property to make sure that the whole system is fault secure (FS). If the checker is both self-checking and failsafe, the overall system is said to be as totally self-checking (TSC). In order to formally define these properties, let us consider the output of the functional circuit shown in Figure 1 to be represented by $G(\mathbf{D}) = G(x, f)$, where x is the input and f is the fault, and then in fault-free operation, i.e., $f = \emptyset$, the output can be represented by $G(x, \emptyset)$. Also, consider the input code space $\mathbf{D} \subseteq X$, output code space $\mathbf{S} \subseteq Y$, and an assumed fault set $\mathbf{F}$; then according to the definition of totally self-checking (TSC), G is

(1) self-testing if for each fault f in $\mathbf{F}$ there exists at least one input code $\mathbf{d} \in \mathbf{D}$ that produces a noncode output; i.e., $\forall f \in \mathbf{F} \, \exists \mathbf{d} \in \mathbf{D} \ni G(\mathbf{e}, f) \notin \mathbf{S}$,

(2) fault secure (FS) if for all faults f in $\mathbf{F}$, and all code inputs $\mathbf{d} \in \mathbf{D}$, the output is either correct or is a noncode word; i.e., $\forall f \in \mathbf{F}$ and $\forall \mathbf{d} \in \mathbf{D}$, $G(\mathbf{e}, f) = G(\mathbf{e}, \emptyset)$ or $G(\mathbf{e}, f) \notin \mathbf{S}$.

In the proposed SEDC-based HW-level fault tolerance system, the CSG circuit is realized by an SEDC check symbol generator (SCSG) circuit, which generates the SEDC code words corresponding to the information bits $G(\mathbf{D})$. We presented a realization of an SEDC encoded SCSG circuit in [27], i.e., an SEDC encoded arithmetic logic unit (ALU) of a microprocessor. The SEDC encoded ALU circuit (SCSG) computes the SEDC codes corresponding to the output of the

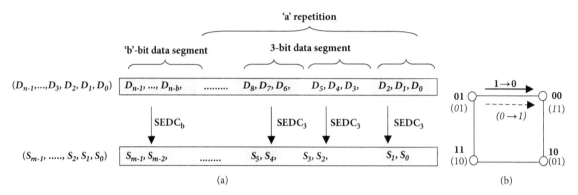

FIGURE 2: (a) SEDC scheme for given data word, and (b) 2D illustration of $SEDC_2$ scheme.

ISG (in [27] a normal ALU). Any fault that causes multiple unidirectional errors at the output of the normal ALU is detected by the SEDC checker. Any logic circuitry including SRAM-based memory cells [28] can be made fault tolerant by encoding them similar to the methods given in [27, 28]. In the next section we briefly introduce the SEDC scheme with an example to encode an adder circuit, while in the rest of the paper we focus on the proposed FS SEDC checker that can be used with any SEDC-based HW-level fault tolerance system.

3. Scalable Error Detection Coding (SEDC) Scheme

The Scalable Error Detection Coding scheme [25] is an AUED scheme formulated and designed in such a way that only the resultant circuit area is scaled, while its latency depends on a small portion of the input data (explained later).

For any binary data $\mathbf{D}$ of length n-bits represented as $(D_{n-1}, \ldots, D_2, D_1, D_0)$ with $D_i \in \{0, 1\}$ for $0 \leq i \leq n - 1$, two parameters, a and b, are computed using

$$a = \frac{n - \max(b)}{3} \quad (1)$$

where parameter a can only take a positive integer value, i.e., $a \in \mathbb{Z}^+$, and parameter $b \in \{2, 3, 4\}$. Satisfying the condition for parameter a, the maximum possible value for parameter b is selected. The SEDC code word $\mathbf{S}$ is represented as $(S_{m-1}, \ldots, S_j, \ldots, S_2, S_1, S_0)$ with $S_j \in \{0, 1\}$ for $0 \leq j \leq m - 1$, where m denotes the length of the SEDC code word and is computed by

$$m = \lceil \log_2(n + 1 - 3a) \rceil + 2a \quad (2)$$

After computing the values for parameters a and b, the SEDC code $\mathbf{S}$ for binary data $\mathbf{D}$ is computed. SEDC is designed to generate codes basically for 2-, 3-, and 4-bit data and is accordingly referred to as the $SEDC_2$, $SEDC_3$, and $SEDC_4$ scheme, respectively. It is then extended for any integer values of n, as shown in Figure 2(a).

3.1. $SEDC_2$ Code. A two-dimensional (2D) illustration of a 2-bit SEDC ($SEDC_2$) scheme is shown in Figure 2(b), where

nodes represent data words, and their corresponding code words are written in brackets.

The SEDC coding scheme assigns code words to different data words with a unique criterion. Whenever there is a change of a bit (or bits) in a data word from "1" → "0," as shown with a bold arrow in Figure 2(b), the change is reflected in the code word in the opposite way; i.e., the code changes from "0" → "1," as shown with the dashed arrow in Figure 2(b), and vice versa. Equation (3) is used to assign 2-bit code words $S_1 S_0$ to the 2-bit data words $D_1 D_0$. Clearly, we can interchange the bit positions of S_1 and S_0 for another variant of $SEDC_2$ codes. This will not affect the code characteristics.

$$[S_1 : S_0] = SEDC_2(D_1, D_0)$$
$$= [XNOR(D_1, D_0) : NAND(D_1, D_0)] \quad (3)$$

In (3), $[S_1 : S_0]$ represent the concatenated SEDC code bits, $XNOR$ and $NAND$ are the logical operations, and $SEDC_2$ is the basic coding scheme.

3.2. $SEDC_3$ Code. $SEDC_3$ code for 3-bit data is computed using (4) as follows:

$$[S_1 : S_0] = SEDC_3(D_2, D_1, D_0)$$
$$= \begin{cases} SEDC_2(D_1, D_0), & \text{if } D_2 = 0 \\ \overline{SEDC_2(\overline{D_1}, \overline{D_0})}, & \text{if } D_2 = 1 \end{cases} \quad (4)$$

where the bar sign (e.g., $\overline{D_1}$) in (4) represents the logical NOT operation.

Figure 3 shows a 3D cube, illustrating the unidirectional error detection mechanism of $SEDC_3$ codes. The same notations are used in Figure 3 as in Figure 2(b). The dashed side of the cube represents the embedded $SEDC_2$ coding scheme in $SEDC_3$. Note that when there is a 2-bit unidirectional change in data word "001" → "111" (the two MSBs changing from "00" → "11"), the code changes in the opposite direction (the least significant bit of the code changes from "1" → "0"). In a similar way, the $SEDC_n$ scheme detects n-bit or all unidirectional errors in the data word $\mathbf{D}$.

3.3. SEDC$_4$ Code. A SEDC$_4$ code for 4-bit data is formulated by (5) as follows:

$$[S_2 : (S_1, S_0)] = SEDC_4 (D_3, D_2, D_1, D_0)$$
$$= \left[\overline{D_3} : SEDC_3 (D_2, D_1, D_0) \right] \tag{5}$$

The MSB of the code word is completely dependent upon the MSB of the data word for SEDC$_4$; hence, any change in the MSB of the data word is detected. The rest of the three data bits are encoded using the same SEDC$_3$ scheme.

It can be observed from (3), (4), and (5) that the SEDC$_2$ is embedded in 3-bit SEDC (SEDC$_3$) and consequently in 4-bit SEDC (SEDC$_4$) to detect all unidirectional errors in 3-bit and 4-bit data, as shown later. This ability to scale codes is not present in any other concurrent error detecting (CED) coding scheme.

In general, for SEDC$_n$, the n-bit binary data is grouped into one b-bit segment and the a number of 3-bit segments, and then these segments are encoded using one SEDC$_b$ and a number/numbers of SEDC$_3$ modules in parallel, as shown in Figure 2(a). It is noteworthy that each group of data segments and corresponding code segments is independent of each other. This independence makes our scheme scalable and able to detect some portion of bidirectional errors (BE) (discussed in Section 5.3).

If we interchange S_1 and S_0 for SEDC$_3$ in Figure 3, the corresponding SEDC$_3$ code is equal to Berger codes for a 3-bit segment, but our way of deriving the SEDC$_3$ code is a lot different from that of Berger codes. SEDC$_3$ codes are basically scaled from SEDC$_2$ codes, and SEDC$_2$ codes have no commonality with 2-bit Berger codes.

3.4. SEDC-Based HW-Level Fault Tolerance System Example. In order to illustrate the designing of a HW-level fault tolerance system using the SEDC scheme, we take the example of a 4-bit adder. Let us consider that this 4-bit adder is a part of a processor which processes big data applications, and we want to make this 4-bit adder fault tolerant against transient errors that arise in its circuitry, so the general HW-level fault tolerance system diagram shown in Figure 1 will be converted to the one shown in Figure 4. As shown in Figure 4, the 4-bit adder acts as an ISG and its equivalent SEDC encoder acts as a CSG. The SEDC encoder or CSG can be implemented using (6) as follows:

$$[S_3 : S_0] = SEDC (\mathbf{A}_{[3:0]} + \mathbf{B}_{[3:0]} + C_{in}) \tag{6}$$

As the output of 4-bit adder is a 5-bit value, hence the equivalent SEDC code has a 4-bit value according to (2). We used Altera's Quartus II software to synthesize the 4-bit adder (ISG), SEDC encoder (CSG), and the SEDC checker shown in Figure 4 and utilized the synthesized circuit for computing the fault coverage of the SEDC scheme, which is presented in Section 5.3. In the next section, we present the proposed FS SEDC checker, which completes the overall proposed SEDC-based HW-level fault tolerance system.

TABLE 1: Code table for FS SEDC$_1$ checker.

G_0	S_0	V_1	V_0
0	0	1	1
0	1	1	0
1	0	1	0
1	1	0	0

4. The FS SEDC Checker

As shown in Figure 4, the FS SEDC checker takes n-information bits and m-SEDC check bits from the functional unit. The FS SEDC checker is also composed of one b-bit FS SEDC checker and a sets of 3-bit FS SEDC checkers. With 1-, 2-, and 3-bit FS SEDC checkers, the output can be directly used as an error indication signal, but for $n > 3$, one level of wired-AND-OR logic gates is used to combine all the output of subblocks of FS SEDC checkers and generate the 2-bit error indication signal. Subsections discuss logic and circuit diagrams for primitive FS SEDC checkers (SEDC$_1$, SEDC$_2$, SEDC$_3$, and SEDC$_4$ checkers) which can be used to scale the SEDC checker to an n-bit FS SEDC checker (i.e., an FS SEDC$_n$ checker).

4.1. The FS SEDC$_1$ Checker. Table 1 shows the logic for a 1-bit SEDC (FS SEDC$_1$) checker. The valid input code words are "10" and "01" and the valid output code word is "10". G_0 denotes the 1-bit information word that is the output of ISG, and S_0 denotes the 1-bit SEDC check bit generated by the SEDC check symbol generator (SCSG). $V_1 V_0$ is the 2-bit error indication signal of the FS SEDC$_1$ checker. V_1 and V_0 signals are generated by the circuits shown in Figure 5(a).

4.2. The FS SEDC$_2$ Checker

$$[V_1 : V_0] = \left[\overline{S_1 . (G_1 + G_0)(S_0 + G_1 G_0)} : \right.$$
$$\left. \overline{(G_1 + G_0 + S_0)(S_1 + G_1 G_0 S_0)} \right] \tag{7}$$

In Figure 5, the symbols P1-P13 and N1-N13 represent the PMOS and NMOS transistors, respectively, and Vss represents the voltage supply. For simplicity, we used the CMOS-based implementation of SEDC checker circuits. Any other technology can be used to design these circuits, but the underlying algorithm, i.e., SEDC, will remain the same.

4.3. The FS SEDC$_3$ Checker. Figure 6(a) shows the block diagram and the logic for a 3-bit FS SEDC checker. Three-bit data $G_2 G_1 G_0$ from the ISG and 2-bit SEDC check bits $S_1 S_0$ from the SCSG are first converted to $G_1' G_0'$ and $S_1' S_0'$, respectively, and then are checked using the same 2-bit FS SEDC checker, as shown in Figure 6(a). When the G_2 bit is "1," $G_1 G_0$ and $S_1 S_0$ are inverted, whereas if G_2 is "0," then $G_1 G_0$ and $S_1 S_0$ remain the same. As the outputs of the XOR gates are fed to the FS SEDC$_2$ checker, any error in the XOR gates is detected. This makes the overall 3-bit SEDC checker FS.

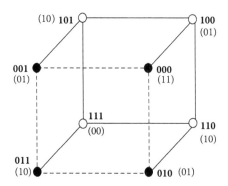

FIGURE 3: 3D illustration of SEDC$_3$ scheme.

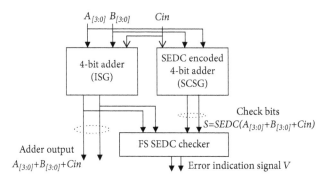

FIGURE 4: Example of SEDC-based HW-level fault tolerance system.

4.4. The FS SEDC$_4$ Checker. A 4-bit FS SEDC checker consists of one FS SEDC$_1$ checker and one FS SEDC$_3$ checker, as shown in Figure 6(b). Both SEDC$_1$ and SEDC$_3$ checkers generate 2-bit output $V_1 V_0$. Because the valid code word is "10," to make sure that both checker units generate the "10" output during error-free operation, we "AND" the V_1 output-bit of the FS SEDC$_1$ checker with the V_1 output-bit of the FS SEDC$_3$ checker. Also, we "OR" the V_0 output-bits of both FS SEDC checkers using wired logic gates. We checked and confirmed by fault simulation that wired-AND and wired-OR gates are also FS for single faults (stuck-at-0, stuck-at-1, transistor-stuck-on, and transistor-stuck-off).

4.5. The FS SEDC$_n$ Checker. Like the SEDC code generator, the FS SEDC checker also consists of multiple 1-, 2-, and 3-bit FS SEDC checkers, depending upon the value of a and b from (1). For example, if $n = 8$ bits, then (1) $\Rightarrow a = 2$ and $b = 2$. This requires one FS SEDC$_2$ checker and two FS SEDC$_3$ checkers to realize an 8-bit FS SEDC checker.

The area of wired-AND-OR gates will also definitely increase as n is increased. Figure 7 shows the block diagram of an n-bit FS SEDC checker. For $n = 8$ bits, there will be total of three FS SEDC checkers, each with 2-bit output; hence, a 3-input wired-AND and a 3-input wired-OR gate is required to compare all V_1 and V_0 bits. In general, for n-bit input, there are "$a + 1$" FS SEDC checkers, each with 2-bit output. So we require "$k = 2 \times (a + 1)$"-input wired-AND and wired-OR gates. With each increasing input to the wired-AND-OR network, one extra transistor is required by each of the wired

gates. This causes the circuit to expand width-wise; hence, the latency of the wired logic remains constant for any value of n.

The size of the load transistor driving these wired-AND and -OR gates will also increase with increasing input, so we consider the maximum fan-in of one gate as equal to 4. For $k > 4$, an extra load transistor is connected in parallel. Generally, for k-inputs we require $r = \lceil k/4 \rceil$ load transistors. A total of $k + r$ transistors is required to design the k-input wired AND-OR network with a constant latency of 1 transistor.

5. Experiments and Results

In this section, we present the experiments we conducted on the proposed FS SEDC checker and the overall proposed SEDC-based HW-level fault tolerance system. The results of each experiment are given along with the experimental details in the subsections below.

5.1. Fault Test on FS SEDC Checker. The FS SEDC$_1$, SEDC$_2$, SEDC$_3$, and SEDC$_4$ circuits in our paper were tested for stuck-at-0, stuck-at-1, transistor-stuck-ON, and transistor-stuck-OFF faults. We assume a single-fault model where faults occur one at a time, and there is enough time between detection of the first fault and the occurrence of another fault [29]. In Table 2, we provide a summary of fault analysis of an SEDC$_1$ checker circuit. We applied one fault at a time in

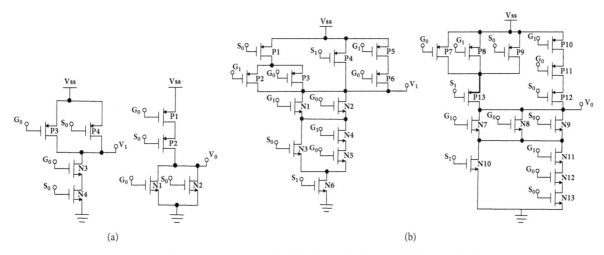

FIGURE 5: CMOS-based circuits of FS (a) SEDC$_1$ checker and (b) SEDC$_2$ checker.

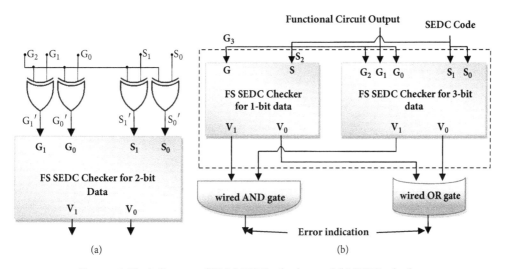

FIGURE 6: Block diagram of FS (a) SEDC$_3$ checker, and (b) SEDC$_4$ checker.

the circuit of Figure 5(a) and observed the output. In single-fault operation, the circuit either produced the correct output or never produced any invalid code words (exhibiting FS property), as shown in Table 2.

Case 1 (transistor stuck ON). In Table 2, we show all six cases of transistor stuck ON faults (one at a time). For the cases with N3 or N4 stuck ON, the circuit shows fault detection by one input code combination (represented with * symbol), and hence, the circuit is self-testing, whereas other cases showed that the circuit is fault secure as well as code disjoint.

Case 2 (transistor stuck OFF). In Table 2, all six cases for transistor stuck OFF faults are shown. In cases where N1 or N2 was stuck OFF, the circuit demonstrates the self-testing property (represented with * symbol) and for the rest of the cases, the circuit is fault secure.

Case 3 (input stuck at 0). When input G_0 or S_0 is stuck at 0, the circuit demonstrates the self-testing property; otherwise, it remains fault secure.

Case 4 (input stuck at 1). When input G_0 or S_0 is stuck at 1, the circuit shows the self-testing property; otherwise, it remains fault secure.

There is one case where the output becomes floating (i.e., P3 or P4 stuck OFF). In either case, if we consider the floating voltage as logic high, then the circuit is fault secure, and if we consider the floating voltage as logic low, then the circuit is self-testing. Hence, we can say that the circuit in Figure 5(a), which is a 1-bit SEDC checker, is FS. Similar analysis was carried out when testing 2-, 3-, and 4-bit SEDC checkers, and we found that all these checkers are FS.

5.2. Area, Delay, and Power Comparison.
In this section, we compare the area and delay of TSC Berger, FS SEDC, and m-out-of-2m code checkers. We use the two possible TSC Berger checker implementations from Piestrak et al. [23] and Pierce Jr. and Lala [26], with the m-out-of-2m code checker from Lala [24] for comparison. For the sake of fairness, the area overhead was measured in terms of the number of equivalent

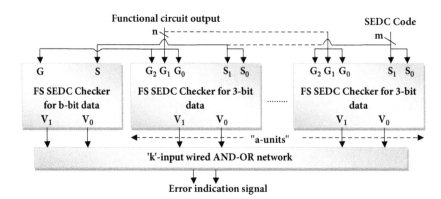

FIGURE 7: Block diagram of FS $SEDC_n$ checker.

TABLE 2: Results of single faults on FS $SEDC_1$ checker.

G_0	S_0	V_1	V_0	G_0	S_0	V_1	V_0	G_0	S_0	V_1	V_0
MOS P1or P2 is stuck ON				*MOS P1 or P2 is stuck OFF*				*Input C_0 stuck at zero*			
0	1	1	0	0	1	1	0	⋆0	0	1	1
1	0	1	0	1	0	1	0	1	0	1	0
MOS P3 or P4 is stuck ON				*MOS P3 or P4 is stuck OFF*				*Input F_0 stuck at zero*			
0	1	1	0	0	1	Floating	0	⋆0	0	1	1
1	0	1	0	1	0	1	0	0	1	1	0
Transistor N1 is stuck ON				*Transistor N1 is stuck OFF*				*Input C_0 stuck at 1*			
0	1	1	0	0	1	1	0	0	1	1	0
1	0	1	0	⋆1	0	1	1	⋆1	1	0	0
Transistor N2 is stuck ON				*Transistor N2 is stuck OFF*				*Input F_0 stuck at 1*			
0	1	1	0	⋆0	1	1	1	1	0	1	0
1	0	1	0	1	0	1	0	⋆1	1	0	0
Transistor N3 is stuck ON				*Transistor N3 is stuck OFF*				-	-	-	-
⋆0	1	0	0	0	1	1	0	-	-	-	-
1	0	1	0	1	0	1	0	-	-	-	-
Transistor N4 is stuck ON				*Transistor N4 is stuck OFF*				-	-	-	-
⋆0	1	1	0	0	1	1	0	-	-	-	-
1	0	0	0	1	0	1	0	-	-	-	-

⋆ The cases where circuit shows self-testing property.

transistors. We made use of the assumptions by Smith [30] to translate gate-level circuits to transistor-level circuits.

Before comparison, we illustrate the functional dissimilarities of the three checkers with the help of Figure 8. Figure 8(a) shows the general block diagram of a TSC Berger code checker. For all the information symbols that the ISG of the functional circuit can produce in normal operation, the check symbol complement generator (CSCG) outputs (S_B') correspond to the bit-by-bit complement of the expected check symbol S_B. The TSC two-rail checker validates that each bit of S_B is the complement of corresponding bit of S_B'. As the size of the input data increases, the length of check symbol S_B also increases, resulting in a longer length for the TSC two-rail checker tree, and hence the resulting delay.

A general block diagram of a TSC m-out-of-2m code checker is shown in Figure 8(b). The checker takes the information bits and check bits S_W and partitions them into two parts. The numbers of 1's, i.e., the weight, of both parts are mapped to a pair of values which in binary belongs to a code, in most cases a two-rail code. The checker consists of a cellular structure of AND-OR gates as given by Lala [24].

Figure 8(c) depicts the general block diagram for an FS SEDC checker that resembles the structure of an m-out-of-2m code checker and differs from a Berger code checker. The FS SEDC checker block receives the information and check bits from the functional unit. If the input data length increases, the size of the FS checker block increases width-wise. The FS $SEDC_n$ block contains "$a + 1$" pairs of small SEDC checkers (subblocks). Each subblock of the FS SEDC checker produces "10" as the valid code output. The overall SEDC checker has a final 2-bit output S_{10}; unlike two-rail

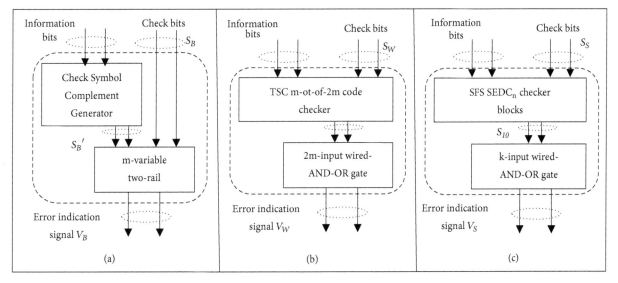

FIGURE 8: Block diagrams of (a) TSC Berger checker, (b) m-out-of-2m code checker, and (c) FS SEDC checker.

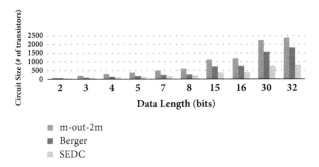

FIGURE 9: Area comparison of area-optimized Berger [23], SEDC, and m-out-of-2m [24] code checkers.

codes, only one of the output combinations "10" is considered a valid code word. A nonvalid checker output "00," "01," or "11" at output S_{10} indicates the presence of a fault in the functional circuit or the FS checker itself. The k-input wired AND-OR network takes the "$a + 1$" pairs of output from each SEDC checker subblock and then converts them into a final 2-bit error indication signal V_S.

5.1. Fault Test on FS SEDC Checker. Area-optimized realization of TSC Berger code checkers in Piestrak et al. [23] showed less area overhead than m-out-of-2m code checkers, which is apparent from Figure 9. But, if we consider the delay-optimized implementation of the TSC Berger code checker from Pierce Jr. and Lala [26], we see that the TSC Berger code checker requires more area than the FS SEDC and m-out-of-2m codes checkers [24], as shown in Table 3. For clarity, we discretely listed the area overhead offered based on code storage area and code checker area in Table 3. Also listed separately are the area overhead required by the TRC tree for the TSC Berger code checker, the wired-AND-OR network for FS SEDC, and the m-out-of-2m code checker.

For a fair comparison, the extra cost of the code storage area is also taken into account. We assumed that 1-bit storage

is implemented by 12-MOS transistors [30]. Table 3 lists the area (in terms of the number of transistors) occupied by FS SEDC, delay-optimized Berger code, and m-out-of-2m code checkers for up to 32-bit data.

The FS $SEDC_n$ checker block shown in Figure 8(c) requires fewer gates, implemented with $[26 + (a \times 50)]$ MOS transistors if "b = 2," $[50 + (a \times 50)]$ MOS transistors if "b = 3," and $[58 + (a \times 50)]$ MOS transistors if "b = 4." The m-out-of-2m code checker implementation of Lala [24] requires $2m^2 - 2m + 2$ gates. The gate-level circuit is also translated to transistor-level circuits using data from Smith [30].

The results show that when scaling a 7-bit 0's counter to an 8-bit 0's counter, 154 extra MOS transistors are required. The m-out-of-2m code checker requires 60 MOS transistors when scaling a 7-out-of-14 checker to an 8-out-of-16 checker, whereas the SEDC checker requires only 18 extra MOS transistors. That is because a 7-bit SEDC checker is implemented with one $SEDC_3$ and one $SEDC_4$ circuit that contain 50 and 58 MOS transistors, respectively (a total of 108 transistors). An 8-bit SEDC checker is implemented using one $SEDC_2$ and two $SEDC_3$ checkers, requiring 26 and 100 (50x2) MOS transistors (a total of 126 transistors). This means that SEDC saves 88% of the number of transistors compared to a Berger code checker [26], and it saves 70% of the transistors when

TABLE 3: Area overhead of Berger [26], SEDC, and m-out-of-2m [24] code checkers.

Data Bit	Berger Code				SEDC				m-out-of-2m			
	Code storage Area	1's counter Area	TRC Area	Total Area	Code storage Area	Checker Area	AND-OR Network	Total Area	Code Storage Area	Checker Area	AND-OR Network	Total Area
2	24	22	4	**50**	24	26	0	**50**	24	36	0	**50**
3	24	80	8	**112**	24	50	0	**74**	36	152	0	**188**
4	36	180	12	**228**	36	58	6	**100**	48	240	10	**298**
5	36	178	16	**230**	48	76	6	**130**	60	300	14	**374**
7	36	396	24	**456**	60	108	8	**176**	84	420	18	**522**
8	48	550	28	**626**	72	126	8	**206**	96	480	20	**596**
15	48	1106	56	**1210**	120	250	14	**384**	180	900	38	**1118**
16	60	1308	60	**1428**	132	258	16	**406**	192	960	40	**1192**
30	60	2586	116	**2762**	240	500	26	**766**	360	1800	76	**2236**
32	72	3048	120	**3240**	264	526	28	**818**	384	1920	80	**2384**

compared to m-out-of-2m code checkers. Although Berger and m-out-of-2m checkers are TSC, while the proposed SEDC checker is only FS, all three checkers provide the same fault security.

5.2.2. Delay. As far as delay is concerned, the FS SEDC checker also performs better than Berger and cellular implementations for an m-out-of-2m code checker, as shown in Table 4. For the sake of uniformity, we designed all the basic gates using the same technology transistors (PMOS = $8\mu/2\mu$, NMOS = $4\mu/2\mu$) and evaluated the worst-case propagation delay of each circuit.

The SEDC checker shows almost a constant delay for n > 3 bits due to its parallel implementation, whereas the delay in the Berger code checker increases owing to an increase in gate levels (from 6 to 16) in the critical path, as shown by Pierce Jr. and Lala [26]. The delay for m-out-of-2m code checkers also continues to increase with increasing data lengths because the cellular implementation requires "m (= input data length)" gate levels in the critical path.

5.2.3. Power Dissipation. In order to evaluate the power dissipation of the three checkers, we used the PowerPlay power analyzer tool. We implemented the Berger [24], m-out-of-2m [26], and SEDC checker using Verilog and synthesized the circuits using Altera's Quartus II software. We targeted the circuit for a Cyclone II EP2C5AF256A7 chip, which has the least power dissipating properties among the Cyclone family. We allowed the synthesizer to create a balance between area and delay while synthesizing in order to get a better power estimate. We also enabled the synthesizer to use synthesizing model that takes intensive steps to optimize power for all three circuits. We clocked the inputs of the circuit with the default toggle rate and estimated the total thermal power dissipation for different values of input data width.

Figure 10(a) shows a comparison of power dissipation between the three checkers. The Berger and m-out-of-2m checkers exhibited a sudden increase in power dissipation

when the input data width was changed from 16-bits to 32-bits, while SEDC showed a minimal change. This happens due to the increase in the number of two-rail checkers in the case of the Berger checker and due to the increase in the checker circuitry itself in the case of the m-out-of-2m checker, which is also evident in Figure 10(b), which depicts an area comparison between the three checkers in terms of # of logic elements (LE) occupied by the checkers.

5.3. Fault Coverage of the Proposed HW-Level Fault Tolerance Scheme. In order to elaborate the effectiveness of the SEDC CSG and its FS checker, we computed the fault coverage of the proposed SEDC-based HW-level fault tolerance scheme. We applied faults in the example circuit of Figure 4, given in Section 3.4. As most of the VLSI combinational circuits designed for mathematical operations, like add, subtract, multiply, division, etc., consist of multiple instances of 1-bit adders (full adders), hence the example circuit, i.e., a 4-bit adder, is a simple and good candidate for presenting the effectiveness of our scheme. We injected two major types of transient errors, i.e., stuck-at-0 and stuck-at-1 [29], at 24 nodes (at 6 nodes per full adder, as shown in Figure 11(b)). We injected these errors using 2-to-1 multiplexers, whose output is given by

$$mux_u$$

$$= \begin{cases} in1 \ (normal \ gate \ output) & if \ select \ (f\_enable) = 0 \\ in2 \ (stuck-at-fault \ f \in \mathbf{F}) & if \ select \ (f\_enable) = 1 \end{cases} \quad (8)$$

In Figure 11(a), the symbols A[3:0], B[3:0], Cin, f_enable, and F[23:0] denote the 4-bits input A, 4-bits input B, 1-bit carry-in, 1-bit fault enabling signal, and 24-bits fault signals, respectively, while Cout is the carry-out and S[3:0] represents the 4-bits sum output of the 4-bits adder. Figure 11(b) shows the detailed schematic of a single full adder.

We considered that the faults can occur at the outputs of the logic gates only and adopted a single-fault model according to which only one fault can occur at a time [29].

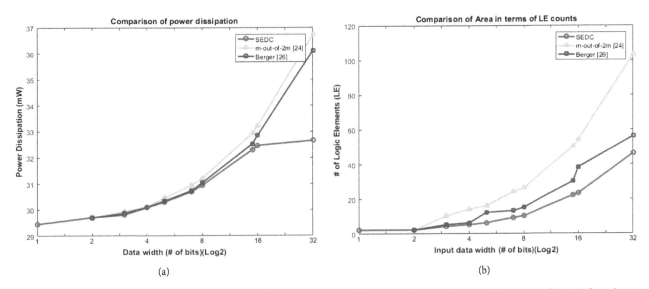

FIGURE 10: Comparison of (a) power dissipation and (b) area in terms of LE counts, between Berger [26], m-out-of-2m [24], and SEDC checkers.

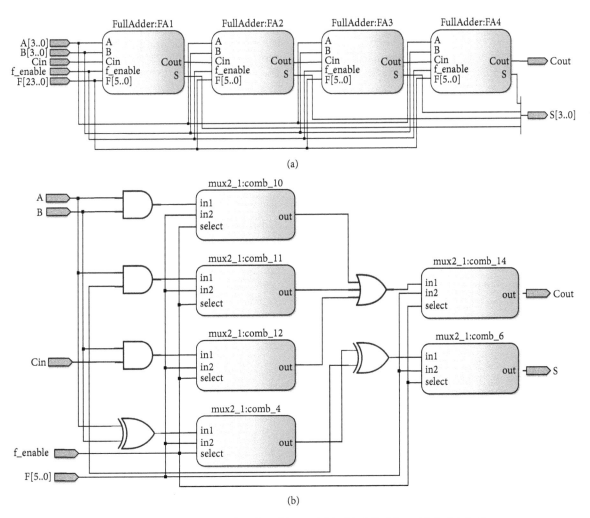

FIGURE 11: (a) RTL schematic of a 4-bit adder, and (b) 1-bit full adder, with fault injection.

TABLE 4: Critical path (CP) delay comparison of Berger, SEDC, and m-out-of-2m codes checker (unit = microseconds).

Data Bits	Berger	SEDC	m-out-2m
2	3.888	0.514	1.024
3	4.151	2.524	-
4	7.741	2.738	5.490
5	-	2.713	5.558
7	7.821	2.77	8.297
8	7.599	2.76	9.284
15	10.566	2.826	-
16	12.956	2.751	
32	17.964	2.771	-

TABLE 5: Summary of fault testing experiment on SEDC-based fault tolerant 4-bit adder.

	(a) Total errors at the output of the adder	(b) BEs	(c) Detected BEs	(d) UEs	(e) Detected UEs	(f) Total detected errors	(g) Total undetected errors
Total	1748	252	120	1496	1496	1616	132
Percentage (%)	100	14.42 w.r.t. (a)	47.62 w.r.t. (b)	85.58 w.r.t. (a)	100 w.r.t (d)	92.45 w.r.t. (a)	7.55 w.r.t. (a)

We used Altera's Quartus II software to design and synthesize the overall system and then simulated the system using ModelSim. We designed a self-checking test bench to evaluate the overall fault coverage. The statistics of the fault injection and its results are summarized in Table 5.

In total, we injected 6425 faults exhaustively, out of which 1748 faults actually caused a logical error at the output of the adder circuitry. Only 14.42% of these injected faults resulted in bidirectional errors (BEs), while most of the faults caused unidirectional errors (UEs). This also proved the fact that most of the errors in VLSI circuits result in UEs at the output [19–21]. Even though SEDC is an AUED scheme, and it provides 100% fault coverage against UEs, it also successfully detected 47.62% of the BEs, as shown in Table 5. This is due to the reason that SEDC partitions the input data word into multiple parts and encodes and decodes each part independently. Consequently, a subset of BEs is also partitioned into multiple UEs and thus detected by the proposed SEDC scheme.

5.4. Cost Analysis: SW-Based Fault Tolerance Versus HW-Based Fault Tolerance.
In this section, we discuss the effect of fault propagation and the estimated cost of recovery from failure (also known as repair time) in big data computing in two cases: (a) when HW-based fault tolerance is applied, and (b) when only SW-based fault tolerance is applied. For simplicity in our analysis, we take the example of a coordinated checkpointing (CC) algorithm, which is widely used in HDFS for data recovery [31].

In HDFS, an image is used to define metadata (which contains node data and a list of blocks belonging to each file), while checkpoint defines the persistent record of the image, stored on a secondary NameNode (SNN) (also called DataNode) or Checkpoint Node, or in some cases on the primary NameNode (PNN) itself. If the PNN uses the CC data recovery algorithm, the checkpoints are distributed among multiple SNNs. During normal operation, the SNN sends heartbeats (a communication signal) to the PNN periodically. If the PNN does not receive a heartbeat from the SNN for certain fixed amount of time, the SNN is considered to be out of service, and the block replicas it hosts are considered to be unavailable. In this case, the PNN initiates the CC recovery algorithm, which includes signaling (sending heartbeats with control signals to other nodes) and replicating the copy of failed SNN data (available on the checkpoint nodes) to the other nodes in a coordinated way [31].

For our cost analysis, we would like to compute the cost associated with the CC data recovery algorithm for which we assume a cloud application, such as a message passing interface (MPI) program that comprises p logical processes that communicate through message passing (heartbeats). Each process is executed on a virtual machine and sends a message to remaining $p - 1$ processes with equal probabilities. We also consider that the message sending, checkpointing, and fault occurrence events are independent of each other. Assuming that a process is modelled as a sequence of deterministic events, i.e., every step taken by the process has a known outcome, and failure only occurs during message passing with equal probability and not during checkpointing or recovery, we use the analytical cost model given in [4] for cost analysis of fault tolerance at the SW level. According to [4], T denotes the total execution time of a process without fault tolerance, while T_{CP} and T_{RO} represent the checkpointing and failure recovery overheads, respectively. Then, the total cost of fault tolerance per process is given by

$$C = \frac{T_{CP} + T_{RO}}{T} \times 100 \qquad (9)$$

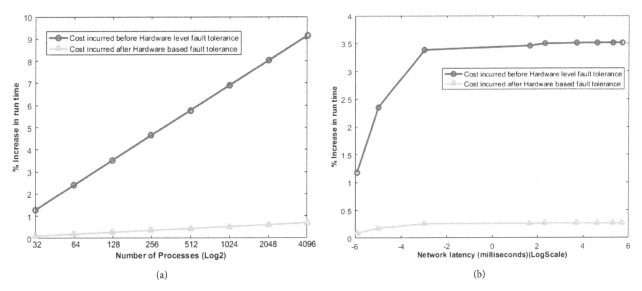

FIGURE 12: Effect of (a) number of processes, and (b) network latency, on data recovery overhead in CC algorithm.

Assuming that the average time to roll back a failed process is C_{rb} and mean time between failures is $1/P(f)$, where $P(f)$ denotes the probability of failure, then according to [4], the average recovery cost in CC per process is given by

$$\overline{T_{RO}} = \frac{C_{rb}}{(1/P(f))} = P(f)\,C_{rb} \qquad (10)$$

Let $P(cp)$ denote the probability that a process starts checkpointing, then $(1 - P(cp))^p$ becomes the probability that p processes do not start checkpointing, while $1 - (1 - P(cp))^p$ becomes the probability that at least one process starts a checkpoint. Consequently, $1/(1 - (1 - P(cp))^p)$ represents the checkpointing interval. A process can be the initiator of checkpointing with probability $1/p$ and generate request (REQ) and acknowledgement signals (ACK) to the rest of the $p - 1$ noninitiators (total $2(p - 1)$ signals) and likewise be a noninitiator with probability $1 - 1/p$ and generate only one ACK signal in response to the initiator. As a result, there are $3(p - 1)/p$ average messages generated per checkpoint, and the average overhead per checkpoint is $C_w + (3(p - 1)/p)C_{nl}$, where C_w denotes the average time to write a checkpoint to a stable node and C_{nl} denotes the average network latency. Then, the average checkpointing cost for a process is given by

$$\overline{T_{CP}} = \frac{C_w + (3(p-1)/p)\,C_{nl}}{1/\left(1 - (1 - P(cp))^p\right)}$$

$$= \left(1 - (1 - P(cp))^p\right)\left(C_w + \frac{3(p-1)}{p}C_{nl}\right) \qquad (11)$$

Using the cost model given in (9), (10), and (11), we carried out the cost of data recovery in the CC algorithm with the parameters, $p = 128$ processes (virtual machines), $P(cp) = 1/15$ (one checkpointing per 15 minutes), $C_{nl} = 20$ $msecs$, $C_w = 1$ sec, $C_{rb} = 2$ $secs$, as given in [4]. We consider the

value of $P(f) = 1/168$ which implies that 100% of the faults in hardware are propagated to the SW level in the absence of HW-level fault tolerance, while each fault occurs after 168 hours (one week's time). After we apply HW-level fault tolerance, the probability of failure $P(f)$ reduces to $P'(f) = 0.755 \times P(f)$, where the value 0.755 signifies that only 7.55% of the faults are unhandled by the proposed HW-level fault tolerance system (see Table 5). We vary one of the above parameters by keeping the other constant and observe the effect of data recovery cost with and without the proposed HW-level fault tolerance.

The graph in Figure 12(a) shows the average cost of data recovery when the number of processes p is increased from 32 to 4096 (virtual machines). We consider that an application is partitioned into p processes and each process runs on a virtual machine. The increase in number of processes causes a sharp increase in data recovery cost in the CC algorithm because every process has to coordinate with each other in case of a failure.

Figure 12(b) depicts the effect of network latency on the cost of data recovery. In this case we increased the network latency from 2 milliseconds to 300 milliseconds. Network latency depends heavily upon the traffic situation, network bandwidth, data size, and number of active nodes in the network. Figure 12(b) shows that increasing network latency has a negative impact on data recovery because it takes a longer time for processes to communicate with each other, resulting in delayed data recovery.

Figure 13 illustrates the situation where we increase the checkpointing frequency from one checkpoint per hour (1/60) to one checkpoint per minute. Even though the increase in checkpointing frequency improves the overall fault tolerance, it also increases the overall fault tolerance overhead, as shown in Figure 13.

Finally, we show the effect of the increasing probability of failure on the cost of data recovery in Figure 14. We varied the failure frequency from one failure per 1024 hours to one

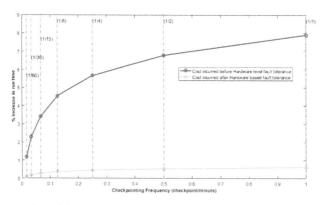

FIGURE 13: Effect of checkpointing frequency on data recovery cost in CC algorithm.

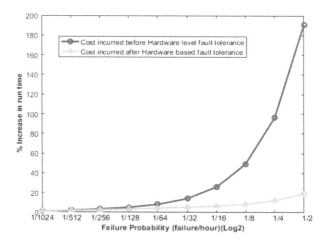

FIGURE 14: Effect of failure probability on data recovery in CC algorithm.

failure per 2 hours, which caused a huge impact on fault tolerance overhead, as shown in Figure 14. But, if we detect most of the errors at the hardware level, the average cost of data recovery reduces to a tolerable limit, as shown in Figure 14.

Because of the errors arising at the HW level, the average cost of data recovery in terms of percent increase in runtime in all of the above cases is much higher if we apply fault tolerance at the SW level only. Among the four parameters, i.e., # of processes, network latency, checkpointing frequency, and frequency of failure, frequency of failure has the worst effect on the average cost of data recovery. The proposed HW-level fault tolerance reduces the average cost to a tolerable limit, which is promising for big data and cloud computing applications. Although there is a one-time cost associated with HW-level fault tolerance, it provides high reliability against potential failures leading to severe socioeconomic consequences in big data and cloud computing.

6. Conclusions and Future Work

In this paper, we presented a concurrent error detection coding-based HW-level fault tolerance scheme for big data and cloud computing. The proposed method uses SEDC codes to protect against transient errors, which is a major

problem in modern VLSI circuits. We also presented an FS SEDC checker that not only detects errors in the functional circuitry but also remains failsafe under s-a-1, s-a-0, s-open, and s-short errors within checker circuitry. We compared the performance of the proposed SEDC checker with Berger and m-out-of-2m checker in terms of area, delay, and power dissipation, which proves the superiority of the proposed SEDC checker. Using the example of a 4-bit adder circuit, we presented a complete SEDC-based HW-level fault tolerance system and computed its fault coverage by exhaustive fault injection. The SEDC-based HW-level fault tolerance method shows 100%, 47%, and 92.5% fault coverage against unidirectional, bidirectional, and total errors, respectively. In order to show the effectiveness of the proposed SEDC-based HW-level fault tolerance method in big data and cloud computing applications, we compared the average cost of fault tolerance overhead with and without HW-level fault tolerance. The results show that HW-level fault tolerance reduces the probability of failure due to transient errors, consequently reducing the average cost of fault tolerance overhead to a great extent when compared with SW level fault tolerance only.

From hardware-level evolution such as microprocessors, memories, and parallel computing devices, to system-level advancements such as networking, data security, resource sharing protocols, and operating systems, the underlying technologies have changed a lot since the emergence of big data and cloud computing. Fault tolerance plays a vital role in big data and cloud computing because of the uncertain failures associated with the huge amount of data, both at SW and HW levels. Given this, we believe that this research opens new opportunities for fault tolerance at the hardware-level for big data and cloud computing.

Conflicts of Interest

The authors declare that they have no conflicts of interest.

Acknowledgments

This study was partly supported by research funds from Chosun University, 2017, Sogang University Research Grant of 2012 (201210056.01) and MISP (Ministry of Science, ICT & Future Planning), Korea, under the National Program for Excellence in SW (2015-0-00910) supervised by the IITP (Institute for Information & communications Technology Promotion).

References

[1] M. Chen, S. Mao, and Y. Liu, "Big data: A survey," *Mobile Networks and Applications*, vol. 19, no. 2, pp. 171–209, 2014.

[2] R. Jhawar, V. Piuri, and M. Santambrogio, "A comprehensive conceptual system-level approach to fault tolerance in Cloud Computing," in *Proceedings of the 2012 6th Annual IEEE Systems Conference (SysCon)*, pp. 1–5, Vancouver, Canada, March 2012.

[3] A. Katal, M. Wazid, and R. H. Goudar, "Big data: issues, challenges, tools and good practices," in *Proceedings of the 6th International Conference on Contemporary Computing (IC3 '13)*, pp. 404–409, IEEE, Noida, India, August 2013.

[4] Y. M. Teo, B. L. Luong, Y. Song, and T. Nam, "Cost-performance of fault tolerance in cloud computing," *Special Issue of Journal of Science and Technology*, vol. 49, no. 4A, pp. 61–73, 2011.

[5] M. Nazari Cheraghlou, A. Khadem-Zadeh, and M. Haghparast, "A survey of fault tolerance architecture in cloud computing," *Journal of Network and Computer Applications*, vol. 61, pp. 81–92, 2016.

[6] J. Deng, S. C.-H. Huang, Y. S. Han, and J. H. Deng, "Fault-tolerant and reliable computation in cloud computing," in *Proceedings of the 2010 IEEE Globecom Workshops, GC'10*, pp. 1601–1605, Miami, Fla, USA, December 2010.

[7] J. Liu, S. Wang, A. Zhou, S. Kumar, F. Yang, and R. Buyya, "Using proactive fault-tolerance approach to enhance cloud service reliability," *IEEE Transactions on Cloud Computing*, p. 1, 2017, http://ieeexplore.ieee.org/document/7469864.

[8] M. Reitblatt, M. Canini, A. Guha, and N. Foster, "FatTire: Declarative fault tolerance for software-defined networks," in *Proceedings of the 2013 2nd ACM SIGCOMM Workshop on Hot Topics in Software Defined Networking, HotSDN '13*, pp. 109–114, Hong Kong, China, August 2013.

[9] R. C. Fernandez, M. Migliavacca, E. Kalyvianaki, and P. Pietzuch, "Integrating scale out and fault tolerance in stream processing using operator state management," in *Proceedings of the 2013 ACM SIGMOD Conference on Management of Data, SIGMOD '13*, pp. 725–736, New York, NY, USA, June 2013.

[10] M. Zaharia, T. Das, H. Li, T. Hunter, S. Shenker, and I. Stoica, "Discretized streams: an efficient and fault-tolerant model for stream processing on large clusters," in *Proceedings of the 4th USENIX Conference on Hot Topics in Cloud Computer*, p. 10, Berkeley, Calif, USA, 2012.

[11] P. Wang, D. J. Dean, and X. Gu, "Understanding Real World Data Corruptions in Cloud Systems," in *Proceedings of the 2015 IEEE International Conference on Cloud Engineering*, pp. 116–125, Tempe, Ariz, USA, March 2015.

[12] P. A. Parker, "Discussion of Reliability Meets Big Data: Opportunities and Challenges," *Quality Engineering*, vol. 26, no. 1, pp. 117–120, 2014.

[13] H. Bauer, P. Ranade, and S. Tandon, "Big data and the opportunities it creates for semiconductor players," in *McKinesy on Semiconductors, BIG DATA for Semiconductors*, McKinesy & Company, 2012.

[14] H. Ueno and K. Namba, "Construction of a soft error (SEU) hardened Latch with high critical charge," in *Proceedings of the 29th IEEE International Symposium on Defect and Fault Tolerance in VLSI and Nanotechnology Systems, DFT '16*, pp. 27–30, September 2016.

[15] S. Mitra, N. Seifert, M. Zhang, Q. Shi, and K. S. Kim, "Robust system design with built-in soft-error resilience," *The Computer Journal*, vol. 38, no. 2, pp. 43–52, 2005.

[16] T. Karnik, P. Hazucha, and J. Patel, "Characterization of soft errors caused by single event upsets in CMOS processes," *IEEE Transactions on Dependable and Secure Computing*, vol. 1, no. 2, pp. 128–143, 2004.

[17] L.-T. Wang, X. Wen, and K. S. Abdel-Hafez, "Design for testability," *VLSI Test Principles and Architectures*, pp. 37–103, 2006.

[18] N. Alves, "State-of-the-art techniques for detecting transient errors in electrical circuits," *IEEE Potentials*, vol. 30, no. 3, pp. 30–35, 2011.

[19] S. Kotaki and M. Kitakami, "Codes correcting asymmetric/unidirectional errors along with bidirectional errors of small magnitude," in *Proceedings of the 20th IEEE Pacific Rim International Symposium on Dependable Computing, PRDC '14*, pp. 159-160, Singapore, November 2014.

[20] B. S. Manjunatha, G. S. D. Pateel, and V. Shah, "Oral fibrolipoma. A rare histological entity: report of 3 cases and review of literature," *Journal of Dentistry*, vol. 7, no. 4, pp. 226–231, 2010.

[21] N. K. Jha and M. B. Vora, "A t-unidirectional error-detecting systematic code," *Computers & Mathematics with Applications*, vol. 16, no. 9, pp. 705–714, 1988.

[22] J. Kim, D.-H. Lee, and W. Sung, "Performance of rate 0.96 (68254, 65536) EG-LDPC code for NAND Flash memory error correction," in *Proceedings of the 2012 IEEE International Conference on Communications, ICC '12*, pp. 7029–7033, June 2012.

[23] S. Piestrak, D. Bakalis, and X. Kavousianos, "On the design of self-testing checkers for modified Berger codes," in *Proceedings of the Seventh International On-Line Testing Workshop*, pp. 153–157, Taormina, Italy, 2001.

[24] P. K. Lala, *Self-Checking and Fault Tolerant Digital Design*, Academic press, UK, 2001.

[25] J.-A. Lee, Z. A. Siddiqui, N. Somasundaram, and J.-G. Lee, "Self-checking look-up tables using scalable error detection coding (SEDC) scheme," *Journal of Semiconductor Technology and Science*, vol. 13, no. 5, pp. 415–422, 2013.

[26] D. A. Pierce Jr. and P. K. Lala, "Modular implementation of efficient self-checking checkers for the Berger code," *Journal of Electronic Testing*, vol. 9, no. 3, pp. 279–294, 1996.

[27] Z. A. Siddiqui, P. Hui-Jong, and J. Lee, "Area-Time Efficient Self-Checking ALU Based on Scalable Error Detection Coding," in *Proceedings of the 2013 Euromicro Conference on Digital System Design (DSD)*, pp. 870–877, Los Alamitos, CA, USA, September 2013.

[28] Z. A. Siddiqui and J.-A. Lee, "Online error detection in SRAM based FPGAs using Scalable Error Detection Coding," in *Proceedings of the 5th Asia Symposium on Quality Electronic Design, ASQED '13*, pp. 321–324, Penang, Malaysia, August 2013.

[29] D. A. Anderson and G. Metze, "Design of Totally Self-Checking Check Circuits for m-Out-of-n Codes," *IEEE Transactions on Computers*, vol. C-22, no. 3, pp. 263–269, 1973.

[30] M. A. Smith, Transistor counts, http://en.wikipedia.org/wiki/Transistor_count, April 05, 2018.

[31] K. Shvachko, H. Kuang, S. Radia, and R. Chansler, "The Hadoop distributed file system," in *Proceedings of the IEEE 26th Symposium on Mass Storage Systems and Technologies (MSST '10)*, 10, 1 pages, Piscataway, NJ, USA, May 2010.

20

Identifying and Analyzing Strong Components of an Industrial Network Based on Cycle Degree

Zhiying Zhang,[1] Xiaozhen Chen,[2] Wenwen Xiao,[1] and Guijie Qi[1]

[1]*School of Management, Shandong University, Jinan, Shandong 250100, China*
[2]*Business School, Shandong Normal University, Jinan, Shandong 250014, China*

Correspondence should be addressed to Xiaozhen Chen; cxz005566@sdnu.edu.cn

Academic Editor: Guo Chen

In the era of big data and cloud computing, data research focuses not only on describing the individual characteristics but also on depicting the relationships among individuals. Studying dependence and constraint relationships among industries has aroused significant interest in the academic field. From the network perspective, this paper tries to analyze industrial relational structures based on cycle degree. The cycle degree of a vertex, that is, the number of cycles through a vertex in an industrial network, can describe the roles of the vertices of strong components in industrial circulation. In most cases, different vertices in a strong component have different cycle degrees, and the one with a larger cycle degree plays more important roles. However, the concept of cycle degree does not involve the lengths of the cycles, which are also important for circulations. The more indirect the relationship between two industries is, the weaker it is. In order to analyze strong components thoroughly, this paper proposes the concept of circular centrality taking into consideration the influence by two factors: the lengths and the numbers of cycles through a vertex. Exemplification indicates that a profound analysis of strong components in an industrial network can reveal the features of an economy.

1. Introduction

With the rapid development of the Internet, Internet of Things, and cloud computing technology, data has the potential for an explosive growth. The big-data era, which depends on cloud computing and cloud storage, has arrived. Large scale, diversity, and fast processing speed are the major characteristics of big data. Currently, data research focuses not only on describing individual characteristics but also on depicting the relationships among individuals [1, 2]. Relational data has been explored in the research of the economic management sector; for example, Acemoglu et al. used a degree sequence of a relational indicator to study the influences of the relationships among different departments on the fluctuation of the total output [3]; Hidalgo et al. studied an industry (product) upgrading issue by studying internet relational stricter among industries (products) [4]; Zhao et al. studied the linkage structure effect of blue economy under the perspective of an industrial network [5]; McNerney et al. studied the structure of interindustry relationships using

networks of money flows between industries in 45 national economies [6]. On the basis of an analysis of industrial relational structures using relational data, this paper proposes the concept of circular centrality to detect unknown and potentially useful circular relational data hidden behind Input-Output Tables and study the topological properties of industrial circulation relationships.

In a connected component of an undirected graph, all the vertices are reachable from each other, but this is not necessarily true for a digraph. When there is no path from one vertex to another in a digraph, it is not reachable from the vertex. If there are mutually reachable paths between two vertices, they must be in the same subdigraph, a strong component. A strong component of a digraph, also known as a strongly connected subdigraph, is a maximally induced subdigraph of the digraph. Because any two vertices in a strong component can reach each other, a strong component has features that are different from other components. These make strong components meaningful to a digraph, especially to the one with practical significance such as an industrial network.

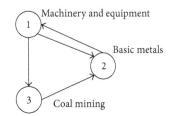

FIGURE 1: Industry circular linkages.

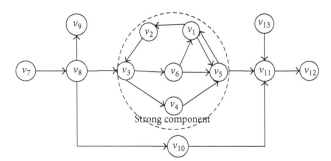

FIGURE 2: An industry network.

With vertices being the sectors and arcs representing significant industrial linkages, an economy can be abstracted into a network—an industrial network. The strong components of an industrial network depict industrial circulation linkages in an economy, where the former sector provides the input for the latter while the output of the latter comes back to the former. As shown in Figure 1, the sectors of coal mining, basic metals, and machinery and the linkages among them make up a strong component, and there are industrial circulation linkages among them. As fundamental linkages, industrial circulation linkages appear in various economic phenomena such as industrial clusters and circular economy [7].

In an industrial network, the general properties of strong components make them an important factor influencing the economy. Since any two sectors in a strong component can reach each other, any change of a sector can be felt by the others, and feedback effects also can influence the initial sector. The effects circulate with diminishing strength, as is shown in Figure 2.

Figure 2 describes an industrial network representing product flows. It contains 13 vertices, and 6 of them are in a strong component, forming vertices set V_c. If any sector of V_c undergoes some changes, such as shrink or expansion, the changes would pass on to all sectors of V_c and pass it on to some vertices outside the strong component. For instance, if sector v_4 alters, all sectors of V_c would change accordingly, and the effects circulate again and again over. As for the sectors outside, such as v_{11}, v_4 would push it along the directed path $v_4 \rightarrow v_5 \rightarrow v_{11}$. When the influence circulates within the strong component and reaches v_4 again, the effects on v_{11} would repeat again with lessened strength.

Any changes of a strong component can influence the circulation of the network. For instance, if v_1 becomes isolated in Figure 2, there would be no circulation, and any

changes of a sector in the network would pass on along unidirectional paths and stop.

Consequently, strong components play significant roles in an economy. Campbell [8, 9] recognized the importance and proposed that a strong component could be regarded as a vertex to build the condensation digraph. Some scholars followed this method, such as Morillas et al. [10]. This approach would do a lot to clarify the relationship structure of the whole network but did not involve the internal structure of a strong component. In order to do further researches on strong components, Zhao et al. [11, 12] developed the concepts of cycle degree and cycle length distribution of sectors and testified their applicability to show the structure of strong components.

Suppose that N is an industrial network, V is the set of all sectors in N, and sector $v \in V$. An industry cycle through v is defined as a directed cycle containing vertex v, where no two vertices are the same. It is obvious that an industry cycle, the fundamental circular unit of an industrial network, is a closed path through v. Any sector in a strong component is in one or more industry cycles. An industry cycle contains two sectors at least (regardless of loops—arcs beginning and ending at the same vertex) and all sectors of an industrial network at most. In Figure 2, there are four industry cycles through v_1, that is, $v_1 \rightarrow v_5 \rightarrow v_1$, $v_1 \rightarrow v_2 \rightarrow v_3 \rightarrow v_6 \rightarrow v_1$, $v_1 \rightarrow v_2 \rightarrow v_3 \rightarrow v_4 \rightarrow v_5 \rightarrow v_1$, and $v_1 \rightarrow v_2 \rightarrow v_3 \rightarrow v_6 \rightarrow v_5 \rightarrow v_1$.

The cycle degree of a sector in an industrial network, denoted by d_c, means the number of industry cycles through the sector, describing the number of circular linkages between the sector and the others. As a sector with bigger d_c can influence more industry cycles, it has greater driving circulating power. In Figure 2, the cycle degrees of sectors v_1, v_2, v_3, v_4, v_5, and v_6 are 4, 3, 3, 1, 3, and 2, respectively. If v_1 becomes isolated, there would be no cycles in the network. It can be seen that the sectors with big cycle degrees have more influences on the strong component. Now that the sectors outside the strong component do not exist in any cycles, their cycle degrees are all 0.

Differing from the degree, the cycle degree of a sector depicts the structure information from the whole network. A vertex with small degree is not necessarily with small cycle degree. With in-degree and out-degree both being 1, maybe a sector is only adjacent to two sectors, but the three sectors are all in multiple cycles, so that the cycle degree of the sector is large still. In Figure 2, with the in-degree and out-degree being 1, $d_c(v_2)$ is 3, while $d_c(v_4)$ is 1.

The concept of cycle degree can depict some features of the strong component, but it is not enough. For a vertex, its impact on circulation is related to its cycle degree, but also to the steps in circulations, which is reflected in the lengths of cycles. The effects circulating in a shorter cycle are stronger than in a longer one. If an indicator can capture the two aspects, it is more accurate. For this reason, the concept of circular centrality is proposed in this paper. In addition, in order to better analyze the strong component of an industrial network, the cycle degree of a strong component is presented too.

In order to analyze the effectiveness of these concepts, some practical calculations are made. With more than 30 years of sustained rapid growth, China's economy has become one of the fastest growing economies in the world. This paper analyzes China's strong components and compares them to those of the US and Japan. The result shows the differences between China and the other two countries.

The organization of this paper is as follows. Section 2 describes the indicators to research strong components based on cycle degree. Section 3 briefly explains the methodology we employed in this study. The next part presents the main empirical results and analyses. Finally, some conclusions are offered.

2. Relevant Indicators to Analyze Strong Component Based on Cycle Degree

Strong components of an industrial network can be analyzed from a vertex or from the whole network. From a vertex perspective, as different vertices play different roles in circulations, it is important to analyze these differences. From the whole network, the strong components with different numbers of cycles create different circular effects. In addition, the distribution of sectors with large cycle degree can also show the characteristic of the economy.

2.1. Circular Centrality. The cycle degree of a vertex depicts the number of closed paths through the vertex in circulations. For a vertex, cycle degree can show its effect on circulation, but that is not wholly so. As is seen in Figure 1, there are two cycles through vertex ①, ① → ② → ① and ① → ③ → ② → ①, but they have difference. Vertex ① gets to itself through two steps along the first cycle, but three steps along the second one. The length of the path affects the linkage between the two sectors. As the path becomes longer, the linkage would be weaker. To a closed directed path, it is obvious that the cycle's length is a factor which can affect the roles of a vertex in circulation. If a vertex is contained in a special long cycle, the effect of the sector on itself would be slow and weak.

In order to express the effect of a sector on circulation, two factors should be taken into consideration, the cycle degree and lengths of cycles through the sector.

Freeman [13] proposed the concept of closeness centrality and suggested that the shorter the distance between a vertex and the others is, the higher closeness centrality it has. A vertex with big cycle degree and short cycles has a high circulation. Considering the two factors, we define the circular centrality of a vertex, which involves the concept of length distribution of cycles [11].

Length distribution of cycles depicts the numbers of cycles with different lengths through a sector. Regardless of loop, the length of the shortest cycle is 2. As the vertices in a cycle are different, the length of the longest cycle is no more than the number of vertices in the strong component, here assumed to be m. Supposing $d_c^k(v)$ denote the number of k cycles through sector v, we get length distribution of cycles $\begin{pmatrix} 2 & \cdots & k & \cdots & m \\ d_c^2(v) & & d_c^k(v) & & d_c^m(v) \end{pmatrix}$. In Figure 2, there are 4 cycles through vertex v_1, with two cycles of the length of 5 and the others of

2 and 4. So, the length distribution of industry cycles through v_1 is $\begin{pmatrix} 2 & 4 & 5 \\ 1 & 1 & 2 \end{pmatrix}$.

Length distribution of cycles involves the lengths of cycles and the corresponding cycle degrees at each length through a vertex. To a certain length, the ratio of cycle degree to its length shows the circular effect. The sum of all ratios depicts the role of the sector in circulation, which is defined as the circular centrality of a sector here. Denote the circular centrality of sector v by cc_v, and then

$$cc_v = \sum_{k=2}^{m} \frac{d_c^k(v)}{k}. \tag{1}$$

The percentage is applicable when the vertices within strong component are compared with each other. The coefficient of circular centrality of sector v, denoted by p_{cc_v}, is the percentage of circular centrality of sector v in those of all sectors in the strong component, and then

$$p_{cc_v} = \frac{cc_v}{\sum_{v=1}^{m} cc_v} \times 100\%. \tag{2}$$

The circular centrality of a vertex is a concept based on cycle degree but involves the lengths of cycles. A vertex with big coefficient of circular centrality plays an important role in circulation.

2.2. The Cycle Degree of a Strong Component. Cycles are the fundamental units of a strong component. There must be some cycles in a strong component, at least one. Complete strong components contain the most cycles. The more cycles a strong component contains, the stronger the circularity is. The number of cycles in a strong component is related to the number of vertices and the features of arcs.

The cycle degree of a strong component, denoted by d_t, is the number of cycles it contains. As the number of vertices in a strong component is constant, it is highly correlated to the arcs there. In general, the cycle degree of a strong component is highly positively correlated to the number of arcs. Sometimes, it is also related to the directions of arcs, and so forth. In Figure 2, if the arc $v_1 \to v_2$ becomes $v_2 \to v_1$, there would remain only one cycle.

As a cycle including several vertices, the cycle degree of the strong component is not the sum of cycle degrees of all vertices there. If there are k vertices in a cycle, the cycle is counted k times, for it is considered in calculating the cycle degree of each vertex in the cycle. In order to calculate it, we can classify all cycles according to their lengths and sum up the cycle degree at each length. Suppose there are $d_c^k(v)$ k cycles through sector v and m sectors in a strong component, $v = 1, 2, \ldots, m$. As the number of vertices is that of arcs in a cycle, the number of k cycles in the strong component is $\sum_{v=1}^{m} d_c^k(v)/k$.

Regardless of loops, arcs beginning and ending at the same vertex, as an industry cycle contains two sectors at least, the length of the shortest cycle is 2. And that of the longest cycle is m, for m sectors in the strong component. So, the cycle

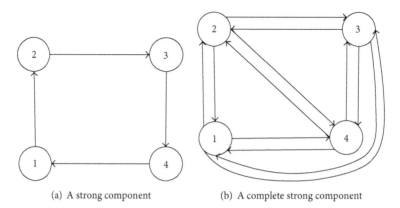

(a) A strong component

(b) A complete strong component

FIGURE 3: Strong component and the corresponding complete subdigraph.

degree of a strong component, denoted by d_t, is the sum at each length. That is,

$$d_t = \sum_{k=2}^{m} \frac{\sum_{v=1}^{m} d_c^k(v)}{k}. \tag{3}$$

The cycle degree of a strong component depicts network connectivity of the strong component. The bigger it is, the stronger the connectivity is.

3. The Methodology to Identify Strong Components and Calculate the Cycle Degree of a Vertex

In order to study strong components, we need to identify them from an industrial network first. In addition, calculating the cycle degree of a vertex is the basis to study the strong component. Here, we employ the methodology proposed by Zhao et al. [11] to do these.

3.1. Identifying Strong Components of an Industrial Network. A strong component should be identified from its unique features. All sectors in a strong component can reach one another along directed paths. If arcs are drawn along all directed paths, a strong component would become a complete subdigraph, where there are arcs between any two sectors, as is shown in Figure 3. In the adjacent matrix attached to a complete subdigraph, the entries off the principal dialogue are all "1." According to this, we can distinguish complete subdigraphs from others and identify the strong components accordingly.

In order to identify the strong component of an industrial network, we draw arcs along all directed paths and get a new network, which is called the expansion network here. In the expansion network, the strong components of the primary network become complete strong components. Suppose that the adjacent matrixes of an industrial network and its expansion network are U and U^*, respectively. In the industrial network, if there are p directed walks, length of k from i to j, the entries at the intersection of row i and column j of U^k would be p [14]. Suppose that an industrial

network contains n vertices; then the length of the longest path (without cycles) of the industrial network will be not more than $n - 1$. The sum of the power sequence of the U^k ($k = 1, \ldots, n - 1$) matrices gives all walks no more than k steps. When arcs are drawn along all paths, the entries of the corresponding adjacent matrix will become 1 at all positive entries of the sum matrix. So we can get the adjacent matrix U^* from the Boolean summation (i.e., $1 + (\#) 1 = 1$) of the power sequence matrices; that is,

$$U^* = \# \left(U + U^2 + \cdots + U^{n-1} \right), \tag{4}$$

where # denotes Boolean summation.

From U^*, we search for all the appropriate j and k for satisfying $u^*(k, j) = 1$ and $u^*(j, k) = 1$. All the vertexes j and k are in one complete subdigraph of the industry linkage expansion network; that is, they all belong to one strong component in the industrial network.

3.2. Calculating the Cycle Degree of a Sector. In a strong component, cycle degree of sector i means the number of all cycles through sector i, denoted by $d_c(i)$. In order to calculate, divide the cycles through sector i into groups according to their length and denote the cycle degree of length k by $d_c^{(k)}(i)$. It is obvious that the sum of cycle degrees of all lengths cycles is the cycle degree through sector i. Consider

$$d_c(i) = \sum_k d_c^{(k)}(i). \tag{5}$$

Ignoring the loops, the shortest cycle is 2 cycles (length of 2), and the longest is no more than the number of vertices in the strong component.

From the adjacency matrix of an industrial network, U, we can get the liaisons of any two sectors. If $u_{ij} = 1$, there is a direct linkage from sector i to j; if $u_{iv_1} = u_{v_1 v_2} = \cdots = u_{v_{k-1} j} = 1$ ($i, v_1, v_2, \ldots, j$ all differ from one another, so that there is a directed path length of k from sector i to j), there is an indirect linkage from sector i to j, as is shown in Figure 4; otherwise, there is no linkage. When sectors i and j are the same one, the directed path becomes a directed cycle. In other words, there is a k cycle through sector i.

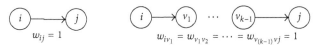

FIGURE 4: Directed path from sector i to sector j.

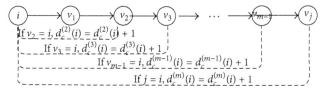

FIGURE 5: Process to calculate cycle degree through sector i.

In order to calculate $d_c^{(k)}(i)$, we search for the directed closed paths $i \rightarrow v_1 \rightarrow v_2 \rightarrow v_3 \rightarrow \cdots \rightarrow v_{k-2} \rightarrow v_{k-1} \rightarrow i$ ($i, v_1, v_2, \ldots$ all differ from one another) first and then count. The number of all these paths is $d_c^{(k)}(i)$, and the sum of all lengths of cycles is $d_c(i)$.

As vertices $i, v_1, v_2, \ldots, v_{k-1}$ are different from each other, the searching process is complex, especially to larger k. But an industrial network has its unique characteristics, which make the calculation possible. Firstly, the number of vertices in an industrial network is clear and small, and so is that of a strong component. Secondly, as industrial networks are sparse, if we only calculate unit entries and omit nil entries of the adjacent matrixes, the calculation will be reduced greatly. The algorithm is as follows.

Suppose that there are m sectors in a strong component, and $\mathbf{W}$ is the adjacent matrix attached to the strong component. Let $d_c^{(k)}(i)$ be equal to 0 for sector i first. As is shown in Figure 5, the steps are as follows.

Step 1. Search for the suitable v_1 for $w_{iv_1} = 1$.

Step 2. Search for the suitable v_2 for $w_{v_1 v_2} = 1$. As no loop is in a strong component, it is certain that $v_2 \neq v_1$. If $v_2 = i$, there must be a 2-cycle; then $d_c^{(2)}(i) \leftarrow d_c^{(2)}(i) + 1$; else, go to next step.

Step 3. Search for the suitable v_3 for $w_{v_2 v_3} = 1$, and $v_3 \neq v_1$. If $v_3 = i$, $d_c^{(3)}(i) \leftarrow d_c^{(3)}(i) + 1$; else, go to next step.

$\vdots$

Step $m-1$. Search for the suitable v_{m-1} for $w_{v_{m-2} v_{m-1}} = 1$, and $v_{m-1} \neq v_1, v_2, \ldots, v_{m-3}$. If $v_{m-1} = i$, $d_c^{(m-1)}(i) \leftarrow d_c^{(m-1)}(i) + 1$; else, go to next step.

Step m. Search for the suitable v_m for $w_{v_{m-1} v_m} = 1$, and $v_m \neq v_1, v_2, \ldots, v_{m-2}$. If $v_m = i$, $d_c^{(m)}(i) \leftarrow d_c^{(m)}(i) + 1$; else, go to next step.

Step $m + 1$. Sum up $d_c^k(i)$ ($k = 2, \ldots, m$); then we get $d_c(i)$.

Applying the procedure to all vertices of a strong component, we obtain all cycle degrees.

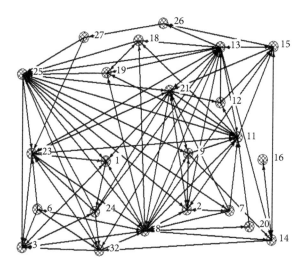

FIGURE 6: Strong component of China's industrial network.

4. Empirical Calculations and Analyses

In order to study the effectiveness of the concepts mentioned, some practical calculations are made. China's rapid development has intrigued a great deal of economists to try to understand the process [15–18]. So we try to analyze China's strong components and compare them to those of the US and Japan.

For comparison purposes, the data employed are derived from the OECD Input-Output Database, which is a part of the structural analysis (STAN) database. Data are used from Domestic Input-Output Tables 2005 of China, the US, and Japan (the 2005 Input-Output Tables were the last ones available). The tables all have 37 homogeneous sectors, as presented in Appendix C, making it possible to provide internationally comparable data for research. In order to find the fundamental relationships from the impacts on total production, we calculate the corrected influence coefficients of industrial linkage (Chen and Zhao [19], see Appendix A), on the basis of which industrial networks are constructed (Zhao et al., 2011 [20], see Appendix B).

4.1. Identifying the Strong Component of China's Industrial Network. Based on the methodology of Section 3, we obtain China's strong component. There is only one strong component, containing 23 sectors and 144 arcs, as is shown in Figure 6. The cycle degree of the strong component of China is 1263356.

4.2. Cycle Degrees of Sectors in China's Strong Component. The lengths distribution of cycles and cycle degrees of sectors in China are calculated, as is shown in Table 1. It can be seen that, to one sector, when the lengths of cycles are short, as the length is growing, the corresponding cycle degrees rise gradually. When the cycle degree reaches the maximum value, it starts to fall until reaching zero with the increase of the length.

To represent length distribution of industry cycles graphically, with abscissa being the lengths of cycles and ordinate

TABLE 1: The cycle degree and length contribution of the industry cycle in China.

SC	CL																				CD
	2	3	4	5	6	7	8	9	10	11	12	13	14	15	16	17	18	19	20	21	
1	2	4	25	107	380	1313	4026	10899	25554	51547	88434	127442	151844	146632	112795	67276	29412	8739	1572	108	828111
2	2	11	40	178	650	2052	5808	14740	32929	63913	106706	150591	176137	167981	127753	74793	31866	9209	1606	108	967075
3	2	11	24	99	351	1243	3906	10886	26291	54313	94775	138083	165730	160852	123523	72857	31344	9141	1596	108	895130
6	1	3	8	24	95	332	980	2530	5762	11366	19176	27400	32520	31793	25109	15151	6547	1931	306	12	181046
7	2	4	18	82	300	989	2884	7511	17328	34788	60037	87754	106841	107042	86807	54980	25545	8039	1522	108	602581
8	5	19	91	360	1239	3794	10271	24579	51524	93889	147017	194780	214946	194481	141537	80104	33293	9447	1622	108	1203106
9	0	1	11	51	197	689	2156	6122	15218	32672	60053	92626	117231	119530	96764	60793	28003	8639	1586	108	642450
11	2	14	64	251	883	2780	7880	19866	43791	83147	134135	181398	203212	186175	136908	78136	32705	9373	1622	108	1122450
12	0	3	12	47	170	560	1692	4590	10896	22583	41000	63044	79701	81707	67046	42191	18606	5413	1138	108	440507
13	7	26	112	412	1351	3976	10489	24674	51229	92888	145253	192679	213173	193435	140944	79708	33142	9435	1622	108	1194663
14	2	3	12	50	197	715	2353	6901	17620	38534	71472	110377	138890	139031	108388	64369	28007	8417	1570	108	737016
15	2	7	30	125	456	1501	4466	11827	27481	55934	98438	145565	176637	172832	133298	78096	33000	9431	1622	108	950856
16	1	0	0	0	0	0	0	0	0	0	0	0	0	0	0	0	0	0	0	0	1
18	1	3	26	113	398	1278	3625	9072	19997	38282	62701	86852	100837	97134	76051	47225	22776	7897	1568	108	575944
19	1	3	26	113	398	1278	3625	9072	19997	38282	62701	86852	100837	97134	76051	47225	22776	7897	1568	108	575944
20	0	0	2	12	58	191	529	1324	2894	5510	9071	12772	15411	15806	13578	9556	5267	2138	606	96	94821
21	2	16	66	252	892	2817	7928	19746	43046	81291	131103	177581	199263	182709	134497	76911	32279	9267	1610	108	1101384
23	1	9	45	179	639	2116	6286	16450	37559	73706	122878	171619	198136	186101	139081	79856	33349	9459	1622	108	1079199
24	2	8	37	136	495	1708	5228	14041	32515	64157	107018	149683	173631	164338	124043	72031	30474	8859	1594	108	950104
25	2	15	87	343	1181	3635	9938	24070	51183	94355	148777	197784	218558	197656	143437	80798	33425	9459	1622	108	1216433
26	0	0	2	14	75	277	913	2658	6953	16234	33021	56729	80801	94058	87068	60555	29345	9157	1622	108	479590
27	0	0	2	14	75	277	913	2658	6953	16234	33021	56729	80801	94058	87068	60555	29345	9157	1622	108	479590
32	1	7	32	133	482	1626	5000	13526	31830	64073	108425	152058	175267	164745	124286	72746	31288	9217	1622	108	956472

Note. SC: sector code; LC: cycles' length; CD: cycle degree.

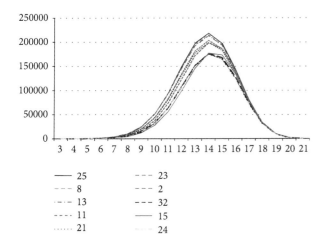

FIGURE 7: Length distribution of cycles of the top ten sectors.

being cycle degrees, we get the line charts of the top ten sectors, as is shown in Figure 7.

From Figure 7, it appears that the curves look like bells, increasing first and then decreasing. In the declining process, several curves overlap gradually. Given closer analysis it can be seen that as cycle becomes longer, there are more sectors in one cycle, so the cycle degrees of the top sectors increase simultaneously.

Dividing curves into halves in the middle parts, it can be seen that the differences of cycle degrees mainly come from the shorter cycles. Since shorter cycles circulate faster than the longer ones, the sectors with larger cycle degrees play more important roles and show greater competitiveness in an economy.

The cycle degree through a sector is an absolute value describing all closed paths through the sector. When we analyze how much a sector impacts the whole structure, relative cycle degree is needed. The relative cycle degree through sector i is the percentage of the cycle degree through sector i in that of the strong component, denoted by $p_{d_c(i)}$; then

$$p_{d_c(i)} = \frac{d_c(i)}{d_t} \times 100\%. \tag{6}$$

The relative cycle degrees of sectors in China are calculated, and the top ten ones are taken out, as is shown in Table 2.

4.3. Strong Component Comparisons among China, the US, and Japan. The cycle degree of the strong component of China is 1263356, while those of the US and Japan are 72712187 and 94706, respectively. It shows that, within an economy, the economic circulation of China is in the middle of the US and Japan. Relatively, Japan is the most dependent on foreign economy, and the US is the weakest.

For comparison, the coefficients of circular centrality and the relative cycle degrees of sectors are calculated and ordered in the three economies. Listing the top ten sectors, we get Table 2.

From Table 2, the top ten cycle degree sectors in the three economies basically share the same rankings with their coefficients of circular centrality. It is thus evident that the sectors with bigger cycle degrees have higher circular centrality generally.

Comparing the ten largest cycle degree sectors in the three economies, we can find that there exist some similarities but more differences in the three economies, as is shown in Figure 8. Overall, there are three common sectors, sectors 23, 25, and 32. They all belong to the service sector.

The distributions of the top ten sectors in the three economies are largely in accordance with their characteristics.

In China, the top ten sectors are distributed in three industries, one belonging to the resource industry, five to the manufacturing industry, and four to the service industry. Sector 2 (mining and quarrying) ranks in the top ten only in China. Of the five sectors belonging to the manufacturing industry, four are in the top five. It is evident that the manufacturing industry is the predominant part in China. The US shows its unique characteristics. Of the top ten sectors, nine belong to the service sector. Obviously, the service industry plays a dominant part in the US. Among them, sectors 28 (real estate activities), 31 (research and development), 36 (other community, social, and personal services), and 3 (food products, beverages, and tobacco) are in the top ten sectors only in the US, and sectors 28, 31, and 36 are even in the top five. Japan is somewhere between the US and China. The top ten sectors are both evenly distributed in the manufacturing and the service industry.

5. Conclusions and Further Research

Strong components are important components of a digraph for the circulations among vertices. Studying the strong components of an industrial network makes it easier to further identify the structural characteristics of the vertices and the whole network. To describe the strong components of an industrial network more accurately, this paper proposes the concept of circular centrality of a vertex and cycle degree of a strong component on the basis of cycle degree. As circular centrality of a vertex takes into consideration the influence by the lengths and the numbers of cycles through the vertex, it can better describe the real world. Using these indicators, the features of the strong components of China are analyzed and compared with those of the US and Japan.

We can analyze the strong components of an industrial network from two aspects: a vertex and strong component. From the viewpoint of a vertex, circular centrality is a concept involving the cycle degree and lengths of the cycles. Generally, a sector with a higher circular centrality has a stronger circulation and a larger influence on the economy. The study on the strong components of China and the other two economies shows that a vertex with a large cycle degree, with a few exceptions, has a high coefficient of circular centrality. From the viewpoint of a strong component, its cycle degree describes the number of circular paths within it. With a constant vertex number, a strong component with a larger cycle degree circulates stronger.

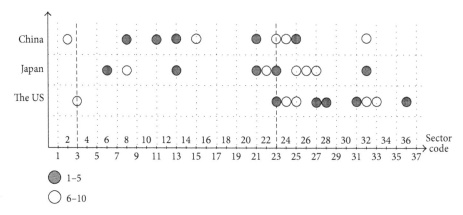

FIGURE 8: The top ten largest cycle degree sectors of the three economies.

TABLE 2: The top ten sectors of relative cycle degree and coefficients of circular centrality.

	China					Japan					The US			
SC	RCD		CCC		SC	RCD		CCC		SC	RCD		CCC	
	(%)	RA	(%)	RA		(%)	RA	(%)	RA		(%)	RA	(%)	RA
25	96.3	1	7.20	1	23	98.3	1	8.0	1	23	23	1	6.24	1
8	95.2	2	7.13	2	21	89.7	2	7.17	2	36	36	2	6.23	2
13	94.6	3	7.08	3	32	89.2	3	7.12	3	31	31	3	6.17	3
11	88.8	4	6.60	4	13	88.5	4	7.04	4	28	28	4	6.01	4
21	87.2	5	6.47	5	6	80.1	5	6.41	5	27	27	5	5.85	5
23	85.4	6	6.28	6	27	78.4	6	6.20	6	33	33	6	5.79	6
2	76.5	7	5.61	7	25	76.8	7	6.09	7	25	25	7	5.1	7
32	75.7	8	5.55	8	22	76	8	5.99	8	32	32	8	4.97	8
15	75.3	9	5.45	10	26	70.8	9	5.52	9	53	53	9	4.53	9
24	75.2	10	5.51	9	8	67.8	10	5.3	10	24	24	10	4.32	10

Note. SC: sector code; RCD: relative cycle degree; RA: ranking; CCC: coefficients of circular centrality.

Although the concept of circular centrality of a vertex can describe strong components thoroughly, the calculation methods also have some limitations. Since the calculation process involves circulation, it may take a long time when there are many vertices and arcs in a strong component. As the intermediate inputs of industries are uneven (see Appendix B), the industrial networks are relatively sparse. This makes the method effective in most cases.

Generally, a sector with higher circular centrality has more competitiveness. In order to improve the competitiveness of an economy, we can try to change some linkages through policy guidance to enhance the circular level of the sector and the whole network. It is meaningful to find these linkages and take appropriate action to change them in future research. In addition, there are probably some vertices with more intimate relationships than others within a strong component. Finding these groups will be useful to further analyze the network.

Appendix

A. The Corrected Influence Coefficients of Industrial Linkage

From the perspective of the total output of an economy, corrected influence coefficients of industrial linkage delineate the effects of the linkages between two sectors on the total output with the unchanged final demand. The hypothetical extraction method (HEM) is a suitable method for quantitatively calculating the coefficients.

The original idea of the HEM is to extract a sector hypothetically from an economy and examine the impact of the extraction on the economy (Schultz [21]; Cella [22]; Clements [23]; Dietzenbacher and Van Der Linden [24]; Miller and Lahr [25]; Cai and Leung [26]). The differences of total output show effect of the linkages.

Similarly, to assess the linkage effect between two specific sectors, we assume that sector j would purchase import goods to substitute for the inputs of sector i completely. Thus, by comparing the total outputs before and after the hypothetical extraction, the linkage between sectors i and j can be calculated. Based on the Leontief model, the industry linkage effect is studied from backward linkages.

Formally, denote the technical coefficient matrix of an economy with n sectors by $\mathbf{A}$, $\mathbf{A} = (a_{ij})_{n \times n}$, and the total output vector by $\mathbf{X}$, $\mathbf{X} = (x_i)_{n \times 1}$, the final total demand vector by $\mathbf{F}$, $\mathbf{F} = (f_i)_{n \times 1}$. The impact of a sector on its own is not considered.

In accordance with the Leontief model, the basic balance equation is

$$\mathbf{X} = \mathbf{A}\mathbf{X} + \mathbf{F}. \qquad (A.1)$$

According to HEM, it is assumed that the technical coefficient matrix $\mathbf{A}$ is partitioned into two groups: group one (g_1) being the two sectors to be studied (sectors i and j) and group two (g_2, $g_1 + g_2 = n$) being the remaining sectors. $\mathbf{X}$ and $\mathbf{F}$ are divided accordingly. Consider

$$\mathbf{A} = \begin{bmatrix} \mathbf{A}_{11} & \mathbf{A}_{12} \\ \mathbf{A}_{21} & \mathbf{A}_{22} \end{bmatrix},$$

$$\mathbf{X} = \begin{bmatrix} \mathbf{X}_1 \\ \mathbf{X}_2 \end{bmatrix}, \qquad (A.2)$$

$$\mathbf{F} = \begin{bmatrix} \mathbf{F}_1 \\ \mathbf{F}_2 \end{bmatrix},$$

where

$$\mathbf{A}_{11} = \begin{bmatrix} a_{ii} & a_{ij} \\ a_{ji} & a_{jj} \end{bmatrix}_{2 \times 2};$$

$$\mathbf{A}_{12} = \begin{bmatrix} a_{il} & \cdots & a_{ik} \\ a_{jl} & \cdots & a_{jk} \end{bmatrix}_{2 \times (n-2)};$$

$$\mathbf{A}_{21} = \begin{bmatrix} a_{li} & a_{lj} \\ \cdots & \cdots \\ a_{ki} & a_{kj} \end{bmatrix}_{(n-2) \times 2}; \qquad (A.3)$$

$$\mathbf{A}_{22} = \begin{bmatrix} a_{lm} & \cdots & a_{ln} \\ \cdots & \cdots & \cdots \\ a_{km} & \cdots & a_{kn} \end{bmatrix}_{(n-2) \times (n-2)}$$

with $l, k, m, n \neq i, j$.

Equation (A.1) can be rewritten as

$$\begin{bmatrix} \mathbf{X}_1 \\ \mathbf{X}_2 \end{bmatrix} = \begin{bmatrix} \mathbf{A}_{11} & \mathbf{A}_{12} \\ \mathbf{A}_{21} & \mathbf{A}_{22} \end{bmatrix} \times \begin{bmatrix} \mathbf{X}_1 \\ \mathbf{X}_2 \end{bmatrix} + \begin{bmatrix} \mathbf{F}_1 \\ \mathbf{F}_2 \end{bmatrix}. \qquad (A.4)$$

Solve (A.4):

$$\mathbf{X}_1 = \mathbf{H}\mathbf{A}_{12}\mathbf{B}_{22}\mathbf{F}_2 + \mathbf{H}\mathbf{F}_1$$
$$\mathbf{X}_2 = \mathbf{B}_{22}\mathbf{F}_2 + \mathbf{B}_{22}\mathbf{A}_{21}\mathbf{H}\mathbf{A}_{12}\mathbf{B}_{22}\mathbf{F}_2 + \mathbf{B}_{22}\mathbf{A}_{21}\mathbf{H}\mathbf{F}_1, \qquad (A.5)$$

where $\mathbf{B}_{22} = [\mathbf{I} - \mathbf{A}_{22}]^{-1}$, $\mathbf{H} = [\mathbf{I} - \mathbf{A}_{11} - \mathbf{A}_{12}\mathbf{B}_{22}\mathbf{A}_{21}]^{-1}$, and $\mathbf{I}$ denotes the identity matrix.

Now, suppose that the input from sector i to sector j is extracted from the economy; that is, $a_{ij} = 0$. $\mathbf{A}_{11}$ becomes $\mathbf{A}'_{11}$, $\mathbf{A}'_{11} = \begin{bmatrix} a_{ii} & 0 \\ a_{ji} & a_{jj} \end{bmatrix}_{2 \times 2}$, and $\mathbf{X}$ becomes $\mathbf{X}'$. Equation (A.4) can be expressed as

$$\begin{bmatrix} \mathbf{X}'_1 \\ \mathbf{X}'_2 \end{bmatrix} = \begin{bmatrix} \mathbf{A}'_{11} & \mathbf{A}_{12} \\ \mathbf{A}_{21} & \mathbf{A}_{22} \end{bmatrix} \times \begin{bmatrix} \mathbf{X}'_1 \\ \mathbf{X}'_2 \end{bmatrix} + \begin{bmatrix} \mathbf{F}_1 \\ \mathbf{F}_2 \end{bmatrix}. \qquad (A.6)$$

Solve (A.6):

$$\mathbf{X}'_1 = \mathbf{H}'\mathbf{A}_{12}\mathbf{B}_{22}\mathbf{F}_2 + \mathbf{H}'\mathbf{F}_1$$
$$\mathbf{X}'_2 = \mathbf{B}_{22}\mathbf{F}_2 + \mathbf{B}_{22}\mathbf{A}_{21}\mathbf{H}'\mathbf{A}_{12}\mathbf{B}_{22}\mathbf{F}_2 + \mathbf{B}_{22}\mathbf{A}_{21}\mathbf{H}'\mathbf{F}_1, \qquad (A.7)$$

where $\mathbf{H}' = [\mathbf{I} - \mathbf{A}'_{11} - \mathbf{A}_{12}\mathbf{B}_{22}\mathbf{A}_{21}]^{-1}$.

The difference between (A.5) and (A.7), denoted by ILE_{ij}, means the industry linkage effect of sectors i and j. Consider

$$\mathrm{ILE}_{ij} = \mathbf{k}\left(\mathbf{X} - \mathbf{X}'\right) = \left[\mathbf{k}_1\left(\mathbf{H} - \mathbf{H}'\right) \right.$$
$$+ \mathbf{k}_2\mathbf{B}_{22}\mathbf{A}_{21}\left(\mathbf{H} - \mathbf{H}'\right)\Big]\mathbf{F}_1 + \left[\mathbf{k}_1\left(\mathbf{H} - \mathbf{H}'\right)\mathbf{A}_{12}\mathbf{B}_{22}\right. \quad (A.8)$$
$$\left.+ \mathbf{k}_2\mathbf{B}_{22}\mathbf{A}_{21}\left(\mathbf{H} - \mathbf{H}'\right)\mathbf{A}_{12}\mathbf{B}_{22}\right]\mathbf{F}_2,$$

where $\mathbf{k}$, $\mathbf{k}_1$, and $\mathbf{k}_2$ are row summation vectors for $\mathbf{g}$, $\mathbf{g}_1$, and $\mathbf{g}_2$.

The corrected influence coefficient between sectors i and j, $ilcic_{ij}$, is the percentage of ILE_{ij} in the total output. Consider

$$ilcic_{ij} = \frac{\mathrm{ILE}_{ij}}{\mathbf{k}\mathbf{X}} \times 100\%. \qquad (A.9)$$

B. Constructing the Industrial Network

The industrial network is a fundamental model to analyze economic structures. With information in Input-Output Tables, the industrial network can be constructed with sectors being vertices, while arcs (directed edges) represent industrial linkages. The numeric values matrices, such as input-output quantitative transactions, or coefficients calculated from them, such as corrected influence coefficients, depict various relationships and determine the existence of arcs between sectors. In principle, with a defined threshold value, a numeric values matrix can be transferred into an adjacency matrix attached to a directed graph, with all positive entries larger than or equal to the filter to unity and the rest of the entries to zero.

It can be observed that the intermediate inputs of any sector are uneven. In the technical coefficient matrix $\mathbf{A}$ of any economy, only few a_{ij} values are large. For instance, in Chinese IO tables for the year 2005 (37×37), the 53 highest intermediate flows comprise 50% of the total intermediate consumption, while the remaining ones (1316) account for the other 50%. Nonuniform inputs make the industrial networks determined by several important relations.

Considering that the inputs have obvious inflection point, Zhao et al. [20] proposed the method to establish networks with Weaver-Thomas index.

TABLE 3: OECD sector classification.

Code	Sector
1	Agriculture, hunting, forestry, and fishing
2	Mining and quarrying
3	Food products, beverages, and tobacco
4	Textiles, textile products, leather, and footwear
5	Wood and products of wood and cork
6	Pulp, paper, and paper
7	Coke, refined petroleum products, and nuclear fuel
8	Chemicals and chemical products
9	Rubber and plastics products
10	Other nonmetallic mineral
11	Basic metals
12	Fabricated metal products except machinery and equipment
13	Machinery and equipment n.e.c
14	Office, accounting, and computing machinery
15	Electrical machinery and apparatus n.e.c
16	Radio, television, and communication equipment
17	Medical, precision, and optical instruments
18	Motor vehicles, trailers, and semitrailers
19	Other transport equipment
20	Manufacturing n.e.c; recycling
21	Electricity, gas, and water supply
22	Construction
23	Wholesale and retail trade; repairs
24	Hotels and restaurants
25	Transport and storage
26	Post and telecommunications
27	Finance and insurance
28	Real estate activities
29	Renting of machinery and equipment
30	Computer and related activities
31	Research and development
32	Other business activities
33	Public admin and defense; compulsory social security
34	Education
35	Health and social work
36	Other community, social, and personal services
37	Private households with employed persons

Source: This sector classification uses the latest version of the OECD I-O tables: 2005 Edition. http://stats.oecd.org/ to obtain the 2005 edition of OECD input-output tables for free.

The Weaver-Thomas index is an effective tool for finding the significant index developed by Weaver first and improved by O. Thomas later. Comparing an observed distribution with an assumed one, the closest approximation distribution is established to identify the key elements in numerical sequences. For the availability of finding crucial factors, it is widely used in regional economics.

Let $\mathbf{C}$ denote the coefficient matrix of an economy with n sectors (it can be technical coefficient matrix, or other matrixes); $C = (c_{ij})_{n \times n}$. According to the sequence from big to small order, rearrange $c_{11}, c_{12}, \ldots, c_{nn}$ and get the vector $\mathbf{C}^*$. Denote the lth element of $\mathbf{C}^*$ by c_{ij}; then the Weaver index is

$$w(l) = \sum_{k=1}^{n^2} \left[s(k, l) - 100 \times \frac{c_{ij}}{\sum_{j=1}^n \sum_{i=1}^n c_{ij}} \right]^2, \quad \text{(B.1)}$$

where

$$s(k, l) = \begin{cases} \dfrac{100}{l} & (k \leq l) \\ 0 & (k > l). \end{cases} \quad \text{(B.2)}$$

Let $w(l^*) = \min\{w(1), w(2), \ldots, w(n \times n)\}$; the l^*th element of $\mathbf{C}^*$, c^*, is the threshold value. If $c_{ij} \geq c^*$, there would be an arc from sector i to sector j in the industrial network with the direction in keeping with the flow. Denote the adjacency matrix by $\mathbf{W}$; then

$$w_{ij} = \begin{cases} 1, & \text{if } c_{ij} \geq c^* \\ 0, & \text{if } c_{ij} < c^*. \end{cases} \quad \text{(B.3)}$$

C. OECD Sector Classification

See Table 3.

Competing Interests

The authors declare that they have no competing interests.

Acknowledgments

This work was supported by the National Natural Science Foundation of China (no. 71371108).

References

[1] X. Su, P. Shi, L. Wu, and Y.-D. Song, "Fault detection filtering for nonlinear switched stochastic systems," *IEEE Transactions on Automatic Control*, vol. 61, no. 5, pp. 1310–1315, 2015.

[2] X. Su, L. Wu, P. Shi, and C. L. Chen, "Model approximation for fuzzy switched systems with stochastic perturbation," *IEEE Transactions on Fuzzy Systems*, vol. 23, no. 5, pp. 1458–1473, 2015.

[3] D. Acemoglu, V. Carvalho, A. Ozdaglar et al., "The network origins of aggregate fluctuations," *Econometrica*, vol. 80, no. 5, pp. 1977–2016, 2012.

[4] C. A. Hidalgo, B. Klinger, A.-L. Barabási, and R. Hausmann, "The product space conditions the development of nations," *Science*, vol. 317, no. 5837, pp. 482–487, 2007.

[5] B. Zhao, W. Xiao, R. Tong et al., "Blue economic connotation in industrial network perspective and its correlation structure effect—a case study of Shandong Province," *China Soft Science*, no. 07, pp. 135–147, 2015 (Chinese).

[6] J. McNerney, B. D. Fath, and G. Silverberg, "Network structure of inter-industry flows," *Physica A: Statistical Mechanics and its Applications*, vol. 392, no. 24, pp. 6427–6441, 2013.

[7] M. Fischer-Kowalski, "On the history of industrial metabolism," in *Perspectives on Industrial Ecology*, D. Bourg and S. Erkman, Eds., Greenleaf Publishing, Sheffield, UK, 2003.

[8] J. Campbell, *The relevance of input—output analysis and digraph concepts to growth pole theory [Ph.D. thesis]*, Department of Geography University of Washington, 1970.

[9] J. Campbell, "Growth pole theory, digraph analysis and interindustry relationships," *Tijdschrift voor Economische en Sociale Geografie*, vol. 63, no. 2, pp. 79–87, 1972.

[10] A. Morillas, L. Robles, and B. Diaz, "I-O coefficients importance: a fuzzy logic approach," *International Journal of Uncertainty, Fuzziness and Knowledge-Based Systems*, vol. 19, no. 6, pp. 1013–1031, 2011.

[11] B. Zhao, X. Chen, and J. Zhang, "Cycle degree of an industry and its algorithm," *System Engineering—Theory & Practice*, vol. 36, no. 6, pp. 1388–1397, 2014 (Chinese).

[12] B. Zhao and J. Zhang, *Introduction to Industrial Network Theory*, Economic Science Press, Beijing, China, 2013 (Chinese).

[13] L. C. Freeman, "Centrality in social networks conceptual clarification," *Social Networks*, vol. 1, no. 3, pp. 215–239, 1978.

[14] F. Harary, *Graph Theory*, Addison Wesley, London, UK, 1969.

[15] Y. F. Lin, F. Cai, and Z. Li, *China's Miracle: The Development Strategy and the Economic Reform*, Shanghai People's Publishing House, Shanghai, China, 1994 (Chinese).

[16] H. Fehr, S. Jokisch, and L. J. Kotlikoff, "Will China eat our lunch or take us out to dinner? Simulating the transition paths of the US, EU, Japan, and China," NBER Working Paper 11668, NBER, 2005.

[17] J. Ren, W. Li, Y. Wang, and L. Zhou, "Graph-mine: a key behavior path mining algorithm in complex software executing network," *International Journal of Innovative Computing, Information and Control*, vol. 11, no. 2, pp. 541–553, 2015.

[18] H. He, J. Wang, and J. Ren, "Measuring the importance of functions in software execution network based on complex network," *International Journal of Innovative Computing, Information and Control*, vol. 11, no. 2, pp. 719–731, 2015.

[19] X. Chen and B. Zhao, "Research on industry linkage correction influence coefficients based on hypothetical extraction method," *Management Review*, vol. 26, no. 6, pp. 23–32, 2014 (Chinese).

[20] B. Zhao, C. Yin, and J. Zhang, "A study on industry complex network and its modeling—on the example of Shandong province," *Economic Management*, no. 7, pp. 139–148, 2011 (Chinese).

[21] S. Schultz, "Approaches to identifying key sectors empirically by means of input—output analysis," *The Journal of Development Studies*, vol. 14, no. 1, pp. 77–96, 2007.

[22] G. Cella, "The input-output measurement of interindustry linkages," *Oxford Bulletin of Economics and Statistics*, vol. 46, no. 1, pp. 73–84, 1984.

[23] B. J. Clements, "On the decomposition and normalization of interindustry linkages," *Economics Letters*, vol. 33, no. 4, pp. 337–340, 1990.

[24] E. Dietzenbacher and J. A. Van Der Linden, "Sectoral and spatial linkages in the EC production structure," *Journal of Regional Science*, vol. 37, no. 2, pp. 235–257, 1997.

[25] R. E. Miller and M. L. Lahr, "A taxonomy of extractions," in *Regional Science Perspectives in Economic Analysis*, Elsevier, Amsterdam, The Netherlands, 2001.

[26] J. Cai and P. Leung, "Linkage measures: a revisit and a suggested alternative," *Economic Systems Research*, vol. 16, no. 1, pp. 65–86, 2004.

21

Index Based Hidden Outlier Detection in Metric Space

Honglong Xu,[1,2,3] **Rui Mao,**[1] **Hao Liao,**[1] **He Zhang,**[1] **Minhua Lu,**[4] **and Guoliang Chen**[1]

[1]*Guangdong Province Key Laboratory of Popular High Performance Computers, College of Computer Science and Software Engineering, Shenzhen University, Shenzhen, Guangdong 518060, China*
[2]*College of Information Engineering, Shenzhen University, Shenzhen, Guangdong 518060, China*
[3]*School of Mathematics and Big Data, Foshan University, Foshan, Guangdong 528000, China*
[4]*Guangdong Key Laboratory for Biomedical Measurements and Ultrasound Imaging, School of Biomedical Engineering, Shenzhen University, Shenzhen 518060, China*

Correspondence should be addressed to Minhua Lu; luminhua@szu.edu.cn

Academic Editor: Michele Risi

Useless and noise information occupies large amount of big data, which increases our difficulty to extract worthy information. Therefore outlier detection attracts much attention recently, but if two points are far from other points but are relatively close to each other, they are less likely to be detected as outliers because of their adjacency to each other. In this situation, outliers are hidden by each other. In this paper, we propose a new perspective of hidden outlier. Experimental results show that it is more accurate than existing distance-based definitions of outliers. Accordingly, we exploit a candidate set based hidden outlier detection (HOD) algorithm. HOD algorithm achieves higher accuracy with comparable running time. Further, we develop an index based HOD (iHOD) algorithm to get higher detection speed.

1. Introduction

In recent years, the rapid growth of multidimensional data brings about increasing demand for knowledge discovery, in which outlier detection is an important task with wide applications, such as credit card fraud detection [1], online video detection [2], and network intrusion detection [3].

As a matter of necessity, the wide use of outlier detection has aroused enthusiasm in many researchers. Over the past few decades, many outlier definitions and detection algorithms have been proposed in the literature [4–6]. Among these, statistics-based outlier detection [7, 8], which initiated a new era for data mining, has attracted an intensive study. Nevertheless, statistics-based outlier detection always depends on the probability distribution of the dataset, which is always priorly unknown.

In order to overcome shortcoming of statistics-based method, Knorr and Ng et al. proposed distance-based definition and the corresponding detection method [9, 10]. According to his definition, an object O in a dataset T is DB(p, D) outlier if at least fraction p of the objects in T lies greater than distance D from O [10]. Soon afterwards, a number of distance-based definitions had been presented [4, 6]. Based on these definitions and their relevant detection methods, many researches significantly improved both outlier detection accuracy and speed.

However, by existing definitions, outliers tend to be far from their nearest neighbors. As a result, if a small number of outliers are close to each other but are far from other points, which also known as outlier cluster, they are not likely to be determined as outliers because of their adjacency to each other. In this case, these points are hidden by each other. In other words, outlier itself has bad influence on detection accuracy [11]. In this paper, we propose a new perspective of hidden outlier that can uncover those hidden ones by traditional definitions and also design a new detection algorithm. Specifically, we make the following contributions:

(1) A more accurate definition of outlier taking hidden outliers into consideration.

(2) An effective detection algorithm for the definition proposed, with higher accuracy only at the cost of a little more time.

(3) An index based HOD (iHOD) algorithm and getting much higher detection speed.

(4) A simple but effective algorithm to select pivot for iHOD algorithm to avoid selecting outliers as pivots.

The rest of this paper is organized as follows. In Section 2, we will discuss several commonly used outlier definitions and relevant detection algorithms, along with their efficiency variants. Section 3 proposes the definition of hidden outlier and Section 4 proposes its detection algorithms. Experimental results are presented in Section 5, followed by conclusion and future work in Section 6.

2. Related Work

As mentioned in the introduction, there are many definitions and detection algorithms for outliers, among which Hawkins's work [12] stands out as the first. Following this work, three major distance-based definitions of outliers have been proposed, namely, k-R outlier [9, 10], k-distance-based outlier [13], and distance sum-based outlier [14].

k-R outlier [9, 10] in a dataset is a point that no more than k points are within distance R to it, denoted as $O_{thres}^{(k,R)}$ [15]. Please note that the definition of k-R outlier is essentially equivalent to definition $DB(p, D)$ [9, 10], by which a point in a dataset T is an outlier if at least a fraction p of all points in T is beyond distance D to it.

k-distance-based [13] outlier in a dataset is the point whose distance to its kth nearest neighbor is the largest among all points. Usually, the distance of a point to its kth nearest neighbor is considered as its outlier degree, and the n points with the largest outlier degrees are determined as outliers, denoted as $O_{kmax}^{(k,n)}$ [15].

The definition of distance sum-based outlier [14] considered the sum of distances from a point to its k nearest neighbors as its outlier degree, and the n points with the largest sums are determined as outliers which can be denoted as $O_{ksum}^{(k,n)}$. Similarly, distance average-based outlier, an equivalent definition in which the average distance to k nearest neighbors is considered, can be defined and denoted as $O_{kavg}^{(k,n)}$ [15]. Because kNN method is easy to implement [16], the above three distance-based definitions become popular.

In addition, density-based outlier is actually distance-based outlier; for example, LOF [17], the most famous density-based definition, was accomplished in detecting outliers from a dataset with different densities, while ordinary definitions are not qualified for this work.

Distance-based outlier detection algorithm was always designed for one or several definitions. Over the past decades, many detection algorithms were proposed since the above definitions emerged, in which the most famous one is ORCA [18]. ORCA has been honoured as the state-of-art algorithm [18] because of its simplicity and efficiency. What is more, it supports any outlier definitions with monotonically decreasing function of the nearest neighbor distances such

as $O_{kmax}^{(k,n)}$ or $O_{kavg}^{(k,n)}$. After that, many variants appeared in the literature, including solving set algorithm [19], MIRO [20], RCS [21], and iORCA [22]. It should be noted that not all the variants support the same definitions as ORCA [18]; for instance, iORCA [22] could not support $O_{kavg}^{(k,n)}$ definition.

For speeding up kNN search [16], some researchers exploit other research methods, for example, index based algorithm. Knorr et al. first bring forward index based method. According to their description, R-tree and k-d tree can be applied [10]. After that, k-d tree based method was proposed and had got a time complexity of $O(nk)$ [23]. Other detection algorithms, including HilOut based algorithm [24], P tree based algorithm [25], LSH based algorithm [26, 27], and SFC index [28], use different index structure to speed up detection. Besides, sample method was applied to reduce distance computations [29].

k-R outlier also attracted many researchers since Knorr and Ng et al. proposed $DB(p, D)$ outlier definition and three relevant algorithms (nested-loop, index based, and cell-based algorithm) [9, 10]. For example, Tao et al.'s SNIF algorithm [30] can detect all outliers by scanning the dataset at most twice and even once in some cases. DOLPHIN algorithm [31] is also an efficient method to detect k-R outlier. However, k-R outlier has a shortcoming that parameters are difficult to set [13].

Similarly, the research works for density-based detection algorithm started from their incipient definition, which is LOF [17]. The variants or improved algorithms included COF [32], MDEF [33], Ensemble method [34], and so forth.

Since this paper aimed at outlier definition, we just took three most popular and simplest algorithms as comparison algorithm: ORCA [18], which is the state-of–art distance-based outlier detection algorithm, LOF [17], the most representative density-based outlier detection method, and iORCA [22], latest index based outlier detection algorithm in metric space. For ORCA and iORCA, $O_{ksum}^{(k,n)}$ and $O_{kmax}^{(k,n)}$ were used as outlier definition, respectively.

3. Definition of Hidden Outlier

In this section, we propose the new perspective of hidden outlier. The basic idea is that once an outlier is detected, exclude it from the nearest neighbors of other points.

3.1. Cause of Hidden Outlier. As is shown in Figure 1, points A and B are outliers, but point C is not. In this case, if we set $k = 2$ and detect TOP 2 outliers by distance sum-based outlier definition, A and C will be detected as outliers, other than B, which is a real outlier. However, A and C will be detected as outliers, other than B, which is a real outlier. The reason is that the existence of A reduces the outlier degree of B, leading to the mistake in detection.

3.2. Definition of Hidden Outlier. If a small number (e.g., equal to or greater than 2) of points are close to each other but are far to other points, they are usually deemed as outliers. However, traditional distance-based definitions of outliers determine an outlier by its distances to its nearest neighbors.

As a result, those small number of points close to each other are usually not outliers according to traditional definitions. In this situation, outliers seem to be hidden by each other, and they can be called hidden outliers.

Our definition of outliers which include hidden ones, denoted as $HO_{k\text{sum}}^{(k,n)}$, is extended from the definition of distance-based outlier. Here we take distance sum-based outlier, $O_{k\text{sum}}^{(k,n)}$, as example to give detailed description. Notation summarizes the notations and their description.

Let D be a dataset, let dist be a distance function, let p be a point, and let $nn_i(p, D)$ be the ith nearest neighbor of p in D. Please note that a point is not considered as a nearest neighbor of itself. Further, let $D_{i,k}$ be the ith outlier by $O_{k\text{sum}}^{(k,n)}$ definition, let $w_k(p, D)$ be the outlier degree of p, and let D_n-outlier be the set of n outliers of the largest values of outlier degree. According to the definition of $O_{k\text{sum}}^{(k,n)}$, $w_k(p, D)$ is given by

$$w_k(p, D) = \sum_{i=1}^{k} \text{dist}(p, nn_i(p, D)). \tag{1}$$

Let $HD_{i,k}$ be the ith outlier by our new definition, let $Hw_k(p, D)$ be p's outlier degree, and let HD_n-outlier be the set of first n outliers.

Definition 1. The definition of outliers include hidden ones, $HO_{k\text{sum}}^{(k,n)}$, defines the outliers in an iterative way:

$$HD_{1,k} = \text{argmax}p(w_k(p, D))$$

$$HD_{i,k} = \text{argmax}p(w_k(p, D - HD_{i-1}\text{-outlier})), \tag{2}$$

$$2 \le i \le n.$$

Definition 2. The outlier degree of p by $HO_{k\text{sum}}^{(k,n)}$ definition, $Hw_k(p, D)$, is defined as

$$Hw_k(p, D)$$

$$= \begin{cases} w_k(D_{1,k}, D), & \text{if } p = D_{1,k} \\ w_k(p, D - HD_{i-1}\text{-outlier}), & \text{if } p = HD_{i,k}, \ 2 \le i \le n \\ w_k(p, D - HD_n\text{-outlier}), & \text{otherwise.} \end{cases} \tag{3}$$

In other words, $Hw_k(p, D)$ is still the sum of distances from p to its k nearest neighbors, while outliers already detected are not considered as p's nearest neighbors. Please note that the sequence of $Hw_k(HD_{i,k}, D), 1 \le i \le n$, might not be in descending order.

The other definition of outliers may be deduced by analogy. For example, $O_{k\text{max}}^{(k,n)}$, we can simply displace the outlier degree of $O_{k\text{sum}}^{(k,n)}$ as that of $O_{k\text{max}}^{(k,n)}$, which is

$$w_k(p, D) = \text{dist}(p, nn_i(p, D)). \tag{4}$$

Then we can give the same definition of hidden outlier and its degree as Definitions 1 and 2. It is worth mentioning that, for simplicity, $O_{k\text{sum}}^{(k,n)}$ based hidden outlier will be called $k$sum hidden outlier, while $O_{k\text{max}}^{(k,n)}$ hidden outlier will be called

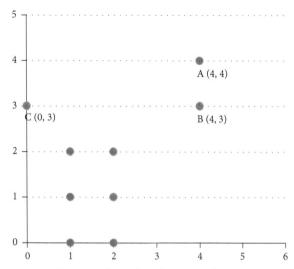

FIGURE 1: A simple 2-dimension dataset.

$k$max hidden outlier. Though both HOD (Section 4.1) and iHOD (Section 4.2) can apply these two definitions, for the limited space, they will only use one definition, respectively, in our experiments.

4. Hidden Outlier Detection Algorithm

In this section, the detection algorithms designed for hidden outlier are proposed, together with several theorems and definitions.

4.1. Hidden Outlier Detection Algorithm. The detection algorithm of $HO_{k\text{sum}}^{(k,n)}$ is presented in this section. We start from a few theorems and concepts together which can be used to speed up the detection.

Theorem 3. *The hidden outlier degree is always no less than the outlier degree or* $Hw_k(p, D) \ge w_k(p, D)$.

The proof is straightforward from the definitions of both outlier degrees and is thus omitted.

Theorem 4. *The ith hidden outlier's outlier degree is no less than that of the ith outlier by* $O_{k\text{sum}}^{(k,n)}$; *that is,* $Hw_k(HD_{i,k}, D) \ge w_k(D_{i,k}, D), \ 1 \le i \le n$.

Proof. (1) if $i = 1$, the equation clearly holds.

(2) If $2 \le i \le n$, one has the following.

(a) If HD_i-outlier $= D_i$-outlier, there must exist t, such that $HD_{i,k} = D_{t,k}, \ 1 \le t \le i$. From Theorem 3 and the definition of $w_k(p, D)$,

$$Hw_k(HD_{i,k}, D) \ge w_k(D_{t,k}, D) \ge w_k(D_{i,k}, D). \tag{5}$$

(b) Otherwise, there must exist t, such that $D_{t,k} \notin HD_i$-outlier, $1 \le t \le i$. From Definition 2, Theorem 3, and the definition of $w_k(p, D)$,

$$Hw_k(HD_{i,k}, D) \ge Hw_k(D_{t,k}, D) \ge w_k(D_{t,k}, D)$$

$$\ge w_k(D_{i,k}, D). \tag{6}$$

$\square$

```
Input: k, n, D
Output: HD_n-outlier
(1)      c ← 0;
(2)      D_n-outlier ← φ;
(3)      B ← φ; //B is a data block of dataset D
(4)      while B ← get-next-block(D) {
(5)        for each d in D {
(6)          for each b in B {
(7)            dis ← dist(b, d); update b.NN
(8)            if MPW_{n,k}(b, D) < c remove b from B; }}
(9)        for each b in B {
(10)         D_n-outlier ← TOP(B ∪ D_n-outlier, n)   //update D_n-outlier;
(11)         c ← w_k(D_{n,k}, D)       //update c;
(12)         for each cs in CS_{n,k}(D) {
(13)           if (MPW_{n,k}(cs, D) < c)
(14)             delete cs from CS_{n,k}(D); }
(15)         if (MPW_{n,k}(b, D) > c)
(16)           insert b to CS_{n,k}(D); }}
(17)     HD_n-outlier ← filtering process(D_n-outlier, CS_{n,k}(D));
(18)     return HD_n-outlier;
```

ALGORITHM 1: Hidden outlier detection algorithm.

For convenience, we introduce two more definitions, *maximum possible outlier degree* and *hidden outlier candidate set*, and related theorems to show their properties.

Definition 5. The *maximum possible outlier degree* of p, $MPW_{n,k}(p, D)$, is the hidden outlier degree of p assuming that all the first $n - 1$ nearest neighbors of p are detected as outliers and thus are excluded from contributing to p's hidden outlier degree. That is,

$$MPW_{n,k}(p, D) = \sum_{i=n}^{n+k-1} \text{dist}(p, nn_i(p, D)). \quad (7)$$

From Definition 5, we give the following obvious theorem without proof.

Theorem 6.

$$Hw_k(p, D) \le MPW_{n,k}(p, D). \quad (8)$$

Definition 7. The hidden outlier candidate set, $CS_{n,k}(D)$, is a subset of D such that, for each $p \in CS_{n,k}(D)$, $MPW_{n,k}(p, D) \ge w_k(D_{n,k}, D)$.

The following theorem shows the purpose in defining hidden outlier candidate set.

Theorem 8. *The hidden outlier candidate sets, $CS_{n,k}(D)$, contains all of the outliers defined by $HO_{ksum}^{(k,n)}$.*

Proof. For an arbitrary outlier p defined by $HO_{ksum}^{(k,n)}$, from definition and from Theorem 4, $Hw_k(p, D) \ge w_k(p, D)$.

From Theorem 6, $Hw_k(p, D) \le MPW_{n,k}(p, D)$.

As a result, $MPW_{n,k}(p, D) \ge w_k(D_{n,k}, D)$; that is, $p \in CS_{n,k}(D)$. □

Our hidden outlier detection (HOD) algorithm (Algorithm 1) is based on the ORCA algorithm [18]. HOD searches $k + n - 1$ nearest neighbors (in consideration of performance, n must be small) of every data block (lines (4)–(7)). Once an object is impossible to become an outlier, it will be removed from data block (line (8)). After processing a data block, HOD gets current D_n-outlier (line (10)) and updates cutoff value c (line (11)) and then maintains hidden outlier candidate set at the same time (lines (12)–(16)), including deleting the objects with smaller MPW than c (lines (13)-(14)) and adding the objects with larger MPW than c (lines (15)-(16)). Finally the candidate set is filtered to get the final results (Algorithm 2).

Algorithm 2 shows how the candidate set is filtered to get the final results. $D_{1,k}$ is first moved from $CS_{n,k}(D)$ to HD_n-outlier (line (1)), because the first outlier of D_n-outlier and first outlier HD_n-outlier are the same. Then the last outlier of HD_n-outlier is checked to see whether it is a nearest neighbor of some objects in $CS_{n,k}(D)$. If yes, it is deleted from that object' nearest neighbors and the hidden outlier degree $Hw_k(cso, D)$ (lines (2)-(4)) is updated. Next, the object with the largest hidden outlier degree in $CS_{n,k}(D)$ is moved to HD_n-outlier (line (5)), and the process goes back to line (2) until there are n outliers (line (6)).

As Bay and Schwabacher indicated, ORCA [18] has $O(N)$ time complexity on average and $O(N^2)$ in the worst case. In contrast to ORCA [18], HOD searches more nearest neighbors and thus costs more time and memory space. Further, HOD prunes less normal objects and results in more distance computations. However, these do not increase HOD's time complexity because as more data blocks have been processed, the cutoff value c becomes larger and more normal objects will be pruned. In other words, the pruning mechanism is the same as ORCA [18]. After searching a data block's nearest neighbors, HOD maintains an outlier candidate set

Input: D_n-outlier, $CS_{n,k}(D)$
Output: HD_n-outlier
(1) $HD_{1,k} = D_{1,k}$, delete $D_{1,k}$ from $CS_{n,k}(D)$;
(2)   Set $i = 1$;
(3)   **for** each cso in $CS_{n,k}(D)$ {
(4)   **if** ($HD_{i,k} \in cso.NN$) update $cso.NN$ and $Hw_k(cso, D)$; }
(5) $i++; HD_{i,k} \leftarrow \text{TOP}(CS_{n,k}(D), 1)$, delete it from $CS_{n,k}(D)$ and insert to HD_n-outlier;
(6)   **if** ($i < n$) **do** $line$ (3)
(7)   return HD_n-outlier;

ALGORITHM 2: Filtering process.

Input: D, $pivot$
Output: index L
(1) $L \leftarrow \phi$;
(2)   **for** each o in D
(3) $L(o) \leftarrow \text{dist}(pivot, o)$;
(4)   sort(L); //sorted by the distance value in
                //descending order
(5)   return L;

ALGORITHM 3: Build index.

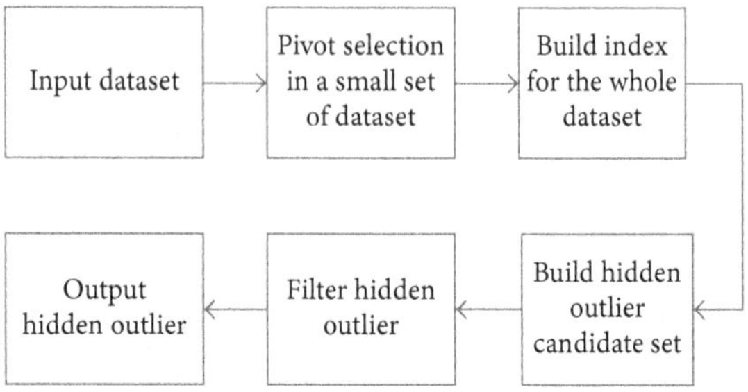

FIGURE 2: The flow chart of iHOD algorithm.

and updates it after updating c, which can be implemented by a fast priority queue. In addition, experimental results show that the candidate set size keeps constant as a whole with various dataset sizes, limiting the overhead of filtering process described in Algorithm 2.

4.2. Index Based Hidden Outlier Detection Algorithm. In order to speed up HOD algorithm, we draw on the experience of iORCA and develop a simple index based hidden outlier detection algorithm. As we discussed in Section 2, iORCA is a very excellent distance-based improvement from ORCA, which is the state-of-the-art method in outlier detection. It is worth mentioning that the build index process (Algorithm 3) of iORCA is very simple and almost costs little time. However, the only fly in the ointment is that iORCA is short of pivot selection method. Addressing this shortcoming, we propose a simple but efficient pivot selection algorithm (Algorithm 4).

The most important idea of iORCA is to update the cutoff value faster. In Algorithm 3, we can see that, in order to achieve this goal, iORCA simply calculates the distance between every object to pivot (lines (2)-(3)) and then sort them from large to small (line (4)). Obviously, both the time and memory consuming of this index are very small.

The largest difference between similarity search and outlier detection is that similarity search procedure may be used many times, for searching different object, while outlier detection procedure may be used for only several times, even just one time. That is a decision that their pivot selection method for building index will be different. Since similarity search always follows the rules of Offline Construction and Online Search [35, 36], it can spend more time to select pivots

and build index, other than outlier detection to save time in this stage.

As Bhaduri et al. said that if we select inlier points as pivots, the points farthest from them will be more likely to be the outliers [22]. To benefit from this, the goal of our pivot selection algorithm is to select density points as pivots. However, the accurate search of density points is too expensive. So, in our pivot selection algorithm, we only find out the approximate density regions (lines (4)-(5)) and then choose the middle point of these regions (line (6)).

In addition, we only take a part of dataset to select pivots, and usually a data block is enough. Due to the small percentage of outliers, it is almost impossible to select outliers as pivots via this subset using our method. The flowchart of iHOD algorithm is shown in Figure 2.

The stopping rule (Theorem 9) of iORCA can be applied in iHOD as well to quickly stop updating the cutoff value.

Theorem 9 (iORCA stopping rule [22]). *Let D be the dataset, let c be the cutoff value, let p be the pivot, and let x_t be any test point currently being tested by iORCA (or iHOD); if*

$$\text{dist}(x_t, p) + \text{dist}(p, nn_k(p, D)) < c \qquad (9)$$

then iORCA (or iHOD) can terminate with the correct D_n-outlier and cutoff value.

In addition, we propose other rules to reduce the distance computing times.

Theorem 10. *If $\text{dist}(x_t, p) + \text{dist}(p, nn_{k+n-1}(p, D)) < c$, then iHOD can stop updating hidden outlier candidate set.*

Theorem 10 can be proved similar to Theorem 9.

Input: D, *pivotNum*
Output: *pivot*
(1) blockIndex $\leftarrow \phi$;
(2) $B \leftarrow$ getPartOfDataSet(D); //B is usually a data block of dataset D
(3) blockIndex $\leftarrow$ buildIndex(B, $B[0]$);
(4) divide blockIndex into *partNum* equal segments;   //*partNum* $\geqslant 2 *$ *pivotNum*
      and 10, every segment has the same number of points
(5) get *pivotNum* segments with smallest skip distance;
(6) *pivot* $\leftarrow$ middle object of every smallest segment;
(7) return *pivot*;

ALGORITHM 4: Pivot selection.

Input: k, n, D
Output: HD_n-outlier
(1) $c \leftarrow 0$; D_n-outlier $\leftarrow \phi$; $B \leftarrow \phi$; //B is a data block of dataset D
(2)   pivot $\leftarrow$ pivotSelection(D, 1);
(3) $L \leftarrow$ buildIndex(D, pivot); //L is a data block of dataset D
(4)   **while** $B \leftarrow$ get-next-block($L(D)$){
(5)   **if** (*Theorem 10 holds for B(1)*) **then** break;
(6)   **else** {
(7) $\mu \leftarrow$ findAvg($L(B)$);
(8) $startID \leftarrow$ find($L \geqslant \mu$);
(9) $order \leftarrow$ spiralOrder($L.id$, $startID$);
(10)   **for** each d in D with order {
(11)   **for** each b in B {
(12)   **if** (*Theorem 11 doesn't hold for d and b*) {
(13) $dis \leftarrow$ dist(b, d); update b.NN
(14)   **if** $MPW_{n,k}(b, D) < c$ remove b from B; }}}
(15)   **for** each b in B {
(16)   **if** (*Theorem 9 doesn't holds for B(1)*) {
(17) D_n-outlier $\leftarrow$ TOP($B \cup D_n$-outlier, n)   //update D_n-outlier;
(18) $c \leftarrow w_k(D_{n,k}, D)$ //update c;
(19)   **for** each cs in $CS_{n,k}(D)$ {
(20)   **if** ($MPW_{n,k}(cs, D) < c$)
(21)   delete cs from $CS_{n,k}(D)$; }
(22)   **if** ($MPW_{n,k}(b, D) > c$)
(23)   insert b to $CS_n, k(D)$; }}}
(24) HD_n-outlier $\leftarrow$ filtering process(D_n-outlier, $CS_{n,k}(D)$);
(25)   return HD_n-outlier;

ALGORITHM 5: Index based hidden outlier detection algorithm.

Theorem 11. *If*

$$\left\| \text{dist}\left(x_i, p\right) - \text{dist}\left(x_j, p\right) \right\| > \text{dist}\left(x_i, nn_k\left(x_i, D\right)\right) \quad (10)$$

then x_j is no longer the k nearest neighbors of x_i.

Proof. Using Triangle Inequality, there is

$$\text{dist}\left(x_i, x_j\right) \geq \left\| \text{dist}\left(x_i, p\right) - \text{dist}\left(x_j, p\right) \right\| \quad (11)$$

so we have

$$\text{dist}\left(x_i, x_j\right) > \text{dist}\left(x_i, nn_k\left(x_i, D\right)\right). \quad (12)$$

In other words, x_j is faster than the kth nearest neighbor of x_i. So x_j is no longer the k nearest neighbors of x_i. □

Our index based hidden outlier detection algorithm (Algorithm 5) combines iORCA (lines (3)–(9)) and HOD (lines (13)–(24)) algorithms and updates them with pivot selection algorithm (line (2)) and Theorem 11 (line (12)), finally resulting in its high performance.

5. Experimental Results

In this section, we compare HOD and iHOD algorithm with ORCA [18], iORCA [22], and LOF [17], three popular distance-based outlier detection algorithms, in both accuracy and efficiency.

5.1. Test Suite. We follow a common way [37] in constructing the test suite. Four popular real world classification datasets are picked from the UCI Machine Learning Repository [38], and then a few objects from a class of small cardinality together with other larger classes are finally picked as the test suite. The first dataset is from the KDD Cup 1999 dataset, used by Yang [37]. The first 20,000 TCP data of its ten percent version, which has 76 abnormal connections or outliers, are picked. The second dataset is from the Optdigits (short for Optical Recognition of Handwritten Digits) dataset. The first 10 records from class 0, served as outliers, together with other 3,447 records are picked. The third one is from the Breast Cancer Wisconsin (Diagnostic) dataset. The first 10 records of the malignant ones, served as outliers, are picked, making 367 as the total number of records. The last one is from the Heart Disease dataset. All records in class 4, serving as outliers, together with other records except in classes 1–3 are picked. Altogether, there are 203 records with 15 outliers in dataset 4.

After a simple constructing, these four datasets are match for Hawkins's outlier definition [12], which is generally acceptable.

5.2. Evaluation Methodology. In statistics, a receiver operating characteristic (ROC) or ROC curve is a graphical plot that illustrates the performance of a binary classifier system as its discrimination threshold is varied. The curve is created by plotting the true positive rate (TPR) against the false positive rate (FPR) at various threshold settings. Calculate the Area Under Curve (AUC), and the larger it is, the better it is.

With regard to outlier detection, as mentioned before, let D be the dataset, let $|D|$ be the dataset size, and let n be the various threshold setting parameter. In other words, when n is set as a specific value, the top-n outliers will be identified as outliers, and other $|D| - n$ points in the dataset are regarded as inliers. So, for a specific n, we can get a couple value of TPR and FPR. Vary n from 0 to $|D|$; we can easily get the ROC curve and then calculate the AUC value.

Obviously, the above calculation is in the case that neighbor number k is specific. If we vary it, then we can get the AUC-k graphical plot, which make us easily see the outlier detection accuracy with regard to parameter k.

5.3. Experimental Results. The experiments were run on a desktop with Intel Core 3.40 GHz processor, 8 GB RAM, running Windows 7 Professional Service Pack 1. The algorithms were implemented in C++ and compiled with Visual Studio 2012 in Release Mode. Unless otherwise specified, both the parameters k in determining nearest neighbors and detecting outlier number n are set as 10. The accuracy is first studied, then the running time and performance of pivot selection algorithm at last.

5.3.1. Accuracy. The accuracy of the five algorithms, namely, HOD, ORCA [18], iHOD, iORCA [22], and LOF [17], is first studied by way of AUC. For each constant value of k, the AUC values of the three algorithms with various values of n are computed. Then the AUC values of various values of k are plotted in Figure 3. Please note that ORCA uses $O_{ksum}^{(k,n)}$ definition, and HOD uses its extensional $k$sum hidden outlier, while iORCA uses $O_{kmax}^{(k,n)}$ definition, and iHOD uses $k$max hidden outlier.

TABLE 1: Rankings obtained through Friedman's test over average true positives of Figure 4.

Algorithm	ORCA	HOD	LOF	iORCA	iHOD
Ranking	3.75	3.25	5	1.875	1.125

It can be seen that HOD and ORCA achieve higher AUC values than LOF for almost all of the cases, for the four datasets. Further, HOD is better than ORCA for most of the cases. For the cases when ORCA is better than HOD, the values are close to 1, and the difference is thus marginal. Also, we can see the appearance of iHOD and iORCA.

To see the difference more clearly, we further compare the three algorithms by way of true positives (Figure 4). Obviously, iHOD is the best in most cases while LOF is the worst for almost all of the cases. Particularly, the true positives of LOF are close to 0 for the KDD Cup 1999 and Optdigits dataset. In Figure 4(c), we can see that HOD and iHOD have got the true positives similar to ORCA and iORCA, respectively. This is because Breast Cancer Wisconsin (Diagnostic) dataset is free of outliers hidden by other ones.

In order to see more details about the performance of iHOD, we also do some Non-Parametric Tests [39], including Friedman's test [40] and Hochberg's procedure [41]. However, even though Hochberg's testing results show that the difference between iHOD and iORCA is insignificant, it can be seen from Figures 3 and 4 that iHOD has actually made improvements from iORCA, which is an excellent outlier detection algorithm. Table 1, which is the rankings of average true positives from Figure 4, also shows that iHOD outperforms iORCA.

5.3.2. Efficiency. As mentioned earlier, an extra piece of work of HOD and iHOD is to filter through the candidate set, which may cost much time if the candidate set size is too large. The candidate size with respect to values of n (Figure 5) and dataset size (Figure 6) are plotted. The Breast Cancer Wisconsin (Diagnostic) dataset and the Heart Disease dataset are not included due to their tiny sizes. Clearly, the candidate set size is not strongly correlated to the dataset size, making its effect to the running time limited.

The running time of the seven algorithms for the KDD Cup 1999 dataset and the Optdigits dataset is listed in Figure 7, respectively. Please note that HOD has better accuracy than ORCA [18] and LOF [17], while iHOD is better than almost all algorithms, as indicated in last section. To make the comparison fair, we extend ORCA and iORCA [22] to HORCA and HiORCA to achieve the same detection results of HOD and iHOD. That is, run ORCA or iORCA n times, while each time only one outlier is detected and is removed from following runs. The running time of HORCA and HiORCA is also listed in the tables.

The figure shows clearly that the running time of LOF increases dramatically as the dataset size increases. HOD, with better accuracy, takes almost 1.5 times of the time as that of ORCA [18]. However, HORCA, with the equivalent accuracy as that of HOD, takes up to 9 times of the running time as that of HOD. To our surprise, iHOD runs even faster

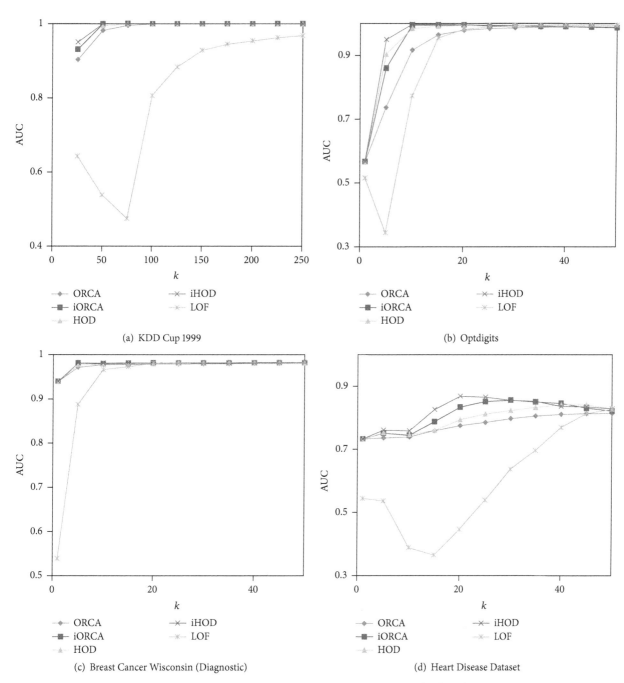

FIGURE 3: AUC values with various values k of five algorithms for four datasets.

than iORCA [22]. This is because iHOD uses Theorem 10 to get a large reduction of distance calculation times.

5.3.3. Performance of Pivot Selection Algorithm.

In order to estimate the performance of pivot selection algorithm, we compare iORCA/iHOD with/without pivot selection algorithm, in both running time and distance calculation times. For the sake of accuracy, we ran every experiment setup for 10 times and then get their standard deviation and mean value.

From Tables 2 and 3, we can see that our pivot selection algorithm makes the experiment results very stable and even

gets better results in mean value of running time and distance calculation times.

As other popular outlier detection algorithms like ORCA [18], iORCA [22], and LOF [17], both HOD and iHOD have two parameters, which are nearest neighbor number k and outlier number n. However, for these two parameters, it is unwise to decrease their value in order to get improvement in efficiency, because it may seriously reduce the detection quality. In fact, k can be set refer to $O_{k\mathrm{avg}}^{(k,n)}$ an so on. Though n is in proportion to candidate set size, thereby increasing the running time. Fortunately, n depends on user's requirement, so it is usually not large.

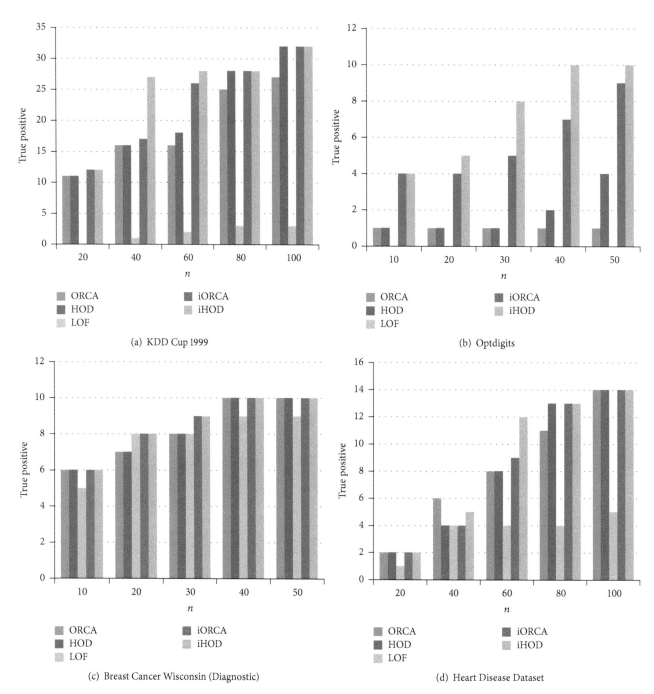

FIGURE 4: True positive values with various values n of five algorithms for four datasets.

TABLE 2: Standard deviation and mean value of running time (milliseconds) over KDD Cup 1999 dataset.

Size	5,000		10,000		15,000		20,000	
Category	Standard deviation	Mean value	Standard deviation	Mean value	Standard deviation	Mean value	Standard deviation	Mean value
iORCA random	16.7	697.60	8.0	1,363.50	21.7	2,040.60	78.5	2,725.40
iORCA psm	4.9	688.10	8.1	1,379.10	34.6	2,098.20	26.1	2,717.60
iHOD random	39.0	216.70	96.4	368.10	54.6	405.60	33.6	458.80
iHOD psm	21.2	232.20	35.9	309.00	83.2	402.60	22.2	441.60

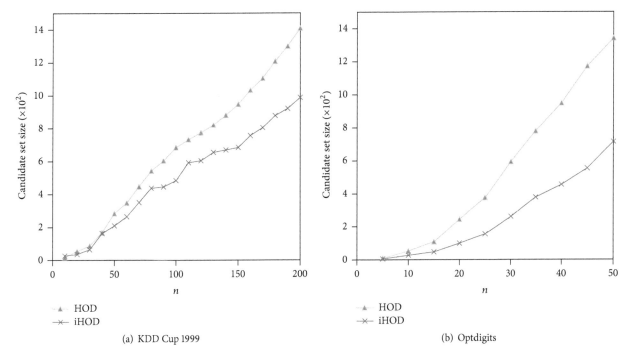

(a) KDD Cup 1999

(b) Optdigits

FIGURE 5: HOD's candidate set size with various values of n.

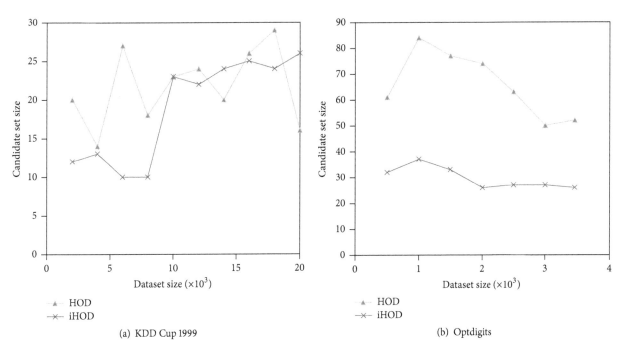

(a) KDD Cup 1999

(b) Optdigits

FIGURE 6: HOD's candidate set size with various dataset sizes.

TABLE 3: Standard deviation and mean value of distance calculation times (10^4 times) over KDD Cup 1999 dataset.

Size	5,000		10,000		15,000		20,000	
Category	Standard deviation	Mean value	Standard deviation	Mean value	Standard deviation	Mean value	Standard deviation	Mean value
iORCA random	5.23	504.1	1.39	1,002.5	0.201	1,502.5	0.332	2,003.3
iORCA psm	0.00	501.4	0.059	1,002.0	0.048	1,502.5	0.157	2,003.0
iHOD random	30.04	124.4	56.23	197.7	28.54	209.8	20.85	223.2
iHOD psm	15.17	137.0	24.59	165.7	46.41	197.6	10.19	211.0

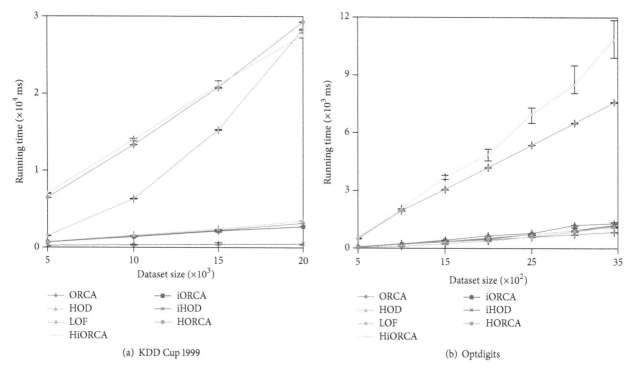

FIGURE 7: Running time (milliseconds) over KDD Cup 1999 and Optdigits datasets with $k = 10$ and $n = 10$.

5.4. Analysis of Mistakenly Detection. As we all know, HOD and iHOD algorithms detect next outlier after excluding the detected outliers, so that they can detect more real outliers. Is there any possibility that the normal objects are mistakenly detected as outliers?

To analyze easily, we let D be the dataset, let $O_{k\max}^{(k,n)}$ be the original outlier definition, and let d be the dimension number of datasets; region D_1 with radius of r consists of n_1 objects, which include outlier p_1. Another region, D_2, with the same radius, consists of n_2 objects, including normal object p_2. According to distance-based outlier definition, there is $n_1 < n_2$.

The expected outlier degree of p_1 and p_2, $E_1(d_k)$ and $E_2(d_k)$, is as follows:

$$E_1(d_k) = r\left(\frac{k}{n_1}\right)^{1/d}$$
$$E_2(d_k) = r\left(\frac{k}{n_2}\right)^{1/d}. \tag{13}$$

After taking out m objects from region D_1 and D_2 separately, the expected outlier degree of p_1 and p_2 becomes

$$E_1(d_k') = r\left(\frac{k}{n_1 - m}\right)^{1/d}$$
$$E_2(d_k') = r\left(\frac{k}{n_2 - m}\right)^{1/d}. \tag{14}$$

The variation of p_1 and p_2's outlier degree should be

$$\Delta_1 = r\left(\frac{k}{n_1 - m}\right)^{1/d} - r\left(\frac{k}{n_1}\right)^{1/d}$$
$$\Delta_2 = r\left(\frac{k}{n_2 - m}\right)^{1/d} - r\left(\frac{k}{n_2}\right)^{1/d}. \tag{15}$$

For ease of analysis, we can set

$$n_1 - m = n_1 m_1$$
$$n_2 - m = n_2 m_2. \tag{16}$$

So that

$$\Delta_1 = r\left(\frac{k}{n_1 m_1}\right)^{1/d} - r\left(\frac{k}{n_1}\right)^{1/d}$$
$$\Delta_2 = r\left(\frac{k}{n_2 m_2}\right)^{1/d} - r\left(\frac{k}{n_2}\right)^{1/d}. \tag{17}$$

Because $\Delta_1 > 0$, $\Delta_2 > 0$, we can compare their value via their ratio

$$\frac{\Delta_1}{\Delta_2} = \frac{r(k/n_1 m_1)^{1/d} - r(k/n_1)^{1/d}}{r(k/n_2 m_2)^{1/d} - r(k/n_2)^{1/d}} = \frac{(1/m_1)^{1/d} - 1}{(1/m_2)^{1/d} - 1}$$
$$= \frac{1 - m_1^{1/d}}{1 - m_2^{1/d}}. \tag{18}$$

Obviously, from formula (16), there is

$$n_1(1 - m_1) = n_2(1 - m_2). \tag{19}$$

Since $n_1 < n_2$, there is

$$m_1 < m_2. \tag{20}$$

As a result, $\Delta_1/\Delta_2 > 1$, which is $\Delta_1 > \Delta_2$.

In other words, the variation of outlier is larger than normal object, so that it is easier to be detected as outlier. However, owing to the complexity of dataset distribution and the limitations of distance-based outlier definition, it remains possible that a very few normal objects may be mistakenly detected.

6. Conclusions and Future Work

In this paper, we propose a new distance-based outlier definition to detect hidden outliers and design a corresponding detection algorithm, which excludes detected outliers to reduce their influence and improve the accuracy. Candidate set based method also avoids repeating detecting the whole dataset. Experimental results show that our HOD algorithm is more accurate than ORCA [18] and LOF [17]. Further, with better accuracy, HOD is much faster than LOF and is of comparable speed to that of ORCA. In addition, to achieve the same accuracy, ORCA takes up to 9 more times of running time than HOD. With the help of Triangle Inequality to reduce the distance calculation times, iHOD gets a much faster speed than iORCA and HiORCA. Moreover, we develop a pivot selection algorithm to avoid choosing outliers as pivots, and in experiments, we also show that our method can achieve stability of the results.

Our definition and algorithm are extended from two distance-based outlier detection algorithms: ORCA [18] and iORCA [22]. The case of hidden outlier also exists for density-based outlier detection, which we will study in the future. Besides, we will further study how to choose right pivots to speed up our detection algorithm.

Notation

$HO_{k\mathrm{sum}}^{(k,n)}$:	Hidden outlier definition; see details in Definition 1
D:	Dataset
dist:	Distance function
p:	An object of dataset
n:	Number of outliers to detect
k:	Number of neighbors for calculating outlier degree
$nn_i(p, D)$:	The ith nearest neighbor of p in dataset D
$D_{i,k}$:	The ith outlier by $O_{k\mathrm{sum}}^{(k,n)}$ definition
$w_k(p, D)$:	Outlier degree of p in dataset D
D_n-outlier:	The set of top-n outliers with respect to traditional outlier definition
$HD_{i,k}$:	The ith outlier by hidden outlier definition
$Hw_k(p, D)$:	p's hidden outlier degree in dataset D; see details in Definition 2
HD_n-outlier:	The set of top-n hidden outliers

$MPW_{n,k}(p, D)$:	Maximum possible outlier degree of p, with regard to dataset D. See details in Definition 5
$CS_{n,k}(D)$:	Hidden outlier candidate set, each object of which has larger maximum possible outlier degree than cutoff value c
c:	Cutoff value, equal to the outlier degree of current nth outlier. Namely, $c = w_k(HD_{n,k}, D)$ or $c = Hw_k(D_{n,k}, D)$ depends on the outlier definition
B:	A data block, that is, a set of objects
L:	Index, for example, $L(D)$, denotes index of the dataset D
blockIndex:	Index of a data block
$partNum$:	Number of segments/partitions
$pivotNum$:	Number of pivots. In this paper, it can only be set as $pivotNum = 1$.

Competing Interests

The authors declare that there are no competing interests regarding the publication of this paper.

Acknowledgments

Dr. Minhua Lu is the corresponding author. This research was supported by the following Grants: China 863: 2015AA015305; NSF-China: U1301252 and 61471243; Guangdong Key Laboratory Project: 2012A061400024; NSF-Shenzhen: JCYJ20140418095735561, JCYJ20150731160834611, JCYJ20150625101524056, and SGLH20131010163759789; Educational Commission of Guangdong Province: 2015KQNCX143.

References

[1] W.-F. Yu and N. Wang, "Research on credit card fraud detection model based on distance sum," in *Proceedings of the International Joint Conference on Artificial Intelligence (JCAI '09)*, pp. 353–356, IEEE, Hainan Island, China, April 2009.

[2] L. Chen, Y. Zhou, and D. M. Chiu, "Analysis and detection of fake views in online video services," *The ACM Transactions on Multimedia Computing, Communications, and Applications*, vol. 11, no. 2, pp. 1–20, 2015.

[3] N. A. M. Hassim, "Rough outlier method for network intrusion detection," *International Journal of Information Processing and Management (IJIPM)*, vol. 4, no. 7, pp. 39–50, 2013.

[4] M. A. F. Pimentel, D. A. Clifton, L. Clifton, and L. Tarassenko, "A review of novelty detection," *Signal Processing*, vol. 99, pp. 215–249, 2014.

[5] M. Albayati and B. Issac, "Analysis of intelligent classifiers and enhancing the detection accuracy for intrusion detection system," *International Journal of Computational Intelligence Systems*, vol. 8, no. 5, pp. 841–853, 2015.

[6] J. Singh and S. Aggarwal, "Survey on outlier detection in data mining," *International Journal of Computer Applications*, vol. 67, no. 19, pp. 29–32, 2013.

[7] V. Barnett and T. Lewis, *Outliers in Statistical Data*, vol. 3, Wiley, New York, NY, USA, 1994.

[8] P. J. Rousseeuw and M. Hubert, "Robust statistics for outlier detection," *Wiley Interdisciplinary Reviews: Data Mining and Knowledge Discovery*, vol. 1, no. 1, pp. 73–79, 2011.

[9] E. M. Knorr and R. T. Ng, "Algorithms for mining distancebased outliers in large datasets," in *Proceedings of the International Conference on Very Large Data Bases*, New York, NY, USA, 1998.

[10] E. M. Knorr, R. T. Ng, and V. Tucakov, "Distance-based outliers: algorithms and applications," *The VLDB Journal*, vol. 8, no. 3-4, pp. 237–253, 2000.

[11] H. Liao, A. Zeng, and Y.-C. Zhang, "Predicting missing links via correlation between nodes," *Physica A: Statistical Mechanics and its Applications*, vol. 436, pp. 216–223, 2015.

[12] D. M. Hawkins, *Identification of Outliers*, vol. 11, Springer, New York, NY, USA, 1980.

[13] S. Ramaswamy, R. Rastogi, and K. Shim, "Efficient algorithms for mining outliers from large data sets," *ACM SIGMOD Record*, vol. 29, no. 2, pp. 427–438, 2000.

[14] F. Angiulli and C. Pizzuti, "Outlier mining in large high-dimensional data sets," *IEEE Transactions on Knowledge and Data Engineering*, vol. 17, no. 2, pp. 203–215, 2005.

[15] L. Cao, D. Yang, Q. Wang, Y. Yu, J. Wang, and E. A. Rundensteiner, "Scalable distance-based outlier detection over high-volume data streams," in *Proceedings of the 30th IEEE International Conference on Data Engineering (ICDE '14)*, pp. 76–87, Chicago, Ill, USA, March 2014.

[16] R. Mao, P. Xiang, and D. Zhang, "Precise transceiver-free localization in complex indoor environment," *China Communications*, vol. 13, no. 5, pp. 28–37, 2016.

[17] M. M. Breuniq, H.-P. Kriegel, R. T. Ng, and J. Sander, "LOF: identifying density-based local outliers," *ACM SIGMOD Record*, vol. 29, no. 2, pp. 93–104, 2000.

[18] S. D. Bay and M. Schwabacher, "Mining distance-based outliers in near linear time with randomization and a simple pruning rule," in *Proceedings of the 9th ACM SIGKDD International Conference on Knowledge Discovery and Data Mining (KDD '03)*, pp. 29–38, ACM, August 2003.

[19] F. Angiulli, S. Basta, and C. Pizzuti, "Distance-based detection and prediction of outliers," *IEEE Transactions on Knowledge and Data Engineering*, vol. 18, no. 2, pp. 145–160, 2006.

[20] N. H. Vu and V. Gopalkrishnan, "Efficient pruning schemes for distance-based outlier detection," in *Machine Learning and Knowledge Discovery in Databases*, pp. 160–175, Springer, Berlin, Germany, 2009.

[21] C.-C. Szeto and E. Hung, "Mining outliers with faster cutoff update and space utilization," *Pattern Recognition Letters*, vol. 31, no. 11, pp. 1292–1301, 2010.

[22] K. Bhaduri, B. L. Matthews, and C. R. Giannella, "Algorithms for speeding up distance-based outlier detection," in *Proceedings of the 17th ACM SIGKDD International Conference on Knowledge Discovery and Data Mining (KDD '11)*, pp. 859–867, ACM, San Diego, Calif, USA, August 2011.

[23] A. Chaudhary, A. S. Szalay, and A. W. Moore, "Very fast outlier detection in large multidimensional data sets," in *Proceedings of the ACM SIGMOD Workshop on Research Issues in Data Mining and Knowledge Discovery (DMKD '02)*, 2002.

[24] F. Angiulli and C. Pizzuti, "Fast outlier detection in high dimensional spaces," in *Proceedings of the 6th European Conference on Principles of Data Mining and Knowledge Discovery (PKDD '02)*, pp. 15–27, Springer.

[25] D. Ren, I. Rahal, W. Perrizo, and K. Scott, "A vertical distance-based outlier detection method with local pruning," in *Proceedings of the 13th ACM International Conference on Information and Knowledge Management (CIKM '04)*, pp. 279–284, ACM, November 2004.

[26] Y. Wang, S. Parthasarathy, and S. Tatikonda, "Locality sensitive outlier detection: a ranking driven approach," in *Proceedings of the IEEE 27th International Conference on Data Engineering (ICDE '11)*, pp. 410–421, Hannover, Germany, April 2011.

[27] M. R. Pillutla, N. Raval, P. Bansal, K. Srinathan, and C. V. Jawahar, "LSH based outlier detection and its application in distributed setting," in *Proceedings of the 20th ACM Conference on Information and Knowledge Management (CIKM '11)*, pp. 2289–2292, ACM, Glasgow, Scotland, October 2011.

[28] M. Radovanović, A. Nanopoulos, and M. Ivanović, "Reverse nearest neighbors in unsupervised distance-based outlier detection," *IEEE Transactions on Knowledge and Data Engineering*, vol. 27, no. 5, pp. 1369–1382, 2015.

[29] M. Wu and C. Jermaine, "Outlier detection by sampling with accuracy guarantees," in *Proceedings of the 12th ACM SIGKDD International Conference on Knowledge Discovery and Data Mining (KDD '06)*, pp. 767–772, ACM, Philadelphia, Pa, USA, August 2006.

[30] Y. Tao, X. Xiao, and S. Zhou, "Mining distance-based outliers from large databases in any metric space," in *Proceedings of the 12th ACM SIGKDD International Conference on Knowledge Discovery and Data Mining (KDD '06)*, pp. 394–403, August 2006.

[31] F. Angiulli and F. Fassetti, "DOLPHIN: an efficient algorithm for mining distance-based outliers in very large datasets," *ACM Transactions on Knowledge Discovery from Data*, vol. 3, no. 1, article 4, 2009.

[32] J. Tang, Z. Chen, A. W. Fu, and D. W. Cheung, "Enhancing effectiveness of outlier detections for low density patterns," in *Advances in Knowledge Discovery and Data Mining*, vol. 2336 of *Lecture Notes in Computer Science*, pp. 535–548, Springer, Berlin, Germany, 2002.

[33] S. Papadimitriou, H. Kitagawa, P. B. Gibbons, and C. Faloutsos, "LOCI: fast outlier detection using the local correlation integral," in *Proceedings of the 19th International Conference on Data Ingineering*, pp. 315–326, IEEE, Bangalore, India, March 2003.

[34] H.-P. Kriegel, M. Schubert, and A. Zimek, "Subsampling for efficient and effective unsupervised outlier detection ensembles," in *Proceedings of the 19th ACM SIGKDD International Conference on Knowledge Discovery and Data Mining*, pp. 444–452, ACM, August 2008.

[35] R. Mao, P. Zhang, X. Li, X. Liu, and M. Lu, "Pivot selection for metric-space indexing," *International Journal of Machine Learning and Cybernetics*, vol. 7, no. 2, pp. 311–323, 2016.

[36] R. Mao, H. Xu, W. Wu, J. Li, Y. Li, and M. Lu, "Overcoming the challenge of variety: big data abstraction, the next evolution of data management for AAL communication systems," *IEEE Communications Magazine*, vol. 53, no. 1, pp. 42–47, 2015.

[37] M. Yang, *Research on Algorithms for Outlier Detection*, Huazhong University of Science & Technology, 2012.

[38] UCI Machine Learning Repository: Data Sets, https://archive.ics.uci.edu/ml/datasets.html.

[39] S. García, A. Fernández, A. D. Benítez, and F. Herrera, "Statistical comparisons by means of non-parametric tests: a case study on genetic based machine learning," in *II Congreso Espanol de Informática (CEDI '07)*, pp. 95–104, Zaragoza, Spain, September 2007.

[40] D. J. Sheskin, *Handbook of Parametric and Nonparametric Statistical Procedures*, CRC Press, Boca Raton, Fla, USA, 2003.

[41] Y. Hochberg, "A sharper Bonferroni procedure for multiple tests of significance," *Biometrika*, vol. 75, no. 4, pp. 800–802, 1988.

Permissions

List of Contributors

Bin He and Yonggang Li
School of Electronics and Information Engineering, Tongji University, Shanghai 201804, China

Jisheng Pei and Xiaojun Ye
Department of Computer Science and Technology, Tsinghua University, Beijing, China

Lifeng Yang
School of Continuing Education, Yunnan Open University, Yunnan, China

Liangming Chen, Ningwei Wang and Zhifang Liao
School of Software, Central South University, Hunan, China

Xun Pu, ShanXiong Chen and XianPing Yu
College of Computer & Information Science, Southwest University, Chongqing, China

Le Zhang
College of Computer & Information Science, Southwest University, Chongqing, China
College of Computer Science, Sichuan University, Chengdu, China

Zhihan Liu, Yi Jia and Xiaolu Zhu
State Key Laboratory of Networking and Switching Technology, Beijing University of Posts and Telecommunications, Beijing, China

I. Gitler and M. Arroyo
Departamento de Matem´aticas, Centro de Investigaci´on y Estudios Avanzados del Instituto Polit´ecnico Nacional (ABACUS-CINVESTAV-IPN), DF, Mexico

C. Couder-Castañeda
Departamento de Matem´aticas, Centro de Investigaci´on y Estudios Avanzados del Instituto Polit´ecnico Nacional (ABACUS-CINVESTAV-IPN), DF, Mexico
Centro de Desarrollo Aeroespacial del Instituto Polit´ecnico Nacional, Belisario Dom´ınguez 22, 06010 M´exico, DF, Mexico

H. Barrios-Piña
Tecnol´ogico de Monterrey, Avenida General Ram´on Corona 2514, 45201 Zapopan, JAL, Mexico

Xu Han, Tao Lv and CongWang
School of Software Engineering, Beijing University of Posts and Telecommunications, Beijing 100876, China
Key Laboratory of Trustworthy Distributed Computing and Service, Beijing University of Posts and Telecommunications, Beijing 100876, China

Zhirui Hu
Department of Statistics, Harvard University, Cambridge, MA, USA

Xinyan Wang
Air Force General Hospital, Beijing, China

Wulamu Aziguli, Yuanyu Zhang, Yonghong Xie, Dezheng Zhang and Chunmiao Li
School of Computer and Communication Engineering, University of Science and Technology Beijing (USTB), Beijing 100083, China
Beijing Engineering Research Center of Industrial Spectrum Imaging, Beijing 100083, China

Xiong Luo
School of Computer and Communication Engineering, University of Science and Technology Beijing (USTB), Beijing 100083, China
Beijing Engineering Research Center of Industrial Spectrum Imaging, Beijing 100083, China
Key Laboratory of Geological Information Technology, Ministry of Land and Resources, Beijing 100037, China

Yao Zhang
Tandon School of Engineering, New York University, Brooklyn, NY 11201, USA

Saeed Ullah, M. Daud Awan and M. Sikander Hayat Khiyal
Faculty of Computer Science, Preston University, Islamabad, Pakistan

Yan Li
School of Business and Management, Shanghai International Studies University, Shanghai, China

Yan Guo
State Key Laboratory of Networking and Switching Technology, Beijing University of Posts and Telecommunications, Beijing, China

Bao Rong Chang, Chia-Yen Chen, Chien-Feng Huang and Hung-Ta Hsu
Department of Computer Science and Information Engineering, National University of Kaohsiung, Kaohsiung 81148, Taiwan

Hsiu-Fen Tsai
Department of Marketing Management, Shu-Te University, Kaohsiung 82445, Taiwan

Lixia Zhang
College of Mathematics and Computer Science, Key Laboratory of High Performance Computing and Stochastic Information Processing, Ministry of Education of China, Hunan Normal University, Changsha 410081, China

Jianliang Gao
School of Information Science and Engineering, Central South University, Changsha 410083, China

Shaymaa Alhayali, Oguz Bayat, and Osman N. Uçan
Altinbas University, College of Engineering, Istanbul, Turkey

Tareq Abed Mohammed
Altinbas University, College of Engineering, Istanbul, Turkey
Kirkuk University, College of Science, Kirkuk, Iraq

Yueqin Zhu and Yongjie Tan
Development and Research Center, China Geological Survey, Beijing 100037, China
Key Laboratory of Geological Information Technology, Ministry of Land and Resources, Beijing 100037, China

Xiong Luo and Zhijie He
School of Computer and Communication Engineering, University of Science and Technology Beijing (USTB), Beijing 100083, China
Beijing Key Laboratory of Knowledge Engineering for Materials Science, Beijing 100083, China

Taeuk Kim, Awais Khan and Youngjae Kim
Sogang University, Seoul, Republic of Korea

Preethika Kasu
Ajou University, Suwon, Republic of Korea

Scott Atchley
Oak Ridge National Laboratory, Oak Ridge, TN 37831, USA

Wanrong Huang, Xiaodong Yi, Yichun Sun, Yingwen Liu, Shuai Ye, and Hengzhu Liu
School of Computer, National University of Defense Technology, Deya Road No. 109, Kaifu District, Changsha, Hunan 410073, China

Bao Rong Chang, Yun-Da Lee, and Po-Hao Liao
Department of Computer Science and Information Engineering, National University of Kaohsiung, 700 Kaohsiung University Rd., Nanzih District, Kaohsiung 811, Taiwan

Zhigang Chen
School of Software, Central South University, Changsha, China

Xu Xia
School of Software, Central South University, Changsha, China
Hunan Vocational Institute of Safety Technology, Changsha, China

Wei Wei
School of Computer Science and Engineering, Xi'an University of Technology, Xi'an 710048, China

Zahid Ali Siddiqui and Unsang Park
Department of Computer Science and Engineering, Sogang University, 35 Baekbeom-ro, Mapo-gu, Seoul 04107, Republic of Korea

Jeong-A Lee
Department of Computer Engineering, Chosun University, 309 Pilmun-daero, Dong-gu, Gwangju 61452, Republic of Korea

Zhiying Zhang Wenwen Xiao and Guijie Qi
School of Management, Shandong University, Jinan, Shandong 250100, China

Xiaozhen Chen
Business School, Shandong Normal University, Jinan, Shandong 250014, China

RuiMao, Hao Liao, He Zhang and Guoliang Chen
Guangdong Province Key Laboratory of Popular High Performance Computers, College of Computer Science and Software Engineering, Shenzhen University, Shenzhen, Guangdong 518060, China

Honglong Xu
Guangdong Province Key Laboratory of Popular High Performance Computers, College of Computer Science and Software Engineering, Shenzhen University, Shenzhen, Guangdong 518060, China
College of Information Engineering, Shenzhen University, Shenzhen, Guangdong 518060, China
School of Mathematics and Big Data, Foshan University, Foshan, Guangdong 528000, China

Minhua Lu
Guangdong Key Laboratory for Biomedical Measurements and Ultrasound Imaging, School of Biomedical Engineering, Shenzhen University, Shenzhen 518060, China

Index

Printed in the USA
CPSIA information can be obtained
at www.ICGtesting.com
JSHW051432221024
72173JS00006B/1448